Fodor's EXPLORING
JAPAN

FODOR'S TRAVEL PUBLICATIONS
NEW YORK • TORONTO • LONDON • SYDNEY • AUCKLAND

WWW.FODORS.COM

Published in the United States by Fodor's Travel, a division of Random House, Inc., and simultaneously in Canada by Random House of Canada Limited, Toronto.

Fodor's and Fodor's Exploring are registered trademarks of Random House, Inc.

Published in the United Kingdom by AA Publishing.

ISBN 13: 978-1-4000-1534-4
ISBN 10: 1-4000-1534-0
Fifth Edition

Fodor's Exploring Japan

Author: **David Scott**
Revision Verifier: **David Scott**
Revision Editor: **Lodestone Publishing Limited**
Cartography: **The Automobile Association**
Cover Design: **Fabrizio La Rocca, Tigist Getachew**
Front Cover Silhouette: **Frangenberg Orient/
   Fototeca 9 x 12**
Front Cover Top Photograph: **AA Photo Library**

Printed and bound in Italy by Printer Trento srl.
10 9 8 7 6 5 4 3 2

A03236

How to use this book

ORGANIZATION

Japan Is, Japan Was
Discusses aspects of life and culture in contemporary Japan and explores significant periods in its history.

A–Z
Breaks down the country into regional chapters, and covers places to visit, including walks and drives. Within this section fall the Focus On articles, which consider a variety of topics in greater detail.

Travel Facts
Contains the strictly practical information vital for a successful trip.

Hotels and Restaurants
Lists recommended establishments throughout Japan, giving a brief summary of their attractions.

ABOUT THE RATINGS
Most places described in this book have been given a separate rating. These are as follows:

▶▶▶   **Do not miss**

▶▶   **Highly recommended**

▶   **Worth seeing**

MAPS
To make the location of a particular place easier to find, every main entry in this book has a map reference to the right of its name. This includes a number, such as 176B3. The first number (176) indicates the page on which the map can be found. The letter (B) and the second number (3) pinpoint the square in which the place is located. The maps on the inside front cover and inside back cover are referred to as IFC and IBC.

Contents

6

A–Z

My Japan

David Scott is a restaurateur and an internationally published writer specializing in Japan, food and travel writing. He has written or co-authored a number of highly successful titles, including *Middle Eastern Vegetarian Cooking, Japanese Cooking, Elements of Zen, Samurai and Cherry Blossom*, and various travel guides to Japan.

Three elderly couples, dressed in white, shared my carriage on the train to Takamatsu, Shikoku's main port town. They each carried a straw hat, a walking stick, and a small bundle of possessions wrapped in a square of blue cloth. They were part way into the famous 88-temple pilgrimage in commemoration of the Shingon Buddhist patriarch, Kobo Daishi. I left them at the station and found an inn. The landlady showed me into a tiny room, followed me in, sat on her heels at a low table, made a pot of green tea with hot water from a flask, and then backed out of the door, bowing. Later, she brought in the evening meal, *sashimi*, *tempura*, vegetables and rice, plus a treat for me: hamburger and eight french fries, garnished beautifully with three perfect strawberries with their stalks!

Chitoshi Funabashi is a respectable suburb of Tokyo. It has narrow streets, small detached houses with tiny gardens and a minature park with a signposted jogging track. I went into a local barber shop, sat down in an empty chair and showed the barber how I wanted my hair cut. He refreshed my neck and face with a hot towel, and then, with great care, cut my hair, expertly shaved me and massaged my face, neck and shoulders. Finally, he massaged my back as I leaned forward in the chair. Before I left he cleaned my spectacles and handed them to me with a bow.

Uwajima is known for its city park and its bull ring. Here, two bulls, like four-legged sumo wrestlers, try to push each other out of its bounds. At the tourist office I got an English-language map. The lady behind the counter giggled when I asked her to locate Taga Jinja. This Shinto shrine is an amusement to local people, for the priest is an avid collector of sexual memorabilia and has built, near the shrine, a museum to house his collection.

These stories illustrate why, for me, Japan is a fascinating country, a captivating mixture of the old and the new coexisting side by side. The Japanese have embraced the most modern technology and ideas, and yet remain a people governed by traditional social values and etiquette. Japan is perhaps unique in being a modern, Westernized state, yet one that is relatively free of crime, litter and drugs. As a result you are free to take in the wonders of the country, so intriguing and sometimes so unexpected.
David Scott

Japan Is

The samurai warriors of old Japan saw the cherry blossom, with its beautiful but short life, as a symbol of their own lives, which could end violently at any moment. It is in this oscillation between beauty and ugliness, tenderness and violence, delicacy and coarseness that many people find the source of their fascination of the Japanese and Japan. The natural physical expression of this union of extremes, and perhaps a potent force in forming the Japanese character, is found in the violence and gentleness of the landscape and the climate of the Japanese islands.

10

You might think of the islands of Kyushu, Shikoku, Honshu and Hokkaido as the peaks of a deeply submerged mountain range, the seas off the coasts plunging to great depths. These peaks are a major presence throughout Japan, and even outside mountain regions the countryside is often exceptionally hilly. The land is either flat or rises sharply, and as a result the population is largely and densely confined to the coastal plains or the occasional areas of flat land found in the mountain

❑ The southern peak of Sakurajima volcano, which is sited on its own broad patch of land across the bay from the city of Kagoshima, still erupts quite regularly. During eruptions, clouds of black ash from the mountain cover Kagoshima in a fine coating of dust and collect in drifts along the store fronts. ❑

Mount Fuji framed by cherry blossoms

ranges. Together, they cover less than one fifth of the land surface.

Many of the mountains within the various mountain chains are volcanic and there are 50 active or semiactive volcanoes scattered throughout Japan. Mount Fuji, Japan's highest peak, last erupted in the 18th century, but Mount Asama, nearby, frequently rumbles and belches smoke. Other active volcanic areas are found in southern Hokkaido, central Honshu and Kyushu.

The Japan coastline is immensely varied in its topography and long in relation to the country's land area. The Japan Sea coast runs smoothly from south to north in an extended line of beaches and wide banks of sand dunes. In contrast, the wind- and tide-beaten Pacific coast is rugged with jutting peninsulas, such as Izu, and deep bays, such as those of Sendai and Tokyo.

The Inland Sea coast is different again. Constant sea erosion, matched by land-forming alluvial mud deposits brought down by the rivers, has formed a flat plain that is nowadays the region of Japan's most extensive industrial zone.

Japan lies directly along a fault line marking the juxtaposition of the Pacific and Asian Plates, which grind against each other and cause earthquakes. The major cities most at risk from earthquakes are Tokyo and Osaka, and the foundations of all their newer buildings are designed to allow them to sway without cracking. Earthquakes under the sea also produce tidal waves (tsunami) that regularly pound the coasts of Japan.

Add to these perils the typhoon winds that occasionally savage the land, heavy snowfalls in the north, torrential summer rainstorms in the south, the heavy humid heat of central and western Honshu and Kyushu, and those who are nervous about visiting Japan may be forgiven their jitters.

❑ More than 20 serious earthquakes struck Japan during the last century, the most recent in Kobe, 1995. The most catastrophic was the Great Kanto earthquake of 1 September 1923, which hit the country's most densely populated area, including the cities of Tokyo and Yokohama. More than 100,000 people were killed, 60,000 in Tokyo alone, mainly as a result of ensuing fires. ❑

In fact, summer heat is the most regular contender. Japanese inventiveness, foresight and experience of natural phenomena have allowed them to adapt to and cope with the other forces.

11

The gentle beauty of Japan: Lake Ashino

For a demonstration of the Japanese approach to business, visit a filling station. A team of attendants runs across the forecourt to meet the car. One fills the tank, another cleans the headlights, windscreen and mirrors, a third empties the ashtrays and cleans the mats, and a fourth takes the money. One of the team then stops the flow of traffic outside the garage, guides the car into the stream of vehicles, and finally waves goodbye.

Eagerness for business is an important factors in Japanese commercial success in world markets. Another is the long-term view taken by Japanese businessmen. Competition is fierce, but it is founded on long-term objectives rather than quick money schemes. First and foremost, customers must be provided with what they want and with the best service possible. Loyalty is nurtured, and from this it has been assumed that profits grow.

POSTWAR SUCCESS After World War II, the Japanese were economically and spiritually broken by their first military defeat in history and by the horrific way in which the war was finally ended. A new start was required and a re-examination of national values was undertaken at every level. As a result, radical changes were made, such as the

constitutional principle forbidding the formation of armed services other than for defending the country. These changes, together with certain qualities inherent in the nature of Japanese society, provided the structure for their future success.

The workforce demonstrated a sense of mutual responsibility and competitiveness, together with an unquestioned acceptance of long working hours and commitment to job and employer. Managers developed a keen understanding of the needs of specific home and overseas markets and the skills needed to fulfil them. By a combination of good marketing, an eye and an ear for what people wanted, the application of new technology, and the ability to produce high-quality goods quickly and economically, the Japanese learned

Bay Bridge, Yokohama

Business on the march in Tokyo

how to dominate world markets. At home, the Japanese government protected its markets from foreign competitors by imposing rigorous import quotas and duties. International pressure is now changing this situation, but the problem for importers remains that the Japanese simply prefer to buy Japanese goods.

FUTURE PROSPECTS Having enjoyed a long postwar period of growth and prosperity, Japan is now a decade into a recession, which has seen the collapse of a number of financial institutions.

There are now pressing demands to review the banking system, the first of many reforms that face Japan as it begins the new millennium.

Technological and social changes mean that Japan will have to rethink many existing policies.

Perhaps Japan's foremost concern, which affects many industrialized nations, is the ageing of society. A decline in the birthrate and a rise in the number of elderly mean that within a few years one-third of the population of Japan will be over 60. Worried that the government will not be able to afford to pay for future pensions, Japan's ageing population prefers to save rather than spend. This adds to the economy's deflation problems.

Assembly-line technology, seen as the way ahead for Japan's economy

❏ A Japanese government commission was formed to make recommendations on Japan's main economic goals for the 21st century. The commission stressed in its report a new emphasis on 'individual empowerment'. This is a very radical view given the Japanese liking for the slogan 'the nail that sticks up must be hammered down'. The commission supported the shift away from traditional egalitarianism towards a system rewarding individual initiative and expertise. ❏

On the street of any Japanese city, the man walking past in a white shirt and blue suit is probably a salaryman. A salaryman would, in the past, have expected lifelong employment with the same company, which he joined in his early 20s. This is changing because of the continuing downturn in the economy. However, the assumption still remains, on both sides, that he will stay there until he retires.

LIFE STYLE Although companies do not provide as much job security as they used to due to downsizing, they do provide salaried employees and their families with health care, housing and leisure facilities. Managers even arrange their staff's holidays. This system is accepted by most Japanese employees, who are used to the conformity it entails.

Salarymen usually work quite late. This is expected if they are to be

> ❏ Wages are calculated on the basis of a salaryman's expected day-to-day domestic expenses, which depend on his job status. Added to this is a twice-yearly bonus for holidays, cars, luxury items, and any other expenses concomitant with a person's position in the company, such as golf-club membership for upper management. ❏

Salarymen are always on call, even when they are on the road

promoted. They may even waste time during the day to be sure of work in the evening. After work, salarymen usually go out to drink with their colleagues. The tradition is provided for by the numerous bars and restaurants in the business areas of large cities. A salaryman's wife expects her husband home late, and may even worry that he is not getting on at work if he arrives home early.

IN THE OFFICE Salarymen expect their bosses to trust them and to leave the responsibility of day-to-day matters solely in their hands. A boss who makes decisions about mundane matters would lose respect. Once employees have grown to trust their managers, their loyalty is total and good relationships between management and staff are normal in Japanese business. Both parties are usually on close terms and go out drinking together. However, even outside work, company status is recognized and deferred to.

Strikes do take place but they are normally only ritualized stoppages.

Every year, during the second week in April, salarymen go on strike for one or two days to support their yearly wage claim; during this time they wear red armbands to signify that they are on strike. Many even stay on the company premises during the day, but they do not work, and do not go out drinking with the management.

STRESSES There is a heavy price to pay for Japan's work culture. Salarymen work long hours, often under competitive and stressful conditions; Sunday is the only day they have to spend with their wives and children. This can put marriages under strain and prevent close

relationships from developing between fathers and children, as well as giving all the responsibility for their upbringing to the mother. Further, deepening recession and rising unemployment are undermining Japan's traditional social fabric and causing a breakdown in life-long employment. Salarymen are losing their financial security as well.

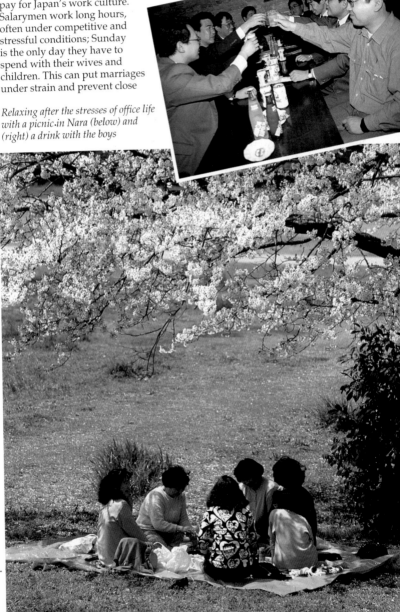

Relaxing after the stresses of office life with a picnic in Nara (below) and (right) a drink with the boys

Japan is a country of tradition and custom, but it is also a hothouse of modernity; a world leader in computer technology, digital hardware and futuristic architecture. Despite the current economic difficulties it remains a country where the future arrives early and where their huge 24-hour neon cities continue to expand.

TRANSPORTATION AND COMMUNICATION

In a world that is rapidly adjusting to the revolution in information technology, Japan heavily emphasizes both research and development in telecommunications and transportation to meet the ever-growing need for faster methods of conveying information and people.

Japan is a world leader in the development of increasingly compact computer and digital hardware. The country that gave the world the Walkman is renowned for its expertise in producing the latest gadgets, and the Japanese are rabid consumers of all types of electronic goods.

In addition, Japan boasts the world's most efficient and reliable transportation network, a crucial factor for any country wishing to compete effectively in international affairs and commerce. The well-known bullet trains, which run regularly and punctually, connect all Japan's major cities and they are constantly being upgraded. Testing is well under way for the new Maglev line (tentatively named) to connect Tokyo and Osaka, allowing businessmen to travel from one city to the other in about one hour (currently a two-and-a-half-hour journey).

FUTURE CITIES

You will most readily notice Japan's international commercial success and the influences of the West in urban and industrial landscapes. In the major Japanese cities, individually designed chrome, marble and glass apartment buildings are replacing the old towering box flats, with their balconies hung with drying clothes and airing futons. Architecturally adventurous office buildings rise in business districts, while environmentally controlled, glass-domed shopping arcades shut out the noise and fumes of traffic in the heart of the cities. Carefully sculpted and tended Zen gardens are still found in the

Train of the future, landscape of the past: A bullet train races past Mount Fuji

Kansai International Airport, Osaka Bay, one of Japan's monumental engineering project

grounds of city temples, but they may now be overshadowed by the razor-sharp images of video advertising screens or the hi-tech dazzle of neon signs. Joggers in designer tracksuits run in city parks among the cherry blossoms while, overhead, helicopters whirl past.

FUTURE DOUBTS Despite the technical expertise of the Japanese and their well-educated workforce, there are doubts about the future. There are three principal problems that the Japanese are having to face.

Firstly, there are growing concerns that the traditional Japanese work ethic is being eroded by influences from the West. Many of Japan's youth are no longer prepared to make the same sacrifices that their parents and grandparents made to create the New Japan. Today's youth values leisure time, and they are not prepared to work the long hours of previous generations.

Secondly, Japan's previous success has been due partly to its emphasis on conformity. The Japanese have traditionally been raised to accept decisions from above rather than to question them. In a world that demands greater flexibility and where successful companies are having to flatten existing hierarchies, many worry that Japan's rigid social structure and emphasis on collective responsibility, qualities that contributed so much to Japan's past economic miracle, could be the very factors that paralyze it in the 21st century.

Finally, Japan is going to have to face the inevitable effect of having an increasingly automated society. With many jobs being rendered obsolete, and with increasing competition both domestically and abroad, the guarantee of lifetime employment will soon be a thing of the past. The future is not all bleak, however. Japan has become even more adept at creating products desired by the rest of the world and continues to be a powerful global commercial force. For young people around the world Japanese products are 'cool'.

Shinto, a religion unique to Japan, and Zen Buddhism, followed for more than a thousand years, have exerted a significant influence on Japanese history. Known by the Japanese as Kami-no-Michi, *'The Way Of The Gods', Shinto has its origins in the myths of ancient Japan. Zen Buddhism is perhaps best known in the West for the inspiration it has provided for Japanese martial arts.*

SHINTO BELIEFS AND RITUALS

Followers of Shinto worship the spirit god Kami, whose nature is manifested in all the things around them, such as rivers, mountains, trees, rocks and animals. Each deity has a place in a hierarchy of power that culminates in the sun goddess Amaterasu, venerated at the imperial shrines of Ise, on the Ise-Shima Peninsula of Honshu (see pages 106–107). The local *kami* are lesser deities, who look after just one village or one family's fields.

There are no fixed scriptures in Shinto. Its rituals and ceremonies, a daily part of Japanese life, are directed at receiving a blessing from the gods for a particular function or event. Shinto priests, wearing long, flowing robes and tall, lacquered silk hats, officiate at all manner of occasions: to bless babies, marriages, children starting school, new construction sites and even new cars.

Confucianism, brought to Japan by Chinese merchants in around AD 400, had an important influence on Shinto beliefs. It emphasized loyalty to the family, with the father as patriarchal head, and demanded reverence and respect for the memory of ancestors.

Offerings are made at Shinto shrines, or *jinja*, either to ancestors or to the guardian spirits of the shrine. Before making an offering, the devotee pours water from a trough by the inner shrine over his hands and rinses his mouth. He then attracts the gods by clapping his hands three times and pulling on a rope attached to a wooden clapper. A silent prayer is then given and an offering of fruit, money, incense, or *fuda* (strips of paper symbolizing purity, sold at the entrance) is made.

With its emphasis on the basic purity of all things, the Shinto religion was fertile ground for the assimilation of Buddhist and especially Zen Buddhist beliefs. The two schools of thought have never

18

Above and opposite: many faces of Buddhism in Japan

exactly merged, but most Japanese follow the Shinto and Buddhist religions, depending on what is customary for the occasion at hand.

ZEN BELIEFS AND RITUALS There are two main branches of Zen: the Rinzai school, founded by Eisai in 1191, and the Soto school, founded by Dogen in 1244. Both traditions developed out of the Chinese Buddhist school of Ch'an.

THE WARRIORS' ZEN The Rinzai school valued sudden enlightenment, using meditation and *koan*, questions not soluble by logical thinking such as 'What is the sound of one hand clapping?' This appealed to the warrior classes of 12th-century Japan, attracted to the principles of sudden inspiration, quick intuition and intense concentration, as opposed to learning. Eisai opened a temple in Kamakura, the site of the new warrior capital; descendants of the warrior class ruled Japan for the following six centuries and Zen became the religion espoused by the ruling classes.

Samurai warriors used Zen meditation to prepare for battle, but their interest in the spiritual essence of Zen increased during the Tokugawa era (1603–1867) and martial arts gradually became a vehicle for expressing Zen ideals.

THE PEOPLE'S ZEN Dogen believed that everyone is enlightened, but ignorant of this fact. He placed great emphasis on the detail of daily activities and saw each moment as an opportunity to express gratitude for our 'Buddha nature'. Now revered as one of Japan's greatest historical figures, Dogen avoided the military and aristocratic power struggles of his day, creating in Soto Zen a 'people's faith'. Soto Zen now has a much larger number of temples and followers than Rinzai.

Taikodani Shrine, Tsuwano

At the age of three or four, Japanese children start to attend kindergarten. The choice of a good school is crucial because, even from this early age, university entrance is the focus of a child's education, and there is intense pressure to do well. The heavy burden that is placed on the shoulders of Japanese youth, especially on young men, of whom most is expected, sometimes has disastrous consequences.

20

READING AND WRITING Despite having the highest literacy rate in the world, problems for the nation's children begin with the Japanese language. Schoolchildren must master four ways of writing: *Kanji, Hiragana, Katakana* and *Romaji. Kanji* are Chinese characters adopted centuries ago and given uniquely Japanese meaning, *Hiragana* are phonetic Japanese characters used to link *Kanji* ideograms, *Katakana* is the phonetic system used to write foreign words, and *Romaji* uses the Roman alphabet to write Japanese. It is estimated that Japanese students need two years more of schooling than their Western counterparts just to grapple with the complications of their own writing system.

❑ There are more than 40,000 *Kanji* Japanese characters, but today only about 3,000 are taught in schools. *Toyo-kanji* are the 2,000 most common characters chosen by the Japanese government for use in popular written books and newspapers. ❑

THE EDUCATION RACE If a child is to do well, from the time he or she starts kindergarten his or her parents need to save to pay for private tutoring and later, possibly, for private college and university. Education is the key to upward social and economic mobility.

Educational pressures start early

❏ *Ronin* was a term originally applied to free-roaming samurai warriors without a master and consequently without status. Today it refers to high-school graduates who have failed their university entrance exams. *Ronin* cram for a year or even two or three to gain entrance at their next attempt. ❏

The importance given to it in this status-conscious country is enormous. This, of course, creates intense competition for good grades, a process that itself devalues qualifications, thereby increasing the competition even more.

At the age of six a child goes to elementary school, which he or she attends from Monday to Friday, 8.40am to 4.30pm, and Saturday mornings. At the age of 12, the child moves to *chugakko*, middle school, for the final three years of compulsory education. Here the pressure begins and many students attend expensive *juku* (private tutoring schools) before and after school and on Sundays.

From *chugakko*, more than 90 per cent of students attempt the difficult entrance examinations for *kotogakko*, senior high school. If they are unsuccessful, students aim for a less demanding, private college. Once in senior high school they sometimes work themselves close to a nervous breakdown in preparation for the forthcoming arduous university entrance examinations. Some go over the edge, and suicide is not uncommon. To fail is to fail one's family and to lose social credibility.

It used to be the case that students could treat university life as a four-year holiday, a break between the rigorous series of examinations during their school years and the long hours that awaited them in their future careers. Employment was largely assured, or at the very least university grades had no bearing on the search for work upon graduation.

This is no longer the case, however. With more and more jobs requiring graduates to enter the workplace partially trained in information technology, modern-day students are

At the age of 12, schoolchildren move to middle school

having to put as much time into their studies as their Western counterparts, and their choices of study are very important as well.

Taking time out from the stresses of studying

From a Western perspective, of all the developed nations, Japan is the country where the question of rights for women has been least addressed. Traditional attitudes are being modified by pressure from women and by wider changes in society as a whole. But the slow pace of change reflects the importance of tradition even in contemporary Japan.

THE TRADITIONAL ROLE OF WOMEN

The traditional role of the Japanese woman has been that of the dutiful wife. Until comparatively recently women who entered the workplace did so for only a few years after university until they had met their husbands. In some cases, women entered companies with the specific intention of husband-hunting. However, working after marriage was a virtual 'no-no' for women, except in clear cases of necessity. Those who attempted to continue to work after marriage invariably met with strong opposition not only from members of their own family but frequently from work colleagues.

Two faces of the Japanese woman: at a traditional wedding…

Until only a few years ago, a Japanese woman was expected to get married by her mid-twenties. Her function in life was to be a good mother, a homemaker. Indeed, the Japanese for 'wife' (*oku-san*) uses Chinese characters making her role in this regard explicit. The pressure to get married was, and in rural areas still is, very strong. For the woman who found herself still single in her late twenties, arranged marriages using *o-miai-san* (go-betweens/negotiators) often resulted. These were set up by anxious parents or even at the request of the woman in question.

THE ROLE OF MARRIED WOMEN

Once married, a woman has to resign herself to domestic chores. Husband and wife live almost entirely separate

...and doing a sharp deal

lives as a married couple. While her husband spends increasingly longer hours at the office and socializing with his work colleagues as he climbs the corporate ladder, the wife is charged with dealing with all aspects of home life. Everything from the day-to-day running of the house to overseeing the education of her children are the responsibility of the wife. As a consequence, although newly-wed Japanese wives tend to be fairly timid, they invariably come to 'rule the roost' and play a key role in decisions concerning family life.

Of particular interest to Westerners is the fact that Japanese women hold the purse strings. A husband's salary is paid into the family bank account from which often only his wife can make withdrawals. Each month the husband has a spending allowance that is determined by his wife.

THE MODERN WOMAN A number of factors have significantly changed the role of women over the last decade, however. Western pressures and influences have encouraged Japanese women to be much more assertive, and increasingly Japanese women are marrying later. The stigma of being a single working woman at the age of 30 and beyond is fast being eradicated. Women can be seen enjoying life more and, perhaps more importantly, enjoying life as single women.

Formerly, a woman's pay was only about 60 per cent of that of a man in a similar position. This clear prejudice is fast being removed. Although the employees of many of the traditional companies are still dominated by men, women can increasingly be found in the service industries and in advertising and design companies. There are even a few companies that employ women exclusively.

As women play an increasingly important role in Japanese society, a number have risen to quite prominent positions. One or two women are achieving political prominence, although government is still one of the institutions least open to change. Japan may someday have an empress as head of state, as the Crown Prince has a daughter to succeed him.

Sumo is Japan's national sport and an integral part of the country's cultural fabric. It can also lay strong claims to being the world's oldest sport. Its roots lie in the realms of mythology, and it is said to have been popular with the gods. Before becoming a sport in the sixth century, sumo was considered to be a form of divination and a way of invoking the good will of the spirits.

THE RITUAL Once started, sumo techniques are executed with great speed, and each bout is over quickly. The *rikishi* (wrestlers) move with consummate skill and their expertise can easily be misjudged by a casual observer.

The fight is the core of sumo, but its attractions for the cognoscenti are the prefight rituals, drawn in part from the battlefield. These rituals demonstrate the Shinto origins of

Careful preparation of a sumo star for the forthcoming show

sumo and also serve to raise the psychological tension between the fighters to fever pitch.

THE RULES The *dohyo*, or wrestling area, is a circular clay ring that is surrounded by rice-straw bales. The rules of the sport are simple. The first wrestler to set a foot or any other part of his body outside the ring, or to touch the ground inside the ring with anything but the sole of his foot, loses. There is no classification by weight; lighter men try to overcome their handicap by making use of superior speed and agility.

Ranking is based on a pyramid system, with teenage beginners (*jonokuchi*) at the bottom and grand champions (*yokozuna*) at the top. Surprisingly, juniors start their training with the same build as ordinary mortals. They then steadily put on weight by eating large quantities of rice and *chanko-nabe*, a hearty stew of meat, fish and vegetables, washed down by large quantities of beer and sake. Dictated by their stable master, their lifestyle is hard and strict.

THE FIGHT Once in the ring, the *rikishi* loosen up with a movement called *shiko*, where each leg is raised sideways to waist height and then brought down with a formidable stamp. This movement is said to drive out stray devils. Salt is then thrown into the air by each man to purify the ring after the last bout's loss. The wrestlers face each other in a low squat in the middle of the ring, each trying to stare the other down. Finally, at a word from the referee, they squat, lean forward, touch

24

hands on the ground, and then crash into each other at full force.

THE CHANGES Sumo is steeped in tradition and ritual, but it is also about professionalism and winning. Of the many hundreds of wrestlers, few become nationally known, but Western attitudes to the sport are beginning to influence the age-old traditions. Even the legendary inscrutability of the competitors has now been breached. Nowadays, winners are sometimes even known to allow themselves a smile in victory and losers a frown in defeat.

In the past, the rigorous discipline of a sumo wrestler's training deterred most *gai-jin* (foreigners) from trying to join their ranks, but this situation is now changing.

The following Tokyo sumo stables allow overseas tourists to view morning training sessions.

❏ Top sumo wrestlers have the status, the media attention, and riches of Hollywood stars, and are treated with the respect and deference usually only accorded to royalty. They have private fan clubs, corporate sponsors and, it is said, the pick of Japanese women. Despite modern influences, the Shinto origins of sumo are still evident, especially in prefight rituals. ❏

A Japanese operator will need to make an appointment by calling: Azumazeki, tel: 03 3625 0033; Tatsunami, tel: 03 3631 2424; or Kasugano, tel: 03 3631 1871, or visit www.sumoworld.com for details.

Crowds enjoy the sumo spectacle at a Tokyo arena

The Japanese have a rich and varied cultural history, and classical performing arts such as noh *and* kabuki *and the elegant pleasures of pastimes such as the tea ceremony continue to flourish. However, the principal source of Japanese entertainment and nightlife is the network of bars, restaurants, coffee shops and tea houses that are an integral part of even the smallest Japanese town.*

WORK AND PLEASURE

Entertainment is a key component of the world of business deals, and corporate entertainment, which is said to drive the economy, always appears as a large (sometimes hidden) debit in the accounts of any successful Japanese company. Company employees usually meet after work for drinks and perhaps to eat, and on these occasions it is quite

❑ The Japanese home is a wife's domain, and Japanese men entertain their friends, business colleagues and acquaintances away from the house at a popular restaurant or bar. If they invite you out, they expect to pick up the bill, just as though they were taking the trouble themselves. ❑

Outrageous facades adorn streetfood and karaoke venues of Osaka

acceptable, after a fair amount of alcohol, to find fault with a superior or colleague (or foreign guest) in a manner that would be inappropriate in the formal atmosphere of work. Tomorrow it will be forgotten.

STREET FOOD AND STRIPTEASE

Cinemas, discos and intimate clubs are to be found in downtown areas alongside 'Soapland' districts, where striptease and massage joints rub shoulders with street-food stands and fast-food restaurants. Historically, sex and eroticism played an important role in the nightlife of male-dominated Japan. Many of the clubs in Soapland areas are owned by the *Yakuza* (the Japanese Mafia).

Prices in restaurants and bars vary widely, and are usually high in places that do not display a price list. The cost of drinks in any bar is high; the cheapest are those frequented by young men and women, office workers and college students. Those that employ hostesses to fill your glass and to make idle chat can be prohibitively expensive. Geisha bars, where expertly trained women entertain with witty conversation, traditional dancing, music and food (but not sex) are not generally open to foreigners unless you have a respected client's introduction.

KARAOKE BARS The Japanese invented and love karaoke. Singing songs to the sound of pre-recorded music, in front of other customers or with friends, is a popular pastime.

PLEASURES SIMPLE AND REFINED
Japanese coffee shops (*kissaten*) are one of the country's best discoveries. They pride themselves on serving exquisite coffee and on providing a first-class sound system, playing jazz, classical, rock, or other music. A cup of coffee is relatively expensive, but once you have ordered you can sit for as long as you wish reading, writing, or looking at the comics and magazines always available. (*Kissaten* frequently offer a good breakfast for the price of a coffee; ask for 'morning service' in English.)

Noh theatre, *bunraku* or 'puppet theatre' (see page 88), and *kabuki* (see pages 58–59) are available in major cities, and although alien in format to most Westerners, they are usually worth seeing both for the spectacle and the insight they give into Japanese culture.

Tokyo's dazzling nightlife

Traditional meals are cooked and presented with the intention of inspiring the spirit as well as the senses. The ingredients and menu are chosen to take into account the season, location and occasion. Tableware is selected to harmonize with the texture and appearance of the food which, according to the Japanese, must be tasted with the tongue, the heart and the eye to be truly enjoyed.

THE BUDDHIST INFLUENCE Japanese cuisine developed in a state of isolation and its style is unique. Buddhist beliefs, which forbade the eating of flesh, together with the nature of the landscape and climate, restricted the choice of food, and the main ingredients of the Japanese diet were rice, noodles, vegetables, pickles, seafood, soya-bean products and fruit. To some degree, this remains the case today, but, ironically, now that such ingredients are highly recommended by nutritionists, the Japanese are adding more and more meat and dairy products to their diet.

> ❏ In Japan, the use of seaweed as a foodstuff is commonplace. *Kombu* seaweed is packaged in fancy boxes and given as presents by dinner guests. Unusually rich in vitamins and minerals, it has both nutritive value and seasoning properties. ❏

COOKING CATEGORIES At a typical Japanese meal, individual dishes are served in smaller amounts but greater variety than in the West. They are all served at the same time, rather than in courses, and the order

A food vendor in Hokkaido

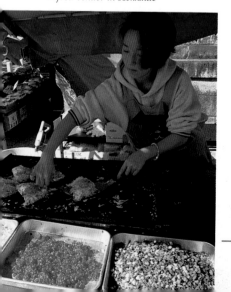

in which they are eaten is a matter of personal choice. Each dish is classified according to the way it is cooked, rather than by the main ingredient. For example, *yakimono* are grilled foods; fish is most widely served this way. *Agemono* are deep-fried dishes, of which *tempura* is the best known and loved. *Nimono*, such as the dish *shabu-shabu*, is food simmered in water or some other liquid such as sake. Diners pick out cooked morsels with their chopsticks and later sip the cooking liquor out of a bowl like soup.

Other categories are *sashimi*, in which pieces of very fresh raw fish are served with *wasabi*, a green Japanese mustard; sushi, vinegared rice patties topped with a variety of foods, particularly raw fish, and *nabe-mono*, one-pot meals such as the well-known *sukiyaki* (pronounced 'ski-yaki').

BASIC FOODS Rice is eaten with every meal, including breakfast. *Han*, the Japanese word for rice, is given the honourable prefix *go*, so that rice is referred to as *go-han*, or 'honourable rice' (*ho han* also means 'meal'). The rice at a meal is usually eaten last, rather than as an

Breakfast at a Minshuku

accompaniment to other foods. It is the core of the meal, and often two or three bowls of it are eaten at a time.

Noodles are eaten almost as often as rice. One of the great delights of being in Japan is to eat a bowl of noodles in one of the inexpensive noodle restaurants that can be found in even the smallest villages. The Japanese eat their noodles quickly, with lots of sucking and slurping noises and 'aahs' of contentment.

Surprisingly few seasonings and condiments are used; the cuisine depends as much on the natural taste of the ingredients, their aroma and visual beauty as on added seasoning. Apart from soy sauce, *miso* (a fermented soya bean paste), and seaweed, the most commonly used seasonings are: *goma*, a mixture of toasted and crushed sesame seeds and salt; *mirin*, a sweet fortified rice wine; ginger root; *togarashi*, a seven-spice pepper-like condiment; and *wasabi*.

O-cha, or green tea, is the usual offering with food in Japanese homes and restaurants. In the latter, green tea is served to guests on their arrival and at the end of the meal, free of charge.

An elegant display of tempura, *the popular deep-fried dish*

Japan is a land of festivals (matsuri) and celebratory events, and even the smallest villages have their own calendars of activities. Most have some kind of historical or religious significance, but they are generally boisterous affairs that provide an excuse for much noise, eating and drinking, and crowd participation.

It is very possible, particularly in summer, that you will accidentally come across a local festival in progress, but for specific information contact the tourist information offices in Tokyo and Kyoto (see page 264), which publish monthly bulletins of events. The larger, better-known festivals mentioned here are always very popular with the Japanese; if you plan to visit one, arrange your hotel and transportation well in advance.

SUMMER Gion Matsuri (16–17 July): This is perhaps the best known of all Japanese festivals. It takes place in Kyoto, and events span a month. The highlight is a huge procession of floats on 17 July. The ceremony, more than 1,000 years old, began as a purification ritual to rid the city of plague. Each of Kyoto's 29 districts builds its own elaborately decorated float for this event.

O-Bon (13–16 August): At this time of the year, the Japanese like to return to their home towns or villages to take part in the O-Bon ceremonies that mark the return to earth of all departed ancestors. At the

Dressed up for Tokyo's White Crane Festival

end of the rituals, candlelit paper lanterns are set to float down rivers and out to sea, to mark the return of the spirits to their own world. Yasukuni Shrine in Tokyo and Nachi Shrine in Katsuura, Wakayama prefecture hold large ceremonies.

AUTUMN Jidai Matsuri (22 October): The Imperial Palace in Kyoto is the start of a large procession to mark the founding of the city. Thousands of people dressed in the costumes of different historical eras march along in this noisy, happy event, finishing at the Heian Shrine.

Shichi-Go-San (15 November): On this day girls aged between three and seven, and five-year-old boys are dressed in their best clothes and taken to city and village shrines and temples, where prayers are offered up for their good health.

WINTER Joya-no-Kane and Ganjitsu (31 December–1 January): On New Year's Eve everybody stays up until midnight, when temple bells ring out 108 times. New Year's Day is seen as an opportunity for renewal: debts are paid and arguments settled. Festivities go on for seven days and most businesses come to a halt. On 2 January, the Imperial Family appears at the Imperial Palace in Tokyo and huge crowds gather to greet them.

SPRING Cherry Blossom Viewing (March to May): At this time of the year cherry blossom (*sakura*) viewing parties take place all over Japan. The exact date depends on the flowering of the blossom in a particular region. Local weather forecasts give updates on the state of the blossom ripeness in each area of Japan.

Kodomo-no-Hi (Children's Day, 5 May): This national holiday focuses around the nation's children, with a special emphasis on young boys (it is sometimes known as Boys' Day). Families fly giant paper *koi* (carp) from their homes to symbolize the strength of manhood. The larger fish represent the eldest sons and the increasingly smaller ones represent the younger children.

NATIONAL HOLIDAYS
1 January New Year's Day;
15 January Coming of Age Day;
11 February Founding of the Nation Day; **21 March** Vernal Equinox Day (varies); **29 April** Greenery Day; **3 May** Constitution Day; **5 May** Children's Day (the period from 29 April to 6 May, called 'Golden Week', is essentially a national week off, and is not a good time to travel); **15 September** Respect for the Aged Day; **23 September** Autumn Equinox Day (varies); **10 October** Health–Sports Day; **3 November** Culture Day; **23 November** Labour Thanksgiving Day; **23 December** Emperor's Birthday.

Karatsu Festival, Kyushu Island

Shinto, the ancient religion of Japan, lays great emphasis on purification and cleanliness. Partly because of this, bathing and the rituals surrounding it are very much a part of the Japanese culture. No other country in the world possesses more natural hot springs, called onsen, *and the popular custom of bathing in them for physical and spiritual regeneration dates back to the distant past.*

PRIVATE BATHING At home, the Japanese find two Western habits particularly difficult to comprehend. The first is that we wear shoes in the house and the second is that we sit in the dirty water in which we wash. In Japan, the bather sits outside the tub on a small stool, scoops water over him or herself, washes, rinses off the soap, and only then, with a clean body, climbs into the tub to both soak and relax in the very hot water.

PUBLIC BATHING Communal bathing is also popular, and *sento* (public bath houses) are places to meet friends, swap gossip and jokes, and to soak away aches, pains and worries. Consider visiting them, not just to get clean, but also to see the

The bliss of an open-air onsen

Japanese at their ribald best. *Sento* are found in cities and small towns, and come in a variety of shapes and forms varying from Gothic-style exaggeration to Zen simplicity. They have recently enjoyed a revival in popularity among young people, and many are being renovated in their original style.

ONSEN There are places to stay for tourists around most of Japan's *onsen* (hot springs). At spas such as Beppu, massive commercial resorts have developed, where the emphasis for visitors is on group togetherness (a sacred concept in Japan). At other, more isolated *onsen*, there may be only two or three thatched-roof cottages with a single *rotemburo* (outdoor bath). Here you come to seek spiritual comfort rather than material comfort.

Japan Was

The prehistoric era of Japan's history usually refers to the age before the first writing system and the Buddhist religion were introduced in the sixth century. Japan's earliest settlers, who arrived about 100,000 BC, are a mystery. They were probably not the ancestors of the predominantly Mongoloid modern Japanese, nor of the Ainu, the earliest known people of Japan (see pages 236–237). A similarity in language may be the only link between these original inhabitants and present-day Japanese.

The emperor Chuai looks towards the West

The near prehistoric era may be divided into three distinct periods. The Jomon age (c10,000–300 BC) was one in which pottery-making (without a wheel) and other crude technical skills emerged. During the Yayoi era (300 BC–AD 300) immigrants and invaders from mainland Asia brought agricultural and military knowledge. The third age, the Kofun period (AD 300–700), was marked by the building of *kofun* (large earthen tombs) throughout Japan and the growing influence of Chinese culture.

JOMON ERA The Jomon people were hunters and gatherers. They lived in small communities, primarily in central Honshu, and had a well-developed religion of nature worship, deifying the sun and moon. During this period, according to Japanese mythology, the sun goddess Amaterasu sent one of her descendants to the island of Kyushu to establish order and to unify the people of Japan. This aim was later partly realized by Jimmu, the great grandson of the emissary and the half-legendary first emperor of Japan.

The sun-goddess Amaterasu

❏ A Chinese visitor to southwest Japan in about AD 200 described what he saw as follows: 'The people live on raw vegetables and go about bare-footed. They smear their bodies with pink and scarlet. They serve food on bamboo and wooden trays, helping themselves with their fingers. Whenever they undertake an enterprise or a journey and discussion arises, they bake bones and divine in order to tell whether fortune will be good or bad...If the lowly meet important men on the road, they stop and withdraw to the roadside.' ❏

YAYOI ERA During the second and first centuries BC, craftsmen and warriors, driven from Korea and China by political turmoil, crossed the Korean Straits to Japan in large numbers. They brought with them mining and metal-working skills, pottery-making with a wheel, cloth-weaving techniques, and rice cultivation in flooded paddies. In their turn, they took up many of the customs and the language of the indigenous people. Japan flourished as a country of many small states, some of which were ruled by women; rule by women continued in outlying regions until almost the ninth century AD.

KOFUN ERA A later development of the Yayoi era was the formation of powerful clans and the development of a military elite skilled in horsemanship and weaponry. At the beginning of the Kofun period, clan chiefs fought to maintain or expand control of their independent kingdoms. By AD 300, however, the chieftain of the Yamato clan, based in the Yamato lowlands, south of Kyoto, had brought many of them under his command. Over the next 250 years, by intermarriage and the exercise of political and military skills, the Yamato unified Japan under a succession of single leaders. It was for the burial of such powerful men

A replica kofun *figure, in Kyushu*

❑ *Kofun* were often encircled with *haniwa*, clay figures of warriors and servants; inside the mounds were bronze mirrors, glass beads and other objects that would be needed by the dead in their next life. You can see numerous *kofun* mounds and *haniwa* at Saitobaru, north of Miyazaki in Kyushu. ❑

that the huge *kofun* burial mounds were created. This era also saw the introduction of Buddhism into Japan and the formation of close cultural links with China, powerfully redirecting Japanese history.

With the introduction of Buddhism and the use of Chinese characters for writing in the sixth century, Japan entered its classical period (710–1185). During this time, the first permanent capital was established at Nara, and later at Heian-kyo (Kyoto). Early in the classical period the Japanese were influenced by Chinese cultural and scholarly ideals, but by the 10th century they had evolved a unique and sophisticated culture of their own.

PRINCE SHOTOKU Buddhism was already known in sixth-century Japan, but it was first fully introduced to the Japanese court by the king of a minor Korean state. In 553 he sent the emperor Buddhist images, vestments, incense, *sutras* (scriptures) and other ritual objects as part of a petition seeking Japanese military aid. Some

❑ The conflict between Buddhism and Shinto was reconciled by the Buddhist monk Gyogi. In 740, he was requested to visit Ise, location of the most important of Shinto shrines (see pages 106–107), to meditate on the propriety of the emperor's plans to erect a giant statue of the Buddha. Gyogi received a message from Amaterasu, the sun goddess, that the two religions were just different forms of the same path. This was widely accepted and, to this day, both religions are followed side by side. ❑

influential members of the court found the new religion attractive, while others remained loyal to their native Shinto (see pages 18–19). Those who followed Buddhism eventually won the struggle for power and in 604 Shotoku (574–622), prince regent to an infant empress, drafted a document, greatly influenced by Buddhist and Confucian principles, calling for political and constitutional reforms. Shotoku founded many Buddhist temples and monasteries, including the famous Horyuji Temple at Nara.

TAIKA REFORM Shotoku's vision was overtaken by political events, and in

Amitabha, the Buddha who guides humans towards the Paradise of the West

645 Emperor Kotoku, backed by traditionalist Japanese nobles, instituted the Taika Reform. All land was declared the property of the throne and its administration was to be controlled by officials appointed by the emperor or his ministers. The reforms were not strictly enforced, but they did eventually create a hierarchical system that became the basis of the feudal system later to dominate Japanese life.

NARA PERIOD In 710, Japan's first permanent capital was established at Nara (see pages 114–115). It was built on the pattern of Ch'ang-an (Xian), the famous capital city of the Chinese Tang Dynasty. With its green-roofed, red-painted buildings, Nara became the focus of courtly and religious life, and this period saw a huge expansion of Buddhist temple construction. Much of the nation's wealth was spent on sculpture, painting, books, lacquerware and other art work to grace these sacred buildings.

As temples and monasteries continued to expand, the power of the clergy increased. In 784, Emperor Kammu decided to move the capital to avoid this influence and increase the authority of the secular government. Supported by the powerful Fujiwara clan, members of which ruled as regents for the emperor, he moved to what became an even grander capital at Heian-Kyo (Kyoto).

In the eighth century, the military order of Samurai were elevated to an elite rank

HEIAN PERIOD Between 794 and 1156, Japan was peaceful and prosperous and enjoyed one of the most culturally fruitful periods in its history. This was partly as a result of the imperial court's decision in 894 to end all official communication with the now failing Tang Dynasty in China. Japan once again became inward-looking, and over the next 300 years a specifically Japanese culture evolved.

Toward the end of the Heian period, the influence of the Fujiwara family waned while other provincial warrior clans grew in military power. Meanwhile, the imperial family and their noble courtiers lost touch with the affairs of the country, and were finally ignored by the warrior families. The Taira and Minamoto clans engaged in a fierce civil war for control of the nation before Minamoto Yoritomo eventually led his side to victory.

He subsequently established a new capital in Kamakura, leaving the imperial court in Kyoto, and formed a military government, becoming the nation's first shogun (see pages 38–39). This was the system of government that was destined to rule Japan for the following 700 years.

Throughout Japanese history the emperor, although spiritually venerated, has rarely had any political power. Overall control was always held by the clan leader (daimyo) with the strongest army. Such leaders became known as the shogun; their warrior soldiers were called samurai.

THE WAY OF THE WARRIOR In the late ninth century, Japan broke off all relations with the rest of the world and embarked on 300 years of isolation. It was during this time that the samurai developed as a distinct warrior class and the ethics of the *bushido* (the Way of the Warrior) evolved.

Samurai means 'one who serves', and each soldier owed allegiance to his *daimyo* (feudal lord). Samurai were divided into three groups. At the top were those who served the shogun, second were the samurai of ordinary *daimyo*, and at the bottom were *ronin*, who had lost their masters through war or politics. *Ronin* roamed about, some working as mercenaries, others turning to crime. Their exploits feature in many Japanese stories, films and plays.

CIVIL WAR From the 12th until the 16th century, Japan suffered almost continuous civil war. Battles were fought between opposing clans seeking overall power or by emperors trying to gain political control to match their spiritual rule of the land. The situation improved in the late 16th century, when General Oda Nobunaga defeated the other most powerful *daimyo* in the country, General Imagawa, to become ruler of virtually all Japan. Nobunaga was both a ruthless soldier and a devotee of the arts. Under his guidance there was a renaissance of interest in poetry, acting, dancing, and fashion, which flourished in the relative peace

38

A full set of samurai warrior armour

❏ During the Kamakura period (1192–1333) there were women among the samurai. Tomoe, a member of the Minamoto, is described in records of the period as having long, black hair and a fair complexion; her face was very lovely and she was a fearless rider, whom neither the fiercest horse nor the roughest ground could dismay. So dextrously did she handle sword and bow, according to the chronicler, that she was a match for a thousand warriors and fit to meet either god or devil. ❏

of his reign. He also encouraged trade with the outside world, and European arts and Christianity became fashionable.

ISOLATION Toyotomi Hideyoshi succeeded Nobunaga in 1582. His was a different outlook, as he believed that foreign influences were weakening Japan, and introduced laws forbidding the Japanese to leave the country and reducing the influx of foreign goods and people, while at the same time reinforcing the traditional feudal patterns of society.

Hideyoshi died in 1598 and was succeeded by Tokugawa Ieyasu, who moved his headquarters from Kyoto to Edo (now Tokyo). From here the Tokugawa family dominated Japanese life for the next 250 years. One after another, the Tokugawa

shogun maintained hostility to all foreign religions and secular influences and carried out a determined policy of national seclusion.

SHOGUNATE OUTDATED The Tokugawa system of government finally broke down in the mid-19th century. The samurai had been emasculated by lack of battle opportunity, and increased interest in the arts of the tea ceremony and calligraphy weakened their authoritarian grip on the country. Both they and the peasants had grown very poor, while a newly prosperous merchant class had emerged as a force of change. Outgunned by Western powers, the Shogunate was forced to sign treaties and Western explorers and traders were again allowed to enter Japan. In 1868, after fighting off Tokugawa loyalists, Emperor Meiji took power and ended the rule of the Shogunate.

A samurai on horseback, armed with bow and arrows

The feudalism that is to some degree still manifest in Japanese society, and the Japanese language, has its origins in the laws enacted by the Tokugawa shogun. It was their intention to control every aspect of Japanese life, in every corner of the land. The place in which people lived, what they ate, the type of clothes they wore, the posture they adopted and the way they slept were all dictated by the State.

At the top of the ladder, emperors and their courts were restricted to Kyoto, their duties confined to the ceremonial. The Tokugawa family maintained the emperor in his position but only to confer the title of shogun (full title: 'Commander-in-Chief for Quelling the Barbarians') on whomever the family nominated.

Like the emperor's, the affairs of military lords were closely monitored by the shogun. They were controlled by the allotment or dispossession of the territories from which they were entitled to collect taxes. Rights to land were given only in exchange for oaths of allegiance. The number of armed men they had, the types of fortifications around their castles, and even their social contacts were controlled. Government inspectors ensured that they upheld their agreements, and if they broke any they were punished by loss of land or exile to a distant part of the country. As an extra safety measure, the Tokugawa shogun maintained control of the three largest cities, Edo (now Tokyo), Kyoto and Osaka, and gave the lands around them to close relatives and loyal allies.

After the emperor and noble lords, the Buddhist and Shinto clergy were the groups most likely to make trouble for the shogun. They were thus split up under the Tokugawa regime into individual sects, which were themselves divided into separate independent units. No co-operation or joint decisions were allowed between sects, and rivalry for land and income was encouraged—a perfect example of 'divide and conquer'.

❑ The samurai class enjoyed many privileges, and during the Tokugawa years (1603–1867) had little to do since there were few battles to fight. They were, however, expected to set a good example to the rest of society and to lead sober and honest lives. In two centuries of relative peace, the samurai brought the art of fighting to a high point of ceremonial and ritual skill, although expertise in real battle fighting and war tactics diminished. Nevertheless, it was samurai from the southern domains of Satsuma and Choshu who carried out the coup d'état of 1867 that brought along the Meiji Restoration of 1868. ❑

Powerful feudal leaders: Ieyasu and Hideyoshi. These great warriors ruled Japan in the 16th and 17th centuries

40

The rest of society was split into four groups. In descending order of status they were samurai, farmers, craftsmen and merchants. Women belonged to the same class as their fathers or husbands. Membership in a particular class was hereditary and fixed. The samurai did not work as such and they considered the pursuit of money to be shameful. They were supported by taxes from the farming class, who suffered considerable hardship maintaining the top-heavy warrior class.

Farmers, the main bulk of the population, although not at the bottom of the social order, were the most exploited of the classes. The rice harvest depended on them and thus the samurai's and the shogun's prosperity. They had to work hard and were not allowed to leave the vicinity of their birthplace. Most lived in considerable poverty.

Craftsmen had lower status than farmers but had more mobility and freedom in the way they led their lives. Master craftsmen, particularly sword-makers, were valued for their skills and lived in the security of their lord's protection.

Merchants were at the bottom of the social ladder, since they produced nothing, were motivated

In the 16th century, Jesuits engaged in trade at great profit to themselves

by profit, and dealt with money. In spite of their lowly position in the social order, the merchants later became the main beneficiaries of the Tokugawa era, and as a group they were responsible for later changes in cultural and social attitudes.

Courtesans of the 18th century

During the 264-year-long Tokugawa era, the Japanese were prohibited from journeying outside Japan and foreigners were not allowed in. In contrast, during the Meiji era (1868–1912), anything Japanese was despised, and many historical buildings and relics were destroyed, while Western cultures were admired. There was even a cult of marrying foreigners to 'improve' the nation's bloodstock.

OPEN AND CLOSED There has been a cyclic character to the history of Japanese culture that follows a three-phase pattern. In the first phase, the country opens itself to outside influences, such as those from China between the sixth and ninth centuries and the West between the 16th and 17th centuries. During these periods the Japanese tend to underrate traditional Japanese values and qualities, although never completely letting them go. This phase is followed by a period of reassessment and consolidation, during which some imported notions are jettisoned and others are subtly altered, acquiring a distinctly Japanese feel. The third stage is a withdrawal from the outside world. The Japanese shut themselves off from the rest of the world and settle down to a life of regularity and security, safe from the risks created by foreign influences. This cycle has repeated itself throughout Japanese history up until the middle of the 19th century when Japan fully entered modern international affairs. Since 1868, the country has been open to the outside world.

CHINESE INFLUENCES The first major influence on Japanese thought and culture, and perhaps the most

Left and below: Commodore Perry and his US Navy ships

42

Empress Shoken and Emperor Meiji

important in its history, came from China. During the sixth and ninth centuries there was active contact with the Chinese governments of the Tang Dynasty, and tradesmen, craftsmen, artists and scholars regularly crossed the waters between the two countries. Confucian principles were introduced into Japanese government, and Buddhism, brought from China, enjoyed a time of great popularity and prosperity.

Nara, the first permanent Japanese capital city, was fashioned on Ch'ang-an (Xian), the gracious seat of the Tang Dynasty, characterized, like Nara, by green-roofed buildings with red wooden walls. During this time contact was also made with countries farther afield than China, and Shoso-in Museum, in the present grounds of the Todaiji Temple, Nara (see pages 114–115), contains beautiful artefacts of the period from Persia (now Iran), India, Greece and Korea.

ISOLATION In the ninth century, Japan broke off all relations with the rest of the world and underwent 300 years of isolation. It was during this time that Kublai Khan made his unsuccessful attempt to invade Japan with more than 100,000 Mongol soldiers. The country was saved by a typhoon wind, which swept away the enemy fleet and earned the name kamikaze meaning 'the Divine Wind'. Japan was not invaded again until the end of World War II.

The Tokugawa shoguns also enforced a policy of national seclusion and it was not until Commodore Perry and his US Navy ships arrived in 1853, demanding that Japan open to overseas trade, that relations with the West were restored.

EXPANSION During his 44-year reign (1868–1912), Emperor Meiji led Japan from being a rural, isolated, feudal society to a powerful nation with a modern navy and army, railways, a parliament and an industrial base.

However, by the beginning of the 1930s Japan's industrial economy needed overseas markets and new sources of raw materials. At the same time, there was a growing militarism, and a sense that Japan was the natural leader of mainland Asia and the Pacific basin. Japan withdrew from the League of Nations, and totalitarian leadership cemented its hold on the country.

The movement was unlike Italian or German fascism, since the emperor remained the secular and spiritual head of the state and the focus of a consensus form of government. Japan invaded Manchuria in 1931, followed by a full-scale invasion of China in 1937. The country eventually joined forces with Hitler, and on 7 December 1941, with the bombing of Pearl Harbor, it entered World War II.

Shinto teachings that the emperor was a living kami (sacred spirit) and that the spirits of the dead were alive contributed to the development of the patriarchal, ancestor-deifying culture of traditional Japan. The emperor, as a living god, was seen as the symbolic and literal father of the family of the Japanese people. Such beliefs lived on in World War II, when Japanese suicide squads sacrificed their lives for the emperor.

44

ANCIENT HISTORY Before the fourth century AD, Japan was a collection of independent states. In time, the various ruling families made alliances, one of them, the Yamato, gradually gaining precedence over the others and winning paramount control. From this background emerged the ancestors of today's imperial family.

Contemporary knowledge of this period is vague, but all lineal ancestors of the present emperor are said to have descended from the same blood line. Whatever the truth, the Japanese imperial dynasty is generally acknowledged as the longest-reigning in world history.

In Japanese mythology, the origins of the imperial family are much more glamorous. The emperor is believed to be a direct descendant of the sun goddess Amaterasu. As such, he is a divine being who has the power to intercede with heaven on behalf of humanity.

The late Emperor Hirohito

❑ Emperor Meiji was succeeded by his son Yoshito, renamed Emperor Taisho, in 1912. Not much is known about Taisho; he suffered from mental illness and was kept out of the public eye. The illness is said to have been caused by lead poisoning; apparently his wet-nurse had used white lead to whiten her breasts, a common fashion of the day. ❑

THE EMPEROR AS FIGUREHEAD In more recent times the emperor did not, despite his divine status, have real political power; this was in the hands of the shogun. During the Edo period (1603–1867) the emperors' upkeep and that of their courtiers was maintained by land grants from the shogun, from which they kept the income. This maintained them in a respectable, rather than a luxurious, lifestyle. An emperor's activities were supervised by government officials and limited to cultural pursuits. Although he was only a figurehead, his title was hereditary and the line of succession had to be maintained. This was a potential danger to the Tokugawa shogunate and did, in fact, lead to its downfall.

POWER REGAINED By the late 18th century, the superfluousness of the samurai and poverty of the peasants had weakened the Tokugawa regime, and in 1867 the young Emperor Meiji was put forward as the country's leader. After fighting off Tokugawa loyalists, he attained full power in

1868 and began his revolutionary reign, the Meiji Restoration.

Emperor Meiji for the first time formally instigated Shinto as the official state religion. Since the Shinto belief is that the emperor is a living god, this gave him total power over the nation. He used it to abolish the old class system, to industrialize the country and to institute new laws and reforms intended to give more human rights to all Japanese.

MODERN TIMES Emperor Hirohito (born 1901) died in 1989 and his son Akihito ascended to the Chrysanthemum Throne in 1990. The protracted enthronement ceremonies culminated in the Daijosai, the Great Food Offering Rite, when, in the dead of night, freshly harvested sacred rice and sake were offered to the gods and other ancient fertility rites were performed. The emperor was transmuted into a 'living god' behind drawn curtains where, alone except for two attendant shrine virgins, he awaited the arrival of the sun goddess Amaterasu.

Emperor Meiji

In 1946, as a term of the peace, Emperor Hirohito declared that he was not a god. For some Japanese, the fact that his son has not followed his lead by diluting the Daijosai ceremony is a disappointment.

Courtesans walking to view peach blossoms, by Ella Du Cane

Japan signed the Anti-Comintern Pact with Germany in 1936 and with Italy in 1937, a union which grew into the Tripartite Pact signed in 1940. By forming these alliances, Japan made obvious its hostility to Great Britain and to the United States, the only country strong enough to prevent Japanese expansion in the Pacific.

PEARL HARBOR Tension between Japan and the US increased in 1940 when the US banned the sale of fuel, iron and steel to Japan, extending this to a total ban on all exports in 1941. The loss of oil was particularly severe, leading the Japanese Navy General Staff to predict that Japan's oil reserves would last only another two years.

As far as the Japanese military was concerned, the survival of their country was at stake. Prime Minister Konoe was replaced by General Tojo Hideki, and the decision was made to go to war. On 7 December 1941, the Japanese attacked the American fleet at Pearl Harbor, Hawaii. Within days they attacked the Philippine Islands and sank two British battleships.

Japanese forces seemed unstoppable, and by 1942 Japan controlled a vast empire reaching 6,430km (4,000 miles) to the south from Sakhalin Island and 9,650km (6,000 miles) to the east from Burma to the Gilbert and Ellice islands (modern Tuvalu and Kiribati). However, national resentments, caused by the economic exploitation of the areas under

Japanese control, coupled with the brutal treatment of their civilian populations, meant that Japanese plans for a 'New Order' in the Far East never had support.

JAPANESE LOSSES The turning point in the war came at the Battle of Midway, 3–6 June 1942. A powerful Japanese naval force attempted to destroy the US Pacific Fleet, but US cryptoanalysts had broken the Japanese naval codes, and the Americans were waiting. During the battle, American planes sank four Japanese aircraft carriers. The loss of its major striking force meant that the Japanese Navy was forced onto the defensive, and slowly but inexorably the Allies moved toward the main Japanese islands.

The Japanese lost almost all of their merchant fleet to Allied aircraft and submarines, which starved Japan of raw materials. The Allied policy of bombing the mainland added to the

American marines watch as shells explode on Japanese troops dug into the hills in southern Okinawa

hardships, but the tenacity and stubborn courage of civilians and troops defending their bases meant that the Allies, even in the face of heavy Japanese losses, could never presume they would surrender. When American forces attacked Okinawa, more than 260,000 Japanese soldiers and civilians died and more than 50,000 American

The battleship West Virginia *burning in Pearl Harbor, Hawaii, after the attack by Japanese planes*

troops were either killed or wounded before the island was taken.

THE ATOM BOMB In July 1945 the Potsdam Declaration was issued, calling for the unconditional surrender of Japan. The Japanese refused. Rather than accept the enormous casualties they expected if forced to invade the Japanese mainland, the Allies dropped an atomic bomb on Hiroshima on 6 August 1945, destroying most of the city and killing 80,000 people. On 9 August a second bomb was dropped on Nagasaki. Faced with such devastation, the Japanese government surrendered on 14 August 1945. Foreign forces occupied the country until 1952, when, under a democratic constitution, Japan regained its independence.

❏ As pressure increased on the Japanese Imperial forces, special attack units known as kamikaze were formed. Named after the 'divine wind' that saved Japan from invasion by the Mongols, these manned planes, boats, or flying bombs loaded with explosives crashed into enemy ships. More than 1,500 planes and flying bombs were used, sinking 34 Allied ships and damaging 288. ❏

Tokyo

- Nishi-Nippori
- Mikawashima
- ARAKAWA-KU
- Minami-Senju
- MEIJI-DORI
- Nippori
- SHOWA-DORI
- Kaneiji Kiyomizudo (Doll Temple)
- Uguisudani
- TAITO-KU
- KOTOTOI-DORI
- Yanaka
- Nezu Shrine
- Nezu
- DORI
- Tokyo Metropolitan Art Museum
- Kokuritsu Hakubutsukan (Tokyo National Museum)
- Nishi-Asakusa
- Asakusa Kannon Temple
- KOTOTOI-
- Ueno Zoo
- Ueno Park
- National Science Museum
- National Museum of Western Art
- Tokyo Festival Hall
- Ueno
- Asakusa
- HONGO-DORI
- Shinobazu Pond
- Shitamachi Museum
- ASAKUSA-DORI
- onga
- Ueno
- Kaminarimon
- Okachimachi
- KASUGA-DORI
- SHUTO EXPRESSWAY NO 6
- Yushima
- Sumida-gawa
- Yamanote line
- SHOWA-DORI
- Ochanomizu
- Akihabara
- Sumo Museum
- Sumida-ku
- Edo-Tokyo Museum
- Sarugakucho
- YASUKUNI-DORI
- EDO-DORI
- Asakusabashi
- Sumo Stadium (Kokugikan)
- Ryogoku
- HAKUSAN-DORI
- Sudacho
- KEIYO-DORI
- Kanda
- Bakurocho
- SHUTO EXPRESSWAY NO 7
- Kanda
- KIYOSUMI-DORI
- East Garden
- Shin-Nihobashi
- Hamacho Garden
- Ningyocho
- Muromachi
- temon Gate
- Nihombashi
- SHIN-OHASHI-DORI
- EITAI-DORI
- CHUO-DORI
- Marunouchi
- Tokyo
- Tokyo City Air Terminal
- Idemitsu Museum of Arts
- Bridgestone Museum of Art
- SHUTO EXPRESSWAY
- Hirano
- SHOWA-DORI
- Yaesu
- Shinkawa
- Hatchobori
- Hatchobori
- NO 9
- i
- Yurakucho
- Hattori Clock Tower
- Antique Shopping Mall
- EITAI-DORI
- Tokyo Disneyland
- Riccar Art Museum
- Sony Buildings
- Kabukiza Theatre
- KIYOSUMI-DORI
- Ginza
- HARUMI-DORI
- Etchujima
- KOTO-KU
- Shimbashi
- Tsukiji
- Shinkansen
- CHUO-KU
- HARUMI-DORI
- Tsukiji Wholesale Fish Market
- Hama Rikyu Garden
- Hamamatsucho
- International Trade Centre
- Harumi-unga
- SWAY NO 1
- EXPRESSWAY
- Harumi Pier
- Tokyo-ko
- 0 — 1 — 2 km
- 0 — 1/2 — 1 mile
- RAINBOW BRIDGE
- D
- E

A-Z TOKYO

Tokyo

Tokyo's Stark Building

50

TOKYO One quarter of all Japanese live within a 50km (31-mile) radius of the Imperial Palace, Tokyo. More than 12 million live in Tokyo itself, one of the world's largest cities and the political, economic and cultural capital of Japan. Unlike the historic cities of Kyoto and Nara, Tokyo is not a place of classic sights and traditional charms; few buildings survived both the great earthquake of 1923 and the bombing of World War II, but it is a powerhouse of creative energy, global influence and wealth.

For the first-time visitor, Tokyo may appear as a disappointing jumble of skyscrapers, concrete overpasses and crowds of pedestrians. However, any exploration on foot, away from modern thoroughfares, reveals it to be a complex metropolis of interconnected towns, each with its own areas of individual character.

For visitors with limited time, the area of Tokyo of most interest and most easily explored is that bounded by the JR (Japan Railways) Yamanote loop line. Within this circle most of the places you will wish to visit are easily reached by subway, taxi, or on foot.

In the heart of Tokyo is the monumental 19th-century Imperial Palace, the seat of the emperor since the Meiji Restoration of 1868 (see pages 44–45). There are good walks near the palace, but the public is not allowed access to the actual grounds, except on 2 January and the emperor's birthday (23 December).

To the southwest of the palace is the Akasaka district, an area of government buildings that includes the Diet (Parliament), expensive hotels and luxurious restaurants. Farther east is the Ginza, Tokyo's world-famous shopping and expense-account entertainment district.

To the south of Akasaka is Roppongi, an area served only by the Hibiya line. It has, nonetheless, become the city's most cosmopolitan and popular nightlife area, especially with young people and foreigners, who are attracted to its art cinemas, experimental theatre and restaurants offering a variety of ethnic cuisines.

HARAJUKU AND SHINJUKU On the western edge of the area bounded by the Yamanote line are Harajuku and Shinjuku. Harajuku is the hub of the teen fashion scene and the site of the historically important Meiji Shrine. Omotesando-dori, a long boulevard lined with designer shops, leads to Yoyogi Park where, until complaints by residents in the area banned such activities, rock bands and Japanese youth gathered on Sunday afternoons to perform. The Aoyama District is similarly fashion-conscious, but is frequented by more affluent Japanese in their twenties and thirties. The shops of some of the top designers are here.

Shinjuku started life as a staging post for Westerners journeying to Edo (Tokyo) and gained a reputation for sleazy nightlife. It has, essentially, outgrown this image and outside the Shinjuku subway station are many good department stores and gift shops, and respectable restaurants and bars. However, the Kabukicho area, within Shinjuku district, is still known for its seedy massage parlours and cheap dives.

Ancient Japan survives in Asakusa

FINDING AN ADDRESS
It is extremely difficult even for local people and taxi drivers to find a place in Japan, and especially in Tokyo, just by its address. There is no logical system of house numbers, and streets do not have names, although some major roads and avenues do. Instead, addresses are by district, and within each district each building has a one- or two-digit (hyphenated) number. The best way to locate an address is to find it on a map of the vicinity. This is made easier when small maps are printed on the back of business cards, restaurant matchbooks, and so on. Otherwise, travel to the general vicinity by bus or train, then for the final part of the journey, take a cab or walk and ask for help.

51

UENO AND ASAKUSA You can get a taste of old Japan in the Ueno and Asakusa districts, in the northeast of the city. Ueno Park is the cultural heart of Tokyo and several of the nation's major art galleries and museums are found in its grounds, as well as the zoo that houses Japan's prized giant pandas. Asakusa is a temple town and home of the famous Kannon Temple, a popular visiting place during holidays and festivals. North of Ueno is Yanaka, where flimsy wooden houses and temples have somehow escaped the bulldozer in old streets that are a popular haunt of photographers and artists.

The Kabukiza Theatre, dating from 1924, is the best-known venue for kabuki *performances*

Tokyo

TEMPLE ORIGINS

According to legend, Asakusa Kannon Temple was established in the seventh century when two local fishermen discovered in their nets a statue of Kannon, the Buddhist Goddess of Mercy. Originally built on this site to house the statue, the temple has been rebuilt and enlarged many times over the intervening centuries. The original image of Kannon found by the fisherman is said to be buried beneath the gold-plated inner shrine found beyond the main altar in the Main Hall, but this has never been verified.

52

Asakusa Kannon Temple: detail...

...and facade

▶▶ Antique Mall Ginza   49D2

1-20-15 Ginza Chuoku
Subway: Ginza 1 chome
Open: Thu–Tue 10.30–7

A popular shopping area with 250 outlets selling a wide range of Japanese and Western antiques, including kimonos, watches and cameras. This type of shopping is a new concept in Japan.

▶▶▶ Asakusa Kannon Temple (Sensoji Temple)   49E5

2-3-1 Asakusa, Taito-ku
Subway: Asakusa
Open: 24 hours

Asakusa district forms part of the old downtown, literally *shitamachi*, section of Tokyo. Settled by merchants, artisans and craftsmen during the Edo period (1603–1867), Asakusa is still an area associated with popular Japanese culture. Asakusa Kannon Temple, in the heart of the district, is the oldest temple in Tokyo, a place of worship held in particular affection.

The Kaminarimon, the Gate of the God of Thunder, hung with a huge, red paper lantern, marks the main entrance to the temple. Nakamise-dori begins inside the gate and leads to the temple compound. Invariably crowded, the street is lined with small stands selling snack foods, traditional gifts and souvenirs.

At the end of the street, the smaller Hozomon gateway opens onto a five-floor pagoda, the temple landmark, and the Main Hall. Both buildings are postwar concrete replicas of original wooden structures. The Main Hall has little architectural merit, but the constant stream of visitors gives it life and energy.

The streets and covered passageways around the temple are teeming with great little shops, restaurants, tea houses, and nightlife (see pages 68–69).

Dembo-in (Abbot's Residence)▶▶ is in the grounds of Asakusa Kannon Temple; pick up a ticket to enter

Robed participants in a procession during Tokyo's White Crane festival

from the Dembo-in temple offices, near the foot of the pagoda. Simply sign the visitors book to get the ticket; then walk back down Nakamise-dori, past the closed front entrance of Dembo-in. Turn right at the next corner and walk down Dembo-in-dori to the entrance gate opposite Asakusa Public Hall. Inside the peaceful grounds is a stroll garden, designed by the tea ceremony master Enshu Kobori (1579–1647). The garden pond contains carp and turtles, and from one angle the Asakusa Kannon pagoda is clearly reflected on its surface. The abbot's wooden residence and guest hall were built in the mid-18th century; the bronze bell at the main entrance dates from 1387.

▶▶ Bridgestone Museum of Art   49D3

1-10-1 Kyobashi, Chuo-ku
Subway: Kyobashi; JR: Tokyo
Open: 10–5.30 (last entrance 5pm). Closed: Mon and 20 Dec–6 Jan
On the third floor of the Bridgestone building, the Museum of Art displays one of Japan's best private collections of painting and sculpture, mainly of the Impressionist school and the *Ecole de Paris*. It includes works by Rodin, Moore, Giacometti, Picasso, Rembrandt, Utrillo and Modigliani, as well as some fascinating post-Meiji Japanese paintings in highly derivative Western styles.

▶▶ Edo Tokyo Museum   49E4

Open: daily, 10–6, Fri 9–6. Closed Mon
Three minutes' walk from Ryogoku station, across from Kokugikan Sumo Hall
Inside a very spacious and futuristic building, life-size dioramas re-create scenes from Tokyo's cultural and commercial past within a gallery as large as a stadium.

TEMPLE FESTIVALS
Major festivals are regularly held at the Asakusa Kannon Temple. The most popular attractions are the Setsubun ceremony on 3 February; the Kinryu-no-mai (Golden Dragon Dance) on 18 March and 18 October; the Sanja festival of Asakusa Shrine on 17 and 18 May; the Shirasagi-no-mai (White Crane Dance) on 3 November; and the year-end Hagoita-ichi market between 17 and 18 December, when vendors sell *hagoita* (paddles) richly decorated with portraits of famous figures from *kabuki*. The paddle is used with a shuttlecock to play a traditional game, similar to badminton, during the New Year Festival.

▶▶▶ Ginza
49D2

Subway: Ginza (exit for the 4 chome intersection)

The most famous shopping and entertainment district in Japan, Ginza contains the largest concentration of department stores, expensive boutiques, galleries, coffee shops, bars and restaurants in Tokyo. It is also an important commercial hub, home to some of Japan's most prestigious companies, as well as the location of several hotels.

Ginza's best-known landmark is the Hattori Clock Tower, which stands at the top of the Wako department store, at the intersection of Harumi-dori and Chuo-dori. The clock was first installed in 1894 and many of the nearby shops are as old or older. The Kimuraya bakery, next door to Wako, opened in 1874 and is still are a very popular place, especially for its tofu (beancurd) bread. Mikimoto (4-5-5 Ginza) sells cultured pearls and was, perhaps, the first shop in the world to do so, having opened in 1899.

The **Sony Building**▶▶, 5-3-1 Ginza, Chuo-ku (*Open 11–8*), contains restaurants and boutiques, in addition to three Sony showrooms (first, third and fourth floors) where new products and developments are displayed to the public.

GINZA SHOPPING
Ginza is one of the most expensive shopping areas in all Japan. The area housed a mint (*gin* means silver) before Western imports and architecture were first displayed here following the opening of the country to foreign trade in the late 19th century. On Sundays and holidays Ginza-dori is closed to traffic and opened to pedestrians only.

Traffic in Ginza-dori (Ginza Street)

▶▶ Idemitsu Museum of Arts   49D3

Kokusai Building, 9th Floor, 3-1-1 Maruno-uchi, Chiyoda-ku
Subway: Hibiya
Open: 10–5. Closed: Sun, Mon (and Tue if Mon is a
national holiday)

On the tenth floor of the Kokusai Building, the Idemitsu is one of the largest and best-designed private museums in Tokyo. It also has one of the best views in Tokyo, looking right over the Imperial Palace. It contains an excellent collection of Zen calligraphy and ink paintings, some of which are by the famous Zen monk Sengai. It also has fine examples of Chinese porcelain of the Tang and Song dynasties and Japanese ceramics. A Japanese tea room is open to the public.

▶▶ Kabukiza Theatre   49D2

4-12-15 Ginza, Chuo-ku
Subway: Higashi-Ginza

Tokyo's best known *kabuki* theatre sits at the intersection of two main streets in Ginza: Harumi-dori and Showa-dori. It first opened its doors in 1889, but was rebuilt in 1924 during a period of Japanese revivalism, in a baroque style inspired by castle architecture of the 16th century. The present building is a 1951 reconstruction of this structure. Kabukiza is one of the best places to see *kabuki* (see pages 58–59). English language notes and an earphone system are available, and there are daily matinée and evening performances all year, except August and December. It is possible to pay to see just one act.

▶▶ Kokuritsu Hakubutsukan
(Tokyo National Museum)   49D5

13-9 Ueno-koen, Taito-ku
JR: Ueno (exit via Ueno-koen)
Open: Tue–Sun 9–4.30, Fri 9–8. Closed: Mon and
25 Dec–3 Jan

The National Museum covers the whole history of Japan and Japanese art from the earliest periods on record. Its collection of archaeology, sculpture, painting, lacquer work, ceramics and armour make it the most complete collection of its kind anywhere in the world. Architecturally, the museum is a mixture of buildings of opposing styles and periods, but the treasures on view are remarkable.

There are four main exhibition areas. Honkan, the main hall directly facing the front gate, is rather gloomy, but a stroll through the 25 rooms of ancient Japanese sculpture, textiles, metalwork, armour, ceramics, paintings, lacquerware and calligraphy is well worthwhile. Hyokeikan, to the left of the main entrance, was constructed in 1909 to celebrate the marriage of the future Emperor Taisho, and houses important Japanese archaeological exhibits. The third exhibition space is the Horyuji Treasure House, open only on Thursday (and not even then, if it is raining heavily or very humid). It contains rare and priceless Buddhist artefacts and works of art from the Horyuji Temple in Nara, said to be the birthplace of Japanese Buddhism. Finally, the Toyokan Gallery of Oriental Antiques specializes in archaeological, historical and cultural objects from China, southeast Asia and India.

MONEY-MAKING
The name Ginza means 'place where silver is minted' and refers to the government mint established in the area in 1612 on land reclaimed from the sea. Ginza in its present role was created in the latter half of the 19th century to serve as a model of the Western culture the Japanese were embracing at the time. Its shops were the first in Japan to employ window displays, and window shopping is still one of Ginza's attractions. It has given rise to the common phrase *Gin-bura*, meaning to stroll aimlessly through Ginza (or any shopping district). A more recent pastime is *depato meguri*, or hopping from one department store to the next.

Samurai armour, Tokyo National Museum

IMPERIAL LINEAGE
Although some women held imperial power in ancient Japan, from the Nara period (710–794) until the present only males have been allowed to sit on the imperial throne. Except for the crown prince and his oldest son, who may not refuse the throne, it is possible for other descendants of the emperor to give up their imperial status and become commoners through marriage.

The Imperial Palace

▶▶▶ Kokyo (Imperial Palace)　　　48C3

Subway: Otemachi
Open (East Garden only): 9–4 (enter by 3pm). Closed: Mon, Fri, and 25 Dec–3 Jan

This is the residence of the reigning emperor of Japan and his family. It is set in extensive grounds right in the heart of Tokyo's business district, on the former site of Edo Castle, the home of the Tokugawa shogunate. Construction of the Imperial Palace began after the Meiji Restoration of 1868, when the emperor moved from Kyoto to Tokyo.

Most of the main buildings were destroyed in World War II, but rebuilding was completed in 1968. The actual palace is closed to the public, and the private palace grounds are open only twice a year, on the emperor's birthday (23 December) and 2 January. Access on these days is via the Nijubashi, a double-arched stone bridge of

German design, one of Tokyo's most familiar sights (reached from Nijubashi-mae subway station).

The Imperial Palace East Garden, formerly at the heart of Edo Castle, makes up one third of the palace grounds, and is open to the public. Popular with Japanese and foreign visitors, and with Tokyoites keen for air and a stroll in the sunlight, the garden is a welcome oasis in the noise and fumes of downtown Tokyo. The most convenient entrance is via the Otemon, once the principal gate to Edo Castle and an impressive example of a *masugata* (defensive) gate.

To the north of the palace lies Kitanomaru Park, formerly the private grounds of the Imperial Guard but now open to the public, and the home of several museums (access via Kudanshita subway station).

▶▶▶ Meiji Jingu (Meiji Shrine)   48A3

1-1 Yoyogi, Kamizono-cho, Shibuya-ku
Subway: Meiji Jingu-mae. JR: Harajuku and Yoyogi
Open: shrine and inner garden daily dawn to dusk, except third Friday of each month. Iris garden 9–4.30, 1 Mar–3 Nov; 9–4, rest of year

This Shinto shrine and its large park are dedicated to the spirit of Emperor Meiji (1852–1912) and his wife, Empress Shoken (1850–1914). Emperor Meiji reigned during Japan's transformation from an isolated nation, unchanged for many hundreds of years, into a modern world power. He and Empress Shoken are buried near Kyoto, but this shrine was completed in his memory in 1920 with a volunteer workforce of more than 100,000 Japanese people. It was destroyed in an air raid in 1945 and rebuilt to the original design in 1958. The grounds are thickly wooded (with many trees and shrubs donated by the various provinces of Japan) and contain a famous iris garden, once frequented by the Emperor and his consort. It is a beautiful and cool retreat, even during Tokyo's hot, humid summer. The approach to the shrine itself is spanned by a huge *torii* gate (see panel), made of cypress wood more than 1,700 years old. Behind the shrine is the Treasure House, in which articles belonging to Emperor Meiji are exhibited.

The shrine is very popular during the New Year festival, and on New Year's Eve trains run to the nearest JR station throughout the night. It is also particularly busy on Sundays, and on Thursdays young couples come here to present their newborn babies in a ceremony known as *miya mairi*; the babies and mothers are often dressed in traditional robes and kimonos.

TORII
Torii, the large gates that stand at the entrances to Shinto shrines, are made of wood, either plain or painted red. Each gate has two round, upright columns and two crossbeams. The purest and most primitive style of *torii* is made of logs with their bark intact. The red *torii* rising out of the sea at Itsukushima Shrine on Miyajima Island is one of the most famous symbols of Japan.

At the Meiji Shrine

Kabuki, *literally 'song, dance, act', is said to have been created at the beginning of the 17th century by Okuni, a temple priestess who was also a skilled Buddhist dancer and a great beauty. She fell in love with a* ronin *(a masterless samurai) and fled with him, finally settling in Edo (Tokyo), where she founded a theatre and began recruiting actors.*

SWORD-FREE THEATRE

A government edict of 1631, forbidding the wearing of swords in the theatre, had the effect of excluding the samurai, who refused to relinquish their weapons. The nobility abandoned the theatre, which became the pastime of the commercial and lower classes. By attending the theatre himself in 1887, Emperor Meiji rehabilitated *kabuki* among the higher social echelons.

THE AUDIENCE

Despite the slow action, a Japanese *kabuki* theatre audience takes great delight in a performance, hissing the villain and appreciating a well-delivered speech. Theatregoers may skip boring acts and return for those they enjoy. In the foyer they can meet friends, chat, drink, and buy food from a great variety of restaurants and stands.

Kabuki *has villains...*

Larger than life Two different types of plays are performed in *kabuki* theatre: plays about everyday life and historical dramas. Whatever the subject, however, the sets and acting are always flamboyant and exaggerated, with the passions, lusts and violence of life amply portrayed. Animals with human speech arrive in clouds of smoke and dance magically; rivers of blood flow from the heads of soldiers fallen to vengeful armies; victories and defeats are interlaced with the tender tragedies of failed love affairs or the triumphant reunion of lost lovers. In old Japanese society, in which social and private lives were rigidly controlled, *kabuki* gave actors and their audience room to vent emotions they could not normally express. See page 55 for details of Kabukiza Theatre.

Men as women In time, women were expelled from *kabuki* and men were required to play their roles. Since then, *onnagata*, men who specialize in female roles, have striven to present the perfect idealized version of universal woman. To play their roles well they study and rehearse traditional female characteristics, even in their daily lives. Yoshisawa Ayame, an early and great *kabuki* artist, said that the ideal woman could be expressed only by an actor; he called it 'the synthetic ideal'. This admiration of the synthetic is frequently encountered in Japan, perhaps because the Japanese are able to judge the artificial and plastic substitute as a thing in its own right rather than as a copy of something 'real'. For this reason, although transvestite clubs and performers are popular all over Japan, they are taken more seriously than their Western equivalents.

Costumes, music *Kabuki* actors wear wigs, heavy make-up and elaborate costumes. The plays unfold very slowly in a succession of tableaux; tension is maintained by the powerfully contained emotions of the actors. The orchestra, composed of traditional instruments, underlines the action and adds to the charged atmosphere. As a performance, the *kabuki* is a mix of classical theatre, opera and music hall.

The 47 *Ronin* One of the plays that is most popular with *kabuki* audiences is *The Adventure of the 47 Ronin*. Its story (outlined below) contains two of the classic ingredients of a *kabuki* play: satisfaction of honour and suicide.

In 1701, in the shogun's palace, Lord Kira insulted Lord Asano. Asano drew his sword and sprang at Kira, who fled. Unable to avenge his honour, Asano had no alternative but to commit *seppuku* (suicide by the sword). His vassals thus became *ronin*. They swore to avenge their lord, and spent two years waiting for their moment. Eventually, one snowy night, they entered Kira's castle and cut off his head. They carefully washed the severed head, for an inferior must appear clean before his superior and Kira had become Asano's inferior. Then they took the head, together with the sword that had been used and a letter recounting what they had done, and placed them all on Asano's grave. Finally, no longer having any aim in life, and to avoid punishment for their crime, all 47 *ronin* committed *seppuku* and were buried beside their lord.

This *kabuki* plot is based on a true story and the graves of the 47 *ronin* are in the Sengakuji Temple in Tokyo (see page 61).

…and heroines, who are all played by men

TRANSVESTISM
The Tokugawa-era government took measures against any trend that threatened class boundaries. In 1667, to prevent over-familiarity between male and female actors, and the appearance in their ranks of prostitutes, the state banned them from appearing on stage together. This action gave rise to the tradition of transvestism in the Japanese theatre.

Quiet streets around Sengakuji Temple

HIROSHIGE

Hiroshige (1797–1858), now one of Japan's most famous woodblock print (*ukiyo-e*) artists, was considered eccentric in his day. Rather than portraying orthodox themes in the conventional symbolic manner, his work dealt with the lives of ordinary people, presented in a realistic manner. His prints were sold in tea houses or shops, and popular editions were published many times. By the time he was 35, Hiroshige was a well-known artist in the Tokyo area, then called Edo. In the late 19th century, Europe began to discover Japanese art and Hiroshige's work was acknowledged for its unusual composition, hues and freshness. His influence can be seen in paintings by Manet, Toulouse Lautrec and Van Gogh. News of Hiroshige's reception in the West increased interest at home and, by 1900, he had become a nationally known figure.

Kyoto Bridge by moonlight, from the series '100 Views of Famous Places in Edo', published in 1855

▶▶ Nihon Mingeikan (Japan Folk Crafts Museum)   48A2

4-3-33 Komaba, Meguro-ku
Subway: Komabatodai-mae
Open: 10–5 (last entry 4pm). Closed: Mon, 22 Dec–3 Jan, and while changing exhibitions

At the turn of the 20th century, Soetsu Yanagi was one of Japan's leading philosophers and critics, and wrote prolifically on Western art, literature and philosophy. He and his circle of friends published a monthly arts magazine with the aim of introducing European culture to Japan, but gradually his interest switched from European to Asian art. He became distressed that the folk art of his own country was swiftly disappearing. Yanagi embarked on a campaign to preserve *mingei*, the term he coined to describe this 'art of the people', and to increase national awareness of the value of its 'everyday beauty'.

Within three decades, he had founded this museum, dedicated not to the fine arts but to the intrinsic beauty of crafts made for daily use. Items are displayed in a replica farmhouse from Tochigi prefecture, north of Tokyo, and include Soetsu Yanagi's own large collection. Exhibitions are rotated four times a year to allow all the examples of pottery, textiles, carvings, furniture, kitchen equipment and such exhibits to be shown.

▶▶ Ota Kinen Bijutskan (Memorial Museum of Art) 48A2

1-10-10 Jingumae, Shibuya-ku
Subway: Meiji Jingu-mae. JR: Harajuku
Open: 10.30–5.30. Closed: Mon, from the 24th to the end of every month, and 20 Dec–3 Jan

The late Seizo Ota, former chairman of Tokyo Mutual Life, left a formidable bequest of more than 12,000 wood-block prints (*ukiyo-e*) and, in the tradition of successful Japanese entrepreneurs, the money to construct this small museum to display them. The galleries are well lit and the prints expertly displayed on a rotating basis, representing most of Japan's best-known print artists. There is a coffee shop in the basement.

Across from the museum entrance is Omotesando Avenue, busy with shoppers and, particularly on Sundays, the young and fashion-conscious. The Ota is in a small side street near Meiji-dori, which is a haven of peace among the trendy streets of Harajuku.

▶▶ Sengakuji Temple 48C1

2-11-1 Takanawa, Minato-ku (turn right from the station and walk up the hill; the entrance is past the traffic lights on the left)
Subway: Sengakuji
Open: 9–4

The 47 *ronin* buried in this temple are revered by the Japanese as examples of truly loyal men (see pages 58–59). An interesting English-language version of the story of the *ronin* and their sacrifice for their master, Lord Asano, who had been wrongly obliged to commit *seppuku* (ritual suicide), is available at the shops near the temple entrance.

To the right of the entrance is a statue of Yoshio Oishi, leader of the *ronin* and Lord Asano's chief retainer. Beyond the main inner gate, and to the left, is the cemetery. On the way you will pass a well where the *ronin* washed the severed head of Lord Kira (Asano's betrayer) before laying it on their master's grave. The head was eventually given back to Kira's family, and in the small museum in the temple grounds a receipt issued by a temple priest for 'one head' is on display in one of the dusty cabinets. The tombs of the 47 *ronin* have become blackened with the smoke from the many sticks of incense burned in tribute over the years.

Sengakuji Temple

Tokyo

SHINJUKU FRONTIER TOWN

Shinjuku was originally a small post town on the Koshu-kaido highway providing horses, brothels, inns and tea houses for passing wayfarers. It became a boom town with the building of a railway station in 1885 and earned a reputation as a brash, free and easy area. A frontier feel is still associated with eastern Shinjuku. Having been spared by the 1923 Kanto earthquake, the district expanded at a faster pace than the rest of the city. The present Shinjuku station opened in 1964.

62

The modern face of Japan at Shinjuku

A statue of warrior Saigo Takemori in Ueno

▶▶▶ Shinjuku
48A3

Subway: Shinjuku (Marunouchi line at the north end of the station, on the east side; Toei–Shinjuku line at the south end, on the west side)

Shinjuku district has the largest, busiest and most chaotic railway station in Japan (see pages 92–93). Railway lines divide Shinjuku into two very different areas. The eastern side is a busy shopping district, with a warren of underground shopping arcades and a lively entertainment district at night. The Kabuki-cho area, on the east side, is notorious for its sex establishments (see pages 244–245). The unplanned, vibrant quality of the east is in fine contrast to the ordered development of the west side, where high-rise offices and modern hotels have earned the nickname 'Skyscraper City'. The city government recently moved there, into the Tokyo Metropolitan Government offices designed by Kenzo Tange.

Shinjuku Imperial Gardens▶▶ (*Shinjuku Gyoen*), an 80ha (30-acre) park at Naito-cho (*Subway:* Shinjuku Gyoen-mae), belonged to a family of feudal lords, then to Emperor Meiji. The gardens were opened to the public after World War II. The northern end of the park has expanses of greenery, and in the east there is a garden in 19th-century French style. Famous for its cherry blossoms (*sakura*) in spring and chrysanthemums in the autumn, the park is treasured by residents of Shinjuku (*Open* 9–4.30; *closed* Mon). South of Shinjuku Gardens are the beautiful National Noh Theatre and gardens, where English-language guides to *noh* theatre are on sale.

►► Shitamachi Museum   49D4

2-1 Ueno-Koen, Taito-ku
Subway: Ueno, Yushima
Open: Tue–Sun 9.30–4.30. Closed: Mon and 29 Dec–3 Jan
Shitamachi translates as 'town below' and refers to the district in a town where the merchant and artisan classes lived and worked. Asakusa and Ueno in Tokyo were such areas. These closely built, densely populated districts developed their own popular culture, customs and social habits, such as being quick to help others or to argue and work hard. After World War II, the characteristic nature of these areas started to disappear and this museum was built to record their heritage.

►► Tokyo DisneySea Park, Tokyo Bay   Off 49E2

For tickets: Hibiya Mitsui Building, 1-1-2 Yurakucho,
Chiyoda-ku
tel: 03 3595 1777; www.tokyodisneyresort.co.jp
Opened in 2001, this is the world's first Disney Park to be inspired by myths and legends of the sea.

►► Ueno District and Zoo   49D5

Ueno station is the gateway from Tokyo to northern Japan. Department stores, shopping malls, restaurants and bars cluster around the station, and behind it is Ueno Park (*Ueno Koen*), Japan's first and largest public park. Within the park are several museums, including the Tokyo National Museum (see page 55) and the Shitamachi Museum (see above), and Shinobazu Pond. The **National Museum of Western Art**►► (*Open* 9.30–5; *closed* Mon), designed by Le Corbusier, houses the Matsukata Collection of 19th- and 20th-century French art; the **Tokyo Metropolitan Art Museum**►► (*Open* 9–5; *closed* every third Mon) exhibits modern Japanese arts, and the **National Science Museum**►► (*Open* 9–4.30; *closed* Mon) houses displays on science, technology and traditional crafts. **Ueno Zoo** (*Open* 9.30–4.30; *closed* Mon) opened in 1882; crowds flock there to see the two giant pandas given by the People's Republic of China.

DOLL TEMPLE
Kaneiji Kiyomizudo temple, in the grounds of Ueno Park, was built in imitation of the famous Kiyomizudera Temple in Kyoto (see page 129). Mothers leave dolls around the altar of the temple to protect the health of their babies. The dolls are collected throughout the year and ritually burned in a rather macabre ceremony every 25 September.

63

Boating in Ueno Park, Japan's largest city park and a good spot for springtime cherry blossom viewing

Tsukiji is Tokyo's wholesale seafood distribution hub and perhaps the biggest, most vibrant, and most exciting fish market in the world. The market opens before dawn, and as business is virtually over by 9.30am, many visitors miss the opportunity of seeing this Japanese institution.

THE OUTER MARKET
In the outer, smaller area of the market are stands and shops providing everything for the catering trade from *bonito* fish flakes to personalized toothpicks. There are also small cafés, bars and coffee shops serving the fish-sellers, buyers and truck drivers. They are the places to go for breakfast after a visit to the inner market.

MOVING HOME
It was announced in 2001 that Tsukiji will move to a new site in Tokyo Bay in 2006 0r 2007. For direct access to Tsukiji take the Oedo subway line to Tsukiji–Shijo station. From there it's a one-minute walk to the main market.

Seafood for sale well before sunrise

To get to Tsukiji market, take a cab from your hotel or a train on the Hibiya subway line to Tsukiji station, two stops past Ginza station. Turn left out of the station, walk down Shin Ohashi Avenue (*Shin Ohashi-dori*) past two sets of traffic lights, turn left again and you will find yourself in the outer market. Cross the blue iron bridge that leads across a small canal to the sheds of the wholesale market. Walk past the lines of vans, piles of styrofoam boxes, and small boxwood fires, built by the truck drivers to keep warm while they wait to return home. Soon you will come upon the frantically bustling market, where more than a thousand fish vendors and streams of buyers and sellers compete for space in a maze of alleyways, while men push and pull carts loaded with huge tuna fish, or stacks of styrofoam boxes full of ice and wriggling fish.

Tuna fish auction The market specializes in *maguro* (tuna fish), sometimes brought to the market straight from the fishing boats that tie up at the dock behind it, though most are flown in from all over Japan and from London, Boston and Africa. The *maguro*, some of them weighing more than 300kg (650 pounds), are auctioned every morning, then pushed on carts to the buyers' stalls. There they are put on marble slabs and sliced with an electric saw; the sections are then cut into smaller pieces with a long and very sharp knife. Only at this stage does the buyer know if the fish has the desired high fat

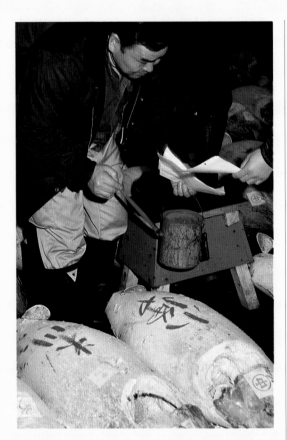

SUSHI AND KNIVES
At lunchtime, the sushi bars around the market sell the freshest sushi you are ever likely to taste. These vinegared rice patties can be topped with a variety of food, but in Tsukiji they are prepared by the *sushi-san* (a sushi chef) with raw fish bought that morning. In winter, sushi is eaten with a hot sake for a perfect lunch. The outer market also has several vendors selling Japanese cooking knives, among the best in the world, beautifully made with plain wooden handles. Blades are marked with the maker's trademark in *kanji*.

Marking tuna with the buyer's sign

content and, thus, whether he has paid a good or bad price for it.

Late at night, trucks from village co-operatives all over Japan start to arrive with their loads of fresh fish. They reach the market and line up to be unloaded between midnight and 4am. Trucks carrying water tanks full of live fish go to the south end of the market, where their catch is placed in aerated holding tanks to await the auction. At around 4am, the trucks leave the auctioneers, and wholesale buyers arrive to look at the produce. The buyers examine the tuna for fat content and take a look inside the boxes of other fish to make sure they are fresh. What they buy, and the prices they pay are crucial to profits they make later in the day.

At 5.20am the auction begins. Tuna fish are auctioned on the ground floor and other fish and seafood upstairs. Meanwhile, at the market, buyers' assistants are clearing up, getting boxes of fresh ice ready, sharpening knives, and preparing for the arrival of the stevedores with the morning purchases. Between 6 and 9am, the retailers, restaurateurs and *sushi-san* (see panel) arrive to buy fish and to catch up on the day's news. By 9.30am the pace in the market is slower, and it is time to leave.

At the entrance to the blue iron bridge leading to the market is the Namiyoke Temple, a Shinto shrine dedicated to the safety of seamen. A stand at its gate sells delicious, freshly baked cakes filled with red-bean jam.

TSUKIJI
Fish is a staple of the Japanese diet, and no world culture is more inventive than this in serving and eating it with relish: raw as *sashimi* or as a topping on rice, as sushi, grilled, smoked, pickled, and dried. Most fish caught commercially for Japanese consumption is rushed to the daily Tsukiji market auction, a remarkable spectacle.

A kamikaze flying bomb on display at Yasukuni Shrine

SUMO AT YASUKUNI SHRINE
Between 21 and 23 April, open-air sumo matches are held every afternoon at Yasukuni Shrine. The event marks the end of a Shinto spring festival and traditionally the best sumo men in Japan dedicate their services freely. Pre-match rituals are shortened, but otherwise the contests are conducted with the usual ceremony. Each sumo stable has its own open marquee, where wrestlers prepare themselves before entering the ring. You can wander freely among the enormous men. Look for top wrestlers arriving in black stretch limousines, a single man filling the whole back seat.

▶▶ **Yanaka District** 49D5

This district, north of the Shitamachi Museum (see page 63) was one of the few in Tokyo to escape most of the destruction of the 1923 Kanto earthquake and World War II bombing. With its narrow streets and old shops and houses, it preserves much of the feel of a Shitamachi area, and is worth exploring on foot, if you do not mind the risk of getting lost. JR Nippori station, on the Yamanote line, is a good starting point.

▶▶ **Yasukuni Shrine** 48C4

3-1-1 Kudankita, Chiyoda-ku
Subway: Kudanshita
Open: shrine 24 hours, Main Hall and museum 9.30–4.30
This Shinto shrine, a national monument in Japan, was built at the request of Emperor Meiji to commemorate Japanese who had died in the battle to reinstate his imperial authority in the Meiji Restoration of 1868. Since then, it has been dedicated to the spirits of all Japanese soldiers and civilians who gave their lives defending the Japanese empire. Many of the 2.5 million souls commemorated at the shrine died in imperialistic wars, and as such their enshrinement is out of step with the postwar Japanese constitution, which renounces militarism and separates the state from religion. As a result of this contradiction, the shrine has been the focus of a number of political controversies.

The official visit of Japan's prime minister in 1985 created an outcry from the government of China and a torrent of protest from Japanese opposition parties, who saw the visit as sanctifying war criminals. Nevertheless, the shrine is regularly visited by many thousands of Japanese, who go simply to pay their respects to lost relatives and friends and to pray for 'the repose of their souls'.

Yasukuni is a complex of buildings that includes the Main Hall, the Hall of Worship, a museum called the Yushukan, a *noh* theatre and a sumo wrestling ring. The Main Hall and Hall of Worship are built in the primitive, unadorned *shinmei* style of the ancient shrines at Ise (see pages 106–107). The Yushukan is essentially a military museum with exhibits such as a tank, a naval gun and the Human Torpedo (*Kaiten*), the submarine equivalent of a kamikaze plane. The most recent addition is a steam locomotive from the Thai–Burma 'Death Railway', built by Allied prisoners of war. The museum's contents in the context of the shrine are, to say the least, disquieting.

Look for the huge steel *torii* (gate) that stands at the entrance of an avenue, lined with stone lanterns and cherry and *ginko* trees; this leads to another enormous *torii* and, finally, the main gate to the inner sanctuary.

▶ Yoyogi Park

48A2

Subway: Omotesando. JR: Harajuku

Once a Japanese army drilling ground, this area was requisitioned by the US Army after World War II and became known as Washington Heights. In 1964, the land was used for the construction of the athletes' Olympic Village, before its final conversion to public parkland. The park is a welcome open space and is of particular interest when it turns a dramatic pink in the cherry-blossom viewing season at the beginning of April. Takeshita-dori, nearby, is a cramped alleyway where cheap boutiques and street vendors sell sunglasses, posters, pins and cut-price fashion clothes: a young teenager's dream.

Rock 'n' roll at Yoyogi Park

Walk

Asakusa

Distance: 2.5km (1.5 miles); time: one hour. Tokyo's 'downtown' shopping and entertainment district, on the banks of the Sumida River, is the spiritual home of the *Edokko*, Tokyo's original blue-collar workers. Asakusa is a great place for inexpensive souvenir shopping, or for the serious cook to look for Japanese additions to the *batterie de cuisine*.

On leaving Asakusa subway station, on the Ginza line, pause to look across the Sumida River. To the left of the bridge stand the **Asahi Brewery Company's** headquarters and the **Asahi Beer Hall▶**, both landmarks of the Tokyo 1980s style, by French designer Philippe Starck. The brewery building is said to represent a glass of beer, complete with a head of foam, while the strange golden object atop the Beer Hall represents a flame.

Turning around, walk two blocks away from the river to find the

Kaminarimon or Thunder Gate, marking the entry to the precincts of **Sensoji Temple**, also known as the **Asakusa Kannon Temple** (see page 52). The approach to the temple on Nakamise-dori is lined with stands selling all manner of traditional

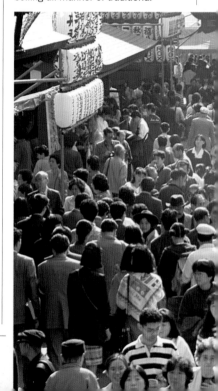

souvenirs and sweetmeats, plus some more way-out articles. About 100m (330ft) along on the left-hand side, a corner stand has an intriguing line in canine formal wear. In common with even the most modest of local shopping streets in Tokyo, Nakamise-dori's decorations change with the seasons.

After visiting the temple and garden, walk around and to the west for three minutes to reach the **Hanayashiki playground▶**, a small children's amusement park. Between Hanayashiki and the Asakusa View Hotel is a group of venues, heart of the Asakusa entertainment district, distinctly different and more welcoming than fashionable Shibuya and Shinjuku. Continue walking along the street to the left of the Asakusa View Hotel, until you come to **Kappabashi-dori▶▶**, the heart of the catering trade wholesale district and the place to go for excellent knives, exotic kitchen utensils, and also the lurid plastic food replicas that grace so many restaurant and cafeteria window displays.

To end the walk, continue south down Kappabashi-dori until you reach Tawaramachi subway station, Ginza line.

Above: the Sumida River
Below: Asakusa Kannon Temple

Walk

Shinjuku

Distance: 3.5km (2 miles); time: one and a half to 2 hours. Relax in the Shinjuku Gardens before taking on Tokyo's busiest shopping and entertainment district.

Start at Shinjuku Gyoen-mae subway station, Maruno-uchi line, and walk one block to the **Shinjuku Imperial Gardens**. This broad, pleasantly landscaped park allows quiet views of the cluster of skyscrapers to the northwest in Tokyo's administrative and business district. Leaving the park, walk back past the subway station and across the main street, Shinjuku-dori, to find the entrance to **Taisoji Temple►►**, originally built in the 17th century and housing a statue of Yama, king of the Buddhist hell.

Continue west along Shinjuku-dori, then turn right into Meiji-dori and head

Metropolitan Government offices

north, crossing the wide Yasukuni-dori, to the entrance to the **Hanazono Shrine►►►**, bright with scarlet *torii* (gates). The shrine is famous for its *Tori-no-Ichi*, held each November, a market for lavishly decorated bamboo rakes sold as good luck charms.

After visiting the shrine, go back across Yasukuni-dori to rejoin Shinjuku-dori and then turn right, to Shinjuku station. Here are the department stores, **Isetan**, **Marui** and **Mitsukoshi**.

Alternatively, turn right along Yasukuni and approach Shinjuku station. The streets to the right make up **Kabuki-cho►**, the city's largest nightlife area.

Either way leads to Shinjuku station. Opposite the east exit stands the **ALTA Building** with a giant TV screen, a popular meeting point. Follow the signs through the station to the west exit. On the lower level, the walkway leads to the right, to an underground link with the business district. Walk to street level to see the marble twin towers of the **Tokyo Metropolitan Government offices►**, a vast and expensive show of architectural bravura. Return by underground walkway to Shinjuku station.

Walk

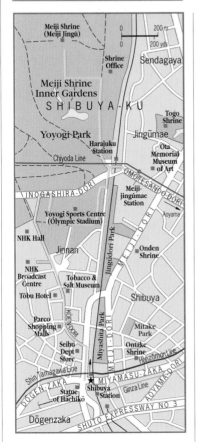

Meiji Shrine
(Meiji Jingū)

0   200 m
0   200 yds

Shrine
Office   Sendagaya

Meiji Shrine
Inner Gardens

S H I B U Y A - K U

Togo
Shrine

Yoyogi Park   Jingūmae

Harajuku
Station   Ota
Memorial
Museum
Chiyoda Line   of Art

INOGASHIRA-DORI

Meiji-
jingūmae
Station

OMOTESANDO-DORI

Yoyogi Sports Centre
(Olympic Stadium)   Aoyama

NHK Hall

Onden
Jinnan   Shrine

NHK
Broadcast   Tobacco &
Centre   Salt Museum

Tobu Hotel   Shibuya

Parco
Shopping   Mitake
Malls   Park

Seibu   Ontake
Dept   Shrine
Store   Hanzomon Line

Shin-Tamagawa Line   MIYAMASU-ZAKA-DORI

DOGEN-ZAKA   Statue   Shibuya   Ginza Line
of Hachiko   Station

Dōgenzaka   SHUTO EXPRESSWAY NO 3

Distance: 2.5km (1.5 miles); time: at least one and a half hours. This walk leads through one of Tokyo's most fashionable districts to the sombre beauty of the Meiji Shrine, then back into the mixture of tacky and high fashion in Harajuku.

Start at the north exit of JR Shibuya station, JR Yamanote line, subway Hanzomon and Ginza lines, by the statue of **Hachiko►**, a dog owned by a college professor, who met his master at Shibuya station every day and continued to wait for him for seven years after his master's death.
    Walk north from Hachiko's statue, along Koen-dori (Park Street), lined

Shibuya and Harajuku

with boutiques and restaurants. Continue walking up the slope, past the **Parco shopping arcades** and the **Tobu Hotel** to the **NHK (Japan Broadcasting System) Broadcast Centre** and the **NHK Hall►►**, one of Tokyo's largest venues for classical music performances.
    Walk northeast to the entrance to Yoyogi Park (see page 67). The **Yoyogi Sports Centre►** was one of three arenas that were used in the 1964 Olympic Games, designed by Kenzo Tange.
    Skirt the Sports Centre and cross the railway tracks by the bridge alongside JR Harajuku station. Left is the entrance to the **Meiji Shrine** (see page 57). A gravel walk, lined with lanterns, leads to the main buildings.
    Walk back to JR Harajuku station and cross into Omotesando Avenue and down the slope to the intersection with Meiji-dori. The streets around this intersection are the youth fashion hub of Japan. Note the tiny, enclosed basketball court on the opposite corner.
    Tucked in behind, off Omotesando-dori, is the **Ota Memorial Museum of Art** (see page 61). End the walk at Harajuku, or continue up Omotesando to the smart residential district of Aoyama.

Modern buildings at Shibuya

Tokyo

In the 12th century, the military leader of Japan, Minamoto Yoritomo, moved the seat of military government away from Kyoto to the isolated village of Kamakura, and established there Japan's first shogun-controlled military government. Over the next two centuries, a number of Japan's most important temples and shrines were built there, as the military and the clergy influenced each other to create a new breed of Zen warriors and warrior monks.

SHOPPING
This area is famous for its *Kamakura-bori*, or finely carved wood. Once finished, every item, such as a decorative box, is painted, usually red and black, and then lacquered to a glossy finish.

Making offerings at the Zeniarai Benten Shrine, Kamakura

Excursions

▶▶▶ Kamakura   95D3

About 50km (30 miles) south of Tokyo

Between 1192 and 1333, Kamakura was the capital city of Japan. Today, it is one of the country's most interesting places, with 65 Buddhist temples and 19 Shinto shrines. It is also an attractive residential town. Being much smaller than Kyoto, Japan's other religious hub, Kamakura is easier to navigate. The local tourist office (left of the main JR Kamakura station entrance) publishes a map of footpaths and rail stops that link the best-known temples. The train (see below) is recommended if you don't feel like exerting yourself.

Getting there JR's Yokosuka line connects Tokyo with Kamakura. Trains run about every 10 to 15 minutes and stop at Tokyo, Shinbashi and Shinagawa stations on Tokyo's Yamanote loop line. A more interesting route, though longer, is to take the Odakyu line from Tokyo station to Fujisawa and change for the Enoden narrow-gauge train, which pulls three wooden cars through small villages to Kamakura station. *En route*, it passes Hase station, the stopping-off point for the Great Buddha and Hasedera temple. Either station is a good starting point.

Among the temples and shrines worth visiting in Kamakura, the following are particularly interesting.

Engakuji Temple▶▶ was built in the 13th century by the Zen warrior Tokimune Hojo, to commemorate the deaths of Japanese and Mongolian soldiers killed during the Mongols' attempted invasion of Japan, and to mark his gratitude to Zen for the calm it had given him during the campaign. Engakuji has large gardens and numerous sub-temples, but Shari-den, the Shrine of the Sacred Tooth of the Buddha (Open 8–5, until 4pm Nov–Mar), is perhaps the most interesting to visit. It is in the Chinese style popular during the Kamakura era, 1192–1333.

TEMPLE FOR BATTERED WIVES
Tokeiji Temple (near Engakuji Temple) became famous during the Tokugawa era as the only legal refuge for women who had left their husbands. Women who managed to reach the safety of the temple grounds escaped the jurisdiction of their husbands and could seek a divorce. Those caught before they reached the temple could be legally punished, and even executed, by their husbands.

Hase Kannon Temple (Hasedera)▶▶ (*Open* 7–5.40, until 4.40pm Nov–Mar), close to Hase station, is set on a hill with fine views of the ocean. The main sanctuary houses the famous 11-headed gilt statue of Kannon, more than 9m (29ft) high and carved from a single log of camphor wood. The many faces of the goddess symbolize various stages of enlightenment. The most beguiling sight in Hase temple is the thousands of tiny statues of Jizo, the guardian deity of children, dressed in tiny clothes and surrounded with children's toys as offerings. Once symbolizing parents' hopes for their children, these Jizo statues now mainly represent aborted or stillborn children.

Above and below: Buddhas at the Great Buddha Shrine

Kamakura's best-known sight is the **Great Buddha▶▶▶**, in the grounds of the Kotokuin Temple (*Open* 7–5.45). This bronze figure of a seated Buddha, the Daibutsu, more than 10m (32ft) high, was cast in the 13th century and housed in a massive wooden temple building. One hundred and forty years later, the temple and Kamakura were flattened by a huge tidal wave that swept inland. The structure that housed the Buddha was washed away, but the Buddha itself remained unmoved, and for the last six centuries it has stood in the open air.

The **Zeniarai Benten Shrine▶▶▶** (*Open* 8–5), also known as the Money-Washing Shrine, is reached through a stone tunnel cut into a steep rock face. Once inside the temple grounds, you pass through a guard of honour of *torii* (gates), erected so close together that they almost form a tunnel. Off the main temple is a cave, into which flows a mountain spring, directed into a channel running around the walls. Here is where the money-washing takes place. Put several coins in a wicker basket, swirl them under the water, and wish for financial success.

Toshogu shrine: an elaborate tower…

Excursions

▶▶ John Lennon Museum   209C1

Saitama Super Arena, 2-27 Kamiochiai
tel: 048 601 0009; www.taisei.co.jp/museum
Open: Mon, Wed–Sat 11–6, Sun 11–8
A unique collection of personal belongings divided into nine areas, each representing a particular stage in Lennon's life. Saitama is 30 minutes from Tokyo via Tokyo or Ueno station.

▶▶▶ Nikko   209C2

About 140km (88 miles) north of Tokyo
Nikko town, in the middle of the 1,407sq-km (543sq-mile) Nikko National Park, has been a religious place since the eighth century. The park's numerous volcanic mountains and lakes include the sacred mountain Nantai-san, at the base of which lies the ravishing Lake Chuzenji and Kegon Waterfall, the highest in Japan. Nikko is a two-hour train journey from Tokyo or Ueno stations; Lake Chuzenji is a bus ride from Nikko along a winding mountain road. To get to Nikko, take the Tohoku Shinkansen line from Tokyo or Ueno stations to Utsunomiya, then change for the local line. Alternatively, take the Tobu line limited express from Matsuya department store in Tokyo's Asakusa district. To reach Lake Chuzenji, take any bus from platforms 1, 2, or 3 of the bus terminal near Nikko station to Chuzenji town, at the east end of the lake.

Toshogu Shrine▶▶▶, ornately decorated in vibrant hues, was begun in 1634 by the grandson of Tokugawa Ieyasu (see panel). A mixture of Shinto and Buddhist elements and elaborate carvings give it a Chinese style;

ONE HUNDRED TOSHOGU SHRINES
The Tokugawa shogunate encouraged the worship of Ieyasu's spirit, and eventually more than 100 Toshogu branch shrines were built throughout Japan. In 1873, Toshogu was dedicated to two other great warlords: Toyotomi Hideyoshi (1536–98) and Minamoto Yoritomo (1147–99).

…and a gate figure

The Kegon Waterfall, at Lake Chuzenji

more than 2 million sheets of gold leaf were used in the gilding that covers it. A Shinto *torii* (gate) and a Buddhist pagoda stand together in front of the black lacquer and gold-leaf adorned Niomon front gate, which bears animal and plant motifs. Nearby, on the lintel of the Sacred Stable for White Horse, is the carving of three monkeys, 'Hear No Evil, See No Evil, Speak No Evil', produced by local craftsmen who regarded them as guardian spirits. Farther into the shrine's compound is Yomeimon, Gate of Sunlight, the lavishly adorned entrance to the inner sanctum and once the limit for lower-ranked samurai (ordinary people were not allowed past the front gate). A succession of chambers leads to the Gokuden (Sacred Palace), which houses the gold lacquer shrine dedicated to the great warriors and leaders Toyotomi Hideyoshi, Tokugawa Ieyasu and Minamoto Yoritomo (see panel).

The entrance to Toshogu shrine is along the broad Ote-dori, and up the Thousand Person stone steps that lead to the front gate. It is part of the **Rinnoji Temple**▶▶ complex. The best way to see the shrine and other sites in Rinnoji is to buy a strip of tickets from the Rinnoji Temple gatehouse, on the right-hand side of Ote-dori before you reach Toshogu shrine (*Open* 8–5, Nov–Mar until 4pm). The **Daiyuin Mausoleum**▶▶, ornate but smaller than Toshogu, is the most aesthetically pleasing of the two.

The bus to **Lake Chuzenji**▶▶ climbs to 1,270m (4,166ft) up a winding road (there is another route for the descent). Near the bus station in Chuzenji town is Kegon Waterfall, where an elevator carries visitors to the bottom of the river gorge. To the right of the lake, Futaarasan Shrine takes the old name of Mount Nantai, the volcanic cone (2,482m/8,143ft) rising above it. In Chuzenji Temple, on the left shore of the lake, is a statue of a thousand-handed Kannon, said to have been carved from a tree by priest Shodo himself.

NIKKO AND THE TOSHOGU SHRINE

Nikko was founded in 782, when a Buddhist temple was erected there by the priest Shodo (735–817). The town was known for its religious pilgrims, but it did not attract prominent national attention until after the death of Ieyasu, founder of the Tokugawa shogunate in 1616. He left instructions in his will that his remains were to be buried in Nikko. Toshogu was built as his mausoleum and as a memorial to his achievements in unifying and governing Japan. It is thus as much a secular as a religious monument, and the shrine is a major tourist attraction, especially on 17 May, the main shrine festival date, highlighted by a procession of hundreds of men in authentic samurai costume.

Samurai from the ruling class were apprenticed to masters of archery and swordmanship, and demanded equipment to match the skills they developed. As a result, there emerged a group of artist craftsmen who manufactured swords and armour combining beauty and function to the highest degree. They developed a technical mastery that far surpassed Western methods of the day, and their swords became renowned throughout the world.

SWORD POWER
A story is told of two famous competing sword-smiths, Muramasa and Masamune, who were almost equal in skill. When a sword made by Muramasa was held upright in a running stream every dead leaf that drifted against its edge was cut in two. However, when Masamune's sword was put to the same test, the floating leaves passed either side of its edge, remaining uncut. Masamune's sword was judged the superior for its spiritual power over the leaves.

Making the sword For the main core of the blade, the swordsmith used a soft, laminated steel that was flexible and tough. The exterior was made of a combination of hard steels that were hammered together, folded over, hammered again, and so on, many times over. This technique formed a skin over the inner blade that was composed of thousands upon thousands of layers of different grades of hard steel welded together. The blade was then hardened even more by heating and cooling. Finally it was coated with clay, leaving only the cutting edge exposed. The clay-coated blade was then heated to the correct temperature and plunged into a tub of cold water. Cooling instantly, the cutting edge became so hard that, once honed, it retained its razor sharpness despite repeated use. The part of the blade covered in clay cooled at a slower rate and retained a perfect degree of softness and flexibility necessary to give the blade 'feel' and durability.

Samurai and sword For the samurai, his sword was not just a weapon but the material symbol of his honour, and he invested it with a spiritual power and surrounded its use with elaborate ritual. To make a binding oath, a samurai swore on his sword. Swords that had been through many battles became objects of reverence and worship, passed from father to son as tokens of loyalty. If beaten in battle, a warrior would pray that his sword might regain its lost spirit. At the birth of a samurai, a sword was placed beside the newborn baby, and at his death a sword was laid by his corpse.

Sword and spirit Because a samurai sword was held to have such spiritual significance, the task of making swords was given mystical importance. The sword-maker occupied a revered place in society and was required to undergo both spiritual and technical training before being entrusted with the job. Only those with the purest hearts and the highest moral standards could become master swordsmiths. The making of each sword was analogous to a spiritual journey and the sword-maker would undergo ritual purification and fasting before he began to make a sword. While at the anvil, he wore white robes and adopted the lifestyle of a monk.

Testing the sword The actual use of the swords was more mundane and bloody. They were fitted with long hilts and wielded with both hands. A good sword could easily lop off an arm, a leg, or a head, and the best could cut through armour and could even slice a man in two at one stroke.

To test a new sword, the swordmaster or samurai would obtain a corpse or, in some cases, a condemned man of low rank. The body, dead or alive, would be hung up and various cutting strokes of different degrees of difficulty would be tried out. Each cut had a name and there was even a table listing cuts in ascending order of difficulty of execution. The simplest cut was 'cutting the sleeve' or chopping a hand off at the wrist. The most difficult was a 'pair of wheels', which required the body to be chopped in half by a stroke across the hips.

DECAPITATION
In battle, cutting off an opponent's head was the most strived-for stroke. The head was taken as a war trophy if the victim had fought with sufficient bravery and was of high enough rank. Samurai wore anti-decapitation collars of steel, and, just in case of failure in battle, would burn incense in their helmets before the fight to ensure that their heads would smell sweet for the victorious enemy.

A 19th-century print by Kuniyoshi showing swordsmen in combat

The New Otani Hotel and garden, Tokyo

Accommodation

In general, there is no shortage of places to stay in Japan. In the cities, and in Tokyo especially, there is a wide variety of options, ranging from hotels that rank with the best in the world to *minshuku*, a Japanese version of bed-and-breakfast.

Major hotels Tokyo itself has hotels throughout the city, but those establishments near the central area are obviously the most desirable. The best areas and those with most major hotels are Akasaka, Ginza, Shinbashi, Shinjuku and around Tokyo station. Reserve in advance for luxury-class hotels, and for all hotels during major festivals and the month of February, when students arrive in Tokyo to take their university entrance exams. The service in the major hotels is invariably first class. They offer a wide range of extras, which may include a health club and massage service, an executive business facility with secretarial services, a guest relations officer to help with any problems, a travel agency, a shopping arcade, cocktail lounges with live music, and Japanese- and Western-style restaurants. Rooms have their own private bathrooms with a bath and shower combination, TV, clocks, and usually radios, hot-water thermos flasks with tea bags and minibars. Because they are accustomed to foreigners, all hotels in this category employ some English-speaking staff. Services provided include laundry and dry-cleaning, and often a complimentary English-language newspaper (such as the *Japan Times*) delivered to your room. Hotels with particular

HOSTEL NETWORK
The International Youth Hostel Federation (IYHF) now has an International Booking Network that includes Japan. A phone call to the YHA in your own country will get you details of how to book rooms and meals in hostels in Tokyo, Kyoto, Nara and more than 30 other cities. Alternatively, visit www.jyh.or.jp for more information.

character or other merits are listed in the Hotels and Restaurants section, (pages 266–268). Whichever class of hotel you choose, you can expect standards of hygiene and service to be excellent.

Other types of accommodation *Ryokan*, traditional Japanese inns, provide the very best of traditional Japanese taste, culture and food. They are usually in beautiful areas and/or overlook elegant gardens. The service is restrained and flawless in its maintenance of correct conduct. Fully fledged *ryokan* are typically expensive, but worth at least one night's stay for the experience (see pages 220–221).

Minshuku are family homes that take guests; these give a closer insight into Japanese life. They provide a room, bed, breakfast and evening meal (see pages 80–81).

Business hotels are straightforward, no-frills, and are clean and efficiently run. Rooms are small but well equipped and the hotels provide facilities such as fax and photocopying machines. Food and room service are not always available. The cost is less than a major hotel, but more than a Japanese inn. For ease of access, business hotels are usually close to railway and subway stations.

The Japanese inn is an inexpensive version of a *ryokan* and recommended if you are on a budget and wish to experience traditional Japanese customs and lifestyle. Tourist Information Centres (TICs, see page 264) at Narita Airport and in Tokyo and Kyoto will make reservations with the Welcome Inn group, an association of independent inn owners.

The best budget places to stay are youth hostels. There are quite a number in Tokyo, and their rules and regulations are similar to those in the West. Youth hostels are convenient for one-night stays, but at busy holiday times they are popular and heavily used and need to be booked ahead. Membership and further information are available at the Japan Youth Hostel Association, Hoken Kaikan, 1-1 Ichigaya-Sadohara-cho, Shinjuku-ku, Tokyo (tel: 03 3269 5831). The National Tourist Office (see page 264) has a free pamphlet listing all youth hostels in Japan, with their locations on a map.

LOVE HOTELS
Because most Japanese live in very small houses or apartments with their families, it is very hard for young unmarried or even married couples to find somewhere to make love privately. Society's solution is short-stay hotels, called love hotels or *avec* hotels. Such establishments are quite common, and you will see their advertisements giving the details of facilities offered in most large cities. The ads are garish, but the hotels themselves are run very discreetly. They are normally surrounded by a high wall and the entrances and exits are separate, to limit the chance of embarrassing encounters. The anonymity of guests is closely guarded, and the management tries to offer all the facilities needed to allow clients to indulge in their wildest fantasies. After 10pm room rates are often lower than those of regular hotels, so if exotic surroundings do not put you off sleeping, they make an inexpensive alternative for a single night's stay.

79

The modern Prince Hotel in Tokyo

Minshuku, *family homes that take in guests, are excellent places to stay for independent visitors to Japan who are on a budget, and who want to gain an insight into Japanese life. Guests are treated with real hospitality and warmth by their hosts, once they have established that their visitors respect and understand their customs.*

80

Enjoying a meal at a minshuku

MISO SOUP

Japanese meals of the type served at *minshuku* are usually accompanied by *miso* soup and are always served with rice. *Miso* is a very popular soup, which is also served for breakfast. Its base is a fish stock, made from the bonito, which is sold in dried flakes in every food store in Japan. This stock is then seasoned with *miso* paste. Floating in the soup are small squares of tofu and strands of seaweed or finely chopped vegetables. In the Japanese manner, the soup is slurped with gusto from the bowl while the solid bits are held back with the chopsticks. Rice is eaten with every meal, including breakfast.

At a *minshuku*, the most important things to remember are to leave your shoes at the door and not to soap yourself in the hot bath tub. You can learn other customs as you go along by being careful and observant.

Shoes In Japanese homes, *minshuku,* and other places such as temples, small hotels and some restaurants, there are rituals attached to the wearing of shoes that need to be observed. On entering a home, leave your shoes in the hall (this is at a lower level than the house itself), then step up into the house and into a pair of slippers that has been placed out for the family and visitors. Wear these slippers unless you are invited to enter a room laid out with *tatami* (closely woven straw floor mats). At the entrance to such a room leave your slippers at the door and enter in your stockinged feet. At the entrance to the bathroom change your slippers for another pair (these are sometimes marked WC on the toe). Change back into the house slippers when you leave the bathroom. Never go into a bathroom barefoot.

Bathing For bathing you will be given a small towel and a cotton dressing gown (*yukata*). Undress in the space provided outside the bathroom. Take the small towel into the bathroom with you. Squat on the low stool placed outside the hot tub and scoop water from the tub over yourself with the small bowl provided; alternatively, use the shower that is set into the wall at knee height. Soap up the towel and use it to wash yourself, then shampoo, shave, and so on. Finally, shower or scoop water from the tub to rinse off all the soap and rinse out the towel. Now sit in the tub, soak and relax. Once out of the tub, wring out the towel and dry yourself with it, before dressing in your underclothes and the *yukata*. Use of the bath tub is generally restricted to particular times in the evening.

Other customs In a *minshuku* you are expected to set out your own futon and bedding, which will be found in a cupboard in your room. Both breakfast and supper are provided, and are served either in your room or in a communal dining area. It is normal for a mixed party of young people to share a room together. This is quite innocent and you will almost certainly be invited to join them for a beer and a chat. The house door is usually locked fairly early (around 11pm).

Finding a *minshuku* Addresses and reservations for *minshuku* can be obtained from the information counters at most reasonably sized railway stations. It is notoriously easy to get lost in Japanese cities, so ask the information clerk to write the address in Japanese on a piece of paper, take a cab and give this to the cab driver. Also ask the clerk to mark the location on a city map. A list of addresses and *minshuku* customs can be obtained from the Japan Minshuku Association, 1-19-5 Takadanobaba, Shinjuku-ku, Tokyo (tel: 03 3232 6561) or from JNTO, or visit Japan Minshuku Centre at www.minshuku.co.jp (tel: 03 3216 6556).

JAPANESE LAVATORIES
Minshuku sometimes have only Japanese lavatories, rather than the Western variety. They are squat, with a hood at one end (face this end). The cistern for flushing is filled through a tap which issues water into a sink set over the cistern; wash your hands under this tap. This ingenious flushing method saves both water and space.

81

A futon bed laid out on tatami (floor mats)

Ready to dig in to a bowl of noodles

ECONOMY

If you are on a budget the following tips may help. Western foods such as bread, cake and cheese are more expensive than traditional Japanese foods. Never order a meal before knowing the cost as only the most expensive restaurants do not display prices. Alcohol is expensive, sometimes exorbitantly so, in Japanese bars and clubs. To drink inexpensively, it is best to buy alcohol from a supermarket or slot machine and drink it in your hotel room. For snacking or self-catering, buy the made-up *bento* boxes of rice, pickles, fishcake, and so on, sold in grocery stores. Finally, one of the many chains of hamburger places in Japan is always involved in a trade war with a competitor, so look for special offers.

Fast food in Shibuya

Food and drink

For Tokyoites, dining out is an integral part of everyday life, and many people eat more often in restaurants than they do at home. As a result, there is an enormous variety of eateries in Tokyo, with something to suit every taste and pocket.

This high density of restaurants, coupled with the size of the city, usually means that the most convenient way to eat out is to explore the area in the vicinity of your accommodation. Two notes of caution: first, avoid the places that provide only Western food, which tend to be expensive; secondly, the Japanese love to eat out and appreciate good food, but they are also happy to pay high prices for ambience and location. Before ordering a meal, always make sure that the price range of a restaurant suits you.

The menu Restaurants in tourist areas have menus written in both English and Japanese. Many restaurants also display plastic models of the dishes they serve that you can point to when ordering. One point worth noting is that the bowls in these displays indicate the country of origin of the food: a large bowl with a design around the rim holds a Chinese dish; smaller, plainer bowls contain Japanese cuisine; and a flat plate holds Western food.

Customs Once seated in the restaurant, you will be given *oshibori*, *o-hashi* and *o-cha*. *Oshibori* are small, napkin-size damp cloths, heated in cold weather and cold in hot weather. Use them to wipe your hands and face, and then as napkins during the meal. *O-hashi* are chopsticks. *O-cha*, or green tea, is an integral part of Japanese life. It is the common offering in restaurants, given out free when you arrive and at the end of the meal.

Places to eat The following are brief descriptions of the various types of Japanese eating establishments.

Sushi-ya, moderately priced sushi bars, are the most atmospheric and distinctive of all small Japanese restaurants. They sell rice delicately seasoned with vinegar, sugar and salt, shaped into rolls, patties, balls, and so on, and topped and filled with slices of raw, boiled or marinated fish, omelette, vegetables and seaweed. They also sell *sashimi*, raw fish served without rice.

Soba-ya are noodle shops, one of the most common types of restaurant in Japan and one of the least expensive (see pages 84–85).

Nomi-ya are small, basic, local bars, recognizable by the large red lantern hanging outside. Mainly for drinking sake and beer, they also serve snacks and are relaxing places in which to sit and take time over a drink.

Koryori-ya serve a small menu of popular Japanese dishes such as seasonal fresh fish and vegetables. *Koryori-ya* are usually small, and each one has a couple of semi-private rooms with *tatami* (straw floor mats), perfect for an intimate, inexpensive dinner.

Chuka Ryori-ya are simple Chinese restaurants, often visited by Japanese families for a cheap meal. They sell Japanese versions of regular Chinese dishes.

Shokudo are small and inexpensive, and sell a selection of the most popular Japanese, Western and Chinese dishes. They always display a complete menu of wax models outside. Their relaxed and friendly atmosphere makes them suitable for unaccompanied visitors and are particularly popular with students.

At the counter in a noodle shop, one of Japan's original and enduringly popular fast-food outlets

SUSHI CHEFS
Sushi preparation is a performing art, and watching chefs assemble sushi on the other side of the bar is good entertainment. Chefs are incredibly deft and quick, and must remember the cost of each person's assortment of orders while preparing and serving the food. The comparative skills of sushi chefs is a popular topic of debate among the connoisseurs.

WHERE TO EAT
See www.bento.com for very comprehensive restaurant guide to Tokyo, listed under both location and cuisine.

Noodles are the original Japanese fast food. Quick-service noodle shops are found even in the smallest Japanese town. Many are just stands or small cafés, while others are more sophisticated establishments with jealously guarded reputations for the quality of their fresh noodles.

SPECIALIST NOODLES

Somen, a very fine wheat noodle used mostly in cold soups, is the only noodle included in traditional Shojin cookery, the vegetarian cuisine of Zen monasteries. In her book *Good Food from a Japanese Temple*, Soei Yoneda mentions that *somen*, in particular, is suited to 'the cooking of nunneries having an Imperial Princess as abbess'. Yellow *somen*, enriched with egg yolk, is called *tamago-somen*; green *somen*, seasoned with green tea and called *cha-somen*, is also available in specialist noodle restaurants.

84

Above: soba noodles on sale
Below: a tempting noodle display

The basic noodle shop menu offers four or five different kinds of noodle, each served in a steaming hot soup with various garnishes on top. This is also the way noodles are cooked and served at home. The garnishes could be thin slices of pork, finely chopped leek, tofu, *nori* seaweed, *kamaboko* (fishcake), *tempura* (vegetables or fish in batter), or other traditional toppings, but connoisseurs tend to prefer good-quality fresh noodles served in a broth, with a little finely chopped spring onion sprinkled over the top, or on their own, with a dipping sauce.

Noodle types Noodles are not differentiated by their shape, as is pasta, but by their ingredients. There are, in fact, only two distinct types: those made with buckwheat flour and those made with wheat flour. The former, called *soba* noodles, are most popular in Tokyo and northern Japan, where the colder climate suits the cultivation of the hardy buckwheat; they are light to dark grey and firm and thin in shape. The most common wheat flour noodle is *udon*, which is soft in texture, flat and round. Other types are the very fine *somen*, the slightly thicker *hiya-mugi*, and the wide, long and flat *kishimen*. Wheat noodles are white and are popular in Japan's wheat-growing areas, which stretch south from Osaka. One other popular type, though not traditional, is *ramen*, a Chinese egg noodle. (The Japanese roll their 'r', even bounce it. If you can't do this, ask for 'damen' when ordering.)

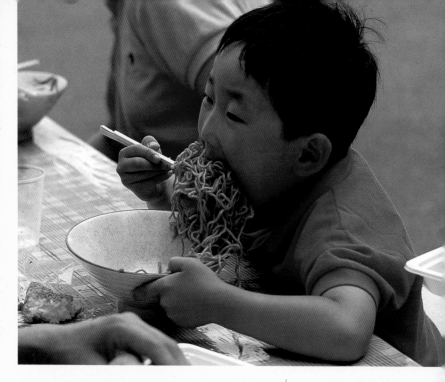

Soba noodles *Soba* is the earliest known variety of Japanese noodle, popular with noodle lovers. Buckwheat was originally made into a gruel, but in 17th-century Edo (Tokyo) a monk called Ganchin discovered that if he mixed wheat and buckwheat flours he was able to make a dough that could be cut into noodles that held their shape. *Soba* noodles became the fashion and there are many references to them in the literature of the time. The best *soba* was (and still is) *ni-hachi* or 'two-eight', meaning two parts wheat flour to eight parts buckwheat. Nowadays, *soba* is served hot or cold, in a broth or with a dipping sauce on the side. Cold *zaru-soba* is served on bamboo lattice baskets, set in a square wooden frame. *Cha-soba*, or green tea *soba*, is made by mixing powdered tea with the buckwheat dough; recognizable by its distinctive green hue, it is often served cold. *Udon*, wheat-flour noodles, are often served hot with tempura. *Udon* and *soba* are interchangeable in practically all dishes.

The art of slurping Eating noodles, Japanese style, requires that you abandon what you usually think of as good table manners. This involves sucking them fast into your mouth, hot and straight out of the broth, while simultaneously drawing in a cooling intake of breath. The result, if done properly, is a loud slurping noise. Once the noodles are finished, the remaining soup is sucked straight from the bowl with equal noise and gusto. For a Westerner, trained to eat quietly, this requires shedding a lifetime's conditioning. To try this without embarrassment, go to any noodle shop in Japan at lunchtime, where you can consume a bowl of steaming noodles among the crowd of customers, with accompanying slurping noises, and not be noticed.

A big helping of noodles for a small mouth

POPULAR NOODLE ORDERS
Kake-soba: noodles in broth with chopped leek garnishing, basic and inexpensive.
Zaru-soba: plain noodles served as *cha-soba*.
Kitsune-soba or *udon:* noodles in broth with fried tofu and leek garnish.
Tempura-soba or *udon:* noodles in broth with *tempura* and leek garnish.
Nabe-yake udon: vegetables, *tempura*, egg and noodles cooked in an earthenware pot.
Ramen: Chinese noodles in pork broth with sliced pork topping and leek or spinach garnish.

Tokyo

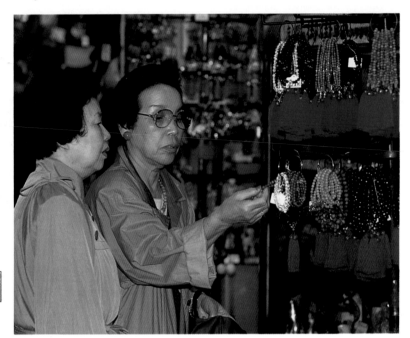

86

A temple tourist shop

GIFTS
Choosing from the
immense range of options
is the biggest problem
when buying gifts. Popular
items include paper
goods, Japanese pottery,
chinaware, chopsticks,
fabrics, lacquerware,
dolls, or *cloisonné* (fine
wire patterned onto a
metal base, with a fired
glass finish filling the
spaces). The following
shops sell traditional folk
arts and crafts: **Bingoya**,
10-6 Wakamatsu-cho,
open Tuesday–Sunday
10–7 (the nearest subway
station is Akebonobashi,
a 15-minute walk away);
and **Oriental Bazaar**,
5-9-13 Jingu-mae, open
Friday–Wednesday
9.30–6.30 (the nearest
subway stations are
Harajuku or Meiji Jingu-
mae, each a few minutes'
walk away).

Shopping

Tokyo shops are wonderful, not only for the amazing
range of goods available but also for the quality of the
service. White-gloved, kimono-clad ladies welcome you
into the smarter shops and department stores. Inside, the
assistants are polite and helpful, and will wrap even the
smallest purchase as though it were a precious stone.

Department stores For presents or souvenirs, it is best to
go to a department store (*depato*). This will save you a lot
of walking, and the vast range of merchandise offers
plenty of ideas. Each store is a self-contained world, in
which all human needs, from baby clothes to funeral
arrangements, are politely and enthusiastically looked
after. Each store has a particular style and price range. But
even the least expensive stores have service and goods of
an excellent standard.

Some of the best-known department stores include:
Mitsukoshi, 1-7-4 Nihonbashi Muromachi, Chuo-ku,
which has its own subway station; **Seibu**, 21-1 Udagawa-
cho, Shibuya-ku, one of the most innovative and modern
(visit the separate hardware section called Loft and the
basement food hall); **Wako**, 4-5-11 Ginza, Chuo-ku, an
exclusive and expensive shop with an amazing range of
watches, known for its prewar clock tower, a meeting
place for couples; and **Takashimaya**, 2-4-1 Nihonbashi,
Chuo-ku, the flagship of Tokyo's department stores, with
opulent decor to match the vast array of famous designer
goods. Most are in the Ginza district.

Fashion and electronics Fashion buildings provide
several floors of fashion boutiques, restaurants, bars

and other facilities. The best known are **Axis** 5-17-1 Roppongi, Minato-ku; **Parco**, 15-1 Udagawa-cho, Shibuya-ku; and **La Foret** (for everything a teenager may wish to buy), 1-11-6 Jingu-mae, Shibuya-ku. **Tokyo Hands**, 12-18 Udagawa-cho, Shibuya-ku, is an astonishing hardware store, said to have more than 3 million different items for sale. **Wave**, 6-2-21 Roppongi, Minato-ku, is a 'concept retailing outlet', with several floors of audio and visual software, such as video tapes and discs, compact discs, sheet music and books (also see Sony Building, page 54).

Teapots for sale

Japan is a world leader in electronic goods, but they are often more expensive in Tokyo than elsewhere. There is, however, an incredible variety of goods available, and the latest models and innovative equipment are often for sale in the showrooms several months earlier than anywhere else in the world. Go to Akihabara subway station and simply choose one of the nearby stores (remember to ask for an export model if the voltage in your home country is not 100V).

Tax-free As a visitor to Japan, you can buy tax-free goods in any store that displays a 'tax-free' sign. Most major department stores, hotel arcades and specialist shops in tourist areas offer this facility. Savings range between 5 and 40 per cent. Take your passport with you to the shop; export forms detailing the goods you have bought will be attached to it. Customs officers may want to see the goods when you leave Japan. Precious stones, electrical goods, cameras and watches are the types of items usually available. In large cities like Tokyo, you will find similar goods in discount stores at reduced or even lower prices.

OPENING HOURS AND SALES

Department stores, and most other retailers, open at 10am, and usually close at 7pm (family-run shops vary widely). Department stores are closed one day a week, and for the New Year (1–2 January). Discounts of 30–50 per cent are common during the summer (mid-July to end August) and New Year (3 January to mid-February) main sales.

A trendy shopping arcade in Shibuya

87

Japan's long tradition in the arts has come to define its culture, not only within the nation itself but worldwide. Among the better known of the fine arts are ukiyo-e (woodblock prints of the Edo period), calligraphy and ikebana, the highly skilled art of flower-arranging. The performing arts are defined by noh theatre, kabuki, and bunraku, while pottery, ceramics, sword-making and lacquerware are the best known of the Japanese crafts.

88

THE ZEN OF CRAFT
In Japanese arts and crafts, the artist or craftsman struggles to extract the essence, or true personality, of the form or material used. The motive is not to dominate the medium, but to work with its nature. Realism, rather than romanticism, is usually the byword.

A TRIP TO THE THEATRE
The National Noh Theatre, 4-18-1 Sendagaya, Shibuya-ku, gives performances four or five times per month. For more details, telephone 03 3423 1331; the nearest subway is Sendagaya.

Traditional tea house with tatami *(straw floor mats),* matcha *(powdered green tea), and a contemplative environment*

Under the banner of *mingeihan*, crafts of the people, many lesser known Japanese craft skills are pursued. In dance and music traditional forms are still maintained and performed, while in the arts of *chanoyu* (the tea ceremony), bonsai and garden design the Japanese exemplify their love of artifice, nature and ritual. The source of this rich heritage is that idiosyncratic Japanese mix of Zen simplicity and Shinto nature worship, together with a class system that ensured the continuity of the master-and-apprentice relationship through many generations.

Woodblock printing *Ukiyo-e* ('images of a floating, transient world') was a school of painters in the 18th and 19th centuries who gave new life to the art of woodblock printing. Renowned for their realism, bold designs and striking hues, they were led by four great masters: Utamaro, Sharaku, Hokusai and Hiroshige, 'discovered' by Europeans in the late 19th century (see panel, page 60).

Theatre *Noh* is a stylized dance drama performed to the accompaniment of music and singing. On a stark stage, actors wear masks and gorgeous, elaborate costumes. Movement is slow and the storyline conveyed by a symbolism sometimes difficult for foreigners to understand. However, *noh* does provide an insight into the contemplative nature of Japanese arts.

Kabuki (see pages 58–59) allows only male actors, who play both male and female roles. They wear traditional costume, and the plays depict either the lives of ordinary people or those of the noble classes in a Japan of earlier times. The dialogue and gestures used to convey the stories are formalized, but there is an energy, vibrancy and accessibility in *kabuki* missing from *noh* theatre.

In *bunraku* (puppet theatre), the main characters are life-like puppets, manipulated by as many as three puppeteers. The stories told are similar to *kabuki* tales, where the scripts are traditional and usually well known by the audience. Osaka is considered the birthplace and capital of *bunraku* theatre (see page 119), although first-class performances are also given in theatres in Tokyo and Kyoto.

The tea ceremony In the authentic setting of a tea garden, the tea ceremony (*chanoyu*), combines the spirit of a religious service with the style of a performing art, and

Putting the finishing touches to Satsuma porcelain

THE RITUAL OF TEA-MAKING

Before the arrival of guests to a tea ceremony, a room or tea house overlooking a garden is set aside and thoroughly cleaned. Utensils are polished, flowers are arranged and the garden is swept. When the guests arrive, conversation is quiet and contemplative. With deft, well-rehearsed movements, the host spoons the green powdered tea and hot water into each guest's cup and whisks it into a foam. As each guest sips tea, comment may be passed on the beauty of the tea cups and other utensils as they are handed around for appreciation. Guests may also express their gratitude to the host and mention the delights of the garden or other natural phenomena such as the sky or moon (see also pages 126–127).

perhaps it best encapsulates all the elements of the Japanese artistic sensibility. At its deepest level, 'the way of tea' aspires to create such an atmosphere of harmony and peace that the participants will experience the same qualities in their own hearts and minds. Tea ceremonies are held in Tokyo and Kyoto for *gai-jin* (foreigners). In this context they are usually rather perfunctory affairs, but nevertheless interesting, and the green tea provides an unexpected buzz.

Kabuki theatre

Tokyo

DISCOS

Entry fees are high for discos, but the price often includes drinks and simple food. Dress is usually smart and the better discos do not welcome unaccompanied males. Roppongi district has many discos, as well as live music dance clubs.

LISTINGS

For more information about what's on, visit www.tokyoq.com for the city's best on-line events guide and www.ciajapan.com for music club listings. www.tokyodoko.com is another useful listings site.

Nightlife

Tokyo's nightlife is lively, and many members of the working population go straight from the office to a bar or club for a drink and a chat before either going home or continuing an evening's carousing. The night starts early, at about 6pm and, for most, ends before midnight.

After midnight, night owls and young people about town head for Roppongi, where the clubs and discos stay open until the early hours of the morning. The Ginza, Asakusa and Akasaka districts provide everything from neon-lit dazzle to the traditional singing, dancing and *samisen-* (lute-) playing of kimono-clad geisha. Massage parlours, sleazy bars and strip joints cluster in Shinjuku, especially its Kabuki-cho area, and the smaller Dogenzaka in Shibuya. These places are expensive and not aesthetically pleasing, but even here you do not need to worry unduly about physical safety or theft.

For cinema, theatre and other cultural events, the monthly *Tokyo Journal*, available in hotels, at the city Tourist Information Centre (TIC) offices, or English-language bookshops, gives comprehensive details of performances, as well as restaurant reviews and up-to-the-minute information on events of interest to English-speaking visitors.

Music Jazz, introduced into Japan during the 1930s and reintroduced after the war by GIs, remains very popular. A number of Tokyo jazz clubs have live jazz, ranging from Dixieland to avant-garde. Japanese jazz fans are knowledgeable and dedicated. Japanese and Western pop and rock is found widely in clubs and at concert venues. Classical concerts are available most nights, with performances by visiting orchestras or one of the many based in Tokyo. Details are given in the *Tokyo Journal*.

A Tokyo nightclub

Practical

Before going to Japan, contact the nearest Japanese National Tourist Organisation office (see page 264) and ask for tourist maps of Japan and Tokyo. If you do not book a hotel in Tokyo in advance, arrive in the city before 5pm in time to visit a Travel Information Centre office where you can get help in finding a place to stay. There is a TIC at Narita Airport and another in the central area.

Information As soon as you arrive in Tokyo obtain, either from the TIC office or from any large railway station, an English-language subway map. This is essential. Before deciding what to do in the city, get a free copy of *Tour Companion*, a weekly English-language newspaper for visitors, and buy a copy of the monthly *Tokyo Journal*. Both these publications contain details of current events, and both are available at TIC offices and large hotels. For taped information (in English) on current events, phone 3503 2911. The Tokyo English Life Line, on 5721 4347, helps with problems. For advice and information on hotels and restaurants contact the TIC office.

Getting about Driving a car in Tokyo is no fun. The traffic is dense, and parking expensive and difficult. Buses are slow because of the heavy traffic, and destination signs are shown only in Japanese. Train and subway networks are fast, efficient, clean and comprehensive, in terms of the places you may wish to visit. Services operate from the very early morning to around midnight. After this time, you can rely on a good taxi service (between 11pm–5am a 20 per cent surcharge is payable so make sure the driver is clear about your destination). See pages 92–93 and 252–254 for more tips on getting about.

Even taxi rides can be slow in Tokyo

Subway signs

Shinjuku, Ueno and Tokyo stations are the three busiest stations in Tokyo, handling more than 3 million passengers a day commuting within the city and visiting places all over Japan.

THE TOKAIDO SANYO LINE

The Tokaido Sanyo Shinkansen train service opened in 1964, just before the Tokyo Olympics. At that time, it linked Tokyo and Osaka, a distance of 552km (345 miles), and followed for most of its length the route of the old Tokaido post road between Edo (old Tokyo) and Kyoto. Nowadays, the line reaches Fukuoka (Hakata station), on the southern island of Kyushu. Trains leave Tokyo station three or four times an hour for the 1,069km (668-mile), six-hour journey.

Shinkansen (bullet trains) grinding to a halt…

Shinjuku station This is said to be the world's biggest and busiest station. It serves nine railway and subway lines, as well as accommodating huge complexes of shops and restaurants, both above and under the ground. There are few signs in English. Shinjuku station is the equivalent of a small city; any visitor who masters it will be able to use the city's other stations with ease.

Shinjuku has two wings, divided by two long parallel passageways, off which runs a maze of underground shopping parades. Subway and surface lines run into the station for both private lines and Japanese Railways (JR itself is no longer owned by the state, but private). If it is necessary to change from a private line to a JR line, you must go out through a ticket barrier, find your next train's line, and purchase a new ticket (this is not needed if you change lines within the same company's network). To buy a ticket, find the correct train or subway line, then use the ticket machine nearest that line's entrance. If you make a mistake (and it is easy to do so, as the signs and instructions are sometimes only in *kanji*), there is a refund office but it is not easy to find. If you do not know how much your ticket will be, buy the cheapest and pay the excess at your destination.

If you get lost, take your time to wander around until you find a signpost in English to help get your bearings. The ticket collectors at the barrier gates are also very helpful and used to dealing with bewildered tourists. Avoid Shinjuku if you have a busy timetable. Otherwise, you can happily enjoy it as a place of interest in its own right. On a rainy day, Shinjuku is a good place for experiencing the lively hustle and bustle of Japanese urban life.

Tokyo station Housed in an old red-brick building, Tokyo station was designed by Kingo Tatsuno, one of Japan's first modern architects. It was completed in 1914, damaged by wartime bombing, and restored in 1954. A new east extension containing the Daimaru department store was added two years later, and there are current plans to renovate and remodel the original building. The bus stop for the Tokyo City Air Terminal (TCAT), where you can check in luggage for some international flights before taking a coach to Narita Airport, is outside the south exit of the station. Buses leave here for Narita Airport.

Maruno-uchi, the district to the west side of Tokyo station, is a major business area. Its name means roughly 'within the castle compound'; it was once within the walls of the Shogun's castle. From Maruno-uchi central exit an avenue leads to the Imperial Palace grounds.

JR Ueno station The JR station at Ueno in northern Tokyo was the gateway to Japan's first public park, museum and zoo and remains the exit and arrival point for visitors to and from Japan's northern provinces. It was completed in 1883 and became a focal point for people migrating to Tokyo from villages in Tohoku to the north. Ueno-Hirokoji, the main thoroughfare of Ueno, runs from the Shinobazu exit (south side) of JR Ueno station. It is lined with restaurants, shops and discount stores, and the back alleys are teeming with small places to eat and drink.

…and speeding off

TRAVEL BY SHINKANSEN
Shinkansen (bullet train) platforms at Tokyo and JR Ueno stations are divided into carriage-length spaces. Above the exact place that each carriage's door will be, there hangs a numbered plate. This relates to the passenger's ticket, and you should wait in the appropriate place, as the Shinkansen pulls into and out of the station within the space of five minutes.

LEAVING TOKYO
JR trains to the Japan Alps (Matsumoto) use Shinjuku station, while the JR Shinkansen and JR express trains on the Tokaido line (to Nagoya, Kyoto, Kobe, Osaka, Hiroshima and the island of Kyushu) use Tokyo station. The JR Shinkansen and express trains on the Tohoku line use Ueno station, as do the JR Shinkansen and express trains on the Joetsu line and the direct Shinkansen line to Nagano.

Central Honshu

94

Grandeur reflected: Mount Fuji

Kantō-sanchi
Kumagaya
Koga
Kinu-gawa
Tsuchiura
Kasumi-ga-ura
Kita-ura
Chichibu
Kasukabe
Ōmiya
Chōshi
Chichibu Kawagoe
Tama Han'ao
Nat Park
Koshigaya
Asahi
Urawa
Matsudo
Sakura
Inubo-zaki
Kōfu
595m
TOKYO
Funabashi
Hachioji
KAWASAKI
Chiba
Machida
Yamato
Tōkyō-wan
Ichihara
Tōgame
Mobara
ji-Hakone-Izu
tional
Atsugi
YOKOHAMA
Park
Fujiyoshida
Fujisawa
Kisarazu
776m
Gotemba
Odawara
Kamakura
Fuji-san
Yokosuka
Bōsō-bantō
Fujinomiya
Hakone
Miura
Futtsu
Katsuura
Kushiro,
Tomakomai
Fuji
Mishima
Kamogawa
Numazu
Atami
himizu
Itō
Sagami-nada
Tateyama
Suruga-wan
Izu-bantō
Fuji-Hakone-Izu
Nat Park
Nojima-zaki
Ō-shima
Irō-zaki
Shimoda
Izu-shotō
Sendai,
Tomakomai
Nii-jima
Kozū-jima
Miyake-jima
Mikura-jima

0   50   100 km
0   20   40   60 miles

D   E

Central Honshu

96

A deity guards the entrance (above) of Horyuji Temple in Nara (detail, below)

CENTRAL HONSHU With its heavy concentration of business, educational and cultural activities, Central Honshu is second only to Tokyo in economic importance and density of population. Historically, it constitutes the geographical, cultural and spiritual heart of Japan, containing within its boundaries the two ancient capital cities of Kyoto and Nara and the sacred mountain of Fuji-san. This chapter concentrates on the Fuji-Hakone-Izu and the Ise-shima National Parks and the cities of Osaka, Kobe, Nara and Nagoya; for convenience of use and clarity, a separate chapter is devoted to Kyoto.

FUJI-HAKONE-IZU NATIONAL PARK This is possibly the most popular excursion destination for residents of the capital, being 96km (60 miles) southwest of Tokyo, and it is flooded with visitors spring and summer. The park includes several distinct areas: Mount Fuji, the Fuji Five Lakes, the Izu Peninsula and Hakone, a hot-spring resort area that lies within a volcanic crater 40km (25 miles) in diameter at the base of Mount Fuji.

OSAKA Japan's major port and commercial hub once had a reputation for being grimy, chaotic and cramped. Some of that description still holds true, but Osaka is a city of immense energy, and the city fathers, with an eye to the economic and sociological importance of ecological issues, are spending considerable sums of money in an attempt to improve the city environment. Osaka is not a tourist town, nor are there many places of scenic or historic interest to visit, but for a keyhole view of real Japanese city life, and the closest there is to a blue-collar Japan, it should not be missed.

KOBE Osaka's main port, built on a hillside overlooking Osaka Bay, Kobe is a major industrial city, a rival to Yokohama as Japan's busiest port. Kobe has a long history as a port city, but real growth began in the late 19th century, when the docks were opened to foreign shipping. Some Western-style merchants' houses still stand in the Kitano district, and Kobe continues to be occupied by a substantial number of foreign residents. Kobe remains a modern, cosmopolitan and sophisticated city, good for shopping, nightlife and international cuisine.

NARA From AD 710 to 794, Nara was the first political and cultural focal point of a united Japan. The capital moved to Kyoto toward the end of the eighth century, and Nara slowly lapsed into relative obscurity. This was a blessing in disguise, as the city escaped much of the damage suffered by other cities in Japan's long civil wars. As a result, Nara and the monastery estates around it contain some of the best examples of traditional Japanese art and architecture. The sights may be roughly divided into two areas. Those in and around Nara Park, a large but not particularly attractive park, well known for its sacred tame and sometimes pushy deer and the southwest district of the city, where several major temples can be found. Modern Nara is a large city with a population of 300,000.

ISE-SHIMA NATIONAL PARK The Shima Peninsula, which juts out into the Pacific Ocean, is home to this park and is the site of the Ise Shrine, the most venerated Shinto shrine in the whole of Japan. This is the symbolic home of Amaterasu, the sun goddess and ancestral divine spirit of the Japanese imperial line. The park itself stretches to the east from Ise to Toba, hub of the pearl industry, then to the south to Kashikojima, famous for its coastline and pine-clad islands.

NAGOYA Japan's third largest city was flattened during World War II by Allied bombs, and rebuilt according to the best city planning theories of the time. As a result, Nagoya is architecturally sterile and uninteresting, an agreeable place to live, but not necessarily to visit. It is, however, a good base for excursions to other towns and areas, especially Gifu for its cormorant fishing.

KANSAI AND KANTO
For practical purposes, Central Honshu is a sensible description of the area covered in this chapter. However, in terms of the way the Japanese divide their country, it straddles two regions: Kansai and Kanto. Kansai, or 'west of the barrier', refers to the region containing the cities of Osaka, Kobe, Nara and Kyoto. Kanto, 'east of the barrier', refers to the region around Tokyo. The 'barrier' is an arbitrary division between Kansai and Kanto, made by the government in the 10th century and marked by three barrier stations along its length.

97

GETTING TO OSAKA
Osaka is connected to Tokyo by more than 100 express trains a day, and international flight connections between the cities are usually free. Prices are a little lower and hotels are easier to find here than in Kyoto or Tokyo, so it can be a convenient base for exploring Kyoto, Nara and Kobe, all within half an hour of Osaka.

GETTING TO NARA
Nara tends to be a place that tourists visit on day trips. The JR Nara line connects Kyoto to Nara (68 minutes); trains run twice an hour. The JR Kansai line connects Osaka to Nara (30 minutes); trains run three times an hour. A city map and walk route is available from the tourist office in Kintetsu–Nara station (upstairs). Services run by Kintetsu (a private railway) are quicker and more frequent than those of JR.

Osaka Castle

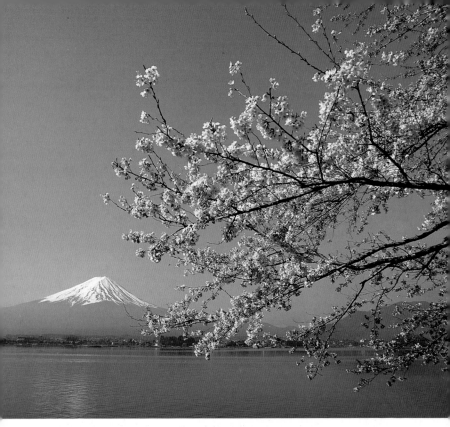

*Mount Fuji and
Lake Ashi*

BACK TO TOKYO
As an alternative to returning to Tokyo all the way by
bus, you can take a bus
from Kawaguchi-ko to
Mishima. The scenic bus
circles Mount Fuji in two
hours. From Mishima it is
just over one hour by bullet
train to Tokyo.

Fuji-Hakone-Izu National Park

This area of crater lakes, volcanic mountain ranges, hot springs and beaches, 100km (63 miles) southwest of Tokyo, is the most heavily visited national park in Japan. The original wildness of the habitat has been sacrificed to some extent to the needs of tourists, but it is still a beauti-ful area. Indeed, the Japanese believe that the symmetrical reflection of Mount Fuji (*Fuji-san*) in the calm surface of Lake Ashi is *the* most beautiful sight in the world. The park can be divided into four distinct areas. Although a grand tour of all of them at once is possible, many visitors prefer to make separate excursions from Tokyo. On pages 101, 102–103, and 108–109 three of the areas, Mount Fuji, Hakone and the Izu Peninsula (*Izu-hanto*), are described individually. The fourth, the Fuji Five lakes, is described below. Throughout spring and summer, the whole park is crowded with visitors, but at other times, partly as a result of the colder weather, it is relatively quiet. See map on page 100.

▶▶ Fuji Five Lakes (Fuji-Go-ko)   100A6

Kawaguchi-ko▶▶, on the southeastern shore of Lake Kawaguchi, is the area's transportation hub, served by train and bus from Tokyo and from other regions of the national park. Buses also go from Kawaguchi-ko station to the other four lakes. The town itself is a busy resort with a mix of *ryokan*, hotels, restaurants, bars and souvenir shops. A 10-minute walk from the station leads to the shore of Lake Kawaguchi, and there are fine views of the lake and Mount Fuji from the observation tower at the top of Mount Tenjo, reached by a cable car (ropeway) operating from the lakeside near the station. From the nearby pier, boats offer 30-minute tours of the lake. Other attractions are the Fuji Museum on the north shore (*Open* 8.30–4), an odd mix of geology and history exhibits and a display of erotica, and the Fuji-kyu Highland Amusement Park, one train stop from Kawaguchi-ko station. Lake Kawaguchi is the most developed and visited of the five lakes.

Lake Shoji (Shoji-ko)▶▶▶ opens on its southeast side onto a glorious view of Mount Fuji, while the other three sides are secluded and enclosed by wooded mountains. The smallest of the lakes, and considered by many to be the prettiest, this is the starting point for the Shoji Trail, which leads through *Jukai*, 'the Sea of Trees' (see panel), all the way to the summit of Mount Fuji. Lake Shoji is 50 minutes by bus from Kawaguchi-ko station. Ice-skating on the lake and fishing (through holes made in the ice) are very popular winter activities for visitors to the area.

Asahigaoka, a commercial district on the southern shore of **Lake Yamanaka (Yamanaka-ko)▶**, the largest of the lakes, is 35 minutes by bus from Kawaguchi-ko. Popular with affluent young Tokyoites, the lake shore is heavily developed with fashionable restaurants, expensive hotels, college and company clubhouses, and villas. Cruise boats from Asahigaoka offer short tours of the lake.

Lake Sai (Sai-ko)▶, the third largest lake, lies to the west of Kawaguchi-ko, 25 minutes away by bus. The lakeside is only moderately developed and, apart from hiking, there is little to do.

The westernmost and deepest of the five lakes is **Lake Motosu (Motosu-ko)▶**. It never freezes over, and is renowned for its beautiful blue waters and fine trout. The bus stop on the eastern shore is 50 minutes from Kawaguchi-ko. Aside from the souvenir shops in the immediate vicinity of the bus stop, the lake shore and surroundings are quiet.

SEA OF TREES
Called the *Jukai* in Japanese, this area is a part of the Aokigahara Forest, between lakes Sai and Shoji. The trees survive on a thin layer of volcanic soil covering a field of lava, which is magnetic and distorts compasses. This makes it easy for you to get lost and difficult for those looking to find you again. Fortunately, you can pick up a marked nature trail at the Fugaku Fuketsu (lava caves) near the Fuketsu bus stop, 40 minutes from Kawaguchi-ko bus station (platform 6).

GETTING TO HAKONE OR IZU PENINSULA
To go to Hakone from Kawaguchi-ko, take the bus to Gotemba. Change at Sengoku for Hakone-Yumoto or Togendai in the Hakone region. The Izu Peninsula is reached by bus from Mishima (see **Back to Tokyo** panel, opposite page).

99

Lake Yamanaka

Central Honshu

Fuji Five Lakes
(Fuji Goko)
1623m
Kawaguchi-ko
Tsuru **Otsuki** *Sagami-gawa*
Tōkyō
Kawaguchi-ko
Shōji-ko *Sai-ko* *1588m*
Fuji-yoshida *1673m*
Motosu-ko Fugaku-fūketsu
Sea of Trees (Jukai)
1468m *Yamanaka-ko* *Tanzawa-ko*
**Fuji-Hakone-Izu
National Park**
Tanuki-ko Kawaguchi-ko
5th Stage Asahigaoka
Oyama TŌMEI EXPRESSWAY
■ **Asagiri-
kōgen** *3776m ▲*
Fuji-san *2693m
▲ Hoei-zan* Yamakita Matsuda
Shin-Gozome **Gotemba** *Tōkyō*
*Shiraito-
no-taki* **Fujikyū-
Highland** **Hakone** **Odawara**
**Fuji
Safari Park** Sōunzan Gōra Chōkoku-
no-mori
Fujinomiya *1507m* Ōwakudani *1438m* Hakone-Yumoto
Shibakawa **Ashitaka-yama**
1248m Tōgendai Miyanoshita *Sagami-
wan*
Hakone-en Moto-Hakone
Ashi-no-ko Hakone-machi
Fujikawa **Susono** **Fuji-Hakone-Izu
National Park**
Yoshiwara Nagaizumi **Himenosawa
Park**
Fuji TŌMEI EXPRESSWAY Yugawara
MOA Museum of Art
Yui Kambara **Mishima** **Atami**
*Shimizu &
Shizuoka* **Numazu** Shimizu Kannami **Atami
Baien**
Nirayama Ose-zaki **Hatsu-
shima**
Izu-nagaoka *Ippeki-ko*
Heda Ōhito **Itō**
Shuzenji Naka-izu **Ikeda Museum
of 20th Century Art**
Toi *Kano-gawa* **Amagi-
kōgen**
**Jōren-
no-taki** *1406m* *Amagi-san*
Kamo Amagi-
yugashima **Atagawa Banana &
Alligator Farm** Atagawa
Suruga-wan **Amagi
Tunnel** **I z u - h a n t ō**
Dogashima **Kawazu-
nanadaru** Higashi-izu
Nishi-izu Kawazu Inatori
Matsuzaki **Fuji-Hakone-Izu
National Park**
Hagachi-zaki **Shira-hama**
Minami-izu **Shimoda**
Yumiga-hama
Irō-zaki ◊ Mikomoto-jima

| 0 | 5 | 10 | 15 km |
| 0 | 5 | 10 miles |

A B C

Mount Fuji is a perfectly shaped volcanic cone that rises to a 3,776m (12,388ft) peak. It is the highest and most popular mountain in Japan, praised by Japanese poets throughout the ages and portrayed in numerous paintings and prints. The summit is frequently covered with clouds, but on a clear day you can see it from as far as 160km (100 miles) away.

Hokusai (1760–1849), the famous *ukiyo-e* painter, immortalized the mountain in two series of woodblock prints featuring *Fuji-san* in all its moods: *Thirty-Six Views of Mount Fuji* and *One Hundred Views of Mount Fuji*.

The ascent Most people climb Mount Fuji (*Fuji-san*) in the hope of witnessing a sunrise from the top. This means either climbing overnight or climbing during the day and staying on the summit overnight in a mountain hut. It is an arduous climb and, once past the tree line, the mountain at close quarters is not beautiful. The rock is black and volcanic and there is no vegetation. Only the view lifts the spirits. The Japanese say that to climb *Fuji-san* once is wise, but to climb it twice is foolish.

During the winter, Fuji is snow-covered from base to peak, and even in summer the summit is never clear.

Mount Fuji is open to the public for climbing from 1 July to 31 August, and every year up to 400,000 people make the ascent along one of the five trails marked off at 10 stations or stages (levels). Kawaguchi-ko 5th Stage, which is halfway up, is the most popular starting level, and can be reached by bus. From Kawaguchi-ko the climb to the summit at a moderate pace is about seven hours; the descent takes half this time. To book into one of the 17 huts *en route*, tel: 0555 22 1948.

SACRED MOUNTAIN
A Shinto shrine to Konohana Sakuya Hime, a divine princess who is the spirit of the cherry blossom, is maintained on the summit of Mount Fuji. The mountain itself is considered sacred by Shintoists, and especially revered by a religious sect known as Fujiko. Pilgrims making the ascent dressed in traditional white tunics and gaiters are a regular sight. Women were not allowed on Mount Fuji or other sacred mountains until the Meiji Restoration (1868).

101

GETTING THERE
The easiest way to reach Kawaguchi-ko 5th Stage is by direct bus from either Hamamatsu-cho or Shinjuku bus terminal, in operation several times a day from 9 July to 31 August. Less frequent bus services are also available from about the end of April to July and again during the months of September and October. Journey times are two and a half hours from Shinjuku and three hours from Hamamatsu-cho.

Opposite: map showing Fuji-Hakone-Izu National Park

Hakone Komagatake Ropeway, with Mount Fuji in the distance

*Contemplating the
view at Lake Ashino*

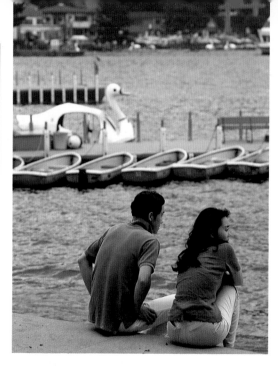

HAKONE SHRINE
The Hakone Shrine was
founded in 757 in Moto-
Hakone, one of the busiest
tourist towns in the
Hakone area. A red *torii*
(gate) out in the lake
provides an obvious land-
mark and a huge Japanese
cedar tree (*Cryptomeria*),
encircled by a sacred rope,
sits in the forecourt.
Known as *Yatate no sugi*
('standing arrow cedar'),
the tree marks the spot
where generals fighting
battles in the area offered
arrows to the gods. The
shrine is also famous as
the site of an act of filial
piety by the two Soga
brothers, medieval warriors
who earned fame for their
military exploits. In the
past, samurai would come
here to venerate the spirits
of these revered men.

102

Q TOUR
For more information, visit
www.odakyu-group.co.jp/
english/index.htm

Shrine detail, Hakone

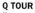

▶▶▶ Hakone   *100C4*

Lying between Mount Fuji and the ocean in Fuji-Hakone-
Izu National Park, Hakone is an area of high mountains
(most over 1,220m/4,000ft), with Lake Ashi nestling in
the middle and Mount Fuji nearly always in view to the
northwest. This is a popular day-trip from Tokyo, and in
summer trains, cable cars, buses and places to stay in the
region are heavily used. However, Hakone's beautiful
scenery, its closeness to Tokyo, and its network of public
transportation make it a very convenient place to explore.

Getting to Hakone There is an 'Odakyu Sightseeing
Service Centre' giving travel advice to individual visitors
journeying to the Hakone area at the Odakyu Shinjuku
station (tel: 03 5321 7887). The cheapest way to get to and
around Hakone is to buy the Hakone Free Pass, or the Q
tour package, available from the Odakyu ticket office in
Shinjuku station. From Shinjuku station in Tokyo,
take the Odakyu private railway to
Odawara (one hour, 25 minutes).
If you travel in the more expensive 'Romance Car', with its
comfortable seating and viewing
windows, go one stop farther to
Hakone-Yumoto. This is the
oldest of Hakone's spa towns,
with a famous *senninburo*
('thousand-people baths') in the
middle. From here or Odawara,
take the Hakone Tozan Tetsudo
line for Gora. The train travels up
steep mountainsides; with each
switchback the views increase in grandeur.
One of the earlier stops is **Miyanoshita▶**, a

more sophisticated, smaller resort than Hakone-Yumoto. Farther along the line is **Chokoku-no-mori▶▶** and the Hakone Open-Air Museum (*Open* daily 9–4.30), with Western and Japanese sculpture in an open, cliffside setting. The train terminus is at **Gora▶**, a town loved by hikers and climbers. From here, take the cable car up to Sounzan, then transfer to the Hakone Ropeway, the longest gondola ride in Japan (33 minutes). Some way out of Sounzan the ropeway crests a ridge and suddenly you are suspended over the **Owakudani Gorge (Great Boiling Valley)▶▶▶**, a long way beneath you. From the gorge floor sulphurous steam spurts out of cracks in the earth and clouds of reeking fumes hover in the air. If you ask the conductor, you can get off at **Owakudani▶▶**, the next stop and the ropeway's highest point. Here you can hike along a nature trail and visit the Natural Science Museum (*Open* daily 9–5).

The ropeway finally descends to Togendai on the shores of **Lake Ashi▶▶▶**. From here, cruise boats travel to Hakone-machi. Look for reflections of the surrounding mountains, particularly Mount Fuji, in the lake surface. The mountains bloom with cherry blossoms in April, azaleas in May and June, and red maple in the autumn.

Historical route The old Tokaido Road between Kyoto and Edo (old Tokyo) ran through Hakone, and one of the most important barrier gates was in **Hakone-machi▶▶** (see pages 104–105). The Barrier Guardhouse (Hakone Sekisho) has been reconstructed and some of the narrow, cobbled Tokaido is preserved. A short walk from where the boat docks, the guardhouse and exhibition hall display mannequins of guards and customers, samurai armour and weapons, and macabre early photographs of crucified and beheaded criminals. For a feeling of old Japan, walk down the nearby tree-lined stretch of the old Tokaido. A bus service runs from Hakone-machi to Hakone-Yumoto (50 minutes) and on to Odawara (one hour). From here, take the Odakyu line back to Tokyo.

VOLCANOES
The Japanese islands lie in the volcanic zone that surrounds the Pacific Rim, and cataclysmic eruptions have always affected the lives of Japanese people. Physically, many volcanoes here are shaped like a cone with a wide base (*Fuji-san* is the best-known example). They are formed by a build-up of layers of lava issuing from an erupting crater. The death and life brought by volcanoes and their imposing presence on the landscape have always given them an elevated place in the Shinto pantheon of divine spirits (*kami*). Many traditions and festivals designed to appease them are still maintained.

103

Mount Fuji provides a dramatic backdrop to Lake Ashi

The second Tokugawa shogun, Iemitsu, inherited his title in 1616. An even more ruthless soldier and cunning politician than his predecessor, Ieyasu, he understood how to maintain and widen his power. With the introduction of his political control system, sankin kotai *or 'alternate attendance', he ensured that the Tokugawa clan would stay in power in Japan for over 200 years.*

ROAD SIGNS

As the remaining short stretch of the original Tokaido Road shows, the Tokaido was not very wide and, because no carts used it, was unsurfaced. Distances were carefully marked, as this quote from a 17th-century Portuguese visitor illustrates: 'There is no need to enquire about distances because all the leagues are measured out, with a mound and two trees to mark the end of each one. Should it happen that a league ends in the middle of a street, they will do no man a favour by making the measurement either longer or shorter, but pull down the houses there in order to set up the sign.'

Sankin kotai required each of the feudal lords, or *daimyo*, of Japan's noble families to build a substantial home in Edo (old Tokyo) and to spend alternate years in residence there while in attendance at the shogun's court. The year in between was to be spent on the noble's own estates. Close family members of the *daimyo* were restricted at all times to their homes in Edo and the surrounding district. At one stroke, the shogun ensured that at any one time half his feudal lords were under his eye at court and for the rest of the time he could, if need be, hold their families hostage. He also required that on his journey from his estate to Edo each *daimyo* should have a stipulated entourage of soldiers, ladies-in-waiting, servants and craftsmen. The size of the entourage was directly proportional to the size of the *daimyo's* estate, and the outlay required to pay for it was designed to ensure the *daimyo* never had enough money to finance an uprising.

The Tokaido Road This law also meant that *daimyo* had to travel between their estates and Edo once a year. There were five main routes radiating from Edo, and the Tokaido, which followed the eastern seaboard to Kyoto, was the most used. It was used not only by nobles from the western provinces but also by normal traffic journeying between the seat of government and Kyoto, the home of the emperor and the religious capital of the land.

The Tokaido followed the coast from Edo to Yokkaichi before striking inland to Kyoto via Kameyama, Otsu, and the southern end of Lake Biwa. The scenery along the way was both picturesque and rugged: open sea, land-locked bays, distant mountains (including Mount Fuji), high cliffs, paddy fields, and many towns and villages all came in and out of view along the route. These different

Hiroshige's changing seasons on the Tokaido

landscapes, the changing light and the human traffic on the road were the inspiration for Hiroshige, the great *ukiyo-e* painter, in his work *Views from the Fifty-Three Stations of the Tokaido*.

Noble progress The journey of a great lord along the Tokaido was an impressive sight. Nobles were carried in beautifully lacquered palanquins. Attendants bore aloft bright banners, and the marching men and samurai on horseback wore full uniform. The whole effect was designed to illustrate the power and authority of the lord.

  A noble procession was heralded well in advance so that post stations and inns could prepare beforehand for the extra provisions, horses and beds that would be required. Others who knew of it would also stay clear of the road, both for their own safety and in order not to hinder the progress of the lordly personage. The procession was preceded by horsemen, who would shout 'Down! down!' and people of inferior rank were required to prostrate themselves on the ground as the *daimyo* passed. Anyone foolish enough to show disrespect and refuse to pay homage in this way was literally chopped down by one of the samurai escorting the lord.

Barrier gates Barriers such as the Hakone barrier gate ensured that none of the *daimyo* could move any of their families out of Edo without permission. This applied especially to womenfolk, and any woman within a procession was subjected to the closest scrutiny. As well as discouraging travel, the system also gave rise to many Japanese stories of intrigue, adventure and thwarted love.

ARISTOCRATIC TRAFFIC
Carriages drawn by oxen were the sole privilege of the imperial court and would usually only be seen in and around Kyoto. If a *daimyo's* procession leaving the Tokaido crossed the path of the carriage of an aristocrat from the Imperial Palace, the *daimyo* himself would have to get out of his palanquin and prostrate himself on the ground. To avoid this embarrassing situation, the *daimyo* would send a guard ahead to offer gifts of money to journeying aristocrats with the suggestion that it was a good time to stop for refreshments.

105

Central Honshu

FUTAMIGAURA

Futamigaura, connected to Ise and Toba by bus or train, is the site of the 'wedded rocks', which represent man and wife. Large straw ropes, used in the Shinto religion to mark sacred spaces and to symbolize marriage, connect the two rocks. On the larger, 'husband' rock is a *torii*, which is also used to denote a sacred space. The Japanese tend to visit at dawn, to see the sun rising between the two rocks.

106

THE THREE SACRED TREASURES

Ise Shrine houses the sacred mirror (*Kagami*), one of the three imperial regalia symbolizing imperial power. According to legend, the sun goddess sent her grandson to Japan so that he and his descendants could rule over the country. Before he left she gave him three insignia: a mirror, a sword and a set of jewels. As she handed him the mirror, she is said to have remarked, 'When you look upon this mirror, let it be as if you look upon me'. The sword is kept in Atsuta Shrine in Nagoya, and the jewels are in the Imperial Palace in Tokyo.

▶▶▶ Ise-shima National Park   94B2

Set on Shima Peninsula, which juts out into the Pacific Ocean south of Nagoya, Ise-shima National Park covers a total area of more than 550sq km (210sq miles). Its fame derives from the Ise Jingu, also called the Grand Shrines of Ise, which enshrine the Sun Goddess Amaterasu o Mikami, the ancestral divine spirit of the Japanese imperial line. Apart from its beautiful coastline and mountainous interior, Ise-shima's other attractions are the cultured pearl farms at Toba, the 'wedded rocks' of Futamigaura, and Ago Bay, at the southern tip of Shima Peninsula, with its host of tiny islands and abundant marine life. The simplest way to tour Ise-shima is to start in the small town of Ise, the northern gateway to the park and home of the Grand Shrines. Then move south down the peninsula to Toba and onto Kashikojima town (on Ago Bay's largest island, connected by bridge to the mainland) for a boat trip around Ago Bay.

Ise is an hour and 25 minutes from Nagoya on the private Kintetsu Ise-shima line, two hours from Kyoto or Osaka on the Kintetsu Yamada line. Trains and buses connect Ise to Toba and Kashikojima. Tour buses travel from the Inner Shrine to Toba along the Ise-shima Skyline Highway, crossing over Mount Asama, the roof of the peninsula.

The **Ise Jingu▶▶▶** are the most important of Shinto shrines, consisting of the Outer Shrine, the Inner Shrine, and more than 100 minor shrines. The Outer Shrine (Geku), first erected in the fifth century, is dedicated to the goddess of food, clothing and housing and is surrounded by a tranquil forest of old Japanese cedars. Each morning offerings of food, attended by a white stallion from the emperor's stables, are made at the shrine. The main building, like that of the Inner Shrine, is made of unpainted cypress wood joined without nails. Both shrines stand on wooden piles and have thatch roofs like ancient Japanese houses. Only members of the imperial family and high-ranking priests are allowed into these buildings, which are surrounded by wooden palisades and are mostly out of sight for ordinary visitors. This does not deter the thousands of Japanese who visit the shrines every year. For them, Ise Shrine and its serene grounds are magical, embodying the very heart of old Japan. The Outer Shrine, 10 minutes' walk from Ujiyamada, Ise town's main station

Shopping in traditional dress at Ise

(where there is a tourist office, *Open* daily 9–5.30), is approached through a large wooden *torii* and down a long avenue lined with various pavilions. You cannot go past the third of the four gates that lead to the shrine.

The Inner Shrine (Naiku), founded in AD 260, is about 6km (4 miles) from the Outer Shrine; the two are connected by a regular bus service. By far the most important of the two, it closely resembles Geku Shrine in its structure, general layout and practical arrangements. Enshrined in the deepest recesses of Naiku is the Sacred Mirror, one of the Three Sacred Treasures of the Shinto religion (see panel). Through the first *torii* and after the second small bridge approaching the shrine, pilgrims and visitors wash and purify their hands and mouths with water from the Isuzu River, whose source lies within the Inner Shrine.

Toba▶ is a prosperous port town, whose main point of interest is Mikimoto Pearl Island, a five-minute walk from Toba station, connected to the mainland by Pearl Bridge. The Pearl Museum and Mikimoto Memorial Hall (*Open* 8.30–5, Mar–19 Nov; 9–4.30, rest of year), on the island, trace the fascinating story of the cultivation of pearls. *Ama* (women divers) in traditional white outfits demonstrate how the women of Shima Peninsula used to dive for oyster pearls as well as abalone, seaweed and other sea foods. Toba Aquarium, five minutes from Toba station, has an impressive collection of sea creatures, including otters and the dugong, a small sea mammal.

Crossing the bridge to the Inner Shrine

RECONSTRUCTED SHRINES
The Inner and Outer Shrines are torn down and rebuilt every 20 years, using the same plans and new wood, in a ritual known as *shikinen sengu*. The present buildings are the 61st in succession. The most recent shrine rebuilding ceremonies were completed in 1993. The most ancient sacred shrines in Japan are thus less than ten years old. For each shrine there are two sites, one occupied and one vacant. The old wood from a demolished shrine is cut into pieces and given to the pilgrims at the ceremony.

Loose tea ready for sale at the Grand Shrines of Ise

▶▶ Izu Peninsula (*Izu-hanto*) 100C3

The Izu Peninsula plunges down from the mainland into the Pacific Ocean in Fuji-Hakone-Izu National Park. It has a mountainous interior, a dramatic coastline, fine beaches and many hot springs. Only about an hour from Tokyo station by bullet train to Atami, at the northern end of the

Erotic art at Ryosenji Temple, Shimoda

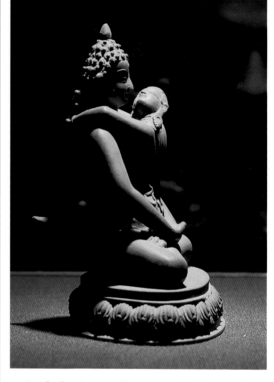

WILL ADAMS
William Adams was born in England in 1564. At the age of 12 he was apprenticed to a shipyard, where he studied astronomy and navigation as well as shipbuilding. In 1598, he set out from Holland as chief pilot of a fleet heading for the Orient. After a long voyage his ship was caught in a gale and washed ashore off the coast of Kyushu. He was taken to Osaka castle and interrogated by Tokugawa Ieyasu himself. The Shogun was so impressed by Adams and his knowledge of ships that he appointed him adviser on foreign affairs. In 1604, on the Shogun's orders, Adams built an 80-tonne Western sailing ship on the estuary of the Matsa-kawa (river) in Ito. Pleased with the result, Ieyasu ordered Adams to build an ocean-going vessel, which the Shogun lent to a Spanish diplomat, who sailed the ship to Acapulco and never returned it to Japan. Adams was rewarded for his services with a large estate and the status of a samurai, and adopted the Japanese name Miura Anjin. He died in Japan of natural causes, aged 56.

peninsula, Izu is a popular resort with Tokyo residents. During mid-July to the end of August, the region is very crowded and to be avoided (at the very least, make sure your accommodation is reserved in advance). Regular train and bus services operate along the scenic east coast from Atami to Ito, a spa resort, and Shimoda, home of the first American consulate. From Shimoda, there are bus services around the southern tip of the coast to Dogashima, a small fishing village on the less developed west side of the peninsula, or through the mountainous interior to Shuzenji, a traditional and rather prestigious spa town. From Shuzenji, there are trains back to Atami or Mishima and on to Tokyo. Alternatively, for a complete peninsula round trip, there is a bus service from Dogashima to Shuzenji. The Izu Peninsula has numerous hotels, *ryokan* and *onsen minshuku*, a sort of hot-spring bed-and-breakfast where your room is in a large house, similar to that of a family house, fitted with a public bath fed by underground hot springs.

Atami▶, one of the largest and best-known hot spring resorts in Japan, is a collection of hotels, souvenir shops, red-light districts, bars and restaurants. Many of the town's visitors are businessmen or workers on company sponsored holidays, and they can get pretty rowdy in the evenings. Unless you wish to visit the MoA (Museum of Art), it is best just to pass through Atami. The museum (*Open* 9.30–4.30; *closed* Thu), is on a hill above the station, and was opened in 1982 by a religious organization founded by Mokichi Okada (1882–1955). It has an excellent collection of Japanese, Chinese and European art, as well as a garden, tea-ceremony room and playhouse for *noh* drama.

In 1604, Will Adams, the English ship's pilot who inspired the novel *Shogun*, built a ship at the old established spa town of **Ito▶** for Tokugawa Ieyasu (see panel). Near the harbourmaster's office a shabby memorial stone records his exploits in Japanese and English. Thirty minutes by bus from Ito station is the Ikeda Art Museum (*Open* 10–5.30, Jul–Aug; 10–4.30, rest of year), which houses a collection of 20th-century Japanese and Western art in an impressive stainless steel building.

Shimoda▶▶ holds an important place in Japanese history, as it was here, in 1854, that the first important trade treaty between America and Japan was signed. All the major sites in Shimoda are linked in one way or another with its American associations (see panel). Shimoda Tourist Office, in front of the station, has an easy itinerary in English.

About one hour by bus from Shimoda, **Dogashima▶▶** is a quiet fishing village in an area of unusual rock formations jutting out from the coast into the sea. A sightseeing boat leaves from the village pier. Dogashima is a place for gentle exploration and relaxation, where you can swim and sunbathe in season.

Shuzenji▶ is a rather expensive inland spa town. The trip there through the mountainous interior from Shimoda is of rather more interest than the town itself (see panel). From Shuzenji, you can travel back to Atami or catch the private railway line to Mishima and change for the bullet train to Tokyo.

THE ROAD TO SHUZENJI
From Shimoda, the road to Shuzenji zigzags up Mount Amagi to Nonadani Bridge near the summit, where the mountain is too steep to continue the road. Four massive steel legs standing on a ledge halfway down the mountain support a double spiral structure that carries the road and juts out over the valley thousands of feet below.

TOJIN OKICHI
In 1857, the first US consul to Japan, Townsend Harris, moved to a village near Shimoda with his Japanese consort, Tojin Okichi. According to the Japanese, she was forced to leave her lover for Harris and, as soon as he left, committed suicide. She has since become a folk heroine. Harris's version was very different. He claimed that he was offered the girl but refused her, and that after his departure she attempted a reconciliation with her lover, which failed. She then opened a restaurant, which was not a success, and finally took to drink.

Fishing boats on the Izu Peninsula

Earthquakes (jishin) are common phenomena in Japan. The country sits over the intersections of four tectonic plates, huge sections of the earth's crust that slip against each other, sometimes gently, occasionally violently. Within the plates are fault lines where slippage is rarer but can be catastrophic. Scarcely a day passes without a tremor in some part of the archipelago. Fortunately, almost all are mild, hardly noticed by the inhabitants.

Top: the Great Kanto
Earthquake of 1923.
Above: an earthquake
cartoon

BEING PREPARED
On 1 September, the anniversary of the 1923 Tokyo earthquake, which left a death toll of more than 140,000, Japan observes Disaster Prevention Day. During the day evacuation procedures are tested and children run through smoke-filled corridors with wet handkerchiefs over their noses and mouths. The Self Defence Force carries out helicopter rescue exercises, and fire departments rehearse their routines. Simulators the size of a small house put people through the experience of a violent tremor while they try to remember the survival drill.

Unpredictably, every 10 or 20 years, a more powerful shock hits a populated area and causes fatalities. At even longer intervals, disaster strikes on the scale of the Great Kanto Earthquake of 1923, which is estimated to have reached 8.2 on the Richter Scale. Its midday timing meant that countless *hibachi* (charcoal grills), ready for cooking lunch, ignited the wooden houses of Tokyo and Yokohama as they collapsed. Far more people died in the resulting firestorms than in the quake itself.

Kobe At 5.46am, on 17 January 1995, the Great Hanshin Earthquake shook a wide area of southern Honshu with a force measuring 7.2 on the Richter Scale. Its epicentre was somewhere under Awaji Island offshore from Kobe, Japan's second-largest port with a population of 1.5 million. Worst hit were the residential areas of the city, built in the 1950s and 1960s. Thousands of wooden houses collapsed, their heavy tile roofs falling on their inhabitants as they slept, causing many of the 5,000 fatalities. Domestic gas heaters running during the cold winter night ignited fatal fires when main gas pipes fractured during the earthquake.

The attitude of the survivors was remarkable, which was a resigned acceptance of their misfortune. In the world's most technologically advanced country, 310,000 people were left with nothing. Their legendary grit was displayed as many walked to work that same morning. If the Japanese reputation for stoicism was reinforced, that for efficiency was undermined. Fire and rescue services were said to be woefully slow to react, and local authorities had to make a written request for help from the Self Defence Force.

Lessons The media savaged the government and bureaucracy for their inadequate response. There was great alarm, too, that buildings, expressways and the tracks of the fabled Shinkansen had not stood up to the shock as well as predicted. What was wrong with the calculations? When cooler assessments were made, it turned out that post-1980 structures, including high-rise buildings, had survived well. More worrying is the evidence that reclaimed land can shake like a jelly, or even behave like a liquid, causing severe damage to Kobe's port installations.

Tokyo In the capital, 20 years of complacency vanished overnight in a shudder of fear. The idea that structures could be 'earthquake proof' had been disproved convincingly. 'Earthquake resistance' is all that can be aspired to now, and levels of that are going to have to be stepped up. Some of the elevated highways date from the 1960s. Plans to strengthen buildings are under way, and there has been talk of relocating the capital somewhere safer, but where? Until 1995, Kobe had been considered safe. Seismology is an inexact science and Japan cannot change its geology. For the moment, though, Tokyo watches and waits for the next inevitable, but unpredictable, earthquake.

*Damage caused by
the Kobe Earthquake*

111

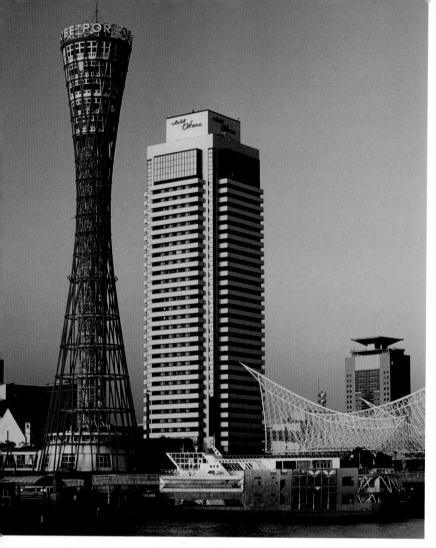

Kobe Port Tower and Osaka Bay

CORMORANT (*UKAI*) FISHING
Trained cormorants on leashes are used to fish for *ayu* (small trout). To prevent them swallowing the fish they catch, the birds are fitted with small rings around their necks. The boats that carry the birds work at night and a bright wood brazier is suspended from the bow to attract the fish.

▶▶ Kobe 94A2

Japan's sixth-largest city prospered as a gateway for trade with China in the 15th and 16th centuries. When Japan's isolation ended in 1868, Kobe was among the first ports to open to Western ships. Many foreign traders settled here and it became a cosmopolitan place, with one of the world's busiest ports. The narrow strip of land between the mountains and the sea was soon outgrown. Residential quarters climbed the slopes, and the port facilities occupied reclaimed land and artificial islands.

As mentioned on page 110, before dawn on 17 January 1995, a devastating earthquake shook the city. Thousands of older houses and small apartment buildings collapsed. More than 5,000 people died. Part of the elevated Hanshin Expressway fell over—train and Shinkansen lines were severed (fortunately the early hour meant that the bullet trains themselves were not running). Buildings put up since 1980, to higher standards of earthquake resistance, survived with little or no damage. Communication networks and damaged buildings in the city proper have now been restored and life is back to normal.

Many restaurants and shops and most hotels are within walking distance of the two central stations, Sannomiya and Motomachi. The lively entertainment quarter, Ikuta, lies west of Sannomiya, and Japan's biggest 'Chinatown' is just south of Motomachi. Main street names are given in English, as well as Japanese.

Bullet trains connecting Kobe and Osaka (15 minutes), Kyoto (33 minutes), and Tokyo (three and a half hours) use Shin-Kobe station, a short subway ride from Sannomiya station. Both have good information desks.

Kobe City Museum▶▶ (*Open* Tue–Sun 10–5), 24 Kyomachi, Chuo-ku, is a 10-minute walk south of Sannomiya station. It specializes in the history of Kobe, the influence of Western taste and techniques on Japanese design, and the way the Japanese viewed Westerners, shown in amusing scrolls and screens. The building and some exhibits suffered damage in the 1995 earthquake and the museum closed for repair, but it is now fully open.

Kitano▶▶ is a hilly district of narrow streets, a 15-minute walk north of Sannomiya, where Western traders and other foreign residents have lived since the 19th century. Some of the houses are open to the public.

▶ Nagoya   94B2

Razed to the ground by Allied bombing during World War II, Nagoya has since been rebuilt and is now the fourth-largest city in Japan. There are few historical attractions beyond its two national treasures: Nagoya Castle and the Atsuta Jingu Shrine. This is, however, a very convenient base for the Grand Shrines of Ise (see pages 106–107), Nara (see pages 114–115) and Gifu (see below). Shinkansen service connects Nagoya with Kyoto (43 minutes), Osaka (one hour) and Tokyo (two and a half hours).

Nagoya Castle▶▶▶ was built in 1612 as a residence and military base for the Tokugawa clan. The five-floor castle was destroyed in World War II, and a copy, built in 1959, houses treasures such as screen paintings and sliding doors. Two bronze dolphins covered with gold scales, reconstructed atop the castle roof, are believed to protect it from fire. Ninomaru garden and Ninomaru Tea House (*Open* 9.30–4.30) are next door.

Atsuta Jingu Shrine▶▶▶, 1-1-1 Jingu, Atsuta-ku (*Open* dawn to dusk; subway: Jingunishi), houses the sacred sword that is one of Japan's most treasured objects (see panel above right).

Gifu▶▶ is 30 minutes by JR train north of Nagoya. The main reason to visit is to view the cormorant fishing on the Nagara-gawa (see panel). This traditional event takes place every evening between 11 May and 15 October. Before and after the fishing, the Japanese gather on the banks of the river to drink, eat and make merry. The tourist office at the station will give you details of how to get to the river and make a hotel reservation.

THE ATSUTA SWORD
Prince Yamatotakeru was a legendary war hero of the third century. The sword that saved his life during a military campaign is that held (but not displayed) in Atsuta Shrine, Nagoya. It is called Grass-Cutting Sword because the prince used it to cut the grass down around him when it was set alight by attacking bandits. The Yamato originated the rule of the Japanese emperors, and the shrine housing the sword was later given the highest rank of a Shinto shrine.

113

Atsuta Jingu Shrine

Horyuji Temple

114

THE GREAT BRONZE BUDDHA
Daibutsu, the bronze Buddha of Todaiji Temple, is 16.15m (53ft) tall, weighs 149,688kg (330,000lb) and took five years to cast. Its completion in 749 was marked by a spectacular ceremony of consecration in 752, attended by the imperial family.

► ► ► **Nara**   94A2

In order to preserve Shinto ritual purity, the imperial court of ancient Japan moved to a different location on the succession of each new emperor. By the eighth century, the size of the state and the administrative arrangements needed to run it finally made this tradition too impractical to maintain. In AD 710, Nara was chosen as the first permanent political and cultural hub of a newly united Japan. There followed a great flowering of every field from art to religion, influenced by the imported culture of the Tang Dynasty in China and Buddhism, which was promoted by the Japanese imperial court as a way of unifying the country. During this period, many remarkable temples and monuments were built, some of which have survived in Nara and are described below. (For details on how to get to Nara, see panel on page 97.)

To the southwest of Nara, **Horyuji Temple► ► ►** is a little off the beaten track, but well worth a visit. It is the oldest intact temple complex in Japan and houses the world's oldest wooden buildings. Horyuji was founded in 607 by Prince Shotoku, a great patron of Buddhist religion and culture, who made his court into a renowned place of learning. The complex is divided into the West Temple, containing the Kondo main hall and pagoda, and the East Temple, mainly comprising the Yumedono pavilion and Chuguji Nunnery. Horyuji owns a magnificent collection of Buddhist art (*Open* 8–5; until 4.20pm 20 Nov–10 Mar; bus from Kintetsu-Nara station, 40 minutes).

Kofukuji Temple► ► is famous for its five-floor pagoda (built in 1426 as an exact replica of the eighth-century original). It is Nara's best-known landmark, and its name, meaning 'Happiness-Producing Temple', dates back to 710, when it was constructed as a teaching temple for the children of the Fujiwara family. Nanendo Hall, which contains a fine gilded statue of Kannon carved in 1188, is a sacred pilgrimage site and is often very crowded. The Kokuhokan Treasure House contains the temple's works of Buddhist art (*Open* 9–5; access from Sanjo Street, running east from Nara JR station).

Founded in 745, **Todaiji Temple► ► ►**, in Nara Park (*Open* 7.30–5.30, Apr–Sep; 8–5, rest of year; walk or take bus number 2 from JR or Kintetsu stations, get off at Daibutsuden), was built to be the headquarters of all temples in Japan. For the Japanese, it remains the most important sight in Nara. Todaiji's main hall, the Daibutsuden, is claimed to be the largest wooden

Detail, Horyuji Temple

Todaiji's Daibutsuden

building in the world. It houses the Great Buddha of Nara, the largest bronze Buddha ever cast, after many years of failed attempts (see panel). Entrance to the temple is through the massive Nandaimon gate; look for the giant wooden statues on either side. Todaiji took a workforce of several thousand, including carpenters and metal-workers, five years to complete. Its cost crippled the economy and led to a peasants' revolt. Nearly all the original buildings were destroyed in 1180 by the Taira clan, to punish the armed monks of Todaiji for their support of the rival Minamoto clan.

Toshodaiji Temple►► (*Open* 8.30–5), near Nishinokyo station on the Kintetsu Kashiwara line, is one of the loveliest of Nara's temples. It was founded in 759 by the Chinese priest Ganjin, who had been invited to Japan by the emperor to spread Buddhism and faced many trials on his journey to Japan, including the loss of his sight. At the age of 66, he supervised the construction of this fine temple. The main hall and lecture hall are national treasures. The eight pillars at the front of Kondo Hall show the influence of Greek architecture, which reached Japan via the 'Silk Road'.

PRIESTLY POWER
The great Buddhist temples of Nara owned large, tax-free estates, and with growing prosperity they became increasingly powerful and avaricious. The priest Dokyo, an eighth-century Rasputin figure, became mentor and love of the empress Koken (718–770). Alarmed by the power of the very temples they had helped to foster, the Fujiwara ruling clan moved the court to Heian-Kyo (Kyoto), and severed the government's strong Buddhist connections.

Kombu-in Temple · Nara Dreamland Amusement Park · Tegaimon Gate · Shoso-in Treasure Repository · Mikasa Onsen · Jukkoku Observatory · ICHIJO-DORI · Sabo-gawa · Daibutsuden · Nigatsudo Hall · 342m Wakakusa-yama · Kaidan-in · Sangatsudo Hall · Todaiji Temple · Tamukeyama Hachimangu Shrine · Prefectural Museum of Art · Neiraku Museum · Nandaimon Gate · Kintetsu–Nara Station · OMIYA-DORI · Kofukuji Temple · Isui-en Garden · Nara · Horyuji Temple · Toshodaiji Temple · Three-storied Pagoda · Five-storied Pagoda · Nara National Museum · Kasuga Taisha Shrine · 498m · SANJO-DORI · Torii Gate · Man-yo Botanical Garden · Kasuga-yama · JR Nara Station · Sarusawano-ike · Ara-ike · Torii Gate · Kasuga Wakamiya Shrine · Sugi-ike · Park · Gokurakobo (Gangoji Temple) · Jurin-in Temple · Shin-Yakushiji Temple · Renjoji Temple · Byakugoji Temple · 0 400 800m · 0 400 800 yards

116

Walk

Nara

Distance: 3km (2 miles); time: three hours. The major historical sites of

Nara are laid out in a huge deer park, with Wakakusa Hill as a backdrop. Despite the sightseers, Nara is imbued with a sense of peace, a comfort for jangled nerves.

Start from the **Nara City Tourist Centre** between JR Nara and Kintetsu–Nara stations. Walk two

Main hall, Shin-Yakushiji Temple

Wooden Buddhist deity at Kofukuji

blocks east to discover the three-floor pagoda of **Kofukuji Temple▶**, founded in 710 and once comprising more than 1,300 buildings. Of the remaining structures, the three-floor pagoda dates from the 12th century, the five-floor pagoda and eastern main hall from the 14th century. The view of the five-floor pagoda from across the Sarusawa Pond is one of the most famous in Nara. From Kofukuji, continue east, passing through the *torii* into the park area, then turn left for the approach to **Todaiji Temple▶▶▶**. The temple's main building, the world's largest wooden structure, houses a 16.2m (53ft) bronze Buddha.

More than 1,000 tame deer roam the park in Nara. From Todaiji, walk southeast through the park to the **Kasuga Taisha▶▶▶**, one of the most famous Shinto shrines, its vermilion lacquered buildings set against the green woodlands. Thousands of stone lanterns line the approach to the shrine, and hundreds of bronze lanterns hang from the eaves of the shrine buildings. The grassy slopes of the 342m (1,122ft) high Wakakusa-yama, north of the shrine, are ritually burned each year on 15 January. South of Kasuga Taisha, outside the park, is **Shin-Yakushiji Temple▶**, another eighth-century monument. Picturesque old houses line the street that leads west from Shin-Yakushiji along the edge of the park. Return to the park, and go back toward the *torii*, passing three ponds to the left. This leads to the **Nara National Museum▶▶**, housing a collection of works of ancient art, including masterpieces of early Buddhist art. The museum's West Wing specializes in objects of archaeological interest.

From the National Museum, walk back past Kofukuji to either station.

BUNRAKU

One of the three classical forms of theatre in Japan, *bunraku*, or puppetry, has been popular since the 17th century. A typical play could deal with a story of tragic love, a well-known historical event, or a comic story of urban life. The puppets, usually dressed in elaborate period costume, are about two-thirds human size, each one made up of interchangeable parts. Each of the major characters is handled by three puppeteers dressed in black. The chief puppeteer (it takes 30 years to become an expert) manipulates the puppet's head, eyes, mouth, and right arm and hand.

NIGHTLIFE

The busiest nightlife area is around the narrow Dotonburi Street, near Namba station. Here there is a hive of bars, coffee lounges, discos and night-clubs, lit up after dark by gaudy neon signs and a huge, open-air video screen. Singles and *avecs* (couples) throng the streets. For low life, the seamy but fascinating place to go is Shin-Sekai, west of Tennoji Park. This is an area of massage parlours, cheap restaurants and strip joints. The Yakuza (Japanese Mafia) control most of the business and occasionally you can see members cruising by in their extravagantly large, chrome-laden Cadillacs.

Osaka facades

►►► Osaka   94A2

For centuries a mecca for merchants, Osaka is Japan's third-largest city. Like Tokyo, it is an important industrial, financial and commercial hub, but it has an energy and pride of its own, and its styles and fashions are very different from those of the capital. Osakans describe themselves as *shominteki*, people with no time for pretensions, and consider Tokyoites to be wimps. It is a crowded, busy city with no obvious town planning, where cherry orchards, Buddhist temples, choked traffic, grimy commercial buildings, and chrome and glass high-technology skyscrapers all exist side by side.

Osaka is famous for its food and its citizens are known to the rest of Japan as *kuidaore*, or those who will eat to physical and financial ruin. There are restaurants of every type and price throughout the city and choice is limitless. Compared with Tokyo, prices are low.

Osaka is a place to wander, shop and eat. Of the tourist sights, the two priorities are Osaka Castle and the National Bunraku Theatre. To find out what is going on in Osaka, pick up a copy of *Kansai Time Out*, a monthly magazine with information on sightseeing, festivals, restaurants and other items of interest, available at bookshops, restaurants and other places frequented by English-speaking visitors.

Getting there and around Osaka is connected to Tokyo by frequent domestic flights and Shinkansen train service (two and a half to three hours). All trains arrive at Shin-Osaka station. Change here and travel a few stops south on the loop line to Osaka station in the middle of town. Osaka also has a futuristic new airport, the Kansai International Airport (see pages 16–17). The Osaka tourist

Downtown restaurant

information office is at the east exit of Osaka station; staff speak English and the office is open 8–7. Osaka City Air Terminal (OCAT) operates check in and transfer services to Kansai International Airport. It is housed in a new building next to Namba station, central Osaka.

Shopping The Umeda area, around Umeda and Osaka stations, is the hub of department stores and high fashion shops. It extends beneath the ground, where there is a maze of streets and arcades. Three of the local department stores have underground basements that descend into this subterranean complex. If you get lost, go to the ground floor of one of the stores and head for an open-air exit.

Sightseeing Osaka is considered the capital of *bunraku* (see panel), and if you are in the city you should take the opportunity to see a play in the **National Bunraku Theatre**▶▶, 1-12-10 Nipponbashi, Chuo-ku. Performances are scheduled for six periods each year, with each production running for two to three weeks. Information is available at the Osaka tourist information office. The theatre is two minutes' walk from Nipponbashi station on the Kintetsu line (exit 7).

Toyotomi Hideyoshi, the warlord who unified Japan, built **Osaka Castle**▶▶ (Osaka-jo) in 1583 on a strategic hilltop in the city's northern district and used it as his headquarters. After he died, armies of the Tokugawa shogunate (1603–1867) took Osaka Castle in 1615. The castle was also damaged in the fighting that led to the Meiji Restoration of 1868. Its main gate and several towers have survived, however, and the eight-floor *donjon*, the main stronghold, was rebuilt in 1931 and extensively renovated again in 1997. Inside the castle is a museum with displays and exhibits relating to old Osaka and the Toyotomi family, but the main reasons to visit are the view from the top of the *donjon* and the castle's majestic exterior. The park that surrounds the castle is also one of the best places in the city for people-watching (*Open* 9–5). To get to Osaka Castle, take the JR loop line from Osaka station to Osaka-jo Koen-mae station and walk up the hill from there.

119

FOOD
Popular local dishes are the street food, *tako yaki*, a wheatflour dumpling stuffed with octopus meat and baked over charcoal; *udon*, a fat, white wheat noodle; and Osaka sushi, squares of sticky sweet rice and raw fish. *Chanko-nabe* restaurants, also very popular, are named after the unpretentious stew that is the mainstay of a sumo wrestler's diet. The stew is not fattening, the huge amount of rice wrestlers eat performs that function, but it is tasty and nutritious. Retired sumo wrestlers often open their own *chanko-nabe* restaurants and jealously guard their recipes.

Detail, Osaka Castle

Kyoto

Koetsuji Temple

Kamigamo
Shrine

Omiya

KITAYAMA-DORI

KITA-KU

Shichku

Kyōto
Botanica
Garden

HORIKAWA-DORI

Imamiya
Shrine

Daisen-in
Temple

Koto-in
Gardens

Daitokuji
Temple

Koyama

Kinkakuji
Temple

KITAOJI-DORI

Murasakino

SHIMAI-DORI

Izumoji

Ryoanji Temple
& Garden

Kinugasa

KITSUJI-DORI

Ryoanji

Hirano
Shrine

Utano

Ninnaji
Temple

Kitano
Temmangu
Shrine

IMADEGAWA-DORI

Nishijin

Nishijin
Textile
Centre

Raku Art
Museum

Kyōto Gosho
(Kyōto Imperial
Palace)

Daikakuji
Temple

Kitano

NISHIOJI-DORI

Omuro

Myoshinji
Temple

Taizo-in
Temple

Taishogun

KAMIGYO-KU

Imperial
Park

Sento
Palace

KARASUMA-DORI

MARUTAMACHI-DORI

Toei Uzumasa
Movie Land

JR SAN-IN

Koryuji
Temple

Tenjin-gawa

Nishinokyo

Nijo Castle

Uzumasa

Tenryuji
Temple

OIKE-DORI

Shinsen-en
Garden

OIKE-DORI

Museum
of Kyōto

SANJO-DORI

NAKAGYO-KU

Yamanouchi

HORIKAWA-DORI

SHIJO-DORI

Kongo Noh
Stage

Saihoji
Temple

Mibudera
Temple

Omuro-gawa

Mibu

NISHIOJI-DORI

Japan
Embroidery
Museum

NISHI-GOJO-DORI

OMIYA-DORI

NISHI-OHASHI
BRIDGE

Yuzen
Cultural
Hall

SHIMOGYO-KU

Higashi-
Honganji
Temple

Katsura-gawa

Nishi-Kyogoku

Suzaku

SHICHIJO-DORI

Nishi-Honganji
Temple

Costume
Museum

i

Central Post Office

Katsura
Imperial
Villa

KATSURA-OHASHI
BRIDGE

HACHIJO-DORI

Umekoji

Karahashi

Kyōto
Railway
Station

KUJO-DORI

MINAMI-KU

Kanchi-in
Temple

Toji Temple

A

B

C

120

Kyoto

▶▶▶ **CITY HIGHLIGHTS**

Kyoto

Kyoto sakura (*cherry blossoms*)

GEISHA

In the Gion quarter of Kyoto, you'll see young girls called *maiko*. These apprentice geisha, aged between 17 and 25, will graduate to full geisha status, when they will probably acquire a rich patron. Geisha are hired, often in pairs, to entertain parties of men after dinner, at a restaurant, or tea house.

MOUNT HIEI

In the eighth century, Emperor Kammu decided to build a new capital city, to be called Heian-Kyo (present-day Kyoto). He ordered a Buddhist monk, Saicho, of the Tendai sect, to establish a temple on Mount Hiei to protect the city from evil spirits. The temple became the heart of a monastery complex that grew in size and importance as rapidly as Heian-Kyo below. By the 11th century Enryakuji contained more than 3,000 temple buildings. The monks had their own army and they warred with any political or religious faction that opposed their control of the city. In 1571 General Nobunaga invaded the mountain, burned every temple to the ground, and executed every monk. Although the monastery was re-established in the 17th century, it never regained its former power.

KYOTO Established in 794, Kyoto remained the hub of civilization in Japan for over a thousand years. Even today, although the capital has now moved to Tokyo, Kyoto retains its unique position as the country's historical and cultural heart, birthplace of much of the spirit and technology of traditional Japan. The Japanese describe the city as *Nihon no Furusato* meaning 'The Heart of Japan'.

The Allies spared Kyoto from bombing during World War II, and it remains a living museum of Japan's great artistic heritage, the setting for historical and religious sites and a vast wealth of traditional architecture, art, crafts, dance and drama.

The original layout of the city was based on Ch'ang-an (modern Xian), the ancient capital of Tang Dynasty China. Its grid plan makes it easy to get around and the mountains that ring Kyoto on three sides help you keep your bearings. On the approaches to these mountains, modern Kyoto gently reverts to its older self, with Buddhist temples and Shinto shrines, villas, gardens, craft shops, Japanese inns and narrow streets of old houses that lead back into the countryside. The most famous mountain, Mount Hiei, rising above the city to the northeast, is the site of the Enryakuji Temple complex, at one time the most influential Buddhist monastery in Japan.

SIGHTSEEING More than 30 million tourists a year visit Kyoto, but there is so much to do (nearly 2,000 temples and shrines alone) that crowds tend to form only at the most popular places. Avoid the city on public holidays and the best-known sites on weekends if you dislike crowds.

The major attractions are the Kyoto Imperial Palace, Nijo Castle and gardens, Daitokuji Temple, with its many sub-temples, Ginkakuji (Temple of the Silver Pavilion), Kinkakuji (Temple of the Golden Pavilion), the sand and rock Zen garden at Ryoanji Temple, the Heian Shrine and Kiyomizudera Temple, built on a steep hillside with wonderful views over the city. Kyoto also has several museums and a botanical and zoological garden.

FESTIVALS AND CRAFTS There are also many popular annual festivals (*matsuri*) held in Kyoto, normally associated with the changing of the seasons or with religious occasions. For the three best known, the Gion (16–17 July), Jidai (22 October), and Aoi (15 May) *matsuri*, make hotel reservations well in advance.

Kyoto is renowned for traditional Japanese crafts, especially pottery, lacquerware, woodblock prints, fans, Yuzen silk-dyeing and Nishijin silk-weaving. Major schools of the tea ceremony, flower arranging, classical dance and *noh* drama have their headquarters in Kyoto.

CONTRASTS Apart from its temples, shrines and gardens, Kyoto is also a city of fashionable shops and restaurants, and a number of modern buildings such as Kyoto Tower, which provides breathtaking views, and spectacular Kyoto Station, which is a marvel of futuristic architecture. The atmosphere of the city is perhaps best captured in the Gion district. Here, a famous venue where the classical Japanese arts are performed is next door to a very busy betting shop, itself adjacent to the entrance of a temple. In the spring, cherry blossoms might be blowing down streets busy with traffic, geisha, monks and visitors, while peace and quiet are found inside the grounds of the temple.

FESTIVALS
15 May: Aoi Matsuri. The *aoi*, or hollyhock, is thought to prevent both hurricanes and earthquakes. This festival is said to date back to the sixth century. People in traditional court costume walk from the old imperial palace to two Shinto shrines.
16 August: Daimonji Gozan Okuribi. Huge bonfires form Chinese characters on five of the mountains that surround Kyoto.
22 October: Kurama-No-Hi-Matsuri. The Fire Festival of Kurama takes place in Sakyo-ku in Kyoto. The main event is a procession of people carrying lighted torches to the gate of Yuki Shrine, passing between rows of bonfires.
See also pages 30–31.

123

Burning incense at a Kyoto shrine

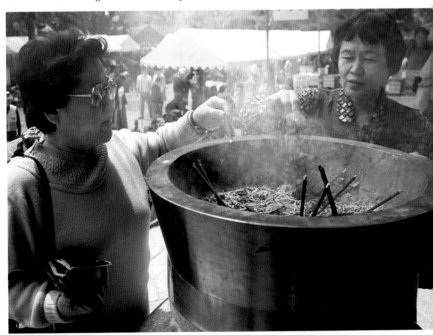

IKKYU SOJUN

Ikkyu Sojun (1394–1481) entered Daitokuji at the age of 20 to study Zen and, according to tradition, achieved enlightenment when he heard crows cawing, while seated in a boat meditating. He constantly criticized the Zen priesthood as corrupt, and scandalized the Buddhist establishment by frequenting the pleasure quarters of Kyoto. When he was an old man he became involved with a young blind singer named Mori and dedicated poems to her in his *Kyounshu* (Crazy Cloud Collection). Ikkyu described himself as:

'Hating incense,
Distrusting Satori,
Disbelieving talk of Zen,
Thoroughly despising
priestly piety,
Wrinkling my nose with
disgust here in the
dimness of the
Buddha Hall.'

THE ZEN LIFE

The Kyoto International Zen Centre offers interested visitors a taste of the Zen life. For information, telephone the Jotokuji Temple on (0771) 24 0152.

*The Zen Garden at
Daitokuji Temple*

▶▶▶ Daitokuji Temple   120B5

Daitokuji-cho, Murasakino, Kita-ku
Bus: 1, 12, 61, 204, 205, 206 to Daitokuji-mae

The Daitokuji (Temple of Great Virtue) is composed of the main temple plus 23 sub-temples (*tatchu*) belonging to the Rinzai sect of Zen Buddhism (only eight of the sub-temples are usually open to the public). Founded in 1319 by Daito Kokushi (1282–1337), the original buildings were damaged by fire in 1453 and 1468, during the Onin Wars. In 1474, the Zen monk Ikkyu Sojun (1394–1481) became head priest of Daitokuji. Although he once said that 'brothels are more suitable settings for meditation than temples', he solicited funds from rich merchants and rebuilt the temple. The great warlord Toyotomi Hideyoshi (1537–98) also contributed to the restoration of the complex; one of the sub-temples, Soken-in, was built by Hideyoshi in memory of his predecessor, Oda Nobunaga (1534–82). Both Nobunaga and Hideyoshi were devotees of the tea ceremony (*chanoyu*), and its greatest master, Sen no Rikyu (1521–91), built tea houses and gardens in the grounds of Daitokuji (see panel, opposite page).

From north to south the temple buildings are: the Chokushi-mon, San-mon Gate, Butsuden (Buddha Hall), Hatto (Lecture Hall) and the Hojo (Abbot's Quarters), which are entered through the Kara-mon (Chinese Gate). The Hojo is open to the public only on 10 October, when its famous collection of paintings is put on display. The Chokushi-mon (Gate of the Imperial Messengers) was originally the south gate of the Imperial Palace in Kyoto. Built in 1590 with curved gables, typical of the style of the Momoyama period, it was given to the Daitokuji by the Empress Meisho in 1640.

Daisen-in▶▶ (*Open* 9–4.30) is a sub-temple of Daitokuji, famous for its eastern Zen garden, created by the founder Kogaku Zenshi with some help from his friend, the artist Soami. The arrangement of rocks (representing mountains), sand (representing a stream of water, the flow of life) and sparse vegetation is symbolic of an individual's journey through life. A rock symbolizing Mount Horai, the home of immortal sages in the Eastern Sea, stands in the northeastern corner. A stream of imaginary water

Stone Buddhist deities...

TEA MASTER
Sen no Rikyu (1521–91) was the greatest master of the tea ceremony. The son of a rich merchant, he became one of Hideyoshi's most trusted advisers, until he was forced to commit suicide by Hideyoshi in 1591. Why this happened is unclear, but it is said that Hideyoshi objected very strongly to walking under a statue of Rikyu that the artist had placed on the upper floor of the outer gate (*san-mon*) of the Daitokuji, thus placing himself 'above' the warlord.

...and a monk at Daitokuji Temple

flows rapidly from the rock, representing youth. Then various obstacles present themselves, with the 'tigerhead stone' representing tragedy. The flow of water is checked and slowed by the stones and a rocky wall, representing doubt and contradiction, and the water eddies and swirls, as if lost and confused. Once the stream moves past this point, it becomes faster and wider, having learned from hard experience. In the middle of this section of the stream, a turtle is observed trying to swim against the flow, demonstrating the pointlessness of trying to return to the past. The southern end of the garden is apparently empty, composed only of white sand, which symbolizes the mind freed from thoughts and emotions.

▶▶▶ Ginkakuji Temple   *121E4*
Ginkakuji-machi, Sakyo-ku
Bus: 5, 17, 203
Open 8.30–5 (last entry 4.30pm)
Ginkakuji (The Temple of the Silver Pavilion) is one of Kyoto's most popular sights. Built originally as a retirement villa for the shogun Ashikaga Yoshimasa (1453–90), it was originally to be covered in silver foil in imitation of his grandfather Yoshimitsu's building, the Kinkakuji or Gold Pavilion. The silver was never applied, but the name survived. Yoshimasa surrounded himself with a circle of artists and aesthetes and devoted his time to the appreciation of women, the tea ceremony, moon-gazing, incense-sniffing and other refinements. The arts that flourished under Yoshimasa's patronage are known as the *Higashiyama Bunka* (Culture of the Eastern Mountains), taking their name from the Higashi mountains that the villa faces.

In 1485, Yoshimasa became a Zen Buddhist monk, and after his death the villa became a Buddhist temple, known as the Joshoji. The gardens are attributed to the artist Soami and are famous for two piles of white sand that sparkle in the moonlight.

One of the most beautiful Zen gardens in Kyoto, and possibly one of the least visited, is that of the Zen temple, Koto-in, a small sub-temple of Daitokuji with only three buildings. The garden is a masterpiece of elegant simplicity, renowned for the beauty of its maple trees in autumn.

CEREMONIAL EXCESSES
During the 14th century, the *chanoyu* or tea ceremony became a social ceremony, a luxurious court ritual. In their splendid apartments, richly decorated and adorned with precious objects, amid the smell of incense, great lords reclining on couches would receive their guests and offer them exotic dishes and tea, whose origin they were supposed to guess to be rewarded with a prize.

Above: Zen garden, Ginkakuji Temple
Below: Daitokuji graves

Early morning reverie The best time to arrive at Koto-in is at around 9am, just as the doors are being opened. Only the doorkeeper is likely to be there. The altar room in the main temple is dark, and you will only just be able to distinguish the Buddhas and other images surrounding the altar itself. The temple rooms are divided by *shoji* (paper screens), which can be opened or closed to make rooms of different sizes, or taken away altogether to make one large room. There is a tangible feeling of peace and calm as you pass over the *tatami* floors onto the veranda overlooking the gardens. Outside, the light strikes the bamboo fences, *shoji*, roof eaves and unpolished wooden beams of the monks' quarters. At this time of the day, if you listen carefully, you may also catch the sound of Zen clappers somewhere in the grounds of Daitokuji, calling the monks to meditation, prayer, or morning tea.

Lord Hosokawa Koto-in was established in 1601 at the behest of a famous military leader, Hosokawa Tadaoki. Hosokawa was a great warrior of his time and one of the

*The stone lantern grave
of Lord Hosokawa and
Lady Gracia, Koto-in Zen
Garden, Daitokuji*

few to survive the bloody civil war that culminated in the establishment of the Tokugawa shogunate. In addition to his martial skills, he was a man of considerable intellectual achievement and an accomplished diplomat. His wife, Lady Gracia, was a devout believer in the then-outlawed Catholic faith, and her father was the disgraced leader of an unsuccessful revolt against the reigning shogun. Hosokawa overcame this potentially fatal association and became a prominent figure in the early Tokugawa regime. He was rewarded with vast domains of land, but later in life devoted himself to the study of Zen under the famous Daitokuji abbot Seigan (1588–1661). He was also noted as one of the most distinguished disciples of the great tea master, Sen no Rikyu. Lord Hosokawa and Lady Gracia are buried in the garden of Koto-in; their grave is marked by a stone lantern.

The tea pavilion Shoko-ken (*Open* 9–4.30), one of the main buildings in Koto-in, is a tea house built by Hosokawa but inspired by the teachings of Sen no Rikyu. During the 15th and 16th centuries, the rituals surrounding the tea ceremony became ever more elaborate and luxurious, finally provoking a return to simplicity and austerity. The reaction was initiated and led by Sen no Rikyu, who devised a set of rules governing the *chanoyu* (tea ceremony) that still applies today. Shoko-ken is reached by a stone flagged path across a small land-scaped garden. It has a tiny kitchen for washing the vessels used in the ceremony, a *tokonoma* (alcove) decorated with an elegant *kakemono* (hanging scroll) and a simple vase with simple flowers, complying perfectly with Sen no Rikyu's rules for the tea pavilion.

TEA CEREMONY
The tea ceremony is a formal ritual for preparing and drinking the bitter-tasting powdered green tea called *matcha*. The ceremony originated in Buddhist monasteries in China, where the monks, on special occasions, shared tea in front of an ink painting of Bodhidharma, founder of the Zen tradition. Sen no Rikyu (1522–91) formalized the Japanese-style tea ceremony that is still carried out today.

Heian Shrine

HEIAN SHRINE FESTIVALS
Emperor Komei is commemorated at a festival on 30 January and Emperor Kammu on 3 April. Perhaps the most interesting festival is the Jidai Matsuri (Festival of the Ages), on 22 October, when men and women wear costumes dating from the end of the Tokugawa period to the Heian period, when Kyoto was founded. Their procession starts at the Imperial Palace at 10am and ends at the Heian Shrine at 3.30pm.

KINKAKUJI ARCHITECTURE
Kinkakuji's architecture is quite unusual. The first floor is built in the Shinden style of the Heian palaces, while the second floor resembles a temple hall and enshrines a statue of Kannon Bosatsu. The third floor is as sparse as a Zen hall, yet contains a statue of a Jodo-style Amida, the Buddha of the Western Paradise, or Pure Land.

▶▶▶ Heian Shrine   121D3
Okazaki Park
Bus: 2, 3, 5
Open (garden): 8.30–5.30, 15 Mar–31 Aug;
8.30–5, Sep–Oct and 1–14 Mar; 8.30–4.30, rest of year
The Shrine of Peace and Tranquillity is a Shinto shrine, built in 1895 to celebrate the 1,100th anniversary of the founding of Kyoto and dedicated to the spirits of Emperor Kammu (781–806), who established Kyoto, and Emperor Komei (1831–66), the father of Emperor Meiji.

Erected as a two-thirds scale replica of the original Imperial Palace (dating from 794 and destroyed by fire in 1227), the Heian Shrine is decorated with vermilion paint and roofed with glazed green tiles, and has an enormous ferro-concrete *torii* (gate). Behind the main buildings, a modern version of Heian period gardens can be found, focused around a large pond spanned by a Chinese-style bridge. Unlike many of the Zen gardens in the Kyoto area, the gardens of the Heian Shrine make extensive use of flowers, and are famous for their display of *sakura* (cherry blossoms) in spring, lotus flowers in summer and maple trees in the autumn.

▶▶▶ Kinkakuji Temple   120B5
Kinkakuji-cho, Kita-ku
Bus: 59 to Kinkakuji-mae, 204 or 205 to Kinkakuji-michi
Open: 9–4.30, Apr–Sep; 9–5, rest of year
The Temple of the Golden Pavilion was built by the shogun Ashikaga Yoshimitsu (1358–1409) for his retirement in 1394. Three floors tall and topped with a bronze statue of a phoenix, the pavilion is covered in gold leaf and extends over a pond that reflects the building. The Golden Pavilion was built according to descriptions of the Western Paradise of the Buddha Amida and is intended to illustrate the harmony between Heaven and Earth.

Like other buildings erected by powerful warriors and politicians, the Kinkakuji symbolizes the mandate to rule granted by Heaven to the Ashikaga shogunate.

On Yoshimitsu's death, his son, obeying his father's wishes, turned the building into a temple known as the Rokuonji. In 1950, one of the temple priests set fire to the building, but an exact replica was built in 1955. Novelist Yukio Mishima based his *Temple of the Golden Pavilion* (1956) on the destruction of the Kinkakuji. The temple was further restored in 1990 and houses many treasures of Buddhist art. The grounds include a beautiful landscaped garden and a large pond.

►►► Kiyomizudera Temple   121D2

Kiyomizu 1-Chome, Higashiyama-ku
Bus: 16, 202, 206, 207 to Kiyomizu-michi or Gojo-zaka
(10-minute walk up Kiyomizu-michi or Gojo-zaka)
Open: 6am–dusk

The Clear Water Temple was established in 780 by a Buddhist priest from Nara named Enchin, who was commanded in a vision to seek the pure source of the Kizu River. In 798, the main hall was rebuilt by General Sakanoue no Tamuramaro, using materials taken from the abandoned Imperial Palace at Nagaoka. Damaged in the power struggles between the monks of Mount Hiei and Nara, most of the present buildings were erected in 1633 by Tokugawa Iemitsu.

Originally the Kiyomizudera was affiliated to the Kofukuji temple in Nara, but it now belongs to the Shingon-Hosso sect, dedicated to the worship of Kannon, the personification of divine mercy. The main attraction for visitors is the *butai* (dancing stage), a large platform in front of the *hondo* (main hall). Wooden scaffolding 12m (40ft) high supports the *butai* above a gorge, giving a panoramic view of Kyoto.

Stone steps lead down from the main hall to the Otowano-taki (Sound of Feathers Waterfall), the source of the pure water found by Enchin. Here pilgrims often drink the water, said to be efficacious for all illnesses.

The streets around Kiyomizudera Temple

129

KIYOMIZUDERA PROVERB
Kiyomizudera is the source of the Japanese saying 'to leap from Kiyomizu's *butai*', which means to make an important decision, or do something that demands great courage.

Kiyomizudera Temple

Kyoto National Museum

NANZENJI 'CATHEDRAL'
Following the Chinese tradition, Zen temples are grouped into fives. Nanzenji Temple was the head of the Gozan (Five Monasteries) of Kyoto and when Ashikaga Yoshimitsu wanted to include the Shokokuji among the group, the Nanzenji was promoted above all others. In effect, Nanzenji acted as a kind of Zen 'cathedral'; whoever was the abbot held the highest Buddhist office in Japan.

BOILED ALIVE
The Sanmon Gate was the hiding place of Ishikawa Goemon, a kind of Japanese Robin Hood. When he and his young son were captured in 1632 they were sentenced to be boiled alive in a big iron tub, but Goemon held the boy above the boiling water until he himself died. His courage is remembered in the *kabuki* play *Sanmon Gosan no Kiri*, and Goemon was the subject of a wood-block print by the artist Kunisada. Goemon's name was also used for the old-fashioned iron baths known as *Goemon-furo*.

▶▶ Kokuritsu Hakubutsukan (Kyoto National Museum)　　121D1
Yamato-oji-dori, Higashiyama-ku
Bus: 206
Open: Tue–Sun 9–4.30 (last entry 4pm)
Established in the second half of the 19th century, the National Museum is housed in two buildings, and its extensive collection is shown in frequently changing displays. Neolithic relics from the Jomon and Yayoi periods can be found in the archaeology section, along with clay figurines (*haniwa*) associated with the burial mounds (*misasagi*) of the early rulers of Japan. The museum is noted for its collection of Japanese pictorial art. The sculpture section is dominated by Heian period statues. There are also examples of metalwork, ceramics, calligraphy and lacquerware from many periods of Japanese history.

▶▶▶ Kyoto Gosho (Kyoto Imperial Palace)　　120C4
Imperial Park
Subway: Marutamachi, Imadegawa
Open: 30-minute tours of the grounds start at 10am; arrive by 9.40am (except Sun and the second and fourth Sat of every month). An English-language tour is available Mon–Fri at 2pm, arrive by 1.40pm
The Imperial Palace was originally built in 794, but has been destroyed by fire on many occasions. The present building was built in 1855. The imperial household moved to Tokyo after the Meiji Restoration, but the Kyoto Gosho is still used for the ceremonies that must be performed when a new emperor ascends the throne.
　Foreign visitors are given preferential treatment for access; they must complete an application form and show their passport. Contact the Imperial Household Agency (Kunaicho), located in Kyoto Imperial Park near the Imadegawa subway station (tel: 075 211 1215).

▶▶ Kyoto Municipal Museum of Traditional Industries　　121D3
Inside the Kyoto International Exhibition Hall near the gate of Heian shrine
Open: 10–6; closed Mon
This new museum displays traditional crafts such as ceramics, Kimono dyeing, bamboo, laquerware and many others. The entrance gallery re-creates a street scene from old Kyoto. Audio-visual sites and free computer databanks allow more detailed investigation.

▶▶▶ Nanzenji Temple　　121E3
Fukuchi-cho, Sakyo-ku
Bus: 5 to Eikando-mae, then a five-minute walk
Open: 8.30–4.30, 6 Mar–15 Nov; 8.30–5, rest of year
Nanzenji (Southern Zen) Temple was built as a retirement villa for Emperor Kameyama (1249–1305) at the base of the hills in the east of Kyoto. The building was given to the Rinzai sect of Zen Buddhism in 1291 at the Emperor's command, and is now the headquarters of Rinzai Zen. During the Onin Wars the temple was badly damaged but was restored in the late 16th and early 17th centuries; the Sanmon (Triple Gate) was built in 1628 and offers a stunning view of Kyoto and the Higashiyama mountains.

Kyoto Gosho

►►► Nijo Castle and Gardens

120C3

Horikawa Nijo, Nijojo-cho, Nakagyo-ku
Subway: Oike, then a 10-minute walk;
bus: 9, 12, 50, 52, 61, 67
Open: Tue–Sun 8.45–4; closed 26 Dec–4 Jan

Built in 1603 by Tokugawa Ieyasu, Nijo Castle has thick outer walls and a moat to defend it. Within the walls, the main buildings are beautifully decorated with paintings by Kano Tanyu (1602–74) and his pupils. The gardens to the southwest of the Great Hall were laid out by Enshu Kobori shortly before Emperor Gomizuno-o's visit in 1626; no trees were used, as falling leaves are suggestive of the transience of life, and the Shogun wanted to impress the Emperor with his power. The central island in the lake is flanked by two smaller islands in the shape of a crane and a tortoise, symbols of strength and longevity.

Entrance is through the East gate, then via the Kara-mon (Chinese Gate) to a diagonal row of five buildings. The Ohiroma Hall contains a reconstruction of the occasion when Tokugawa Keiki returned power to the imperial line.

SQUEAKING FLOORS
While Nijo Castle may not have been built primarily as a fortress, it does contain surprises for any potential spy or assassin. Every building contains hidden rooms, where the shogun's samurai could observe visitors for signs of treachery, and many of the corridors were constructed with 'nightingale floors' (*uguisubari*) that squeak when walked upon to warn of anyone approaching.

PATH OF PHILOSOPHY
Nanzenji and Ginkakuji Temples are linked by a canalside path about 2km (1.5 miles) long, known as Philosopher's Walk (see page 136). It was named after Nishida Kitaro (1870–1945), a noted philosopher who was known for his comparison of Western and Zen philosophies, and who enjoyed walking along this route. The walk is now lined with cherry trees, interesting shops and coffee bars, and is busy with visitors as well as academics.

131

Nanzenji Temple

▶▶ Nishiki-Koji Market
121D2

Open: daily, early morning–7pm. Some outlets close on Sun, others on Wed

In the heart of town on Nishiki-Koji-dori, this fresh produce and fish market is the main place to buy food for the city's restaurants and hotels, as well as for the general public. Vendors, selling everything from seaweed to beans, line the market lanes.

Nishiki-Koji Market

▶▶▶ Ryoanji Temple and Garden
120A4

13 Goryoshita-machi, Ryoanji, Ukkyu-ku
Bus: 59 to Ryoanji-mae
Open: 8–5, Mar–Nov; 8.30–4.30, rest of year

The Temple of the Peaceful Dragon was founded in 1473. Once the estate of Katsumoto Hosokawa (1430–73), it became a Zen temple of the Rinzai sect on his death. The main attraction is the famous rock garden. Attributed to the artist Soami, it was created in the 16th century in a space of 30m by 10m (100ft by 33ft). Following the *kare-sansui* (waterless stream) style, the garden is composed of 15 rocks set into raked white gravel. Simply sit and enjoy the view, but arrive early to avoid the crowds and try to ignore the intrusive explanations that are broadcast over the loudspeakers, destroying the peaceful mood of the place (see also pages 134–135).

RYOANJI TEA HOUSE
In the small garden behind Ryoanji there is a tea house, the Zoroku, whose stone wash basin (the *tsukubai*) has a unique inscription arranged as a rebus around the rim, which can be translated as 'I learn only to be contented'. In Zen, he who achieves contentment is considered to be spiritually rich. The *tsukubai* is said to have been given to the temple by the *daimyo* Tokugawa Mitsukuni (1628–1700), remembered as the compiler of the great history of Japan, the *Dai Nippon Shi*. Copies of the inscription can be purchased as souvenirs.

▶▶▶ Sanjusangendo
121D1

657 Sanjusangendo, Mawari-cho, Higashiyama-ku
Bus: 206, 208 to Sanjusangendo-mae, or 15 minutes' walk east of Kyoto station
Open: 8–5, 16 Mar–31 Oct; 9–4, rest of year

Sanjusangendo, the Hall of the 33 Bays, is also known as the Rengeo-in Temple; its popular name derives from the 33 spaces between the 35 pillars found in the hall, which is 118m by 18m (387ft by 59ft). Thirty-three is also the number of the manifestations of Kannon, the Buddhist goddess of mercy to whom this Tendai sect temple is dedicated. A gilded statue of the 1,000-armed Kannon, carved by Tankei (1173–1256) in 1254, is enshrined in the middle of the hall surrounded by 1,000 smaller gilded statues of Kannon, the work of 70 sculptors supervised by Tankai and his father Unkei. A tradition has developed among visitors to the Sanjusangendo of trying to find the features of a relative or friend among the faces portrayed on the statues.

The Sanjusangendo was originally built by the emperor Goshirakawa (1126–91) in 1164. It was burned down and rebuilt in 1266, when the statues of Kannon were placed in the middle of the hall and the statues of the 28 guardians of Buddhism were erected in the corridor behind the main hall. Many of the guardians are derived from the Hindu pantheon, such as the bird-man playing the flute, Karurao (Garuda), and the emaciated holy man, Basusennin.

▶▶ Zenrinji Temple   *121E3*

Shishigatani-dori, Higashiyama (north of Nanzenji Temple)
Bus: 5 to Eikando mae, then a 15-minute walk
Open: 9–4.30

At the end of the Philosopher's Walk (see panel, page 131), is Zenrinji Temple, also known as Eikando. Established in 836 by the priest Shinsho, the buildings were destroyed during the Onin Wars (1467–77) and rebuilt during the 16th century. The temple enshrines a statue of the Amida Buddha with his face turned to the side as if he is looking over his shoulder. According to legend, this came about when the statue came to life and joined a group of devotees who were dancing in praise of the Amida Buddha. The dancers were led by the priest Eikan, who stood still in surprise. The statue looked back to encourage Eikan to keep dancing, and when he climbed back onto his pedestal he retained the twist in his neck.

If you have the energy to climb the stairs to the top of the pagoda, you'll get a superb view of Kyoto. The excellent gardens include many maple trees that burst with a multitude of tints when the leaves begin to turn in the autumn.

ARCHERY CONTEST
Sanjusangendo is the site of an archery contest first held in 1606. On 15 January and 2 May, archers gather at the temple to see who can fire the greatest number of arrows at a target placed at the end of the hall's outer veranda. The record of 8,133 bull's eyes established in 1686 has yet to be beaten, but the upright wooden posts bear the scars of many misdirected shots.

TEMPLE FOOD
Two restaurants that serve vegetarian and tofu dishes typical of the meals served in Buddhist temples can be found on the road leading to Eikando Temple, to the north of Nanzenji Temple. The Okutan Restaurant is the most famous and most expensive. Less expensive is the nearby Koan restaurant, which also serves good vegetarian meals and tofu.

Sanjusangendo

There are three basic types of Japanese garden: the tea garden, usually designed by tea masters as a site for the tea ceremony; the hill garden, designed for private estates as a small park with miniature artificial hills; and the flat garden. The Zen garden at Ryoanji is a famous version of the flat garden.

GARDEN TOURS IN KYOTO
A convenient way to see a variety of gardens in Kyoto is to take a guided bus tour. The commentaries are in Japanese, which actually leaves you more time to enjoy the gardens in your own company. All buses leave from the front of Kyoto station (Keihan Bus Company, tel: 075 672 2100). Ask at the TIC across from the station for more details.

Above: taking tea in Daitokuji Temple's Zen garden
Below: Ryoanji Garden

134

Ryoanji Garden In the flat garden style few shrubs are used and the most common elements are stones, sand and gravel. They are designed, like a painting, for contemplation. Several of the best Zen gardeners were also well-known painters in ink, and in this medium they intended, with just a few strokes of black ink on white paper, to evoke an atmospheric natural scene. Their gardens were three-dimensional evocations of the same idea, using sand or gravel instead of silk, and shrubs, trees, or stones instead of brush strokes. The stones they chose were also charged with different meanings according to their shapes, their textures and the angles at which they were placed. Also see page 132.

The garden at Ryoanji was said to have been created by Soami, a famous ink-line artist (although this is by no means certain). It consists of raked gravel and 15 stones in five groupings, and certainly obeys the injunction of an anonymous 16th-century painter and gardener: 'Caution should be taken not to be too anxious to overcrowd the scenery to make it more interesting. Such an effect often results in a loss of dignity and a feeling of vulgarity.' The temple authorities publish a small pamphlet describing the garden as symbolizing 'a group of mountainous

Daisen-in Zen Garden

TOUR ITINERARIES
F: Kyoto station–
Tenryuji Temple–
Ryoanji Temple–
Daitokuji Temple–
Daisen-in Temple–
Myoshinji-Taizoin Temple–
Kyoto station (9.30am;
five hours, 30 minutes,
including a Japanese
lunch).
J: Kyoto station–
Hakusasonso–
Konchi-in Temple–
Nanzenji Temple–
Shoren-in Temple–
Daigo Sambo-in Temple–
Kajyuji Temple–
Kyoto station (10am; six
hours, including a
Japanese lunch).
R: Kyoto station–
Tenryuji Temple–
Ryoanji Temple–
Zuihoin Temple–
Kyoto station (2pm; three
hours, 30 minutes).

islands in a great ocean, or mountain tops rising above a sea of clouds. We can see it as a picture framed by the ancient mid wall, now in itself regarded as a national treasure, or we can forget the frame as we sense the truth of this sea [the grave] stretching out boundlessly'.

Daisen-in Zen Garden Soami was an official painter in the court of Yoshimasa, the eighth Ashikaga shogun. In 1480 he designed and built one of the earliest and, to this day, most famous Zen flat gardens for the abbot's residence at Daisen-in, a sub-temple of Daitokuji Temple (see pages 124–125). At the time, Soami was influenced by Chinese Song period paintings which, by their portrayals of dramatic and awe-inspiring mountain landscapes, highlight human vulnerability. His garden at Daisen-in, designed to be viewed from the veranda of the abbot's quarters, rather than to be walked around, is constructed of rocks and sand. Unlike the abstract garden of Ryoanji Temple, it is a three-dimensional representation of a Song-style painting featuring a mountain (Mount Horai, the mythical home of enlightened beings), a river and a boat with a cargo of treasure. It has been suggested that the garden may be seen as a representation of the bridge between being and nonbeing. As such, it rewards quiet contemplation, and it is a good idea to visit Daisen-in early in the day and to avoid weekends and public holidays.

Like other Zen gardens, Ryoanji and Daisen-in *kare sansui* ('waterless stream gardens') were designed to promote meditation among Zen monks. Rock and sand gardens, unaffected by the changes of the seasons, gave the monks a sense of the calm of eternity.

The perfect precision of Ryoanji Garden

Walk

trendy coffee shop along the way, allowing you make a stop if you wish After it passes the **Kano Shoju-an** Japanese patisserie, with its elegant tea room, the canal goes underground by the entrance to the **Nyakuoji Shrine**. Turn right, then turn left, to pass the gate to **Zenrinji Temple** (see page 133). To the right is the **Nomura Art Museum▶▶**, which has a collection of tea-ceremony arte-facts. The lane bends to the right and then left before reaching the entrance to **Nanzenji Temple** (see page 130), where the massive **Sanmon gate**, **Konchi-in Temple**, and the Abbot's quarters are well worth a visit. The latter two have exquisite Zen gardens. The restaurants at the entrance to the temple specialize in *yu-dofu*, a Buddhist vegetarian dish.

From Nanzenji, walk away from the entrance, past Yachiyo *ryokan's* elegant forecourt on the left, then turn right and walk for three minutes to the Eikando-mae bus stop to catch City Bus 5 back to Kyoto station.

As evening descends, paper lanterns (chochin) are lit to decorate a canal-side restaurant

136

Along the old canal

Distance: 1.6km (1 mile); time (excluding temple visits): 50 minutes. This pleasant canal-side stroll follows the Path of Philosophy, from Ginkakuji, the Silver Pavilion, to Nanzenji Temple.

Begin at bus stop A-1, Ginkakuji-michi (City Bus 5), and walk in the direction of the entrance of **Ginkakuji Temple**. On the right-hand side, before the park-ing area for buses, is the pleasant and modest **Hakusa-Sonso Garden▶**, once the home of the early 20th-century painter, Hashimoto Kansetsu. Ahead are the immaculate hedges that form the entrance to the **Ginkakuji Temple** (see page 125). From Ginkakuji, walk back to join the path that runs south along the little canal. This is the start of the **Path of Philosophy** (see panel, page 131), linking **Ginkakuji Temple** and **Nanzenji Temple**.

The canal passes through a quiet, residential district with the occasional

Kinugasa

Ryoanji

Utano

0 | 200 | 400 | 600 m
0 | 200 | 400 | 600 yards

Kinkakuji Temple

Daitokuji Temple

★ Kinkakuji-machi

KITSUJI-DORI

Wara Tenjin Shrine

Domoto Art Museum

Ryoanji Temple & Garden

Hirano

Ritsumeikan University

Hirano Shrine

Ninnaji Temple

Yomei Bunko

Toji-in Temple

Komatsubara

Kitano Shrine

NISHIOJI-DORI

Tenjingawa

Toji-in

Kitano

Ryoanjimichi Station

Omuro Ninnaji

Myoshinji Station

Toji-in Station

Kitano Hakubaicho Station

IMADEGAWA-DORI

Omuro Station

Walk

Kinkakuji Temple and Ryoanji Garden

Distance: 1.6km (1 mile); time: about one hour, including visits to both the temples. This walk in the western foothills links two of Kyoto's most celebrated monuments: the dazzling Golden Pavilion and the Ryoanji rock garden at the Ryoanji Temple.

Start from Kinkakuji-michi bus stop, B-3 (City Bus 59 or 205). A driveway lined with low, clipped pine trees and hedges leads to the entrance, to the left of where the tour buses are parked. Bamboo groves and tile-capped walls striped in ochre and white line the approach path to **Kinkakuji** (see pages 128–129), built as a villa retreat at the end of the 14th century by the third Ashikaga shogun. Once through the gate, the path turns sharply right. A high bamboo fence obscures the view until suddenly the Golden Pavilion appears, floating above its reflection in the lake. Covered in thick gold leaf, the pavilion glows even under rainy skies.

The path skirts around the lake, with the main temple buildings to the right, past the pavilion, then winds up and around the garden, past a lotus pond and a tiny thatched tea house, before leading to a flight of steps back to the entrance. In the gardens of the temple, visible from the path, is a large pine tree in the shape of a boat. The gift shop has a surprisingly good selection of high-quality souvenirs.

Leaving the temple, walk back to the main road and turn right. Follow the road, which curves along the hillside, past the **Domoto Art Museum▶** and on to **Ryoanji Temple and Garden** (see pages 132 and 134). From Ryoanji, the walk can be extended, turning right along the main road to **Ninnaji Temple▶▶**, first built in the ninth century and famous for its late-blooming cherry trees. From Ninnaji, take City Bus 26 back to the city.

Kinkakuji Temple

138

The view of Kyoto from the Mount Hiei cable car

▶ ▶ ▶ Mount Hiei (*Hei-san*)

Sakamoto Honmachi, Otsu, Shiga Prefecture
Bus: 16, 17, 18 to Yase-Yuenchi stop. Entrance to Keifuku cable car on the left; departs every 30 minutes. Transfer at Hiei to the Hiei-zan Ropeway to the observatory on the summit; from there follow the path down to Enryakuji
Open: 8.30–4.30, Mar–Nov; 9–4, rest of year

Standing to the northeast of Kyoto, Mount Hiei is, at 850m (2,790ft), the second-highest mountain in the vicinity of the city. Its location is significant, as the northeast was feared as the 'Devil's Gate' (*Ki-mon*), through which all malevolent forces entered the city. Even today, buildings in Kyoto can be seen that have the northeast corners cut off to ward off evil.

The Emperor Kammu (737–806), concerned for the city's safety, ordered the priest Saicho (767–822) to build a temple on Mount Hiei to protect the city from malign influences. Saicho built a small meditation hut on Mount Hiei in 785, which he enlarged three years later into a small temple. When the temple was inaugurated in 794, the Emperor climbed Mount Hiei to attend the inauguration ceremony.

In 797, Saicho was appointed one of a group of 10 'imperial monks' and Kammu ordered that his temple be supported by funds gathered from Saicho's home province of Omi. The temple was renamed Enryakuji in 823 after Saicho's death, and Saicho was given the posthumous title of *Dengyo Daishi* or 'Great Teaching Master'.

Saicho was the founder of a new sect of Japanese Buddhism known as Tendai. He believed that the world was coming to an end and was convinced that the only way to avert this catastrophe was to unify all the sects of Buddhism. He went to China in 804 and studied Buddhism at Mount T'ien-t'ai. In the summer of 805 he returned to Japan with over 460 works on Buddhism, Taoism and various schools of Chinese philosophy. Within a very short time, Tendai was acknowledged as an independent sect by the court, and the temple on Mount Hiei became the recipient of a great deal of patronage by the court and aristocracy.

Within two centuries or so, the complex of temples on Mount Hiei had become very wealthy. To protect their wealth, the monks established their own army of *sohei*, fierce warrior-monks willing and able to fight and destroy anyone who offered any kind of threat to their power and authority. Emperor Shirakawa (1053–1129) once said that there were three things he could not control: the fall of dice when gambling, the floodwaters of the Kamo River and the monks of Mount Hiei.

Eventually the arrogance of the monks proved their undoing. They challenged the might of Oda Nobunaga (1534–82), who ordered his forces to destroy the monastic complex of over 3,000 buildings and slaughter the monks. In response to protests from some of his advisers, he said 'I am not the destroyer of this monastery. The destroyer of the monastery is the monastery itself'.

Set among towering cedar trees, Enryakuji was later rebuilt on a smaller scale. Most of the buildings seen today date from the 17th century. From the railway station the path leads to the Daidoko (Great Lecture Hall), rebuilt after a fire in 1956. Climb the hill to the Kaiden-in, built in 1604 as the ordination hall for Tendai priests. Following the path through the trees, turn left at the Sanno-in (the Temple of the Mountain King) and down the stairs to the Jodo-in (Pure Land Temple), founded by Saicho and rebuilt in the 17th century. His tomb can be found behind the main hall. Go down the steps to the Kompon-chudo (Fundamental Central Hall), erected in 1642, which contains paintings of flowers on the ceiling 'donated' by all the *daimyo* (great landowners) at the command of the Tokugawa shogunate.

Enryakuji Temple

MISCREANT MONKS
The monks of Mount Hiei influenced Japanese political and religious life until the 16th century and the arrival of General Oda Nobunaga. He is quoted as saying: 'If I do not take them away now, this great trouble will be everlasting. Moreover, these priests violate their vows: they eat fish and stinking vegetables, keep concubines, and never unroll the sacred books. How can they be vigilant against evil, or maintain the right? Surround their dens and burn them, and suffer none within them to live.' Nobunaga invaded the mountain, burned every temple to the ground, and executed every monk.

Sandals at Enryakuji

Kyoto

Pavilion in Katsura Imperial Villa garden

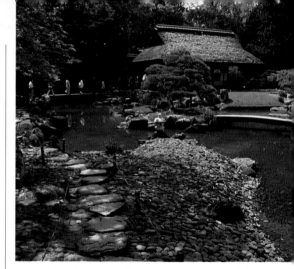

THREE CONDITIONS
It is said that when Kobori Enshu was commissioned by Hideyoshi to build the Katsura Villa he imposed three conditions on his employer: no limit on expense, no limit on time, and no interference until the building was completed. Hideyoshi died before the work was complete and he never saw the building that he paid for.

▶▶▶ Katsura Imperial Villa 120A1

Katsura Shimizu-cho, Ikyo-ku
Train: Katsura station on the Hankyu Arashiyama line
(10-minute walk from station), Kyoto station (5km/3-mile cab
ride); bus: 33 from Kyoto station to Katsura Rikyu-mae
Open: tours on weekdays at 10am and 2pm, Sat at 10am
Closed: Sat afternoon, Sun, national holidays and 25 Dec–
25 Jan; see below

Katsura Imperial Villa, in western Kyoto, was originally built at the beginning of the 17th century by Prince Toshihito, the brother of Emperor Goyozei. Set on the banks of the Katsuragawa, it is constructed from carefully selected materials so that the buildings and gardens harmonize elegantly with their natural surroundings, within sight of the Arashiyama and Kameyama hills.

The Katsura garden is judged to be the masterpiece of Kobori Enshu, Japan's greatest landscape gardener. Each turn of the path that meanders through the garden brings a new view. Stone lanterns, carefully cultivated trees, bridges gracefully arching over water, and a number of rustic tea houses are all cleverly arranged to provide viewers with an aesthetic experience reminiscent of the tea ceremony. The garden is built around a central pond with tea houses designed to reflect each of the four seasons. Katsura has been described as the epitome of Japanese culture and aestheticism, and many contemporary Western architects have been drawn to it and influenced by its elegant simplicity, its use of natural materials, and the harmony of interior and exterior design. For example, the ground running away from the building is laid in strips of bare earth, pebbles, stepping stones, and then moss with the intention of gradually leading one away from the human order of the house to the naturalness of the garden or vice versa.

Special permission is needed to visit the villa and details can be obtained at the Kyoto TIC on the ground floor of Kyoto Tower opposite JR Kyoto station. Visitors must be aged at least 20 and must take their passports when collecting permits. Tours are in Japanese, but information is available on an English-language video tape that is played in the waiting room before the tour begins. Apply for a permit in advance.

BORROWED SCENERY
In contrast to Katsura Imperial Villa, Shugakuin is reputed more for its gardens than for its architecture. They make particularly good use of the style of landscaping known as *shak kei*, or borrowed scenery, in which views of distant hills in and, in this case, of Kyoto itself, are incorporated into the design.

▶▶▶ Shugakuin Imperial Villa   *121E5*

Shugakuin Muromachi, Sakyo-ku
Train: Eizan Railway from Yase Yuen station to Shugakuin-mae station, then a 30-minute walk; bus: 5 from Kyoto station to Shugakuin Rikyu Michi bus stop, then a 15-minute walk from there
Open: tours in Japanese at 9, 10, and 11. On Sat extra tours are held at 1 and 3. Closed: Sun, national holidays, 25 Dec–5 Jan. Permission must be obtained from the Imperial Household Agency (see Katsura Imperial Villa)

This villa in northeast Kyoto was built in 1659, on a foothill of Mount Hiei by the Tokugawa shogunate, as a retirement home for Emperor Go Mizuno-o. The grounds are divided into three large gardens, each with its own tea house. The upper garden, which is the largest, is set around a lake with islands, bridges, waterfalls and a long winding path through the gardens that gives fine views over Kyoto to the surrounding hills.

The Rakushiken pavilion, in the middle garden, was built for the Emperor's daughter, Princess Ake. When she became a nun, the building was converted into a temple for her use. Jugetsukan pavilion in the lower garden contains only four rooms. The rooms are laid out in an 'L' shape and surrounded by a veranda. The three raised and framed mats in the 15-*tatami* (closely woven straw floor mats) room were the Emperor's sitting place.

From the back gate of the lower garden you step onto a pretty patio area that gives unimpeded views of far-off mountain ranges.

IMPERIAL PATRONS OF THE ARTS
Emperor Go Mizuno-o and his empress Tofukuman-in designed Shugakuin themselves and continued to visit their 'rustic' retreat after their retirement from office and into old age. Both were avid patrons of the arts, especially the tea ceremony and flower-arranging, and were also the driving force behind the 17th-century rebuilding of Kyoto after the ravages of many centuries of war.

141

The view across the lake from Shugakuin Imperial Villa

Ana Hotel, Kyoto

Accommodation

The hotels and *ryokan* of Kyoto are renowned for their impeccable service and hospitality. However, Kyoto is essentially a tourist town and space is at a premium. Rooms are not large and during the peaks of the spring and autumn seasons and over public holidays the best places need to be reserved in advance. Fortunately, Kyoto is also rich in a variety of places to stay. If you travel on a flexible timetable you will find, except at exceptionally busy festival times, somewhere to rest your head, even if it is only a dormitory-style lodging (see pages 80–81). *Ryokan*, traditional Japanese inns, are found in a wide range of price categories in Kyoto; if you particularly wish to stay in one, Kyoto is the ideal city (see pages 220–221). For hotel, inn and *ryokan* web addresses, see page 266.

TEMPLE LODGING
Temple lodging is popular Kyoto. Rooms are small, in the traditional *tatami* style, and the lodgings are usually located in temple grounds, often in a quiet garden setting. Facilities may or may not include a bath or shower, but one or the other will be available nearby. Breakfast is provided if required and in some places an evening meal may be ordered. Prices for lodging and food are usually very reasonable (see Hotels and Restaurants, pages 269 and 278).

Budget accommodation The Japanese Inn Group has a number of member inns in the Kyoto area, providing simple and inexpensive *tatami* (floor-mat) rooms and communal dining areas in hostel-like environments. These are a good choice if you are on a budget and want to meet fellow visitors. Other tips to help keep down your costs: reserve a room without a bathroom; in more expensive hotels ask for a smaller, less expensive room, so that you can enjoy the facilities without paying the full price; do not use the hotel telephones, bars, or restaurants. Many *ryokan* and hotels are focused around the Kyoto station area, but as Kyoto is not a large city, and is served by an excellent bus network, it is not essential to stay in the heart of the city, and some places are less expensive farther out.

Gion Hotel, Kyoto

The best First-class hotels in Kyoto are excellent and the services they provide are of a high standard. English-language television, English-speaking staff, well-stocked information desks, computer equipment for businesspeople, rapid room service and guest relations officers are all standard, even in the less than top-notch establishments. Tea bags, instant coffee packets and thermos flasks of hot water are provided in the rooms of every category of hotel. A 3 per cent government tax is added to all Japanese hotel bills and, for hotels in Kyoto, a further 3 per cent city tax is added to bills over ¥15,000. The highest-class establishments also add a 10 to 15 per cent service charge. Tipping is not expected.

Accommodation

Where to stay The Kyoto bus network operates on a grid pattern and is easy to follow. Maps of the bus routes are available from the Tourist Information Centre. If, however, you have only a few days in Kyoto and wish to explore on foot, it would be best to choose one area and to stay in that vicinity. For most visitors the eastern district, Higashiyama, provides the best cross section of attractions, including Gion, an area with many traditional shops and a geisha entertainment quarter, plus some of the most famous sights in Kyoto, such as Ginkakuji Temple (Temple of the Silver Pavilion) and the Heian Shrine. Central Kyoto has a similar mix of shopping, evening entertainment and major sights, while western and northern Kyoto are the places to stay if you want a quieter experience of Kyoto.

HOTEL-CHECKING
If you are visiting Japan as part of an arranged trip or for business reasons, your travel agent will book you into an approved hotel. Some offer Japanese as well as Western-type rooms; if you want a room with a *tatami*-covered floor and sunken bath tub, request a reservation in a Japanese-style room.

Kyoto Tower

O-BENTO AND EKI-BEN

O-bento are everyday lunch-boxes prepared at home or bought in local shops. *Eki-ben* are lunchboxes specially for train trips. They are sold on train platforms, in and around stations, and on express trains. The boxes themselves are made from thin, unpainted wood or, for the deluxe version, lacquered wood. Inside they divide into neat compartments and contain such foods as sushi rice, mushrooms, smoked fish, grilled chicken, pickled plums, and fresh and cooked vegetables. They are sold neatly wrapped in decorative paper and tied with string. Each region of Japan has its own version of *o-bento* and *eki-ben*, containing a particular selection of food and one or two local delicacies.

Kyoto noodle restaurant

Food and drink

Food in Kyoto is derived from that of the imperial court and the vegetarian food of Buddhist temples. *Kyo-ryori* or Kyoto cooking is the most refined of all styles of Japanese cooking, the *haute cuisine* of culinary traditions.

Kyoto's cuisine can be divided into two categories: *shojin-ryori*, Zen-style vegetarian dishes developed to serve the needs of monks and pilgrims; and *kaiseki-ryori*, food originally prepared for the tea ceremony, but eventually evolving into an elegant full-course meal, popular with the nobility. A restaurant advertising *kyo-ryori* will usually offer a selection of each of these styles of cooking. Many of Kyoto's traditional Japanese restaurants are in the heart of the city. *Yusoku-ryori*, cooking inspired by the dishes of the imperial court, is not now generally available and only one restaurant, the Mankamero (see **Hotels and Restaurants**, from page 266), specializes in this style of cuisine. The Kyoto Tourist Information Centre publishes a *Kyoto Gourmet Guide* that is worth picking up.

Zen food The *shojin* cook emphasizes the importance of simple meals prepared from local foods. These include rice, fresh vegetables, pickled vegetables, sea vegetables (seaweed), and soya-bean products such as *miso*, tofu (beancurd) and *shoyu* (soy sauce). The cook strives to create a harmonious balance out of five tastes from *shoyu*, sugar, vinegar, salt and spices (ginger root, sesame seeds and *wasabi*, a Japanese mustard) with other ingredients to make a vegetarian meal that is appropriate to the season, good to look at and nutritious. Local *shojin-ryori* dishes are *yu-dofu*, a pot of tofu cooked at your table, and other tofu dishes (see pages 146–147); *fu*, a glutinous wheat cake, and *yuba*, dried soya-bean milk skin.

HEALTHY COOKING
Shojin cookery is also
sometimes referred to as
yukuseki or 'medicine'.
Food selection and its
preparation are seen to
be inseparable from the
treatment of disease and
the cultivation of good
health. The traditional
Chinese medical view is
the same: 'If one falls ill
one should first examine
one's diet, then choose
well, chew carefully, and
give thanks. In this way the
curative powers of nature,
with which mankind is
blessed, are given full rein
to act and nearly all
diseases are conquered.'

145

Tea ceremony food *Kaiseki-ryori* is often very expensive,
but it is an essential experience for visitors to Kyoto. The
meal consists of a procession of tiny courses, each presented in carefully selected porcelain dishes or lacquered
bowls, chosen to match in shape and size their portions of
vegetable, fish, or other foods. The ingredients of the
dishes are valued for their scent, texture, taste and
seasonal freshness. Ideally, a *kaiseki-ryori* should be
presented in a traditional *tatami* room decorated with a
hanging scroll and flower arrangement, within earshot of
running water. The Miyako Hotel (see page 270) offers the
tea ceremony every day. Reservations are necessary.

If you are on a budget, try a *kyo-bento*, or lunchbox, a
commonly available version of *kaiseki-ryori* (see panel).
These are very popular in Kyoto and are available
in the basement food halls of most of the city's department stores.

Tradition and convenience Many of the restaurants in
Kyoto have been in business for generations and old ways
die hard. Several still do not accept credit cards, so check
ahead if you plan to use one. The better places expect you
to dress reasonably formally and tend to serve dinner
early (7–8pm). If you wish to try a variety of Japanese
cooking styles, visit the inexpensive restaurant complexes
in the Hankyu department store (see page 149) or the
Kintetsu Mall, under the tracks on the west side of Kyoto
station. In eastern Kyoto there is a variety of informal
restaurants selling temple-style *shojin-ryori* food in and
around the Kiyomizudera temple.

There are also outlets of many familiar American fast-
food chains.

Daily special The *teishoku* is a daily, fixed-price menu that
many Japanese restaurants present at lunchtime. The
menus of expensive restaurants offering *kaiseki-ryori*
meals are also often much better value at lunchtime than
in the evening.

…and presentation

Tofu (beancurd) is rich in vitamins and minerals, and is fat-free. This wonderfully versatile food can be used fresh or deep fried, grilled, baked, or simmered, and is one of the world's best sources of vegetable protein. Once all Japanese towns and villages had their own tofu-maker. This is less common now, but in Kyoto, where the tofu has the reputation of being the finest in Japan, the tradition is still alive and thriving.

.

146

TOFU-MAKING CONTESTS
In the past, each year throughout Japan, tofu-making contests were held among master craftsmen. First on the city, then on the provincial, and finally on the national level, master craftsmen met for a period of several days and were judged by retired masters on the speed and accuracy of their cutting, and, above all, on their ability to make tofu with fine taste, texture, bouquet and appearance.

TYPES OF TOFU AND DISHES
Momengoshi-dofu: regular cotton-strained tofu.
Kinugoshi-dofu: delicate silky tofu.
Aburage: thin sheets of deep-fried tofu.
Nameage: thick blocks of deep-fried tofu, soft in the middle.
Ganmodoki: deep-fried balls of tofu and vegetables.
Goma-dofu: sesame-tasting tofu.
Yu-dofu: tofu heated in seaweed water and served with soy sauce, grated ginger root, *bonito* (dried fish) shavings and chopped onion.
Hiyayakko: chilled tofu, served as *yu-dofu.*
Agedashi-dofu: tofu dipped in potato flour and deep fried, served with soy sauce and grated *daikon* (a type of white radish).

The raw materials: soya beans

Tofu is made by soaking and grinding soya beans, then extracting the milky liquid from the resulting mixture, and curdling it. The set product is pressed into slabs to produce soft-textured, delicate-tasting, pale cream tofu, which is sold the day it is prepared.

The tofu shop At the Morika tofu shop (42 Fujinoki-cho, Ukyo-ku, *Open* 8–6) on the outskirts of Kyoto, the family tradition of tofu-makers has been maintained and the shop is owned and run by brothers whose father was a tofu master. Work starts at 5am, and by 6.30 the shop is a hive of activity. The stone floor of the work area is awash with water from the rinsing of beans, buckets and wooden storage boxes. Deep tanks of water hold huge slabs of tofu, ready to be cut into standard 400g (17.5oz) blocks. Large drums hold soaking soya beans that will later be crushed between stone rollers and boiled, before filtering through a cotton cloth into a steel mould. The hot soya milk collected in the mould will be set with *nigari* (magnesium chloride), an almost tasteless salt that serves the same function as rennet in cheese-making, before being pressed under weighted wooden boards.
   Fresh tofu made in this way and seasoned with a little good-quality soy sauce is delicious and creamy and as

different from day-old tofu as newly baked French bread is from a stale baguette.

The tofu-maker's wife Traditionally, the tofu craftsman's wife has complete responsibility for all deep-frying work, and at Morika the mother of the family is still in charge of this task. Apart from their reputation for the highest standards of cleanliness, tofu shops are known for their lack of waste; the mother at Morika is also responsible for collecting tofu left from the previous day and that day's offcuts. She crumbles and mixes it with slivers of vegetables, forms the mixture into small balls and deep fries them golden brown to make *ganmodoki*, a popular tofu snack and lunchbox food.

Tofu seasons For the tofu-maker, the year has a rhythm. January and February, when the air and water are cold, are the best months for making regular tofu (*momengoshi* tofu) and keeping it fresh. With the arrival of spring, the demand starts for *kinugoshi*, a silky smooth, more watery tofu supplied throughout the summer. During the hot months the tofu-maker begins work even earlier to take advantage of the cool, pre-dawn air. Autumn finds *kinugoshi* replaced with grilled tofu (*yaki-dofu*), a firmer ingredient for winter vegetable stews. In November, the new crop of soya beans arrives and then the tofu has an added sweetness and aroma. Near the last day of the year, demand for *yaki-dofu* peaks, as it is a traditional New Year food. From New Year's Eve, the tofu shops all over Japan are closed and the tofu-maker and his family take a well-earned break.

Making tofu, the traditional way

ORIGINS OF TOFU
Tofu is said to have been discovered in about 200 BC in China by Lord Liu of Huai-nan, a Chinese scholar, philosopher and ruler. He was a Taoist and undertook experiments to make tofu in order to introduce variety and nutrition into a meatless diet. In the craft tradition of old Japan, the daily work of the craftsman was regarded as part of a spiritual path that had as its goal self-realization and liberation. The paths of the swordsmith, the potter, the calligrapher and the tofu-maker were united by this same underlying principle.

Gift shop sign, Kyoto

SHUENSU
The *shuensu* is a brocade-covered booklet of blank, heavy paper sheets, available at any stationery store and many temples. Used as a passport to collect ink stamps from places visited, the *shuensu* is very popular with the Japanese; most sights and places of interest provide stamps and ink stamp pads.

148

Antiques on sale in Kyoto

Shopping

For more than 1,000 years, while Kyoto was the nation's capital, a collection of the best craftsmen of each generation lived in the city and satisfied the demands of the imperial court. Even today, Kyoto is a focus for artistry and refinement, and the place to shop for all traditional goods, as well as contemporary craftware.

Specialist shops The largest concentration of small shops is in the Gion district, along both sides of Shijo-dori, which runs east–west, and Kawaramachi-dori running north–south. In the square formed by these two avenues and Sanjo-dori and Teramachi-dori are shops selling everything from lacquerware to combs to swords. The square also encloses Shin-Kyogoku, an arcade with many souvenir shops. For the latest in modern shopping arcades, try the huge underground one, named Porta, at Kyoto station. The shopping avenues radiate, like subterranean catacombs, out from the Karasuma (north) side of the station. There are more than 200 boutiques and restaurants. For pottery shops, food shops and tea houses the establishments that line the steep roads leading up to Kiyomizudera Temple in Higashiyama-ku district are the places to explore.

Art and antiques Head in the direction of Shinmonzen-dori, also in the Gion district, for art and antiques. This unprepossessing street of two-level wooden houses runs parallel and to the north of Shijo-dori. The shopkeepers here have an excellent reputation for selling authentic goods at the correct price. Together they publish a free booklet called *Shinmonzen Street Shopping Guide*. Copies are available at the TIC and from some hotel reception desks. *Netsuke*, woodblock prints, scrolls, paintings and antiques are some of the goods that the traders specialize in.

NETSUKE
Netsuke are carved, ornamental ivory toggles by means of which purses, pouches, or medicine boxes were suspended from waist bands. During the Tokugawa regime they were popular with merchants, who wore them to vie with the ornamental sword guards of the samurai. Later, *netsuke* carving developed into a specialized art form. The international trade ban on ivory has reduced the number of contemporary practitioners of *netsuke* carving.

Nishijin Textile Centre

Department stores Kyoto department stores are not as large or glamorous as their Tokyo counterparts, but they are the places to visit for modern goods, clothing and accessories. The basement floors are always given over to a cornucopia of food counters. Many offer free samples of their particular foodstuffs, and are good places to wander, to taste, and to put names to the strange and wonderful array of foods that are often uniquely Japanese. **Takashimaya** department store (*closed* Wednesday), right in the heart of Kyoto, is one of the oldest such stores in Japan, and has a good selection of traditional and modern goods, a money-exchange facility, and an information counter with English-speaking staff. **Hankyu** department store, right across from Takashimaya, has two floors devoted to a variety of restaurants, each with window displays showing the types of dishes available and their prices, which are usually very reasonable.

Silk Kyoto is celebrated for its silk and in the Nishijin silk-weaving district, to the west of Horikawa-dori and north of Ichijo-dori, the sound of looms fills the air. The **Nishijin Textile Centre**, in central Kyoto on Horikawa-dori, Imadegawa-minamiiru, and Kamigyo-ku (*Open* 9–5. *Admission free*), is a museum established in 1915, where a large display of Nishijin products is exhibited and kimonos are on sale. Note that new silk kimonos are *very* expensive; used kimonos are much less so. **Aizan Kobo** (Omiya Nishi-iru, Nakasuji-dori, Kamigyo-ku; *Open* 9–5) is the home of a traditional weaving family, who show and sell a variety of hand-woven and dyed silk goods and garments.

FLEA MARKETS
On the 21st day of each month a famous flea market is held at the Toji Temple, 15 minutes' walk southwest of Kyoto station. Renowned throughout Japan, it is said to be part of a tradition going back several hundred years. The market opens from dawn to dusk and is the place to buy old kimonos at a fraction of the cost of new ones (the Japanese are not fans of second-hand goods and old bric-à-brac is very cheap). There is another good flea market held on the 25th day of each month at the Kitano Temmangu Shrine.

Focus On   Gifts

Gifts are an important part of Japanese life and ritual. Meeting for dinner at a friend's house, saying goodbye, meeting someone important for the first time, thanking someone for help or a service provided are all occasions marked by giving or receiving a gift, and as a place to buy appropriate Japanese presents, Kyoto is second to none.

GIFT-WRAPPING
In Japan, the wrapping of a present is an art form in itself. Whether you buy from an expensive department store or a street vendor, your goods will be deftly, swiftly, and beautifully wrapped. When receiving a gift, unwrap it with care and respect.

150

SOUVENIR SHOPS
One of the features of Japanese life is the many small souvenir and gift shops found near temples and railway stations and in the resorts. They provide for the tiny numerous presents (*miyage*) bought to take home to relatives and friends after a day out or a weekend away from home. For the Japanese, one of the joys of tourism is the purchase of such gifts.

The art of giving Before leaving home, it is useful to buy a number of small, lightweight gifts with some characteristic of your home country. Always wrap your gift and do not press the recipient to open it while you are there. As with much else in Japanese life, there are many subtleties to present-giving that you will not understand, but the one golden rule to remember in this situation, and others, is that neither party should be embarrassed or lose face.

Kyoto craftware The boundary between art and craft is not clearly defined within the tradition of Japanese craftwork, and nowhere is this more evident than in Kyoto, where craftsmen serving the imperial court left a legacy of artistry and refinement maintained to this day. Locally made craftwork is prefixed with *kyo*, for example, *kyo-yaki* are ceramics made in local kilns. Such items are relatively expensive but renowned throughout Japan for their craftsmanship.

Traditional gifts Dolls are generally regarded as works of art to be appreciated for their beauty, rather than played with. Expensive dolls are often encased in glass cases and displayed in Japanese homes. *Kyo-ningyo* are display dolls, produced in Kyoto since the ninth century, made of wood coated with a white paste and dressed in traditional costumes of the finest materials.

Souvenir ideas: ceramic objects...

Lacquer, the sap of the lacquer tree (*urushi-no-ki*), has been used in Japan since the sixth century to coat both precious and well-used objects to give them a beautiful appearance and to protect them from the elements. Lacquerwork is commonly decorated with designs created by sprinkling gold and silver powders onto damp lacquer; mother of pearl, ivory and metals are also used. While decorative and often precious, lacquerware is intended for daily use. *Kyo-shikki*, Kyoto lacquerware products, include cabinets, writing boxes, bowls, serving trays and spoons.

The two most common types of Japanese fan are the folding fan and the flat fan. The former, called *sensu*, are used on ceremonial occasions by men and women alike. They are given as presents on auspicious occasions and used as accessories in the *noh* play and classical Japanese dance and as props in story-telling. *Kyo-sensu* are decorated folding fans made by Kyoto craftsmen.

The craft and art of making pottery and ceramic objects has attained an exceptional degree of refinement in Japan. Skills flourished particularly in the 16th century with the popularity of the tea ceremony. In the Kyoto region especially, numerous kilns produced tea bowls, serving dishes, tea storage jars, and so on. Feudal lords competed with one another to have the finest wares, and their demands inspired technical and artistic enterprise. The most popular *kyo-yaki* products are perhaps the hand-painted red, green and blue on white tableware, made in the Kiyomizu district. The area around Kiyomizudera temple is also a good place to look for shops specializing in *kyo-yaki*.

Kimonos Nowadays, most Japanese wear Western clothing and only put on their kimonos for special occasions such as the New Year Festival or a wedding. New kimonos are extremely expensive, but second-hand kimonos can be a tenth of the price and are frequently in perfect condition.

...or wind chimes...

151

MONEY AND TIPPING
If you receive a present and plan to give one back, it should be of approximately the same value. If you plan to give money to someone Japanese, be it to a child or for exceptional services rendered, always present it enclosed in an envelope. Remember, however, that tipping is not a custom in Japan and tips will not be expected or, in some cases, accepted.

GOOD-LUCK DOLL
The papier-mâché *daruma* (*dharma*) doll is a popular good-luck figure and present, named after the legendary monk Bodidharma. A *daruma* doll is always painted red, with a fierce, bearded face. It is weighted at the base and if pushed over will right itself.

...or Japanese parasols

Gifts

Kyoto

Kyoto after dark

GEISHA

Gei means culture and *sha* person; a geisha is therefore a person well versed in the arts. The profession of geisha is traditionally respected in Japan and the young ladies who follow it are highly esteemed. Most geisha never marry, although some may form a liaison with a regular client and prominent Japanese men may sometimes maintain a geisha as a sort of social secretary. Nowadays, it is said that a few geisha do in fact accept sexual assignations outside their professional activities. Yet a geisha is never obliged by the terms of her contract, and *makura* (geisha cushions) can be summoned as stand-ins, if necessary, after dinner. Seasonal dances (Miyako Odori and Kamogawa Odori) performed by geisha and their apprentices to celebrate spring and autumn are held in Kyoto in April, May, and October. These ravishing spectacles are held at the Gion Kaburenjo Theater, Gion Hanamikoji, Higashiyama-ku and the Pontocho Kaburenjo Theatre, Pontocho Sanjo-sagaru, Nakagyo-ku.

LISTINGS

For more details, pick up a copy of the *Kyoto Visitor's Guide* or *Kansai Time Out*.

A maiko in Gion

Nightlife

Kyoto is not noted for its nightlife, nor does it aspire to be, but, for those who wish it, there are enough bars, restaurants, geisha houses and hostess bars. For a more cultural experience, the Gion quarter after dark gives a real taste of old Japan, as well as the opportunity to see performances of traditional theatrical arts. Strolling the streets of Kyoto or the banks of the Kamo River on a lively evening is an excellent way of finding free entertainment. For a range of Kyoto night-time entertainment, from pool to disco to karaoke, you can go to the eight-floor entertainment building **Imagium**, Shijo-dori, Kobashi-nishi-iru.

Culture Gion, a small district of Kyoto, is the geisha entertainment quarter of the city. Here, especially in the evening, you can see geisha and their *maiko* (young apprentices), dressed in gorgeous kimonos with beautiful hair and make-up, on their way to work. Gion Corner, a theatre in the heart of Gion, presents one-hour shows that give a brief taste of a variety of Kyoto's performing arts. Dancing, puppet theatre, court music, demonstrations of the tea ceremony, flower arrangement and comic routines are all included. The show is very good value. Tickets are available at most hotels, travel agents and Gion Corner. Two performances are given nightly, at 7.40pm and 8.40pm, 1 March–29 November (no performances on 16 August or from December to February).

Bars and clubs Kawaramachi-dori and the area around it, including Kiyamachi-dori to the east, is a district of small, inexpensive drinking clubs, bars and restaurants. Those with red lanterns outside are the most reasonable. If you are unsure of the cost, order a drink and then ask for the bill. In hostess bars, you will quickly be offered tiny titbits to eat. Avoid these places unless you have plenty of yen to spend.

Tourist Information Centre, Kyoto

Practical

Avoid Kyoto on public holidays and avoid the best-known temples on weekends. Otherwise, it is very easy to get around on foot, by bus, subway, or hired bicycle or, if you are in a hurry, by taxi.

What's on The once dowdy Kyoto station was rebuilt in 1997 and is now a suitable entranceway to this important city. There are two tourist information offices in the station complex: **Kyoto Tourist Information**—operated by Kyoto Prefecture, 9F, JR Kyoto Station, Shimogyo-ku (tel: 344 3300; *Open* daily 10–6; *closed* second and fourth Tue of month, and year-end and New Year public holiday); and **Kyoto City Tourist Information**—operated by Kyoto City, 2F, JR Kyoto Station, Shimogyo-ku (tel: 343 6655; *Open* daily 8.30–7). At either office you can obtain street and subway/railway maps and copies of *Kyoto Visitors Guide*, a monthly publication in English.

Walking and riding It is best to see the city in sections and to get a real feeling for the place at a meditative pace, rather than rushing from point to point. A fun way to get around is to travel by bicycle. There are several places where you can rent a bicycle by the day, including **Nippon Rent a Car** (tel: 672 3045), across from the Hachijo exit of Kyoto station; **Kyoto Cycling Tour Project**, 3-2 Kinugasa Tenjinmori-chou (tel: 467 5175), which will arrange to pick up and deliver bicycles anywhere in Kyoto; and **Rent Pia Cycle**, Kyoto station (tel: 672 0662).

GETTING TO KYOTO
Journeys to Kyoto take about two hours, 40 minutes (514km/319 miles) from Tokyo station, 45 minutes (148km/92 miles) from Nagoya, and three hours, 20 minutes (663km/412 miles) from Fukuoka (Hakata), by the 'Hikari' on the JR Shinkansen. The new Haruka Express train now also links Kyoto with Kansai International Airport in just over one hour. A long-distance night bus leaves from Tokyo station, arriving in eight hours, and a bus from Nagoya takes two hours, 40 minutes.

153

TAXIS
Taxis in Kyoto come in three different sizes, increasing in price from the smallest to the largest category. Taxis are readily available from taxi stands and hotels, or they can be flagged down.

City traffic

Oki-shotō

Dōgo
Saigo

Dōzen

Daisen-Oki
National Park

Jizō-zaki

Shimane-hantō
Sakaiminato
Mino-wan

Hino-misaki
Hirata
Shinji-ko
Matsue
Yonago

Izumo-Taisha Shrine

Izumo

Ōda

Daisen-Oki
National Park

Hino-kawa

1126m
Sambe-san

1269m
Dōgo-san

Gōtsu
Gō-gawa

Hamada

Taishaku-kyō

Shōbara

Mi-shima

Chūgoku-sanchi

Miyoshi

Kibi-kōgen

Masuda

Fuchū
Ibara

Susa

Sandan-kyō
Kake

Tsuwano

1339m

Hiroshima

Higashi-Hiroshima

Fukuyama

Onomichi

Nagato
Hagi
Atō
Chōmonkyō

Takehara
Mihara

In'noshima

Hōhoku

Akiyoshi-dō

Ōtake
Miyajima
Kure

Ōmi-shima

Hibiki-nada

Mine

Yamaguchi

Nishiki-gawa
Nomi-jima

O-shima

Huichi-nada

Toyoura

Ogōri

Tokuyama
Iwakuni

Kurahashi-jima

Imabari

Onoda
Ube
Hōfu

Kudamatsu

Setonaikai

Takanawa-hantō
Tōyo

Niihama
Saijō

Shimonoseki

Hikari
Yanai

Hōjō

Dogo
Onsen

Matsuyama

KITAKYŪSHŪ

Yashiro-jima

National Park

Suō-nada

Iyo

1982m
Ishizuchi-san

Shikoku

Yukuhashi

Omogo-kei

Niyodo-gawa

Tagawa

Iyo-nada

Uckiko
Kuma

Ino
Tosa

Nakatsu

721m
Kunisaki-hantō

Ōzu

Usa
Kitsuki

Sadamisaki-hantō

Yawatahama

Susaki

Aso-Kuju
National Park

Misaki

Sada-misaki

Uwa-kai

Uwajima

Kubokawa

Hita

Beppu
Ōita

Hōyo-kaikyō

Tsushima

Shimanto-gawa

Saga

KYŪSHŪ

Usuki

Nakamura

Aso-Kuju
National Park

1791m
Kujū-san

Ashizuri

Sukumo

Aso

Taketa

Saiki

Tsurumi-saki

Bungo-suidō

Tosashimizu

1592m
Aso-san

Takachiho

Uwakai
National Park

Ashizuri-misaki

5
4
3
2
1

A
B
C

Kyōga-misaki

San'in-kaigan National Park

Tango-hantō

Kasumi

Iwami

Kumihama

Toyo'oka

Miyazu

Akasaki

Kurayoshi

Tottori

Wadayama

Ayabe

1730m
Dai-sen
Daisen-Oki National Park

1510m
Hyōno-sen

Fukuchiyama

Chizu

Ikuno

Sanda

1240m

Tsuyama

H O N S H Ū

Kasai

Kabe-gawa

Nimi

Tatsuno

Himeji

Ono

Takahashi

Bizen

Aioi

Akō

Kakogawa

Miki

KŌBE

Sōja

Okayama

Akashi

Osaka

Kurashiki

Kojima-wan

Uno

Setonaikai
Harima-nada

Kasaoka

Seto-
ōhashi
Bridge

Shōdo-shima

National Park

Ōsaka-wan

Yoshino-gawa

Sumoto

Sakaide

Yashima

Awaji-shima

Marugame

Takamatsu

Wakayama

Kan'onji

Zentsūji

Hiketa

Kotohira

Naruto

Naruto-kaikyo

Kawanoe

Sanuki-sanmyaku

Dōchū

Iyomishima

Yoshino-gawa

Komatsushima

Koboke

Tokushima

Aridai

Anan

K i i - s u i d ō

Gobō

Oboke

1955m
Tsurugi-san

Kamoda-misaki

Hinomi-saki

-sanchi

Hiwasa

Monobe-gawa

Kōchi

Ryūga-dō

Tōkyō

Aki

Nankoku

Kaifu

Katsurahama

Yasuda

S H I K O K U

Tosa-wan

Muroto

Muroto-zaki

Tōkyō

0   20   40   60   80   100 km

0   20   40   60 miles

Hyūga
Naha

D

E

Western Honshu and Shikoku

156

Miyajima

WESTERN HONSHU This region is divided down the middle by a chain of mountains running from east to west. The San-yo region on the southern coast, facing the Seto Inland Sea, is a corridor of heavy residential development and industry. The San-in region, which stretches along the northern coast and faces the Sea of Japan, is, by contrast, a less developed area where tourists are few and agriculture and fishing remain the major economic activities.

SAN-YO COAST The JR Shinkansen express Tokaido train line, from Tokyo to Kyushu, runs along the San-yo coast. Three of the main stops, Hiroshima, Okayama and Himeji, are also the cities of most interest to visitors.

For the Japanese, Hiroshima has been an important town since the early 16th century; to the rest of the world it is known and visited as the target of the first nuclear weapon attack in history. Apart from a trip of homage to the dead, one of the reasons to visit Hiroshima is to take an excursion from there to Miyajima, a picturesque small island in the Inland Sea. Miyajima is traditionally regarded as one of the top scenic attractions in Japan.

Okayama is of interest chiefly for its Korakuen Gardens, which were laid out on the banks of the Ashigawa 300 years ago, and are one of the three most famous gardens in Japan (Kenrokeun in Kanazawa and Kairakuen in

One section of the vast Seto-Ohashi bridge

Mito, being the other two). After a visit to Korakuen Gardens in Okayama, Kurashiki is a good place to spend the rest of the day and the following morning. Fifteen minutes from Okayama JR station, it is an oasis of traditional Japan amid the industrial development of the San-yo coastal plain.

Himeji is the site of perhaps the finest surviving castle in Japan, the second largest after Osaka Castle. Set on a hill overlooking the city, the castle goes by the name of Shirasagi, the White Egret (or Heron). Train service to Himeji is excellent, and you can arrive, visit the castle and leave within a morning or afternoon.

SAN-IN COAST There is much to see of ordinary Japanese rural life along the San-in coast. The main reason to go there is to enjoy a quiet part of Japan that *gai-jin* (foreigners) don't often see. There are three towns and a famous shrine worth special visits: Matsue, a pleasant, busy town best known for being the home of Lafcadio Hearn, the 19th-century writer-expatriate, and for its hot springs; Tsuwano, a small, well-preserved castle town; Hagi, a castle town and port, and Izumo-Taisha Shrine near Matsue, a celebrated Shinto shrine to which many Japanese travel to pray for good fortune in marriage.

THE INLAND SEA Separating western Honshu from Shikoku island (see pages 168–177), the *Setonaikai* (Inland Sea) is about 500km (315 miles) long and ranges in width from 64km (40 miles) to just 6km (4 miles). Mountainous coastlines and more than a thousand small, pine-covered islands, scattered throughout its length, add to the beauty of this area, which has been designated a national park. Nevertheless, the once abundant marine life has been decimated by pollution and over-fishing. Increased environmental awareness and the growth of fish-farming make the sea's future look brighter. In the past, the Inland Sea was the major route for the distribution of goods and the spread of culture between Kyushu and the old capitals of Nara and Kyoto in Honshu. Sightseeing cruises are available from Hiroshima and Takamatsu, on Shikoku.

THE SETO-OHASHI BRIDGE
Seto-Ohashi, the longest bridge in the world, is actually composed of six bridges that connect a series of small islands in the Seto Inland Sea, using them as stepping stones from western Honshu to Shikoku. Claimed to be virtually earthquake-proof, the bridge was built using enough cable to wrap around the earth several times. The authorities proudly advertise that construction costs measured in ¥10,000 notes would create a stack three times as high as Mount Fuji. Train and bus service from Okayama to Takamatsu, on Shikoku, cross the bridge.

San-in Region

▶▶▶ Hagi
154A3

In 1604, the Mori family built their castle at Hagi. Suspicious of the Tokugawa shogunate, they selected a defensive site bounded by the Hashimoto-gawa and Matsumoto-gawa (rivers) on two sides and the Sea of Japan on the third. For tourist information, contact the Hagi Ryokan Association (tel: 0838 22 7599). Their office is to the left of the Higashi-Hagi station, near the entrance of the Rainbow Plaza shopping arcade. Hagi downtown

Tokoji Temple

area is a 30-minute walk from the station or a short cab ride. Tamachi Mall is the busiest shopping street, with shops offering everything from French ball gowns to local craft products, particularly pottery (Hagi is best known for a pinkish-beige tea ceremony stoneware).

Westernmost Hagi is equally accessible by either bus or train. Express buses run from Ogori (one hour, 15 minutes), from Tsuwano (one hour, 50 minutes) and from Akiyoshi-do (one hour, 10 minutes). By train there is a JR San-in line express from Masuda (one hour, 10 minutes) and from Shimonoseki (two hours).

Hagi Castle▶▶ was built in 1604 and dismantled in 1874; only the massive outer walls and moat now remain, and the grounds have been turned into the Shizuki Park. From the castle walls there are wonderful views of Hagi, the Sea of Japan, and the mountains that surround the city on three sides.

Horiuchi▶▶▶ is an old samurai quarter southeast of the castle ruins, between the castle moat and the main town. Once the domain of high-ranking samurai of the Mori Lords, this area is a maze of the earthen walls that surround each residence. There are three imposing samurai mansion gates still standing.

Tokoji Temple▶▶▶ is a simple but impressive Zen temple of the Obaku sect. The austere but grand tombs of five of the Mori Lords stand at the end of a pathway lined with 500 stone lanterns donated by the Lords' retainers. Each year, on 15 August, all the lanterns are lit. Toko-ji is east of the *Matsumoto-gawa* (Matsumoto River) along the road that crosses *Matsumoto-bashi* (Matsumoto bridge).

LAFCADIO HEARN
The son of an Irish father and a Greek mother, the writer Lafcadio Hearn (1850–1904) spent his childhood years in Greece and later visited Britain and the United States. Having arrived in Japan in 1890 and taken a teaching post in Matsue, he met and married a Japanese woman who had nursed him during a bout of illness. Hearn took Japanese citizenship and the name Koizumi Yakumo, and started to write about Japan. His accounts, including *Glimpses of an Unfamiliar Japan* (1894) and *A Japanese Miscellany* (1901), captivated Westerners and the Japanese, who were fascinated to see themselves through the eyes of a foreigner. Hearn's books are still in print in Japan and the US.

▶▶ Matsue   *154C4*

Set on the Ohashi River in the middle of the Sen-in coast, Matsue is best known as the home of Lafcadio Hearn, a European-born writer who took Japanese nationality in the 1890s (see panel). Somewhat off the beaten track for Westerners, this relatively small town is a well-known resort to many Japanese who spend their summer holidays here.

The simplest way to visit Matsue is by train. From Tsuwano, southwest of Matsue, it takes three hours, 30 minutes. From Okayama the trip takes three hours, and the single daily express from Hiroshima takes one hour. On arrival, visit the tourist information office in the station (*Open* 9.30–5.30), where English-language brochures and maps of the city are available. Most of the sights are within walking distance of each other and the station and there is a good bus network.

Lafcadio Hearn's residence, **Koizumi Yakumo Kyukyo▶▶** (*Open* Thu–Tue 9–12.30, 1.30–4.30), is a former samurai dwelling, across from the northern moat of the castle. The house has been preserved as Hearn left it in 1891, and next door is a memorial hall where items of memorabilia concerned with his life and work are collected.

Matsue Castle▶▶ was built in 1611 and partially restored in 1642. Never taken or damaged, the castle's five-floor facade actually contains six levels. There is a collection of samurai arms and armour on the lower floors, and the view from the top floor makes the climb worthwhile. Take the bus to Kencho-mae from stop 1 or 2 outside the JR station, then walk to the castle in Jozen Park. The Western-style building within the grounds is a fascinating museum of local history. There are displays of items from everyday life and photographs covering the period 1808 to the present day (*Open* castle and museum 8.30–5, 8.30–6, Apr–Sep).

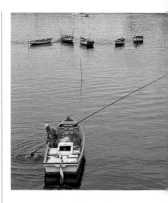

Boats at Matsue

CASTLE AUCTION
Matsue Castle is one of the few original Japanese castles to have survived without major reconstruction or rebuilding. In 1875, it was sold at auction for 90 US dollars to an individual who planned to demolish it. Fortunately, it was saved for posterity by a group of interested local people, who pooled their money to buy it from the successful bidder.

159

Matsue Castle tea house

Focus On — Izumo Taisha Shrine

Izumo Taisha is the oldest and largest Shinto shrine in Japan and the second most important, after the imperial shrines at Ise. The original buildings collapsed in 1031 and were later rebuilt on a smaller scale, the main shrine being built in 1744, and other important buildings dating from 1874.

DAIKOKU
To the northwest, behind the main shrine buildings, the former Treasure House (Shokokan) contains a large collection of images of Okuninushi-no-mikoto in the form of Daikoku. This happy, chubby character stands on a number of rice bales, holding a sack over his shoulder with one hand and a mallet in the other. He is normally accompanied by his son Ebisu, who stands beside him with a fish under his arm.

GETTING THERE
Izumo Taisha is several miles northwest of Izumo, and is served by the Ichihata Izumo Taisha rail station, the JR Izumo Taisha rail station and a bus terminal. A more or less straight road leads up to the shrine, and you can find a good range of lodging and restaurants in the shrine area. A tourist information office can be found on the main street close to the shrine entrance.

Happy marriage Set in pleasantly wooded grounds against a backdrop of the Yakumo Hill, Izumo Taisha is dedicated to the worship of Okuninushi-no-mikoto (Master of the Great Land), the *kami* (spirit god) of fishing, silk production and marriage. According to legend, Okuninushi-no-mikoto was a descendant of Susa-no-o, a *kami* of the Yamato line who married an Izumo princess. In time, Okuninushi-no-mikoto married a Yamato princess and agreed to serve the Yamato line, as long as he was venerated at a great shrine. Scholars believe that this tale reflects the struggle for dominance between rival clans during the earliest period of Japanese history, and that Okuninushi-no-mikoto's acceptance of Yamato authority reflected the emerging political and military dominance of the Yamato clan. The legend has led to the belief that a visit to the shrine is extremely beneficial to those who are contemplating marriage or promoting harmony for any union. Visitors to the shrine clap four times instead of the normal two to attract the deity's attention; twice for themselves and twice for their intended partner or partners.

Taisha architecture The shrine buildings are constructed according to the Taisha style, an ancient form of architecture thought to be purely Japanese. The Haiden (Hall of Worship), with extremely heavy, tapering *shimenawa* (sacred twisted straw ropes) hanging over the entrance, is the first building you will see inside the entrance *torii* (gate). The Honden (Main Hall) is not open to the public. Along the sides of the shrine compound are *juku-sha*, special buildings or shelters erected to house the eight million *kami* that are said to assemble at Izumo every year. To the southeast is the Shinko-den, or Treasure House (*Open* 8–4.30), which contains a collection of shrine artefacts.

Hanging good luck notes at the shrine

▶▶▶ Tsuwano
154B3

This small town in a narrow valley, high in the mountains, is nicknamed 'Little Kyoto' and preserves many features of the past, including large numbers of carp, originally bred as food in case of siege. They live in the water channels flowing through the old samurai quarter, Tonomachi. There are good mountain walks, well maintained temples and castle ruins above the town. The tourist office has maps and details of bicycle rental shops.

Tsuwano is just over one hour by train by JR from Ogori, which is on the Shinkansen line, 40 minutes west of Hiroshima. From 29 April to 5 May, and 20 July to 31 August, and on Sundays and national holidays in May, September, October and November, you can make the trip from Ogori, on the last steam locomotive in Japan.

Maria Sei-do▶▶ is a tiny chapel on a hill east of the station, built in 1948 by a German Catholic priest in memory of Japanese Catholics who were exiled to Tsuwano.

High on a hillside above Tsuwano, the vermilion red **Taikodani-Inari Shrine▶▶▶** is reached by stone steps and through a long tunnel of more than a thousand small, red *torii*. The steps, which are quite steep, start behind the Yasaka Shrine, on the river bank.

Tsuwano Castle▶▶ was originally built over a period of 30 years and completed in 1325, but was dismantled during the Meiji Restoration. The grounds, high above the town, offer spectacular views, and are reached by a steep walk or by chair lift, followed by a 10-minute walk.

Detail of the tunnel of torii (gates) at Taikodani-Inari Shrine

161

THE OGAI MORI CONNECTION
Yomeiji Temple, a Soto Zen temple to the east of Tsuwano station, has a charming garden and a handsome thatched-roof main hall, but is best known as the tomb of Ogai Mori (1862–1922). One of the leading literary figures of the Meiji Restoration, Ogai Mori spent his childhood in Tsuwano. On Tonomachi Street, lined with the whitewashed walls that used to surround samurai residences, the Yorokan Museum was once Ogai Mori's house and the local samurai school. It now houses exhibitions of folk craft in what was once the fencing *dojo* or training hall (*Open* 8.30–5.30).

Taikodani-Inari Shrine

Himeji Castle

San-yo Region

▶▶ Himeji   155E3

Himeji was severely bombed during World War II and has little of interest except its magnificent castle, which has survived almost intact. Bullet trains run here from the following major cities: Tokyo (four hours), Kyoto (one hour), Okayama (30 minutes) and Shin-Osaka (40 minutes). The private Hankyu line also operates a service between Kobe and Himeji. A tourist information office is to the right of the north exit of Himeji station.

Himeji Castle▶▶▶ (*Open* 9–5) is also known as Shirasagi Castle, or 'The Castle of the White Crane', because of its white plastered walls and silhouette from a distance. One of the few original medieval castles remaining in Japan, and one of the most beautiful, its first fortifications were erected in the 14th century and extended by Hideyoshi in 1581. The main tower is supported by three smaller towers and three rings of defensive compounds, which feature loopholes for firing guns or arrows at the enemy as well as *ishiotoshi*, openings through which rocks or boiling oil could be dropped on to attackers. Altogether, the castle presented the best defensive system of its day in Japan. From the central, north exit of Himeji station, the castle is a 15-minute walk.

Housed in a fine building in the northeast corner of the Himeji Castle grounds, the **Hyogo-kenritsu Rekishi Hakubutsukan (Hyogo Prefectural Museum of History)**▶ (*Open* 10–5; *closed* Mon) contains material from prehistoric times to the present, including displays of Himeji Castle and other castles from around the world. There is also a splendid exhibition of puppet heads, used in *ningyo joruri* (puppet drama), from Awajishima, an island in the Inland Sea, where the art originated.

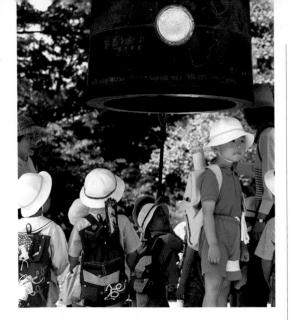

Hiroshima's peace bell

KOREAN VICTIMS
As well as the Japanese killed by the A-bomb, there were 20,000 Koreans who had been brought to Japan as a slave workforce during World War II. Koreans and their descendants still suffer discrimination in Japan, and were ignored by the authorities until 1970, when a cenotaph for Korean victims was erected outside the Peace Memorial Park.

A-BOMB CHILDREN
The statue of the A-Bomb Children in the Peace Memorial Park was inspired by Sadako, a girl dying from radiation poisoning who believed that if she folded 1,000 paper cranes she would recover. She died after folding 664 cranes. Children now fold paper cranes in her memory and the statue is surrounded by millions of paper cranes.

Founded in the 12th century, the large complex of temples making up the **Shoshazan Enkyoji▶▶** includes the oldest surviving Kamakura-period (14th-century) structure, the Yakushido, and the Kongo Satta Buddha, carved in 1395. To get there take a number 6 or 8 bus from the front of Himeji station to the Shosha bus stop. Walk to the temple grounds or transfer to the ropeway by the bus stop, which takes you to the temple. Alternatively, take one of the horse-drawn carriages usually waiting at the stop. They are as cheap as the ropeway.

▶▶▶ Hiroshima   154B3

The city of Hiroshima is known worldwide as the target of the first atomic bomb ever used in a war. The bomb was dropped by the Allies during World War II on 6 August 1945 at 8.15am, killing half the population of 400,000 people (about 80,000 people died immediately) and almost totally destroying the heart of the city. Hiroshima has been rebuilt, but the charred and twisted skeleton of the Industrial Promotion Hall, renamed the A-Bomb Dome, has been allowed to remain as a reminder of the destruction.

A new airport was opened in Hiroshima in 1993, connected by flights to Tokyo (Haneda Airport), Kagoshima (Kyushu) and Sapporo (Hokkaido). Bullet trains run from the following major cities: Tokyo (four hours, 30 minutes), Kyoto (two hours), Fukuoka/Hakata (one hour, 20 minutes). Two tourist information offices in Hiroshima station provide maps and English brochures. They also offer goodwill, free city tours.

A visit to the **Peace Memorial Park▶▶▶** is solemn and sobering. In the heart of town, it contains a number of monuments, including the Peace Memorial Museum and the Peace Memorial Hall, all concerned with recording and describing the story of the A-bomb that devastated the city. A Peace Flame burns in front of the Memorial Cenotaph, never to be extinguished until all nuclear weapons are abolished.

Paper cranes in the Peace Memorial Park

Kurashiki Toy Museum

▶▶▶ Kurashiki   155D3

'Warehouse Village' was originally an important focal point for the rice trade. Surprisingly, it escaped war damage and many of the large rice granaries still exist in the old part of the town, known as the Bikan Historical Area. They and many other Edo-period buildings have been turned into museums, shops, *ryokan* and restaurants. Kurashiki is famous for its museums and art collections; it is also a picturesque and charming town, and its tourist appeal now sustains the Kurashiki town coffers.

Bullet trains run from Kyoto (two hours) or Tokyo (four hours, 30 minutes) to Shin-Kurashiki station. Here you change for the local train to Kurashiki station (departure every 15 minutes). There is also a frequent commuter train service from Okayama JR station to Kurashiki station, journey time about 15 minutes. The tourist information office, on the third floor of Kurashiki station, has maps and information available in English.

Kurashiki Folkcraft Museum▶▶▶ (*Open* 9–5, Mar–Nov; 9–4.30, rest of year; *closed* Mon) is well worth a visit. It houses a collection of Japanese and foreign items to tie in with its slogan, 'Usability Equals Beauty'.

The **Nihon Kyudo Gangukan (Japan Rural Toy Museum)▶▶▶** (*Open* 8–5) contains a fine collection of more than 2,000 toys from all over Japan and other countries, and sells Japanese rural toys.

▶▶▶ Miyajima   154B3

'Shrine Island' is considered to be one of the three most beautiful scenic attractions in Japan. The entire island has been consecrated as a shrine, and is also the site of the famous Itsukushima Shinto Shrine, noted for its huge *torii* set in the sea.

The easiest way to visit the island is to take the JR Sanyo line from Hiroshima station to Miyajima-guchi station (25 minutes); from there, it is a short walk to the pier and the ferry to the island (22 minutes). A tourist information

SACRED MIYAJIMA
Miyajima is considered so sacred that it has no cemeteries. The heavily pregnant and those near death are not allowed to stay for fear they might die while on the island.

Feeding deer on Miyajima Island

office is in the JR ferry terminal, which can be visited on arrival in Miyajima.

The island is 30km (20 miles) in circumference, with Mount Misen at its heart rising to 530m (1,740ft). Although its beauty has been tainted by tourist attractions, this is still a lovely place and worth a day's visit or an overnight stay.

To the west of the ferry pier, **Itsuku Shrine▶▶▶** is approached through Miyajima Village (a tourist trap) and then a park where many tame deer roam. Originally built in AD 593 and last rebuilt in the 16th century, the shrine is dedicated to the three daughters of Susano-o-no-Mikoto, the Shinto god of the moon and oceans. Most of the shrine is private, but the five-floor pagoda and Senjokaku Hall, which are on a hill above the shrine, are open to the public.

▶▶ Okayama   155D3

This major city lies on the Inland Sea and is famous for Korakuen Gardens. Shinkansen run to Okayama, taking four hours from Tokyo and just under one hour from Hiroshima. The tourist information office is near the central exit of the east side of Okayama station.

Okayama is a busy commercial city, not a tourist destination, but it is worth visiting **Korakuen Gardens▶▶▶** (*Open* 7.30–6, Apr–Sep; 8–5, rest of year), constructed between 1687 and 1700 and considered to be one of the three most beautiful landscape gardens in Japan. The 11ha (27 acres) are composed of streams, a pond, bamboo groves, pine, plum and cherry trees, as well as 'borrowed views' of the surrounding hills and Okayama Castle. The park gets crowded on weekends and national holidays.

Okayama Castle▶▶ (*Open* 9–5), or 'Crow Castle', was destroyed in World War II and rebuilt in 1966. Painted black to contrast with Himeji's famous castle, Okayama-jo houses a collection of samurai arms and armour, palanquins, and so on. There is also an elevator to the top of the *donjon*.

ITSUKUSHIMA *TORII* (GATE)

The Itsukushima gate is the subject of countless photographs and many paintings, always taken or painted when the tide is in and the *torii* shimmers above the water. In fact, it stands most of the time in mud flats. From inside the Itsukushima Shrine grounds there is a good view of the brilliant vermilion gate. Offerings are made by individuals or companies to keep the lanterns in the shrine galleries lit at night, producing a spectacular sight if viewed on a dark night at high tide.

165

The striking torii *(gate) at Itsuku Shrine on Miyajima*

The Japanese approach to landscape gardening has traditionally veered away from military precision and geometric perfection. Forcing mechanical order on nature is unattractive to the Japanese spirit, and it is also felt to be wasteful in terms of time and energy. Japanese landscape gardeners thus aspire to work with nature, extending and enhancing natural beauty.

GARDEN POEMS
Japanese poets have always been inspired by a love of nature. The garden, reflecting nature, has served as inspiration for a number of poets. The following poem from a Zen master catches the immediacy of the Zen experience:
'The spring flowers, the autumn moon
Summer breeze, winter snow
If useless things do not clutter your mind
You have the best days of your life.'

Artificially natural Japanese landscape gardeners design their work as microcosms of the real world, aiming to show nature on a small scale. For example, when Muso Soseki laid out the gardens of the Saihoji Temple (the 'Moss Temple' of Kyoto), he did not first level the ground to form a flat surface. Instead he allowed the moss to follow the natural undulations of the ground, and to display a wide range of different shades of green, complementing and contrasting with one another. Trees and stones were then placed subtly among the moss, so that they would seem quite natural; the hand of the landscape gardener is unseen.

As well as moss, Japanese gardens make extensive use of trees such as pine and maple, and bamboo groves, small streams and ponds, rocks, stones and sand. The materials are arranged so as to represent mountains, rivers, lakes and waterfalls, and are planted with a variety of flowering trees such as cherry, peach and plum. Other features are flowering shrubs such as azaleas, wisteria, camellias, and rhododendrons and evergreen plants and ferns, usually planted alongside streams and ponds. From these components three basic types of garden evolved: the *tsuki-yama* (hill style), *kare sansui* ('waterless stream gardens', see pages 134–135) and the *cha-niwa* (tea garden).

Hill gardens The *tsuki-yama* style of garden typically has streams with stepping stones and a bridge leading to a small island set in a pond. A twisting path leads you from one feature to another past ever-changing scenes. Some gardens imitate in miniature places of beauty famous in Japanese art or literature. One variation of the *tsuki-yama* style of garden is known as the *kaiyu* or 'many pleasure' style. Popular with the *daimyo* (feudal lords) of the Tokugawa shogunate, the *kaiyu* has several gardens built around a central pond. Often one or more of them incorporates views that lie outside the garden itself, a technique known as *shakkei* (borrowed views) or *ikedori* (capturing alive). This feature is often seen in gardens in the Kyoto area, where the spectacular mountains that surround the city are seen framed by gateposts and trees.

Tea gardens The *cha-niwa* is designed to enhance the peaceful, spiritual nature of the tea ceremony, hence its description as the 'fourth wall' of the tea house. The traditional *cha-niwa* is always planted with ferns, moss,

A gardener maintains a water feature

*Rikugien Garden
in Tokyo*

A WESTERN VIEW
In his book *Around the World Through Japan*, written at the turn of the 19th century, Walter Del Mar described the requirements of a Japanese landscape garden as: 'a cart-load of rocks, a pail of water, a modicum of ingenuity, and unlimited imagination—all concentrated on a space the size of a mat'. A more elaborate garden would need a dwarf pine, tortured out of its natural shape with permanent bandages and bits of wood and string, or some that 'the patient gardeners have bent, interlaced, tied, weighed down, and propped up the limbs and twigs'. Multiplied by 10, these would provide 'a leafy, lake-centred paradise, and a marvel of artistic arrangement'.

evergreen trees and shrubs set against bamboo fences and stone lanterns. You move through the *cha-niwa* to the tea house along stepping stones placed asymmetrically on the ground. You then encounter a *machiai* (waiting room), separated from the inner garden around the tea house by a *chumon* (small gate). Within the inner garden there is a stone water basin, used to wash hands and rinse the mouth before entering the tea house. The tea gardens of the Kinkakuji Temple and the Katsura Imperial Villa, both in Kyoto, are among the most famous in Japan (see pages 128–129 and 140).

*Kenrokuen Garden,
Kanazawa*

Shikoku

CLIMATE
Shikoku has two climatic regions, separated by the mountain ranges that run east to west across the island. The Pacific Coast area, to the south, is sub-tropical, with hot summers and mild, wet winters. The Inland Sea region, to the north, is less rainy and most days are bright and sunny.

PAPER CRAFTS
Shikoku, and especially the Kochi area, is renowned for its paper products. The raw material is pulp from Japanese mulberry trees, cultivated on the mountain slopes of Shikoku's interior. High-quality paper is used to make many goods, including *shoji* (screens), lanterns, paper wallets, *daruma* dolls and masks. Small, flat paper items make excellent, lightweight presents to take home.

Aspects of Shikoku: a floating restaurant...

SHIKOKU The smallest of the four main islands of Japan hunkers under the San-yo coast, across the Inland Sea from Western Honshu. It is a mountainous, wooded island, lacking in natural resources, limited in industrial development and restricted in inter-island communications. Except for its major sights, Shikoku is still relatively unexplored by foreign and Japanese visitors. However, in 1988, after ten years of construction, the Seto-Ohashi Bridge connecting Shikoku with Honshu by road and rail was opened and tourism has vastly increased in that area.

GEOGRAPHY The northern coast has attracted most of the island's industry and is the site of its two largest cities, Takamatsu and Matsuyama. Here also, rice, wheat, mandarin oranges and tobacco are farmed on terraced mountain slopes and any flat land not taken by housing or industry. The interior of the island, to which access is difficult, is a place of clean rivers, Buddhist temples, small villages and remote hiking trails. The southern half of the island, except for the Kochi plain, is steeply mountainous and, outside of the few towns, sustains a small population of rice farmers and fishermen.

KOBO DAISHI To the Japanese, Shikoku is best known as the focal point of Shingon Buddhism. Every year thousands of followers make a pilgrimage by walking tour (or, more recently, bus tour) of the island's 88 temples in memory of Kobo Daishi, founder of the sect (see pages 178 and 184–185). Many temples offer overnight lodging. Devout pilgrims believe that by visiting all 88 temples they will be released from the cycle of birth and death.

MAIN TOWNS Takamatsu is a medium-size town and a pleasant, convenient base for exploring the rest of Shikoku. Ritsurin Park is the town's main tourist destination. After dark, Takamatsu has a busy nightlife and the 'entertainment area' is a maze of neon-lit, pedestrian-only arcades lined with bars, restaurants and late-night shops. **Matsuyama** is Shikoku's largest city, but with more of a country town feel than Takamatsu, and is famous for its Dogo Onsen, one of the best-known hot-spring resorts in

…dramatic mountain scenery…

HAIKU POETRY

Haiku is a highly stylized and refined form of Japanese poetry, in which the poet aspires to express deep and spontaneous insights about nature and human life. The *haiku* always consists of 17 syllables, arranged in three lines, the first of five syllables, the second of seven, and the last of five. It is traditional to use the name of a flower, animal, custom, or event that invokes the feeling of a particular season. Matsuo Basho (1644–94) is considered the father and greatest exponent of *haiku* in its present form. Here are two examples of his poetry:

> The sea dark
> The call of the teal
> Dimly white

> Soon it will die
> Yet no trace of this
> In the cicada's screech.

Japan. A unique cultural aspect of Matsuyama is the local love of *haiku* poetry.

Kotohira, also in the north of the island, is a small town nestling beneath the nationally revered Kotohiragu shrine to Omononushi-no-mikoto, the Shinto protector of wayfarers and sailors, whose popular name is Kompira-san. For tired pilgrims, there is a *kago* service (a chair suspended from poles and carried by porters) up the hundreds of stairs to the shrine summit. Kotohira also has one of the oldest *kabuki* theatres in Japan.

Uwajima is the last stop on the railway line west from Takamatsu: a five and a half hour journey. Trains leave Takamatsu about five times daily for this small country town, well known locally for its bullring (two bulls, like four-legged sumo wrestlers, try to push each other out of a small ring). Outside Uwajima railway station is a small tourist office. Taga Jinja is the local Shinto shrine.

Kochi, in the south of the island, is a friendly market town. The major attraction is Kochi Castle.

…and hay stacks

GETTING THERE A direct train to Takamatsu leaves Tokyo station every night at 9.05, arriving at 7.35 the following morning. There are regular services to Takamatsu from Okayama station (one hour). JR ferry and hovercraft services connect Uno on Honshu to Takamatsu. Uno is connected to Okayama by a frequent train service, and Takamatsu is connected by an air service to Osaka and Tokyo. Shikoku's three main railway lines begin at Takamatsu: the JR Yosan line to Matsuyama; the JR Dosan line to Kochi; and the JR Kotoku line to Tokushima.

Bargaining at Kochi's Sunday market

DOG-FIGHTING
Dog fights are popular in particular areas of Japan. Among aficionados, top dogs and their owners achieve the same status as star sumo wrestlers. A sumo ranking system is used and winning dogs are even paraded around the ring in miniature sumo-style aprons. Fights take place on a caged circular stage, surrounded by tiers of seats. The dogs, which unexpectedly do not bark, weigh in at around 150kg (330lb); they jockey for a grip on one another's shoulders and then try to throw the other dog down. The fight is over when one dog stays down. A judge sits in a high chair within the caged stage, punishing illegal moves such as nose- or testicle-biting by spraying the nose of the offender with a sting-ing liquid.

▶▶ **Kochi**   *155D2*

This castle town is on the central southern coast of Shikoku, two and a half hours by train from Kotohira. The local microclimate is subtropical and farming and agriculture are the main industries in the lush and fertile surrounding countryside.

Almost every day of the week there is a street market in Kochi; the biggest is on Sunday morning, on palm-lined Otesuji-dori, near the heart of town. *Onagadori* show birds (see panel on opposite page) may also be on display.

Kochi Castle▶▶ (*Open* 9–4.30), in the middle of Kochi Park on the west of the city, dates from 1603. There is a panoramic view of the city from the top of the intact five-floor keep (*donjon*), as well as a museum in the grounds with much information about Lord Sakamoto Ryoma (1835–67), a local swashbuckling hero who helped topple the shogunate. The Lord's Residence, Kaitokukan, is open on the second floor of the *donjon;* kept in its original condition, it acts as a window onto the life of the *daimyo.*

Katsura-hama▶▶, a white, coarse-grained, sandy beach, 35 minutes by bus from Kochi station, is popular with locals in the summer, particularly for swimming, and in the autumn for gazing at the moon. Kochi is famous for breeding the Tosa fighting dog.

▶▶▶ **Kotohira**   *155D3*

Kotohira, 45 minutes by JR Dosan line express from Takamatsu, is best known for its Kotohiragu, one of the oldest and grandest Shinto shrines in Japan, and for the Kyu Kompira Oshibai, the only complete Edo-period *kabuki* playhouse left in Japan.

Known as Kompira-san, **Kotohiragu Shrine**▶▶▶ was originally founded in the 11th century. It is dedicated to Omononushi-no-mikoto (nicknamed Kompira), the guardian of seafarers, who would visit the shrine to pray for safe journeys at sea. Part of the shrine complex houses models and photographs of boats left there by fishermen soliciting protection. Nowadays, Kompira's aid is sought by all who travel, and by those seeking good fortune.

The shrine is built on the slopes of Mount Zozu and the main complex is at the top of 785 stone steps. Turn left out of Kotohira station, under a *torii*, and then turn right down a narrow shopping street, where you will quickly come to the steps. The climb will take 30–40 minutes and is quite daunting if you are not in shape. Litter-bearers will carry you up in a *kago* for a reasonable sum, given the arduousness of the task. The steps are lined with souvenir shops, inns and refreshment vendors, but once through the main gate the atmosphere becomes more refined. At the top, there are wonderful panoramic views of the surrounding Sanuki Plain, the Inland Sea to the north, and the Shikoku mountain ranges to the south.

Near the first flight of steps leading to Kotohiragu Shrine is the **kabuki** playhouse▶▶ (*Open* 9–5; *closed* Tue), built in 1835 in traditional style, with paper lanterns, *tatami* and sliding *shoji* to adjust the light. The revolving stage, which has two trap doors, is turned by eight men in the basement. The entrance to the building is small, to keep out gate-crashers. Plays are staged once a year in April, but it is open daily for viewing.

Kotohira's kabuki *playhouse lit by lanterns*

LONG-TAILED ROOSTERS
An unusual feature of Kochi is the rearing of *onagadori* (long-tailed roosters). The tradition began with the wish to provide decorative features for the local *daimyo*. Three centuries later, selective breeding has produced roosters with tails as long as 10m (33ft). You will find *onagadori* at the Nagaodori Centre (*Open* Tue–Sun 9–5).

KOTOHIRAGU
The inner shrine complex includes the Treasure House, which contains scrolls, sculpture and *noh* masks; Shoin, the original reception hall, housing paintings by Maruyama Okyo, an 18th-century artist; Asahi-no Yashiro, a carved hall, dedicated to Amaterasu, the sun goddess; and Ema-do, a pavilion containing ship models and old photographs, offered by pilgrims.

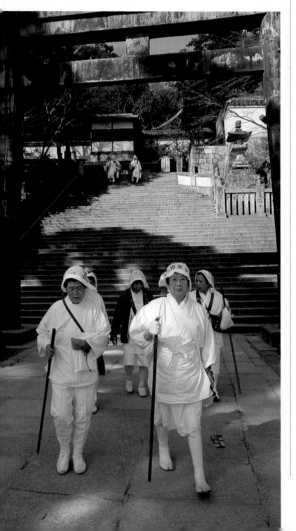

Pilgrims at Kotohiragu Shrine

SWORDS AND ARMOUR
Omishima Island is one hour by hydrofoil boat from Imabari Port, which is 40 minutes on the JR Yosan line from Matsuyama. The boat docks at Miyaura and from here it is a short cab ride to Oyamazumi Shrine. There, most unexpectedly, housed in the shrine treasure hall, is the best collection of swords and armour in Japan. For many centuries Oyamazumi was a popular place of worship for emperors and shogun and it became a tradition for them to donate swords and armour to the shrine. Today 80 per cent of the nation's most treasured items of this type are to be found here, including armour worn by Minamoto Yoritomo, first shogun of the Kamakura period (1192–1333).

172

▶▶▶ Matsuyama   *154C2*

Matsuyama, on the northwest coast of Shikoku, is the island's largest city, renowned in the past as a city of art and literature. The most convenient way to get there is by train from Okayama, Honshu (two hours, 40 minutes) or Takamatsu, Shikoku (two hours, 50 minutes). The city tourist information office is just inside the JR station. The main sights in town are Matsuyama Castle, one of the finest surviving feudal castles in Japan, and Dogo Onsen, a celebrated hot spring. Matsuyama has an excellent network of cable cars and finding your way around is quite easy. World War II bombing devastated the city and postwar planners were keen on practicality, hence the characterless network of straight boulevards and avenues, broken only by the cable cars.

Matsuyama's local crafts include *iyo-kasuri*, an indigo-dyed cotton once used to make working clothes for farming women, *tobe-yaki*, a thick porcelain decorated with brushed cobalt-blue designs on a white ground, and oval-shaped dolls designed is a tribute to Empress Jingu, who visited Dogo Onsen when she was pregnant. For these and other items from the Ehime Prefecture, visit the Ehime no Bussan store, Ichiban-cho 4-chome (Kencho-mae cable-car stop; *Open* Mon–Fri 8.30–5).

Matsuyama Castle▶▶▶ (*Open* 9–5) was constructed in 1603 by the head of the Matsudaira clan and later destroyed by fire. The stone walls, turret and keep, all in good condition, dominate a hill in the middle of the city and command fine views of the Inland Sea and the central mountain ranges of Shikoku. A castle museum exhibits the armour and swords of the Matsudaira family, and the surrounding park is worth exploring. Cable car 5, from the square in front of the station, takes you to the entrance to the castle grounds; from here you can take the steep walk or a cable car to the castle summit.

Dogo Onsen▶▶▶ is one of the best-known hot spring resorts in Japan. (A cable-car line runs here from the railway station.) Part of the baths, still preserved and open

*Looking out over
Matsuyama from the
castle*

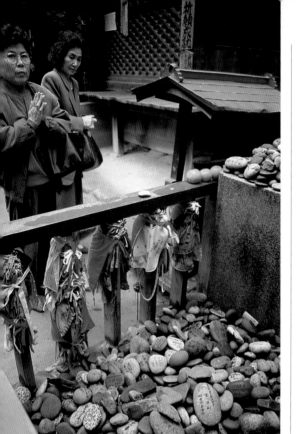

Ishiteji Temple, near Dogo Onsen, is the 51st on the Shikoku pilgrimage route

HAIKU MASTERS
Matsuyama was the birth-place of many famous *haiku* poets, including Masaoka Shiki (1867–1902) and Takahama Kyoshi (1874–1959), and the people of Matsuyama have special affection for *haiku* poetry (see panel, page 169). Throughout the city you can see stone monuments inscribed with the finest poems of the great *haiku* masters. The city even organizes *haiku* contests with special '*haiku* mailboxes' for residents to submit their entries.

173

for viewing, was originally set aside for the exclusive use of visiting royalty from Kyoto. This area is ornate, but the section open for public bathing is simply designed in the best tradition of functional Japanese architecture. At the entrance, you pay a small fee, and collect soap and a miniature towel. This is used for washing, then wrung out for drying, and also as a cover-up while in the spa. In the pools, the natural mineral water is just cool enough to sit in and the salts it contains soften and vitalize the skin. For an extra fee, you can gain access to a communal *tatami* (mat) room on the second floor; a more expensive private room, with tea and access to the imperial pool, is also available.

Slippers from the weary feet of pilgrims

Ishiteji Temple►►, a short walk east of Dogo Onsen station, is the most interesting of eight temples in Matsuyama that are part of the Shikoku pilgrimage. Built in 1318, it is a fine example of Kamakura archi-tecture, with a three-floor pagoda, main gate, hall and bell tower. The deity has a reputation for relieving aching legs, and the straw sandals of many elderly Japanese hoping for a cure for their failing legs hang from the main gate.

Japan sits on a geological region of intense volcanic activity, which gives rise to many hot springs (onsen). Spas, fed by these natural sources of mineral-rich hot water, are popular with the Japanese for their curative, health-giving and relaxing properties. Public washing baths, sento, were invented as a public service when most houses had no bathrooms. They provide hot running water for washing and a large bath full of very hot water for soaking in. Many also have mineral baths, whirlpools, electric baths and cold plunges.

174

ROTEMBURO ETIQUETTE
Young women do not generally swim in outdoor pools during the day, but in the evening mixed groups gather in the pools. After dinner sake, floated from person to person in tiny wooden tubs, is drunk, inhibitions drop away, singing may start up and formal conversation gives way to gossipy chatter and heart-to-heart revelations.

Dogo Onsen, *where the emperor had his own baths built*

Onsen Built near or directly above a hot spring source, *onsen* are Japanese inns where guests hope to benefit from the water's health-promoting qualities, as well as enjoying the regional food. Some of the larger *onsen* are built like modern hotels, attracting large family groups and parties of company workers; others are set deep in the mountains, in beautiful, isolated areas. The latter are usually composed of three or four thatched wooden buildings around a series of *rotemburo* (outdoor pools).

For the cognoscenti, exploring such places in search of the ultimate spa can be akin to a spiritual journey. Most *onsen* are open all year round, and in the smaller country establishments you may sit in the winter in a steaming outdoor pool, surrounded by snow-covered rocks and trees.

Onsen cities The Japanese love to do things together, not only as a way of socializing but, particularly with company and sports parties, to engender solidarity. For this reason, many of the best-known *onsen* have become resort areas with hotels, busy nightlife districts, and huge bathing halls with an exotic variety of pools. The Arita Kanko Hotel in Kinki district, Honshu, has hot baths inside a cable car that rises high above a very dramatic coastline. Famous resorts such as Beppu in Kyushu, Noboribetsu in Hokkaido, and Atami in Honshu are often vulgar, gaudy and kitsch, but they have their own charm, and offer the chance to join in with ordinary Japanese letting their communal hair down.

Sento For independent tourists on a budget, *sento* are excellent places to relax and to experience something quintessentially Japanese. *Sento* can be identified by their tall, narrow, metal chimneys and the distinctive flame logo painted over the entrance. In the last few years they have become fashionable with young people, and, like old cinemas, are being renovated in their original style.

Nowadays, *sento* are not mixed, and the men's and women's baths are usually looked after by an *obasan* (old woman), who sits on a platform inside the entrance astride the wall that divides the two sides. Men enter on the right, and women on the left. The *obasan* takes entrance fees and sells shampoo, soap and razors. Towels are available for rent, but most Japanese make do with a small piece of cotton towelling called a *tenugui*, used initially as a flannel and then as a towel.

Bathers put their clothes in a locker and lock it with a numbered wooden key, which is kept on the wrist. Inside the bathing area, plumbed into the walls, is a series of pairs of hot and cold taps. Sit at one of these on a low plastic stool and pour water over yourself with one of the small bowls scattered around the floor, before rubbing soap into the *tenugui* and soaping yourself all over. Then rinse the soap off thoroughly and sit in the hot tub, adding cold water if the heat is unbearable. Use the same facilities and washing procedure at *onsen* before and after entering one of the communal hot-spring pools.

Thermal baths outdoors…

MASSAGE CHAIRS
Many *sento* provide a massage armchair in the changing rooms to relieve backs stiff from too much walking. To use one, put the correct coins into the slot in the arm of the chair and adjust yourself against the moving rollers. They can be moved up and down by using the control lever near your right hand.

…and indoors

▶▶ Takamatsu 155D3

The second-largest town in Shikoku, Takamatsu is the most convenient arrival point and base for exploring Shikoku. It was bombed flat in World War II but rebuilt, exceptionally, on a human scale. And fortunately Ritsurin Park, in the north of the city, famous even outside Shikoku, escaped damage. The main railway station, the ferry port, the commercial and nightlife area, and the park are all within walking distance. For travel directions to Takamatsu from the main island of Honshu, see page 169.

Crossing the bridge at Takamatsu

Ritsurin Park▶▶▶ is part of the former estate of the Matsudaira clan, originally designed as a summer retreat. An unusually wide variety of tree and flower species grows in the park, including Neagari Kashi oak trees, with exposed, leg-like roots, and Hako Matsu pine trees, characterized by their surreal branch configurations. Plum trees bloom in February, followed by camellias and yulan in March, cherry blossoms in April, wisteria and azalea in May, irises and water lilies in June, and lotus flowers in August. Work was begun on the park in the early 17th century, and was not completed on the formal gardens until more than 100 years later. Two distinct areas make up the park. The south garden is of classical design featuring the landscaping, rock arrangements, ponds and artificial hills of the kind popular in the early and middle part of the Edo period. Winding paths and bridges lead past striking, stark trees with sculpted branches, over ponds stocked with carp and through flower beds of seasonal flowers. Be sure to stop at the Scoop The Moon Tea House (*Kikugetsu-tei*) for some whisked green tea and some bean-jam cake. The north garden is landscaped in a more

Ritsurin Park

open, European style. It was originally designed for wild duck hunting parties led by the *daimyo* of Takamatsu. Nowadays, the open spaces are used for picnics, park games, and, in season, for cherry blossom viewing festivities. The park is open daily from dawn to dusk.

Very near the entrance to Ritsurin Park is **Sanuki Mingeikan**▶▶ (*Open* 8.45–4), a folk art museum that exhibits handicraft products from Sanuki (the old name for the Kagawa Prefecture, of which Takamatsu is the capital) and sells a range of locally made pottery.

Zentsuji Temple▶▶, a short distance west of Zentsuji station, 40 minutes south of Takamatsu on the JR Dosan line, is the birthplace of Kobo Daishi, who founded the temple in AD 813, and the 75th station of the 88 temples (see pages 184–185). An imposing statue of the saint holding a cane guards the entrance to the main temple. Within the complex is a five-floor pagoda and a treasure house exhibiting various 'Important Cultural Properties', including Buddhist artefacts brought back from China by Kobo Daishi. The two large camphor trees growing in the grounds are said to have been planted at the time of the temple's foundation.

Near the main entrance are two wooden cut-outs of traditionally dressed pilgrims with holes where their faces should be, offering a photo opportunity for visitors. If offered a little money, one of the temple monks may agree to lead you through a 'secret' tunnel that runs beneath the main temple. A pitch-black passage, its walls worn smooth by countless searching hands, the tunnel leads to the back of the main altar. The tunnel darkness is said to inspire reflection on the human condition, while the tunnel itself represents life before and after the light of spiritual enlightenment.

RITSURIN PARK AND MOUNT SHIUN
The original design of the park incorporated the green backdrop provided by the adjacent Mount Shiun and took into account the way it would influence views from particular vantage points in the garden. To appreciate this aspect of the design, walk to your right around the garden.

The imperial emblem at Zentsuji Temple

Kobo Daishi is the posthumous name of a Buddhist monk known as Kukai (AD 774–835), born in Zentsuji in Shikoku and famous as the founder of the Shingon (True Word) sect of Buddhism. Kobo Daishi, or Dharma-Spreading Great Master, is the name by which he is best known. It was given to him in AD 921, nearly a century after his death.

MOUNT KOYA (*KOYA-SAN*) MONASTERY

Kobo Daishi petitioned Emperor Saga to give him Mount Koya, claiming that: 'According to the meditation sutras, meditation should be practised preferably on a flat area, deep in the mountains. When young, I…often walked though mountainous areas and crossed many rivers. There is a quiet, open place called Koya, located two days' walk to the west from a point that is one day's walk south from Yoshino. High peaks surround Koya in all four directions; no human tracks, still less trails are to be seen there. I should like to clear the wilderness in order to build a monastery there for the practice of meditation, for the benefit of the nation, and of those who desire to discipline themselves…'

A statue of Kobo Daishi at Takamatsu Temple

At 19 Kukai abandoned his study of Confucianism and Taoism and a potential career in the government bureaucracy to become a pupil of the Buddhist priest Gonso. In 795, he was ordained as a monk at Nara's Todaiji (Great Eastern) Temple, taking the name Kukai ('Sea of Void').

In 804, Kukai joined the retinue of the Japanese imperial ambassador to the Tang Court and journeyed with him to China, where he studied esoteric Buddhism under Hui-kuo, the seventh patriarch of a line of teachers that had originated in India. Kukai was an exceptional student. He collected many scrolls of esoteric lore and ritual and studied tantric Buddhist traditions from Central Asia. When Hui-kuo died in 804, Kukai was chosen to be the eighth patriarch of the sect and entrusted with the task of introducing its teachings into Japan.

Return home Kukai returned to Japan in August 806. He settled in Kanzeonji Temple in Kyushu and sent a list of the Buddhist sutras and other works to the Japanese court. As a result, Kukai's esoteric teaching earned the support of the court and in 823 Emperor Saga gave Kukai a new temple: Toji (Eastern Temple), in Kyoto, which became the headquarters of the Shingon sect.

Death and reincarnation Kukai died on 20 April 835, at the age of 61. His followers claim that he did not actually die, but went into the meditative state known as the Diamond Meditation, from which he will return as the Buddha Maitreya. His remains were entombed on Mount Koya, where his grave is now a shrine for the faithful.

▶▶ Uwajima
154C1

This small, charming country town is the last stop on the JR Yosan line west of Takamatsu (five hours) and Matsuyama (two hours). It is worth visiting for its castle, bull-fights, and the outrageously explicit sex museum at Taga Jinja, a local Shinto shrine. You can walk easily between sites or rent a bicycle at the Information Office, just south of the exit to JR Uwajima station.

Although it is one of the few surviving feudal strongholds in Japan, **Uwajima Castle▶** was never a great castle. To defend its lands, it depended on its excellent position on a promontory once surrounded by interlocking sea moats. The castle is a short walk from the middle of town.

Uwajima is famous for **Togyu bullfights▶▶▶**, in which two bulls test their strength by locking horns and trying to push one another out of the ring. Tournaments are held six times a year, usually on 2 January, the first Sunday in March, April and November, the third Sunday in May and 14 August. The bullring, or Togyu-ju, is at the base of Mount Tenman, a cab ride or a 30-minute walk from the middle of town. Dozens of bouts take place, and the atmosphere is usually less than sober.

Taga Jinja▶▶▶ (*Open* 8–5), a Shinto shrine 10 minutes' walk from the station (directions from the tourist office), is said to be something of an embarrassment to local people, for the priest in charge is an avid collector of sexual paraphernalia. Next to the shrine he has built a three-floor museum to house his collection, which includes perhaps the only classified display of pubic hair in the world. At the entrance, a statue of a masturbating Buddha sets the tone for what follows. Cabinets display sexual gadgets, sexually explicit statues, and representations of penises and vaginas of all sizes and shapes, and the walls and ceilings are covered with pornography. Taga has become a fertility shrine and nowadays infertile couples and newly weds make up the shrine's and the museum's usual customers.

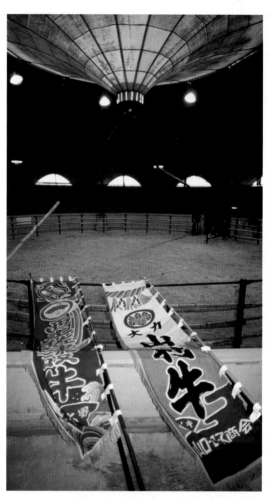

The bullring, Togyu-ju

DUTCH BULLS
Bullfighting started here in the 19th century with a gift of bulls from a Dutch sea captain, saved from a typhoon by Uwajima fishermen. Bulls were new to the Japanese, and were set to fight each other because they were so fierce.

FESTIVAL
Uwajima's biggest festival, Warei Jinja Matsuri, is held on 23–24 July at Warei Jinja Shrine. The main features include bullfights, and an appearance by *ushi-oni*, or ox demons.

In Japan, sex is not something to be shy about, nor is it separated from the spiritual life. The traditional belief is that we have two souls. One is timeless and sublime and the other is earth-bound and pleasure-seeking. Both parts of our being need nourishment. Within this context, romantic love and male and female sexuality have been equally celebrated in Japanese cultural and religious life.

180

EROTIC ART

Remains of erotic pictures of sexual activity have been preserved in Japan from as early as the eighth century. Of the two earliest complete *shunga* (a general term for erotic art painted or printed onto scrolls to be viewed horizontally), one, *The Phallic Contest*, depicts a test of male sexual powers by ladies of the imperial court, while the other, *The Catamites*, portrays the homosexual activities of Buddhist monks.

Soft-porn Manga comic

In the past in Japan, the sexual emphasis has always been on male gratification; the woman's role was to fulfil a man's needs. Until recently, this was the view generally accepted and approved by society. Lack of inhibition and a confidence in his role gave the Japanese male a reputation for coarseness in his bold approach to sex, while the female became known for her demure-ness and her willingness to please. There is still some belief in these notions, but the reality of sexual relations in Japan can be as paradoxical as it is everywhere else.

Sex comics and prudery One of the shocks to a Westerner visiting Japan is to flick through the popular sex comic books sold at all newspaper outlets and available to read in many coffee shops. Glossy nude female pin-ups are followed by cartoons and a picture story, in which the woman heroine undergoes all sorts of sexual humiliations at the hands of an evil monster or pervert.

Neither Japanese men nor women (nor children, who do read them) seem embarrassed or surprised at these comics; neither do they take them seriously. A more recent development is the arrival of the sadistic heroine. The suitably attired dominatrix, usually a successful sports or business woman in her ordinary life, ritually humiliates a male slave. He normally turns out to be a corrupt politician or ruthless financier.

In real-life, sexual violence directed at women is rare in Japan. Assaults are virtually unknown and women are generally safe to move around at any time of the day or night without fear of violence or theft.

Another paradox, given Japanese ribald history and the explicit nature of their comics (and some Shinto shrines), is the prudery of the authorities regarding the genitals. As a result of this, cartoonists and film-makers are experts at being titillating without being explicit.

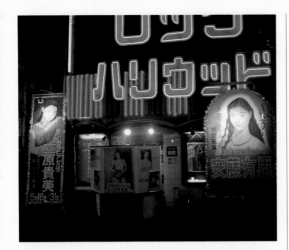

Personal relations It is more common for Western men to date Japanese women than vice versa, but either circumstance is generally considered socially acceptable. However, public displays of affection are usually embarrassing for the Japanese. Kissing and hugging is frowned on and holding hands is about as far as you should go.

Gay sex Homosexuality is neither discouraged nor flaunted in Japanese society. In the past, some Buddhist sects taught that homosexuality was natural and even virtuous compared with sex with women. These teachings were mainly from Buddhist sects forbidding sexual relations with women, but they did for a time influence the samurai of the period, who developed a school of thought that homosexual love was purer than the heterosexual variety.

THE FLOATING WORLD
Ukiyo, 'The Floating World', was a description of the areas officially designated by the Tokugawa shogunate (1603–1868) for sex and entertainment. The name carried the sentiment that life is short and that one might as well enjoy its pleasures while one can. Tea houses, playhouses and bath houses were the venues, and money and sex the catchwords. Woodblock print (*ukiyo-e*) artists of the era are well known for their portraits of the women and *kabuki* actors of the pleasure quarters. 'Water trade' was the phrase used to describe the night-time world of bars, adult entertainment and sex found in 'soapland' districts of Japanese cities.

181

Taga-jinja Shrine, Uwajima

A fisherman's house, Shodo-shima

Excursions

►► Shodo-shima   155D3

Northeast of Takamatsu, 19km (12 miles) off the coast, Shodo-shima is the second-largest island in the Inland Sea (there are almost 1,000 in all). There is a frequent ferry service from Takamatsu Pier to Tonosho port, on the western side of the island, which takes approximately one hour (or 35 minutes on the high-speed ferry). The island has a warm, dry, almost Mediterranean climate and it was here that olives were first cultivated in Japan. Shodo-shima is best known for its scenic beauty.

The main attraction is **Kankakei Gorge►►►** ('Cold and Misty Valley'), found in the central mountainous region of the island. Imprisoned by mountainous rock faces, eroded into surreal shapes by the weather, the gorge is brightened by wild cherry and azaleas in the spring, and pine and maple trees in the autumn. A one-hour bus journey from Tonosho takes you to a nerve-racking aerial ropeway ride up and over the gorge to the summit of a precipice. There is a bus back to Tonoshu from the summit via Kusakabe.

A shorter bus ride from Tonosho (25 minutes), *en route* to Kankakei, takes you to **Choshikei Gorge►►**, which lies on the upper reaches of Denpo River and is known for its spectacular waterfall and profusion of spring and autumn tints. Nearby is the Monkey Park (*Osaru-no-Kuni*), a reserve where wild Japanese monkeys roam freely and show off for the visiting humans.

An extensive public network of buses operates from Tonosho for all the island sights and along the coast to the east. Buses on the coastal route depart for Sakate every 30 minutes, passing Futagoura Beach, just outside Tonosho.

▶▶ Yashima and Shikoku Mura   155D3

Yashima station is 20 minutes by train on the JR line east of Takamatsu station. On the hill outside the station is **Shikoku Mura▶▶▶** (*Open* 8.30–5, Apr–Oct; 8.30–4.30, rest of year), an exceptionally good open-air museum, exhibiting a collection of reconstructed Shikoku architecture brought from all over the island. Included in the display are thatched-roof farms and fishermen's houses dating from the Edo period, an open-air *kabuki* theatre, a sugar mill, a tea house, a paper-maker's hut, and a suspension bridge made of vines, a feature once common across the many rivers, valleys, and gorges of Shikoku. Near the entrance to the 'village' are two restaurants, one of which is designed as a traditional farmhouse and sells good *udon* noodle dishes.

Yashima was formerly an island, but is now a headland connected to the Shikoku mainland. Its summit plateau is the site of the 12th-century battle in which the rival Taira and Minamoto clans fought for the supremacy of all Japan. The Minamoto family won and went on to establish the country's first shogunate in Kamakura. **Yashimaji Temple▶▶**, the 84th of Shikoku's 88 temples, on the southern ridge of the plateau, close to the cable car, houses a collection of relics of the land and naval battles fought by the two opposing clans. It was originally constructed in 754. Views from the top of the hill are extensive.

YASHIMA AND MINAMOTO

In 1182 Taira Munemori, third son of the then head of the Taira clan, was pursued out of Kyoto by warriors of the Minamoto clan. Among his party was Emperor Antoku, son of Munemori's sister. They fled to Yashima and there enlisted the aid of clan chiefs from Shikoku. With new forces they moved their headquarters back to Kobe on the Honshu mainland, but were defeated again by Minamoto forces and fled back to Yashima. It was here, in 1185, that the Taira clan was finally destroyed by its old foes, easing the way for Minamoto Yoritomo to unite Japan under his command and become the country's first shogun.

Cleaning the nets, Shodo-shima

The pilgrimage around the 88 temples of Shikoku is the most famous of the Japanese Buddhist temple pilgrimages. It is part of a tradition of religious discipline that has a long history in Japanese Buddhism. The journey is undertaken on foot, and pilgrims dress in white breeches and jackets, straw sandals, and straw hats. They carry no money and depend on charity for all their needs.

NAKED FESTIVAL
Every year, on the Saturday closest to 20 January, the *Hadaka Matsuri*, or 'Naked Festival', is held at Zentsuji Temple, the 75th temple on the route and the site of Kobo Daishi's birthplace. In the bitter cold, hundreds of young men dressed only in white loin cloths (nakedness symbolizing innocence and white cloth purity), fight over two 'good luck sticks' blessed and tossed into the crowd by the abbot of the temple. The winners, known as the 'fortunate men', carry good luck with them throughout the following year. Zentsuji is 20 minutes' walk from JR Zentsuji station, which is 40 minutes from Takamatsu on the JR Dosan line.

Most pilgrimages are connected with Kannon, the Goddess of Mercy, who is regarded as the deity of the common people, but the Shikoku route is inspired by the Shingon patriarch, Kobo Daishi (see page 178). The journey does, however, attract Buddhists of all sects.

The pilgrims' route The 88 temples are visited along a 1,450km (960-mile) route, taking between 40 and 60 days on foot. Nowadays most people travel by bus or taxi and wear everyday clothes, with perhaps just a white scarf to indicate their purpose. This is not surprising, since the walk is long and arduous and Shikoku is an island of high mountains, deep valleys and a rugged coastline. If you wish to follow some or all of the route, problems increase, since maps and instructions are essential and all those available are published only in Japanese. Traditionally, there are two pilgrim seasons: spring and autumn. At the respective equinoxes, pilgrims are presented with gifts and goods by people living near the temple where they are spending the night. Generally, lodgings are available in and around all the temples.

Best foot forward on the pilgrims' route

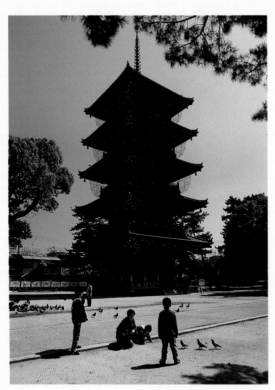

ORIGIN OF THE PILGRIMAGE

In the spring of 835, Kobo Daishi (*Daishi*, or 'Great Master', is a title given by the imperial court to the most accomplished Buddhist priests) announced that he would die on 22 April of that year. He bade farewell to the ruling emperor and the two retired emperors, appointed successors to maintain his spiritual legacy, made a will, and then retired to a monastery on Mount Koya, south of Osaka, where his tomb had been prepared. He died on the predicted day, and soon after his death many disciples began the pilgrimage to places on Shikoku associated with his name, as a mark of their commitment to the spiritual path he had established.

185

A four-temple alternative To give some idea of the variety of style and location of the 88 temples, it is possible to reach four temples by bus from Kochi. The same bus connects all four or you may walk between them.

Hotsumisakiji Temple (24), Murotomisaki-cho, Muroto City, takes two hours by bus from Kochi City and 40 minutes on foot from the bus stop. Located at the cliff top, Cape Muroto, it is often called the Mecca of the pilgrims. The temple's local name is Higashi-dera, or 'East Temple'.

Shinshoji Temple (25), Murozusakai, Muroto City, is one hour and 50 minutes by bus from Kochi City and then 10 minutes on foot. Called Tsuji by locals, Shinshoji Temple is known for its image of Jizo, guardian deity of children. It is also popular with those making a living from the sea.

Kongochoji Temple (26), Moto, Muroto City, takes one hour and 40 minutes by bus from Kochi City. Found at the top of Cape Gyodo, its local name is Nishi-dera ('West Temple'). The treasure house contains important Shingon artefacts, and there is a whale museum in the temple grounds.

Konomineji Temple (27), Tonohama, Yasuda-cho, is one hour and 20 minutes by bus from the JR Gomen station, 15 minutes from Kochi station on the JR Dosan line. Once considered to be one of the five temples most difficult to reach, it is now accessible by road. The temple's principal deity is the 11-faced image of Kanzeon.

For more information, visit Kochi tourist information office, just outside Kochi station exit. All buses for these temples travel in the Muroto direction.

Feeding the birds at Zentsuji Temple

Kyushu and Okinawa

HONSHŪ

Yamaguchi
Mine
Kure
Iwakuni
Tokuyama
Shimonoseki
Hōfu
Kudamatsu
Ube
Hikari
Yanai
Kanda
Suō-nada
Setonaikai
Yukuhashi
Matsuyama
Kunimi
Buzen
Nakatsu
Iyo-nada
Usa
721m
Kunisaki
Aso-Kuju
Kunisaki-
National Park
hantō
Yawatahama
Ōzu
Hiji
Kitsuki
SHIKOKU
Hita
Beppu
Beppu-wan
Sada-misaki
Yufuin
Uwa-kai
Kusu
Yufu-dake
Ōita
Saganoseki
Uwajima
Ogumi
Usuki
Aso-Kuju 1791m
National Kuju-san
Tsukumi
Aso ●Park
Ono-gawa
Taketa
Mie
Saiki
Tsurumi-
1592m
1756m
saki
Aso-san
Sobo-san
Takamori
Takachiho
Kobe, Ōsaka,
Tokyo
Gokase-gawa
Nobeoka
1739m
Hyūga
Mimi-gawa
Kawasaki, Ōsaka
ŪSHŪ
1721m
Omaru-gawa
Saito
Takanabe
Kobayashi
Sadowara
Hyūga-nada
Oyodo-gawa
Miyazaki
Miyakonojō
Nichinan
Shibushi
Kushima
Koyama
Shibushi-wan
Toi-misaki

Hoyo-kaikyō
Bungo-suidō
Kyūshū-sanchi

| 0 | 20 | 40 | 60 | 80 | 100 km |
| 0 | | 20 | | 40 | 60 miles |

kaikyō   D   E

Kyushu and Okinawa

THE BOMB
Kumamoto is said to
have been the original
target of the atomic bomb
later dropped by the US
Airforce on Hiroshima.
On the day of the flight,
Kumamoto was covered
in cloud and the bombers
passed it by. A peace
pagoda, donated by the
Indian government, has
been erected in memory
of the event on a hill
overlooking the city.

188

*Kagoshima port, on
Kyushu Island*

KYUSHU AND OKINAWA The most southerly and third
largest of the four main islands of Japan, Kyushu is
separated from the main island, Honshu, by the 2km (1.2-
mile) wide Kammon Strait. Rail and car tunnels connect
the two islands. Four great volcanic ranges cross the
island from north to south.

Okinawa is the largest and most developed island of the
Ryukyu archipelago, a group of subtropical islands
stretching south from Kyushu through the Pacific and
East China Sea, almost to the tip of Taiwan.

FOREIGN INFLUENCES Due to its geographical position,
Kyushu became a stage post for the transmission to Japan
of Korean and Chinese cultural ideas, influences that
significantly shaped the development of early Japanese
civilization. The first European explorers, traders and
missionaries to Japan also arrived via this island, and its
people are traditionally less xenophobic and easier to get
to know than their northern cousins.

Kyushu is mountainous and volcanic. The mountain
ranges contain many peaks more than 1,525m (5,000ft) and
the caldera in Aso-Kuju National Park, with the active
volcano, Mount Nakadake, at its heart, is the largest in the
world. There are hot-spring resorts on the island, and the
spas of Kyushu are popular with Japanese tourists.

FUKUOKA A modern, commercial city, Fukuoka is the
gateway to Kyushu and a good base from which to explore
the island. The rewards of the economic success of Japan
have been put to unusually good use in this city. Stylish
modern architectural developments and a state-of-the-art
subway system have been happily married to older dock-
land, residential and parkland areas. There is also a
thriving night and street life. The Kyushu Shinkansen, a
249km (155-mile) high-speed rail link between Fukuoka
and Kagoshima (see page 198) is currently being built. The
section between Kagoshima and Yatsushiro is now open.

KUMAMOTO Kyushu's third-largest city is at the heart of the island both geographically and administratively and was once important as the southwestern headquarters of the Tokugawa shogunate. You can base yourself there as an alternative to Fukuoka. Kumamoto lies at one end of the scenic Yamanami Highway, which splits Kyushu in two.

NAGASAKI This lovely cosmopolitan town was the first Japanese port to establish trading contacts with foreign countries, and during the 220 years of Japanese seclusion from the rest of the world one tiny island in Nagasaki Bay was allowed to continue as a trading post. Ironically, given its history of communication with the West, Nagasaki was the second target, after Hiroshima, for atomic bombing.

OKINAWA The climate of the Ryukyu archipelago group of Japanese islands is subtropical and luxurious plants and fruits thrive all year round. Many of the islands are surrounded by coral reefs and fringed by sandy beaches. Okinawa, in Okinawa prefecture, is the largest and by far the most heavily developed island of the group and the one most popular with mainland Japanese visitors, who go not only for the sun, sea and nightlife, but for Okinawan arts, crafts and customs, all of which are markedly different from their own. Okinawa is also the focal point for a network of inter-island ferries that make even remote and barely inhabited islands accessible. US forces occupied the island until 1972, when it was handed back to the Japanese. It is still the site of several US military bases.

Dragons and lions adorn the ancient city in Naha, Okinawa

OKINAWAN TRADITIONS
Okinawan culture has survived the influence of mainland Japan, especially on the more remote of the surrounding islands and in small towns and villages. Festivals of folk dancing and music, contests such as tug-of-war and boat races, and various craft exhibitions are popular forms of local entertainment. Often based on ancient Shinto ceremonies, they provide a happy mix of noisy religious ritual and other, more earthly pursuits.

THE EIGHT HELLS
Beppu's most popular attractions are eight hot springs known as Jigoku (Hell Pools), in which the waters reach boiling point. Each pool has a particular characteristic, for example, Chino-ike Jigoku (Blood Pond Hell) runs blood red as a result of dissolved clay. The Eight Hells are a year-round attraction and are almost always crowded. Regular sightseeing bus tours taking in the pools and other major sights run from Kitahama bus station, just east of Beppu JR station. The Beppu city information office, in Beppu JR station, has maps and leaflets in English.

OLD AND FANTASTICAL BATHS
One of the oldest baths in Beppu is the Takegawa bath house, built in 1879, with an interior reminiscent of an old, well-used boxing gym. Takegawa is best known for its sand baths, where attendants bury you in hot, black sand up to the neck and leave you to sweat for 10 minutes. Afterwards there is plenty of hot water to wash it all off. The most fantastical baths are in Suginoi Palace, adjoining the Suginoi Hotel. Two aircraft-hangar-size baths provide every variety of hot-spring and other bathing experience (including a coffee bath for improving the complexion). One bath is for men, the other for women, and as each one is different, the facilities are alternated each day.

▶▶▶ **Aso-Kuju National Park**   *187D4*

Aso-Kuju National Park lies in the heart of Kyushu between Beppu and Kumamoto, and it is best to plan a trip there in conjunction with a visit to one or both of these towns. Mount Aso (*Aso-san*) is a joint name for five volcanic peaks, all sitting in the world's largest crater basin (technically a caldera). The most central peak, Nakadake, is a very active volcano. There is a cable-car service to the rim of its crater, where you can catch glimpses, through the rising steam, of the green lake at its bottom, smell the lake's sulphurous fumes and sometimes even hear the mountain's portentous volcanic rumblings. On a clear day, the outer rim of the Aso caldera, 128km (80 miles) in circumference, is also visible. The floor of the caldera, 125m (410ft) deep at its lowest point, is undulating grassy meadowland, a rare landscape feature in Japan. Grazing cows and horses bear *kanji* (ideogram) brand marks.

From Kumamoto there is a regular service on the JR Hohi line to Aso town (one hour). Aso itself is not a place of great interest, but from just outside the JR station there is a frequent bus service to the Aso-san Nishi ropeway (cable car) station (40 minutes). From Kumamoto there is also a direct bus service to the Nishi ropeway station (one hour, 30 minutes). If the volcano is too active, the cable car does not operate, and the road and rail links may even be closed. This is unusual, but you may wish to check with your hotel or local tourist office before leaving for Aso.

The journey to Mount Aso from Kumamoto is itself interesting, passing through areas of traditional farmland neatly planted with crops of rice, tobacco and bamboo. Within the park, the designated sights have not been sensitively developed (the power of Nakadake overwhelms most human interference) and are usually crowded, but outside these areas, particularly in the southwest around Takamori, there are delightful old-fashioned, rustic hot-spring *minshuku*, inns and hotels. Takamori is 30 minutes by train, or 40 minutes by bus from Tateno (which is between Aso and Kumamoto). Takamori is connected to Takachiko, another small *onsen* (hot-spring town), by a very scenic bus route along back roads (one hour, 30 minutes).

►► Beppu

187D4

Set on the east coast of Kyushu, Beppu is Japan's most popular hot-spring resort. With more than 3,000 hot springs, Beppu can accommodate the 12 million or so tourists who visit the resort each year to relax in the waters of the public bath houses, or in the private baths of their hotel, inn, or *ryokan*. Baths in mineral-rich waters, mud and sand as well as steam rooms, outdoor pools, saunas and virtually any other form you can imagine, are all available in Beppu. Many of the hot springs are said to have healing properties, and the University of Kyoto runs an institute there to study the therapeutic benefits of mineral baths. In contrast, the town itself is an unattractive place of souvenir shops, garish signs, pinball arcades, neon lights and amusement parlours. The only way to enjoy Beppu is to enter into the unsophisticated spirit of it; the town may be gaudy, but its position on Beppu Bay, with the sea on one side and mountains behind it, is glorious.

Beppu is connected to Kumamoto by the JR Hohi line (three hours) and to Hakata station in Fukuoka by the Nichirin limited express train (two hours, 30 minutes). Bus services also operate between Beppu and Kumamoto (via Aso on some journeys) along the Trans-Kyushu Highway (three hours, 55 minutes).

Mount Naka trail

191

YUFUIN SPA TOWN

Yufuin is a quiet, rural and elegant spa town, one hour by bus from Beppu. It sits on a highland plateau and contains delightful, traditional Japanese inns and *minshuku*, as well as a thatched-roof public bath house.

NAKADAKE TRAIL ROUTE

From the cable-car terminus on the rim of Nakadake there is a path up to the highest point of the mountain. From here, a trail leads to Mount Taka, then on to Sensui-kyo, a volcanic gorge, and finally to Miyaji JR station, one stop down the line from Aso station. The route takes from five to six hours and covers some rough ground. Few people follow it, but the views are exhilarating.

Coastal Beppu

SHOPPING IN FUKUOKA

Fukuoka's best-known local products are silk textiles (*Hakata-ori*), Hakata dolls and kimono sashes (*Hakata-obi*). Hakata silk is not as smooth as most Japanese silk, and it is this slight roughness in texture for which it is valued. *Hakata-obi* are woven from local silk, and Hakata dolls are made from fired clay and then hand-painted. Their trademarks are bright paint, characteristic expressions and depiction of geisha, women and young girls. The Iwataya department store, in the Tenjin district, stocks a wide selection of local products.

▶ ▶ ▶ Fukuoka-Hakata   186C4

Fukuoka is the largest city on Kyushu Island and Kyushu's gateway to the rest of Japan. Fukuoka and the port of Hakata, now connected, were once separate cities, hence the confusion between the two names that sometimes arises in train timetables and maps.

This is a modern, commercial city, a good starting point and base for exploring the island. The people here (and in Kyushu generally) are said to be straightforward and warm-hearted; they certainly retain a friendliness to foreigners, perhaps lost in the more cosmopolitan cities of Tokyo and Osaka.

The bullet train terminates at Hakata (Fukuoka) station. Journey times from Tokyo and Osaka are six hours, 10 minutes and three hours, 20 minutes, respectively. By air to Fukuoka Airport, the only international airport in Kyushu, travel times are reduced to one hour, 40 minutes and one hour, five minutes, respectively. If you have the time, the train journey is an interesting way of seeing the area. All the main cities in Kyushu are connected to Fukuoka by train and bus.

There are two subway lines in the city. Line 1 links Hakata station to Tenjin, a major dining, shopping and nightlife area, and to Ohori Park, the attractive city park surrounding Fukuoka Castle. Buses and tour buses leave from the Kotsu bus station opposite Hakata station and the Tenjin bus station near the subway stop. There is a tourist information office in Hakata station, where English is spoken and good maps of the city and surrounding area are provided.

Fukuoka is well known for its tented **food carts▶ ▶** that illuminate and line the streets at night. Under canvas, customers squash onto a bench seat in front of a low counter, while the cook prepares local delicacies on a mobile gas range and serves beer and sake (hot in the winter months). Shunko-bashi Street, at the southern end of Nakasu-kawa-bata (subway line 1) is the best-known place for outdoor eating carts.

A tented food cart dishes out the goods in Fukuoka

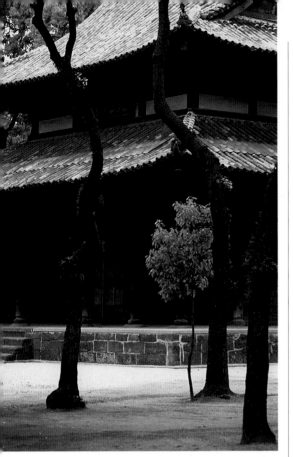

Shofukuji Temple, the oldest Zen temple in Japan, once the monastic home of Sengai Gibon, the famous ink painter

193

SENGAI, SHOFUKUJI ABBOT
Sengai Gibon (1750–1837), one of Japan's most famous ink painters and calligraphers, was a Zen monk, having become a novice at the age of 11. His final formal position as a monk was as abbot of Shofukuji Temple in Fukuoka. Sengai retired in 1811, aged 61, and devoted the rest of his life to his work, which is renowned for its spontaneity and light-heartedness. A large collection of his art is on display in the Idemitsu Art Museum, Tokyo (see page 55).

Fukuoka Castle and Ohori Park►►, 20 minutes by subway from Hakata station, provide an oasis of greenery for city residents. Only a few gates and a simple turret remain of the castle, but its position on a high hill commands a view of Fukuoka in every direction. The park was originally part of the castle's outer defences and some of it has been planted over the site of the old moat. In the middle is a large pond surrounded by willow and azalea trees. More than 2,500 cherry trees grow here and in early April the park is well-loved for raucous cherry blossom viewing parties. Facing the lake to the southeast of the park is the Fukuoka City Art Museum (*Open* 9.30–5.30; *closed* Mon), containing a collection of modern and Buddhist Japanese art and tea-ceremony utensils.

Shofukuji Temple►► is believed to be the oldest Zen temple in Japan. It was founded in 1195 by the priest Eisai, who went on to establish many other important Rinzai sect Zen temples in Kyoto and Kamakura. Eisai spent four years in China and returned not only with Zen Buddhism (known as Chan in China), but with the seeds of the country's first tea plants. The temple itself now seems rather neglected, although the bronze bell in the belfry is designated an important cultural property. However, to anyone interested in Zen it is an important shrine. Shofukuji is 15 minutes' walk from Hakata station and easy to find with a city map.

EXAMINATION SHRINE
Temmangu Shrine in Dazaifu, the ancient capital of Kyushu and within easy reach of Fukuoka, is dedicated to the god of scholarship. High-school students sitting the tough college entrance examinations come here in droves to pray for help, and local restaurants sell good-luck noodle dishes. The grounds of the shrine, planted with many cedar trees, are spacious and worthy of a long stroll. Dazaifu is 30 minutes by train from Nishitetsu Fukuoka station in Tenjin.

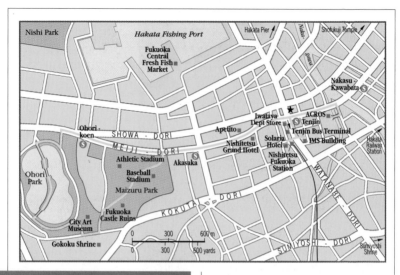

Walk

Fukuoka

Distance: 3km (2 miles); time: about one hour, 30 minutes.
This walk leads through Fukuoka's busy downtown shopping area, then follows the route of the old castle

moat to Ohori Park and the castle remains.

Start at the **Tenjin Iwataya department store▶▶**, which is above the Tenjin subway station. There is an especially good food hall in the basement and there are occasionally cultural exhibitions on upper floors. From here, walk south past the bus terminal, with the **Solaria Hotel Building▶** on your right, a recently constructed modern hotel built around a central well, with glass-walled elevators. There is a sports facility and swimming pool open to nonresidents, as well as boutiques, restaurants, three cinemas, an exhibition space and an arena with fountains. On the opposite side of the street is the **Intermedia Station (IMS)▶▶**, a new, open-plan example of modern Japanese architecture. IMS contains many shops, restaurants, galleries, a car and motorcycle showroom with the latest models, a music store and, on the eighth floor (the Rainbow Plaza), a free library with newspapers, videos and an information desk (at which English is spoken).

From Intermedia Station, walk north to **ACROS (Asian Crossroads Over The Sea)▶▶**, a vast building with four basement floors and 14 floors above ground devoted to all things Asian, including cultural events, conventions, company

The Intermedia Station: outside…

...and inside, with its dazzling galleries, stores and showrooms

offices, restaurants and films. Walking west to Fukuoka Castle, you will pass the **Nishitetsu Grand Hotel**▶ on your left, where there is a reasonably priced piano bar with views over the city, and the **Apetito**▶▶, a Western bakery and restaurant, on your right.

Continue to Ohori Park, passing the moat of the old castle. Inside the park, there is a **coffee shop**▶▶ with a terrace overlooking the lake and distant mountains. After a rest, visit the remains of **Fukuoka Castle** (see page 193 for information on the castle and park), which has good views over the city from its highest point.

POTTERY PRISON

Okawachi-yama village, a short bus or cab ride from Imari, was both home and prison for the many Korean potters brought here by the Nabeshima *daimyo*. A reconstruction of a porcelain factory here illustrates the conditions in which they worked out their lives. Okawachi-yama is still a functioning pottery village with 20 kilns in operation, and its narrow streets are crammed with shops and studios. Maps and information are available from the community showroom (*tenjikan*).

196

Hard at work in the Kyushu Ceramic Museum

Excursion

▶▶ The Saga pottery towns   186B4

Saga prefecture, in northwest Kyushu, is one of Japan's most important areas for the production of traditional porcelain and pottery. The two best-known kiln sites are Karatsu and Arita, each of which has given its name to a particular ceramic style. Imari, the port town from which all Saga ceramics have been shipped to the rest of Japan, has benefited by association, and Imari-yaki is also a famous name in Japanese porcelain.

Until the 17th century, the Japanese imported porcelain from China and Korea. Saga, which lies only 250km (156 miles) from the Korean Peninsula, was a base for Japanese invasions of Korea, and many potters from that country were brought back there as captives and obliged to teach their techniques to the Japanese. One of their number, Ri Sanpei, discovered kaolin, the raw material of porcelain production, near present-day Arita in 1616. The Nabeshima family, the local ruling clan, ensured that the Saga district retained a monopoly on porcelain by keeping their Korean artisans under close guard.

Nearby, Karatsu also benefited from Korean know-how, and the town's elegant stone pottery, much influenced by Korean Yi dynasty ware, is highly valued, especially by devotees of the tea ceremony.

The suggested itinerary for this excursion is Fukuoka–Karatsu–Imari–Arita–Fukuoka. To visit all three places in one day, you will need to use cabs to travel from Imari to Okawachi-yama (see panel), from there to Arita, and for travel around Arita itself. Each of the towns has a tourist office in or near the station.

Karatsu Depart from Hakata station, Fukuoka, initially by subway line 1 to Mei Hama, and then on the JR Chikuhi

*Finished ceramics
on display*

JAPANESE CERAMICS
The Japanese ceramic
aesthetic is nothing, if
not sublime. The earliest
ceramics date back to
the beginning of the
13th century with the
introduction of Chinese
techniques. The develop-
ment of a true Japanese
style, with its freedom,
simplicity, and conscious,
gentle irregularity of design
and manufacture, was
catalyzed 300 years later
by the popularity of the
tea ceremony.

197

line (one hour, 20 minutes in all). Karatsu, in northwest
Saga, was for many centuries an important focus of trade
and commerce with China and Korea. It remains a relatively busy fishing port, but is best known as a summer
beach resort. For pottery fans, two local kilns are particularly worth visiting. **Nakazato Taroemon kiln▶▶** (*Open*
8.30–5.30), a 10-minute walk or a short cab ride from
Karatsu station, has been with the same family for 13
generations. When the immediate past master, Nakazato
Muan, was still alive he was designated a 'Living
National Treasure' for his artistry. There is a gallery
exhibiting work for sale by the present master, Muan's
son, and apprentices, and an area where visitors may
watch potters at the wheel.

   Ryuta-gama kiln▶▶ (*Open* 8.30–5.30), a 15-minute cab
ride from Karatsu station, is run by Nakazato Takashi,
one of the younger sons of Nakazato Muan. The Ryuta-
gama kiln incorporates a gallery, workshop and potter's
house. The work here demonstrates the best of traditional
techniques as well as a freedom of spirit. Imari is one hour
by JR Chikuhi line or by bus from Karatsu.

Arita Reached by train (20 minutes), or bus (40 minutes)
from Imari, or by cab (20 minutes) from Okawachi-yama
(see panel), Arita is the birthplace of Japanese porcelain.
Over 150 kilns still operate in and around the town. The
Kyushu Ceramic Museum▶▶ (*Open* 9–4.30; *closed* Mon), a
short walk (10 minutes) from Arita station, gives a good,
clear introduction to the development and various characteristics of particular Arita kilns, as well as to the
ceramic art of Kyushu as a whole. The **Ceramic Art
Museum▶**, 15 minutes' walk from Kami-Arita station
(three minutes by train from Arita station), exhibits a
collection of Arita porcelain dating from the 17th century
to the present day. The nearby **Izumiyama Jisekiba▶▶**,
the quarry discovered by Ri Sanpei, is still open, with a
working kiln museum alongside.

ARITA PORCELAIN
The first porcelain
products made in Arita
were influenced by Korean,
and later Chinese designs,
but in the 1640s the
Japanese potter Sakaida
Kakiemon (1596–1666)
introduced Japanese
motifs and a technique of
overglaze decoration. His
own trademark hue was
persimmon red but as
his methods inspired his
contemporaries, Arita ware
came to be associated
with bright pieces
decorated in patterns and
influenced by Japanese
textiles, especially those
incorporating birds and
flowers. The fine clay and
translucent glazes that
typify Arita ware came to
the notice of the West
and, following its acclaim
at the Philadelphia
Exhibition in 1876,
became much valued by
collectors.

TATSUDA SHIZEN PARK
This natural park (as opposed to a formal landscaped park, such as Suizenji Park) in Kumamoto contains the burial temple of the Hosokawa family, who took control of the district from the Kato clan, as well as the grave of Hosokawa Gracia (1563–1600), one of Japan's most famous female converts to Catholicism. Gracia was killed by order of her husband to ensure her freedom from capture by his enemies. Mariko, the heroine in James Clavell's book *Shogun*, was based on her. The park is a 15-minute cab ride from the city.

Pruned trees, shaped bushes and a traditional stone bridge in Suizenji Park, a strolling garden constructed in the 17th century

▶ Kagoshima 186C2

This small, modern but relaxed city at the southern tip of Kyushu is a terminus for trains and national highways, and a main port for boats to Okinawa and other islands of the Ryukyu group. Mount Sakurajima, across the Kinko Bay from Kagoshima, is an active volcano that occasionally showers the city with black ash. Its last big eruption in 1914 generated enough lava flow to form the land bridge that now connects Sakurajima to the mainland. Kagoshima boasts no particular tourist attractions but it is off the beaten track and has a distinguished, cosmopolitan history. The three-hour train trip from Kumamoto passes through picturesque mountain and coastal terrain. JR Nishi Kagoshima station is a short walk from the city; the local tourist office is next to it.

▶▶▶ Kumamoto 186C3

Kumamoto was badly damaged during World War II but the modern city, with its many tree-lined avenues and open spaces and a convenient cable-car network, has developed its own character. This was once a nationally important political hub and castle town, and retains the strong sense of identity and independence such power brings. The city's main attractions are the castle and the landscaped gardens of Suizenji Park, both dating from the early 17th century. During this time the city was chosen as the site of the southwestern headquarters of the Tokugawa shogunate. Despite its loss of national influence, Kumamoto remains at the geographical and administrative heart of Kyushu and provides a good alternative to Fukuoka as a touring base for the island. Kumamoto is one hour, 30 minutes from Hakata station, Fukuoka, on the JR Kagoshima line. Within the city, there are two cable-car lines that connect all the main places of interest. The tourist information office is in a booth in front of the JR station entrance.

Mount Sakurajima

KAGOSHIMA AND THE MEIJI RESTORATION
For almost 800 years from the late 12th century, Kagoshima was the feudal seat of the Shimazu family. In 1868, the Shimazu, with the samurai chief Saigo Takamori at their head, rebelled against the shogunate. Saigo negotiated the surrender of the shogun's army and was treated as a national hero. But he wanted to end all foreign influence and provoked a further revolt, this time against the Meiji government that he had helped to establish. After this uprising was suppressed, he committed *seppuku* in Kagoshima, in 1877.

BEST BUYS
Kumamoto is famous for its *higo zogan* products, in which gold and silver are inlaid on black iron. *Obake no kinta*, a toy ghost, is another local product. Goods are sold at the crafts building, next to the Kumamoto Castle Hotel, 3-35 Chiga-jo, Kumamoto (*Open* Tue–Sun 9–5).

Shrine offerings at Kumamoto Castle

Kumamoto Castle►►► (*Open* 8.30–5.30, Oct–Mar until 4.30pm), right in the heart of Kumamoto, was burned down in 1877 after a long siege, but the reconstruction (unlike other examples) has been well managed, and walking around the castle gives visitors a real sense of its former magnificence. The original fortress was built in 1607 by Kiyomasa Kato, feudal lord of the prefecture and a recognized master of castle architecture. It was originally constructed with 49 watchtowers (11 survive), 29 castle gates and remarkable concave defensive walls (fitted with overhanging eaves and missile-dropping openings), which rendered conventional siege tactics almost useless. Nowadays, there are two main entrances to the castle, the most impressive being the southwest. From the top of the castle, there is a magnificent view of Kumamoto and Mount Nakadake smoking in the distance. A museum within the walls exhibits relics of the castle's military past.

Suizenji Park►►► was constructed in 1632 as part of the villa grounds of the Hosokawa clan. It is designed as a miniature version of the old Tokaido highway, between Kyoto and Edo. Generations of gardeners have created a completely artificial landscape here from a natural habitat. Each pruned tree, hill, patch of water, or stone has been designed or chosen to represent a natural feature along the Tokaido. A tea house with *tatami* (straw floor mats) and fine views is near to the pond. To reach Suizenji Park, catch cable car 2 or 3 from outside the castle to Suizenji-koen-mae stop.

Much of the history of Japan is a history of war-fare. Over the centuries powerful landowners, warriors and clerics fought to control the rich rice-producing regions that would in turn give them political control of the country. The earliest types of castles (shiro) were built mainly from wood and earth, and during the Sengoku Jidai, *the Age of the Country at War (1490–1600), large numbers of castles were built by* daimyo *to protect their domains from enemy attack.*

THE WOODEN WARRIORS
During the 14th century, Kusunoki Masashige defended Chihaya Castle against large numbers of Hojo samurai. He put life-sized dummies in armour behind shields near the castle walls. At dawn, the samurai saw what they thought was the defenders fleeing, and they attacked. As they drew close, hidden archers opened fire and dropped rocks from the walls, injuring or killing more than 800 of the attackers.

*Above: detail of Himeji Castle
Below: Kumamoto Castle*

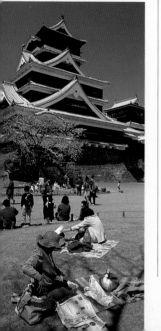

Early construction Building techniques were originally quite simple. Large wooden posts were driven into the earth at intervals of one *ken* (2km/1.25 miles). Between the large posts a framework of lighter bamboo poles was inserted, to which bundles of bamboos and reeds were tied. The walls were then coated with a mixture of red clay and stones to give them greater strength. Defensive towers and other buildings were made of wood. Walls built using this kind of wattle-and-daub technique were highly susceptible to weather damage, and a great deal of work was required to maintain the castles ready for battle.

As warfare increased both in intensity and duration during the Sengoku Jidai period, *daimyo* began to build more permanent and more powerful castles. Western techniques of fortification were introduced through the efforts of Portuguese Jesuit missionaries, and *hirajiro* ('castles on the plain') and *hirayamajiro* ('castles on the plateau') made their appearance. Whenever possible, natural features such as rivers, lakes, hills, mountain crags and the sea were incorporated into the fortifications, which in a typical castle would consist of a moat surrounding a number of concentric courts protected by massive stone walls. In the middle, stood a central compound (*honmaru*), within which a large central tower (*tenshu*) was built on a platform of pounded earth covered with huge stones.

Defending castles Attackers faced a formidable number of fortifications and obstacles. Openings (*hazama*) were left in the walls as loopholes through which archers and gunners could shoot down into the ranks of the enemy. Special chambers (*ishiotoshi*) were constructed over the walls with openings in the floors through which large stones or boiling water could be dropped onto the enemy. In some castles, the inner courtyards and buildings were constructed in such a way as to confuse any attackers who might breach the outer walls. By abrupt changes of direction enemy troops were forced into killing grounds, where they could be attacked by archers and gunners firing from strongholds built into the walls.

At the heart of the castle stood the main tower, consisting of a number of floors of decreasing size, with curving roofs and overhanging gables. The *tenshu* was the command post and watch tower from which troops defending the castle would be controlled. When Hideyoshi built his massive castle at Osaka in 1583 as both the seat of his government and as a symbol of his power, the *tenshu* was more than 80km (980ft) high, in blue and gold.

Castle-smashing Hideyoshi, one of the greatest of castle builders, was also a castle destroyer; a reflection of his political savvy. As Hideyoshi increased his power, he sent out 'castle-smashing commissioners' (*shiro wari bugyo*) to destroy the fortifications built by his defeated enemies. This policy was continued by the Tokugawa shogunate after they came to power. They decreed that each *daimyo* could only retain a single castle in his domains; all others had to be demolished. The surviving castles became hubs of trade and industry, and *joku machi* (castle towns) grew up around the castles to supply the *daimyo* and his retainers.

Many surviving castles have been almost completely rebuilt, but some remain in their original state. Probably the most famous of all Japanese castles is Hideoshi's Shirasagi Castle (Castle of the White Crane), in Himeji (see page 162).

THE LAST SIEGE
In 1877, Satsuma samurai under the leadership of Saigo Takamori rose in rebellion against the imperial government of Emperor Meiji. Imperial troops held Kumamotojo Castle against a rebel force three times larger, who attacked the castle with both traditional and modern weapons. In an echo of the past, both attackers and defenders used troops equipped only with swords, who fought man to man on the battlements. Eventually the rebels were defeated and the castle retrieved.

Matsumoto Castle

DUTCH IN NAGASAKI

During the period of Japanese seclusion between 1639 and 1854, the only Westerners allowed by the Japanese to trade with Japan were the Dutch, who were restricted to a small, man-made island called Dejima in Nagasaki port. Only traders and prostitutes were allowed on and off Dejima, which has since been swallowed up in a land reclamation scheme and is marked only by a cable-car stop. There is, however, a reconstruction of the island at the Dejima Historical Museum (cable car 7 to Dejima; *Open* 9–5, *closed* Mon). Oranda-zaka, or Hollander Slope, a cobbled street behind the station, is lined with 19th-century Dutch residents' houses, and Nagasaki Holland Village, an hour by bus from Nagasaki station, is a complete reconstruction of a genuine Dutch village.

▶▶ Miyazaki   187D2

At Miyazaki, the administrative and economic heart of Miyazaki prefecture in southern Kyushu, the climate is subtropical year round. The town's broad avenues are lined with palm trees, lush greenery abounds and flowers are always in bloom. A seaside promenade and a beautiful coastline, designated as the Quasi-National Park, stretch to the south. Miyazaki was once a popular honeymoon destination, but nowadays Japanese couples prefer the more exotic shores of Australia and Hawaii, or the capital cities of Europe. Nevertheless, Miyazaki remains principally a Japanese tourist destination and very few foreigners visit. Nearby Sengai resort is a popular spot, especially the nightly shows at the Ocean Dome.

There are direct trains from Hakata station, Fukuoka (six hours), Beppu (three hours, 45 minutes) and Kagoshima (three hours), and direct flights from Tokyo (one hour, 30 minutes). Tourist offices can be found at the JR station and at the airport.

▶▶ Nagasaki   186B3

Nagasaki, the target of the second atomic bomb dropped by the Allies on Japan in World War II is a city of many particular sights. Its history, coastal location, scenery, old city, foreign quarters and the warm climate, tempered with sea breezes, make it a perfect place for relaxed exploration on foot or by cable car or rickshaw. The city is easy to navigate and many signs are in English.

Nagasaki is two hours by train from Hakata station on the JR Nagasaki line. The railway station is connected to the city by cable car, part of a system that links all the main sights. Most shopping, dining and cultural activities are to be found in the south of the city. North of the city is the Peace Park and to the west Inasayama, a mountain-top park offering splendid views. A tourist information office is outside Nagasaki station.

Glover Garden▶▶ (*Open* 8–6, Mar–Nov; 8.30–5, rest of year) is an open-air museum that displays Western-style

Glover Mansion

NAGASAKI AND THE PORTUGUESE
Francis Xavier was the first missionary to set foot in Japan. He arrived in 1549 and left in 1551, leaving converts to continue his work. By 1579, Japanese Christians included six *daimyo* among their numbers. One of them, Omura Sumitada, ruled a remote area of northwest Kyushu, where the coastline was blessed with a good natural anchorage. Here, with Portuguese help, Omura built the port of Nagasaki, which attracted the majority of Japan-bound Portuguese ships and quickly became a rich melting-pot of Eastern and Western cultures.

Detail, Kofukuji Temple

TOJIN YASHIKA ATO
In 1698, the shogunate ordered all Chinese in Nagasaki to live in a walled compound in the Tojin Hashika Ato quarter, in the southeast, an area evocative of an old Chinatown settlement. Nearby, Shinchi-machi is the present-day Chinatown, an excellent place for Chinese food.

houses built in the 19th-century Meiji period. The main attraction is the oldest Western-style building in Japan, Glover Mansion, built by Scotsman Thomas Glover in 1863, and still much as it was in his day. The park grounds that overlook the city are well maintained and peaceful, if somewhat spoiled by the hillside escalators leading to Glover Mansion. Take cable car 5 to Oura-Tenshudoshita stop to reach the gardens.

The **Kofukuji Temple▶▶▶** (*Open* 8–5.30) is in Teramachi, the Nagasaki temple district, and was an important Obaku-Zen temple in the style of the Chinese Ming dynasty. Kofukuji is a 10-minute walk from the Kokaido-mae cable-car stop. A 20-minute walk south through the Teramachi district leads to **Sofukuji Temple▶▶▶** (*Open* 8–5), the first Obaku-Zen temple in Japan, founded in 1629 by a Chinese monk. Attractive, grassy gardens with tropical palms surround the temple, whose beautiful, red-painted main hall was constructed by Chinese carpenters.

The bomb that the Allies dropped on Nagasaki on 9 August 1945, was three times more powerful than the one that was dropped on Hiroshima, but it missed the main city and fell on a village on the outskirts of town. Even so, more than three-quarters of the population of Nagasaki died (150,000 people). **Peace Park (Heiwa-koen)▶▶▶** was built on a hill near the site of the explosion. A bronze statue stands as a symbol of hope for peace, and several other sculptures have been given by foreign countries. In the International Culture Hall (*Open* 9–6), there is a display of records and relics of the attack. Take cable car 1 or 3 to Matsuyama-cho stop.

Kyushu and Okinawa

BATTLE OF OKINAWA

The final land battle in World War II between Japan and the Allies took place on Okinawa. The American flag was raised on 22 June 1945, after 82 days of fierce fighting. The Japanese commander, General Ushijima, committed suicide, as did many soldiers and civilians. More than 250,000 Japanese died; 12,500 Allied soldiers were killed and 37,000 wounded. Despite such losses, the Japanese on the mainland did not surrender and the US Command decided to drop atomic bombs on Hiroshima and Nagasaki.

204

OKINAWAN SAKE

Okinawan islanders make a variety of very potent sake. Two of the strongest are a sake matured in jars full of garlic cloves, and a concoction known as 'snake juice', matured in a wide-necked jar containing the coiled body of a small, dead, poisonous snake. After 10 years' maturation the flesh is dissolved and only the bones remain.

Iriomote Island

▶▶▶ Okinawa   186A1

Okinawa is the largest island in the Ryukyu archipelago, which stretches south 1,300km (812 miles) from Kyushu through the Pacific and East China Sea, almost to the tip of Taiwan. Like the rest of the Ryukyu group, its culture has been influenced as much by China as by Japan.

Okinawa is a tropical island, warm in any season and scorchingly hot in July and August. The south of Okinawa, particularly around the capital, Naha, is heavily developed and ugly. However, in Naha itself the jumble of hotels, temples, hamburger bars, ice-cream parlours, Shinto shrines, Japanese tourists, strip joints, karate *dojo* (gyms), elderly men and women in kimonos and dense traffic, all fit comfortably together. The city is a great repository of Okinawan culture and has the best of Okinawa drama, dance, music and cuisine.

Much of the north of the island is now also developed, but there are still a few small, traditional fishing and farming villages, surrounded by sugar cane and pineapple fields, and unspoiled beaches (nowadays often annexed by the fancy hotels). Coral-diving and tropical fishing are popular pursuits. Okinawa is also the birthplace of Japanese karate (see pages 206–207). To experience the unique Sino-Japanese lifestyle of this archipelago, you should travel to other islands in the Okinawan prefecture, such as Kumejima, Taketomi and Iriomote. Okinawa is the hub of ferry and air services to these islands.

Getting there There are direct flights and sea ferry services to Okinawa from Tokyo, Osaka and Fukuoka. Flight times from mainland Japan are between one and three hours; the ferry takes more than two days from Tokyo, and more than a day from Fukuoka. Ferries from Okinawa link all the inhabited islands of the Ryukyu group. An air service links the larger islands. Tourist information is available at Naha airport (15 minutes by bus to Naha centre) or Naha bus terminal.

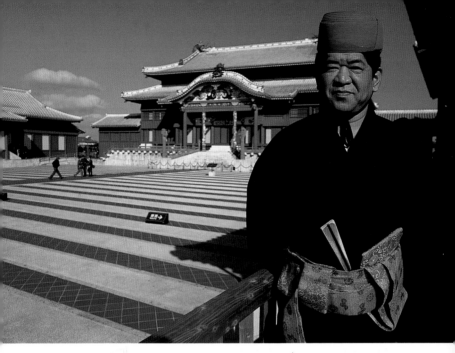

Northern Okinawa The least spoiled part of the island, this is the most satisfying area to explore. Unfortunately, access to the north by public transportation is difficult and services are infrequent.

Hedo Misaki►► is the island's northernmost headland, where a clifftop road affords spectacular views of blue sea and outlying islands. The road circles the headland and passes through the tiny village of Oku, worth visiting for its traditional Okinawan houses. To reach Hedo Misaki take bus 20, 21, or 77 from Naha to Nago (two hours, 20 minutes), bus 67 Nago to Okuma Beach (two hours, 50 minutes), and bus 69 from Okuma to Hedo Misaki-iriguchi. From here, it is a 15-minute walk to the cliff.

Kijoka►►, a traditional village in northern Okinawa, is famous for *bashofu*, a textile similar to linen but made from banana fibre. Take bus 73 or 74 from Nago to Kijoka (one hour).

Southern Okinawa The island's principal craft, fashion shopping and dining thoroughfare is Kokusai-dori, the long main street of **Naha►►**. Along its east side is Heiwa-dori, the middle section of a network of covered alleys and passageways that make up the market district. Selling everything from obscure Okinawan vegetables to baseball caps, this area is the heart of the city.

Shuri, now a district of Naha, was the capital of the Ryukyu dynasty (1429–1879). The once royal city was used by Japanese high command as their headquarters and destroyed by American Forces during World War II in 1945 in the Battle of Okinawa. Parts of the castle, such as some exterior walls and two castle gates, have been restored. *Shurei-mon*, the Gate of Courtesy, a typical example of Okinawan architecture, was restored in 1958 and represents a symbol of the islanders' culture and independence.

Above and below: traditional costume in Shuri

FESTIVALS
Okinawa calendar of events: *Jiriuma* (20 January) a parade of women dressed in bright *bingata* kimono; *Hari* (3 and 4 May) dragon-boat races; *Naha Otsunahiki* (10 October), two 250m (820ft) long fat ropes, one 'male', one 'female', are intertwined, and a tug of war ensues between thousands of people.

Japanese martial arts are now studied worldwide as methods of self-defence, self-discipline and sport. While the classical systems of swordsmanship and related methods attract a devoted following, the systems of judo, kendo, aikido and especially karate are the most popular, and highly skilled non-Japanese teachers and practitioners can be found in countries throughout the world.

206

UECHI-RYU KARATE
One of Okinawa's most popular karate styles, Uechi-Ryu, was developed by Kanbun Uechi (1877–1945). He studied Chinese boxing at the Central Temple in Fukien province, China, where he was a student of Chou Tze-ho. After training with him for 13 years, Kanbun Uechi returned to Japan and became a farmer near Osaka. A young Okinawan persuaded him to start teaching and soon he opened a school. He taught there for 24 years before returning to Okinawa.

Weapons used in Okinawan karate

Okinawan karate origins Karate developed in Okinawa in the 19th century from a fusion of Chinese martial arts, brought by Okinawans from the Fukien province of mainland China, and an indigenous Okinawan system of empty-hand fighting called *te*. *Te* and simple weapon systems using farming and fishing implements were developed in response to a decree by the Chinese invaders of Okinawa that forbade the use by the islanders of swords and other orthodox weapons.

In 1921, Crown Prince Hirohito visited Okinawa and for the first time saw a demonstration of karate by some school children. The demonstration was arranged by Funakoshi Gichin, then the chief instructor of a karate school on the island. It was a great success and Funakoshi went to Tokyo in 1922 to demonstrate his skills. This was the start of karate in Japan and around the world.

Modern karate Karate stresses kicking and punching, although some styles also teach throwing techniques, arm and wrist locks, and the use of traditional Okinawan weapons, such as the *bo* (staff), jointed *nunchaku* (flail), or *tekko* (brass knuckle).

Following the example set by the founders of judo, Funakoshi Gichin and other karate masters wanted karate to be seen as something more than simply a method of fighting. The development of a strong fighting spirit was important, but this had to be accompanied by an equally strong spiritual and moral element to avoid the misuse of the art.

Funakoshi Gichin wrote a code of 20 precepts, among which he said 'Karate begins and ends with courtesy'; 'There is no first attack in karate'; and 'Karate is an auxiliary of justice'. The teachings and methods of the arts of the sword were applied by him to the art of the empty hand; by so doing he hoped that karate would become a means of developing and preserving the samurai spirit.

In the West, karate is most commonly taught as a sport, but the older ideals of self-defence and self-discipline still have many followers.

Other martial arts Judo was described by its founder Kano Jigoro (1860–1938) as 'The Way of Gentleness or of first giving way in order ultimately to gain the victory';

judo today is a competitive sport, in which the aim is to throw or lock an opponent according to strictly defined rules. The martial element has gradually declined because of this stress on judo as a sport, especially since judo became an Olympic event in 1964.

Aikido, 'The Way of Harmony', was created by Ueshiba Morihei (1883–1969). As a young man, Ueshiba studied a number of ju-jitsu systems, as well as swordsmanship and spear-fighting. The techniques of aikido include rapid turning movements, designed to blend with an attacker's movements so as to throw or unbalance him or her. Aikido masters are often compared with the eye of a hurricane: quiet in themselves, but difficult to approach because of the tremendous forces swirling around them.

Kendo, 'The Way of the Sword', is very popular in Japan and has a growing number of followers in the West. Generally, kendo is taught as a sport *cum* combat, in which the practitioners wear protective armour and try to score points on designated targets with a bamboo sword (or *shinai*). Kendo is derived from the older, classical systems of swordsmanship, and kendo practitioners generally regard the sports side of their art as the least important part of the discipline.

Martial artists

EVERYDAY KARATE

Karate on Okinawa is an everyday part of many people's lives. Training sessions do not have the obvious intensity and seriousness evident in Western and mainland Japanese schools. This sometimes disappoints Western visitors, who expect tough training schedules and strict discipline. Okinawan *karate-ka* train steadily, year in, year out, working on form, strength, body conditioning and speed, and developing a style that looks deceptively relaxed.

SAMURAI KENDO

It is common for kendo practitioners also to train in *ken-jutsu*, which involves training with a real blade in techniques designed to dispatch an enemy as quickly and effectively as possible. The methods taught in the older *ken-jutsu* styles are the same techniques as taught to the samurai, and are based on the condi-tions and circum-stances likely to be faced by a samurai on the field of battle.

A karate staff swinging into action

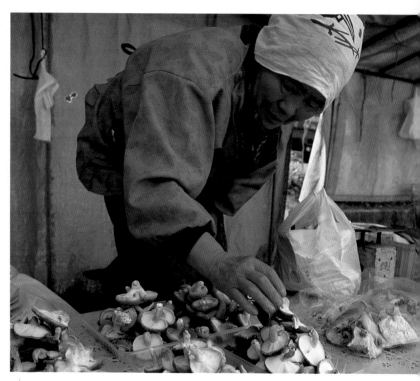

208

Wild mushrooms for sale

HOKKAIDŌ

Hakodate

Ōma
Shimokita-
hantō
Mutsu
Shiriya-zaki

Muroran
Tomakomai

5

Tsugaru kaikyō

Tsugaru-
hantō
Mutsu-wan

Goshogawara
Aomori
Noheji
Ogawara-ko
Misawa
Towada

Henashi-
zaki
Sukayu onsen
Hirosaki
Oirase
keiryu
Towada-ko
Hachinohe

Ōdate
Towada-
Hachimantai
National
Park
Ninohe
Kuji

Noshiro
Yoneshiro-gawa

Nyūdō-
zaki
Goshogake
onsen
Obuke
Fudai

Oga
2041m
Iwate-san
Morioka
Miyako
Rikuchū-

4

Akita
Tazawa-ko
Kakunodate
Ōmagari
Hanamaki
kaigan

Honjō
Yokote
Kitakami
National

Kisakata
Tobi-
shima
Ogachi
Yuzawa
Mizusawa
Kamaishi

Sakata
Ichinoseki
Naruko
Hiraizumi
Ōfunato
Park

Tsuruoka
Shinjō
Kesen'numa

Awa-
shima
3
Dewa Sanzan
1980m
Gas-san
Obanazawa
Furukawa

Bandai-
Asahi
Nat Park
Tendō
Matsushima
Ishinomaki
Ojika-
hantō

Murakami
Yamagata
Sendai
Tomakomai

Iwanuma

Shibata
Yonezawa
Shiroishi

Niitsu
Bandai-Asahi
2128m
Nat Park
Sōma

Kitakata
2035m
Azuma-san
Fukushima
Haramachi

Aizu-
Wakamatsu
Inawashiro-ko
Namie

Kōriyama
Nagoya

Sukagawa

Nikkō
National Park
Shirakawa
Iwaki

Kuroiso
Nakoso

2578m
Nikkō
Yaita
Takahagi

Chūzenji-ko

Utsunomiya
Hitachi

Kiryū
Shimodate
Mito

Oyama

Kumagaya
Tsuchiura
Kasumi-ga-ura

Ageo
Ōmiya
Kawagoe
Koshigaya

TŌKYŌ
Matsudo
Chōshi

Tokyo-
wan
Bōsō-
hantō

KAWASAKI
Chiba

YOKOHAMA

0   50   100 km
0   50 miles

C

D

The Japan Alps town of Takayama (see pages 214–215)

NORTHERN HONSHU The Tohoku region, in northernmost Honshu, has severe winters and a mountainous terrain, and remains one of the areas of Japan least affected by industrialization. The Hide, Kiso and Akaishi ranges of mountains, known together as the Japan Alps, rise in a series of high, jagged snow-capped peaks strung across the middle of the southern end of northern Honshu. They cover a vast area and provide a wide range of hiking, climbing and skiing challenges. Nagano prefecture, within the Japan Alps, was selected to host the 1998 Winter Olympics.

TOHOKU Until the late 19th century, Tohoku was inhabited mostly by nomadic tribes of people known as Ainu. Gradually, Japanese settlers from the south drove the Ainu north to the island of Hokkaido, but the very cold, snowy winters and the distance from Tokyo continued to restrict Tohoku's settlement and commercial development. Even today, the area retains its long-standing traditions of farming and local crafts. It has a relatively rural, untouched air, marred only by some tourist facilities in the most popular national parks and historic towns.

Getting into Tohoku is quick and convenient on the Tohoku Shinkansen (bullet train), but once there and off the beaten track, local train journey times are slow and route-planning more complicated.

The main tourist season is the summer, which tends to be mild and dry; the first ten days of August are particularly busy, with big festivals in Sendai, Akita and Aomori.

SENDAI The largest city in Tohoku, Sendai was flattened in World War II and has since been rebuilt along the lines of most modern Japanese cities, with no exceptional features. It is, however, a reasonably good base from which to explore the rest of Tohoku and especially the

TOHOKU BACK-COUNTRY
Tohoku is the collective name given to the six prefectures of northern Honshu. It was once known by the Japanese as Michinoku, or 'the end of the line'. This image still sticks and, as a consequence, the area is avoided by conventional Japanese visitors, despite the many attractions of the region and the remarkable friendliness of the people.

Yamagata prefecture, a rural district where life is very much in traditional Tohoku style. Sendai is two hours by Tohoku Shinkansen from Tokyo's Ueno station.

JAPAN ALPS Mountains in Japan were once believed to be the sacred dwelling places of divine spirits. Some were climbed, consecrated and made places of religious pilgrimage, but most mountain summits were avoided. However, in 1896 the Reverend Weston, a British missionary and mountaineer, set out to explore the area now known as the Japan Alps, and in the process popularized mountain-climbing in Japan (see panel, page 212). Matsumoto, an old castle town on a high alpine plateau, is the gateway to the Japan Alps and a good base for exploring central Honshu, to the east. Takayama, in the heart of the Hida mountains, is another town worth visiting. Despite its popularity with Japanese visitors who know it as 'little Kyoto', it is not as popular with foreign visitors.

KANAZAWA Although well-liked by the Japanese, Kanazawa is mistakenly neglected by foreigners. Partly an old Japanese castle town, with a thriving reputation as a hub of traditional religions and arts and crafts (especially *noh* theatre), and partly a very modern city with sophisticated shops and nightlife, Kanazawa is of manageable size and is best explored on foot. The city is five hours by train from Tokyo across the Japan Alps.

SADO Off the coast of Niigata prefecture, in the Sea of Japan, Sado Island was once a place of banishment for criminals and those unpopular politically. It is a beautiful island with a slow pace of life, even between May and September, when there is usually a large influx of visitors.

ALPINE TOUR

Tateyama–Kurobe Alpine Route Tour takes a spectacular journey through the mountains using various modes of transportation. Tickets for the whole trip can be bought from Shinano-Omachi train station (one hour from Matsumoto on the JR Oito line), where the tour starts; it ends at Toyama, having proceeded *en route* by bus, cable car, train and foot. The route is open from the end of April to the end of November, but is expensive and busy during holiday periods.

Vegetable handcart, Sado Island

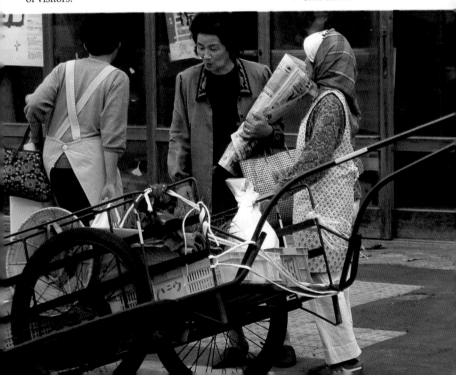

FATHER OF THE MOUNTAINS
The Reverend Walter Weston popularized the term 'Japan Alps' that fellow Englishman William Gowland had coined. Weston's 1896 book *Mountaineering and Exploration in the Japanese Alps* sparked much interest in Japan, and it earned him the title 'Father of Mountaineering'. Until that time the Japanese had seen their mountains as the sacred haunts of gods and spirits. In recognition of his exploration, he was awarded the Order of the Sacred Treasure (Fourth Class) by the emperor and a memorial was erected in his name in Kamikochi.

The Japan Alps

▶▶ Kamikochi   *208B1*

This village, really a collection of inns and lodges, shares its name with the high valley in which it stands. The area provides excellent hiking and climbing, and there are trails and mountain routes for every level of expertise.

Kamikochi is reached via Matsumoto by the private Matsumoto Dentetsu line to Shin Shimashima station (30 minutes) and then by bus (one hour, 20 minutes). The bus route takes a narrow and twisting mountain road and the scenery for the last 30 minutes of the journey is stunning. The road is closed by snow during the long winter months and opens only from the end of April to the beginning of November.

Since hotel development has been limited in Kamikochi, in summer there are few places to stay. Early spring and early October are the best times to visit. Camping and hiking equipment are available to rent and maps, route directions and provisions may be collected from local shops. Mountain huts with comfortable facilities are found along the hiking trails.

▶▶ Matsumoto   *208B1*

Once an important castle town, Matsumoto is now a modern city in an alpine setting on a high plateau near many hot-spring resorts. As one of the gateways to the Alps, and the hub of an excellent communications network, this is a particularly fine base for exploring both the Alps, to the west and north, and central Japan (Chubu district), to the east.

Matsumoto is two hours, 20 minutes by JR Chuo line limited express from Nagoya and two hours, 50 minutes on the same line, but from the opposite direction (Tokyo, Shinjuku station). There is a tourist office at Matsumoto station.

Matsumoto Castle▶▶▶ (*Open* 8.30–5) is one of the oldest, best preserved and most architecturally beautiful

The beautiful Matsumoto Castle

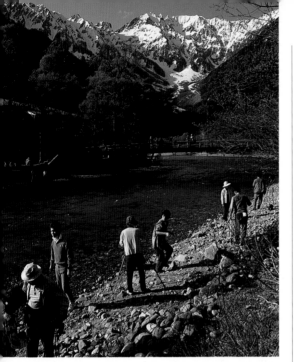

SACRED MOUNTAINS
The habit of leaving
a monetary offering on
mountain peaks is
common throughout
Japan. Many peaks have
religious associations,
and shrines and objects
of veneration may be
encountered (along with
more worldly items such
as vending machines) on
some of the highest
peaks. The first woman
to climb Mount Fuji, in
1867, was Lady Parkes,
the wife of the British
ambassador, who ignored
the taboo that prohibited
women from sacred peaks
(it was believed that the
resident god abhorred
'red pollution', or
menstrual blood).

castles in Japan. Also known as Crow Castle (*Karasu-jo*), because the exterior walls are mainly black, it was begun in 1504, while the impressive six-floor *donjon* was completed in 1597. Climb the *donjon's* narrow, steep wooden staircase for panoramic views of the city. Matsumoto Castle was built for serious combat and its walls are peppered with battlements from which arrows and guns were fired and stones dropped on the attacking forces. To avoid crowds at the castle, go out of season or early in the day. The castle is a 20-minute walk through old Matsumoto, north and east of the railway station; a map is available from the tourist office.

The **Matsumoto Folk Art Museum**▶▶ (*Open* 9–5; *closed* Mon), a 15-minute bus ride from the station to Shimoganai Mingeikan Guchi bus stop, exhibits domestic products of wood, bamboo, glass and porcelain from Japan and other Asian countries.

▶ Nagano   208B1

Nagano prefecture was selected in 1991 to host the 1998 Winter Olympic Games. The resulting construction work included a new Shinkansen (bullet train) line from Tokyo to Nagano, as well as sporting facilities in surrounding alpine towns. Nagano's main attraction, 10 minutes by bus or cab from Nagano station, is the famous **Zenkoji Temple**▶▶▶ (*Open* 5.30–4.30), founded in the seventh century by Yoshimitsu Honda. One of the most important pilgrimage temples in Japan, it is attached to no particular Buddhist sect and is equally accessible to women and men. Millions flock to the Zenkoji Temple every year. The main hall is generally thick with the smoke of incense and the drone of Buddhist chanting. Unusually, in Japan's increasingly secular society, real religious enthusiasm can be experienced here.

KEY TO PARADISE
The object for most
pilgrims visiting Zenkoji
Temple in Nagano is
to touch 'the key to
paradise', and ensure
their salvation. The key
is a specific stone set in
the wall of a tunnel that
runs below the floor of
the main hall. Devout
pilgrims, most of whom
are elderly, wend their
way to the key along a
pitch-black passageway.

Northern Honshu

Thatched farmhouse in Ogimachi

PRAYING ROOFS
The steep roofs of the thatched farmhouses in Shirakawago are designed to prevent a build-up of the snow that blankets the valley throughout the winter. They are described as *gassho-zukuri* meaning 'hands held in prayer'. (See pages 226–227.)

SAKE BREWERIES
The many traditional sake brewers in Takayama old town work from small home breweries, indicated by balls of woven cedar fronds hung from the roof eaves. The fronds are cut at the beginning of the brewing cycle, and by the time the sake is ready to drink have turned from green to brown. Brewers welcome visitors inside to look around, to taste and, if they wish, to buy their sake.

FESTIVAL CARTS
Takayama's famous festivals, the spring Sanno Matsuri (14–15 April) and autumn Yahata Matsuri (9–10 October), feature elaborate and gorgeous floats (*yatai*), which are among the finest in Japan. Four floats designed in the early 19th century are on display at the Takayama Yatai Kaikan, up the street from Yoshijima House (*Open* 8.30–5). The guardian shrine of Takayama, Sakurayama Hachiman-gu, celebrated in the autumn festival, is housed next door.

▶▶▶ Ogimachi   208A1

This village is set in the Shokawa Valley, a two-hour bus ride from Takayama (see below). Surrounded by high mountains, the narrow valley is dotted with thatched *gassho-zukuri* farmhouses (see panel), terraced rice paddies, vegetable gardens and flower beds. About 150 thatched dwellings have been built here, many serving as *minshuku*. The farmhouses were constructed to hold extended families and living space was below, while the upper floor was used for storage and craft work.

Ogimachi is well off the beaten track and a visit is best planned in conjunction with a trip to Takayama. To reach the village, take a bus from Takayama to Makido on the Nohi bus (one hour, 35 minutes) and a bus from Makido to Ogimachi (one hour). Buses are infrequent; plan your trip in advance. There is a tourist office in the village square.

▶▶▶ Takayama   208A1

Takayama is a highland city in the heart of the mountainous Hida district of west central Japan. The city has been modernized but retains a compactness and richness of traditional architecture and culture, earning its nickname 'little Kyoto'. The old town, set around two narrow streets called Sannomachi and Ninomachi, contains many well-preserved old inns, tea houses, shops and merchants houses with the latticed windows and overhanging roofs characteristic of the Edo period.

There is much to see in Takayama, but one of the joys of being here is just to wander around on foot or rented bicycle. The city is laid out in a grid pattern and is easy to negotiate. English-language booklets and maps are available from the tourist office at the station, and there are several bicycle rental shops in the area. The Sannomachi district and most of the best sights are east of the station.

Takayama is two hours, 45 minutes by JR Takayama limited express from Nagoya. The bus journey from Kamikochi (running from May to October) is in two stages: first a bus to Hirayu Onsen (one hour, 15 minutes), then a bus to Takayama (one hour, 10 minutes).

The **Hida Minzoku Mura Folklore Village**▶▶▶ (*Open* 8.30–5) is an open-air museum of old thatched Hida farmhouses that demonstrates how farmers and craft workers would once have lived and worked in this region and gives a vivid account of rural life in medieval Japan. The village is within bus, cycling, or walking distance, west of Takayama station.

One daily **Morning Market (Asa-ichi)**▶▶ (7–noon) is held along the east bank of the Miyagawa River and in front of Takayama Jinya. Vendors sell local produce, flowers and crafts brought in from the surrounding countryside.

Sanmachi Suji▶▶▶ (*Open* 9–5; *closed* Tue and Dec–Feb) was the merchant area during feudal times. Yoshijima House, at the north end of Shimo-Ninomachi Street, was built in 1905 as the fine but rustic home and factory of the well-to-do Yoshijima brewing family. Kusakabe merchant's house, next door, is less rustic and more imposing (same opening hours).

Once the residence of the *daimyo* of Hida, **Takayama Jinya**▶▶▶ (*Open* 8.45–5, Apr–Oct; 8.45–4.30, rest of year), a group of whitewashed buildings, is perhaps the best example of provincial Edo government offices in Japan. They were in use until 1969, and the audience chambers, the interrogation rooms (which contain instruments of torture), the gardens and the rice stores, where the shoganate's rice tax was stockpiled, are open to visitors.

Making rope sandals at the Hida Minzoku Mura Folklore Village

SHORENJI TEMPLE
The Zen Shorenji Temple was transported to Takayama in 1961 from the Shokawa Valley, part of which was flooded to make a reservoir. *Shojin-ryori* (Zen vegetarian food) is served at the temple (*Open* 8–6, Apr–Oct; 8.30–5, rest of year).

215

Takayama's Asa-ichi (morning market)

Map: Nakatsugawa · Eishoji Temple · Toson Memorial Hall · MAGOME · Magome-koge · Kumano Shrine · Toge Chaya Teahouse · Temple · Me-daki · O-daki · Kudaritani · Otsumago · Milestone · Kotokuji Temple · Wakihonjin · Okuya · Nagiso · TSUMAGO

Map not to scale

Walk

Kiso Valley

Distance: 9.3km (6 miles); time: three hours (wear hiking boots in winter). This gentle hike between two post towns in the Kiso Valley follows the Magome Pass, tracing the path of the old Nakasendo Highway, a major route between Edo (Tokyo) and Kyoto during the 18th and early 19th centuries.

To get to Magome, take the Chuo Honsen line from Nagoya to Nakatsugawa station (one hour, 15 minutes). From there, take the bus to Magome (35 minutes). From Tsumago, take a bus to Nagiso station on the Chuo Honsen line and then back to Nagoya or Matsumoto.

Leaving Magome, follow the main street away from the bus station past houses that appear ancient, but which are actually faithful copies of those destroyed by fire at the end of the 19th century. Once clear of the town, walk for 50 minutes along the paved road to the **Magome Pass (Magome-koge)▶▶▶**. Past the Toge Chaya Teahouse, take the path that drops away to the right from the main road. From here, the walk is downhill all the way to Tsumago.

The path leads past a small temple on the left, then, farther along, the site of a guardhouse that controlled the movement of timber from the Kiso Valley and meted out severe punishments to anyone smuggling timber.

After about 45 minutes, having twice crossed the paved road, the path comes to two waterfalls, the **O-daki** and **Me-daki▶▶**, one male, one female. Farther on from these is a marker at a fork in the road, recording the distance in ri (79 *ri* or 320km/200 miles) from the capital, Edo (Tokyo). Take the right fork of the path, and walk for another 30 minutes to reach **Tsumago▶▶▶**.

The second post town from the south on the Nakasendo Highway, Tsumago retains the atmosphere of an Edo-era post town. Its main street, which is lined with dark, wooden, shuttered houses, is particularly evocative. Although it is now enjoying new prosperity as a thriving tourist spot, Tsumago was virtually deserted by the mid-1960s, due both to its position, far away from the main transportation routes, and to the massive migration to the big towns and cities during the post-war years. All of Tsumago's buildings are now under a strict preservation order.

Above and below: views of Tsumago, which still has the air of an old Edo-period town

The Chubu Coast

▶▶▶ Kanazawa 208A1

This important provincial city, bordering the Sea of Japan in the Chubu region, is partly an old castle town and partly a modern city with busy department stores and a thriving nightlife. For those wishing to explore both modern and traditional Japanese cultures and architecture, it is an excellent place to visit. Off the main thoroughfare, which differs little from those of other Japanese cities, there are winding streets, dead-end alleyways and moats designed to confuse would-be attackers of the central castle site, now marked only by its original eastern entrance, the Ishikawa-mon gate. Kanazawa is most easily reached by JR limited express from Kyoto (two hours, 30 minutes) or Nagoya (three hours). Alternatively, if you have visited Ogimachi and do not wish to return to Takayama, you can catch a direct bus to Kanazawa (three hours). There is an information office by the Kanazawa station exit.

The **Eastern Pleasure Quarter▶▶** in the Higashiyama district was set aside in 1820 by the Maeda government as an entertainment area for high-ranking citizens. The most talented and beautiful of 'free' geisha provided evenings of music, dancing, conversation and perhaps other more intimate pleasures. The area is distinguished by a neat row of geisha tea houses, each with a slatted wooden facade and an oblong paper lampshade over its entrance. Rising costs and a demand for sleazier entertainment have reduced business, but some of the old atmosphere can still be experienced along Higashi main street. Shima-ke (*Open* Tue–Sun 9.30–5), the fifth house down the street on the left going east, is an elegant former geisha house open for viewing.

Beneath the castle mound is **Kenrokuen Garden▶▶▶** (*Open* 6.30–6, 16 Mar–15 Oct; 8–4.30, rest of year), Kanazawa's most famous attraction. Once the private

218

REBELLION
Five hundred years ago, rebellious priests and peasants overthrew Kanazawa's feudal lord. They established an independent republic, which survived for 100 years until subdued by the warlord Oda Nobunaga, who awarded the city to his retainer, Maeda Toshiie.

Above and below: one of the geisha quarters

Kanazawa Market

garden of the Maeda lords, who ruled the city for three generations, Kenrokuen is officially categorized as one of Japan's three best gardens, and is said to combine perfectly the six qualities by which a park is judged: size, seclusion, running water, views, artificiality and age. The best time to visit is early morning, before the arrival of parties of Japanese visitors. The moss-covered earth will still be moist with dew and you can sit in solitude in the Moonflower Pavilion tea house and order bean-jam cakes and green whisked tea. Flowers bloom all year round.

The ordinary-looking **Myoryuji Temple▶▶** (*Open* 9–4; tours last 30 minutes) is, in fact, a complex of secret chambers, trap doors, hidden tunnels, staircases and a maze of corridors. It was constructed to confine and hold off invaders while the Maeda *daimyo* made his escape in the event of invasion of the city castle. Myoryuji, also called Temple of the Ninja (*Ninja-dera*), was connected to the castle by a tunnel. To get there, take a cab from the station or a bus to Nomachi Hirokoji stop and a further five-minute walk. Reservations are required (stop by the temple or telephone 41 2877), but generally a few last-minute walk-ins can be accommodated.

The old **Nagamachi Samurai District▶▶▶** is in the area that begins just behind the 109 Korinbo department store in the heart of Kanazawa. Nowadays it consists mainly of one street, lined with traditional, privately owned samurai wooden houses, each hidden behind roof-topped mud walls. Fortunately, the Nomura Family House (*Open* 8.30–5.30; *closed* first and third Wed of the month), once the home of a well-to-do samurai warrior, has been maintained in its original condition and is open to visitors. The design of the interior of the house is severe but extremely elegant, making extensive use of cypress, ebony and persimmon wood.

EASTERN TEMPLE QUARTER
Rising behind the Eastern Pleasure Quarter, overlooking Kanazawa, is Utatsuyama mountain, scattered with 40 Buddhist and Shinto temples and shrines. Some are still in use; others are in decay. An exploration along the spiral roads and wooden paths reveals a history of changing architectural styles and old statues of Japanese heroes. On the flat summit is a park with trees, shrubs and some grass to sit on, which is a rare freedom in Japanese parks.

WESTERN PLEASURE QUARTER
This district was inhabited by enslaved, as opposed to 'free' geisha, and was guarded by heavy gates. Its narrow streets and the temple quarters of the adjacent Teramachi district border the city on the western bank of the river.

Ryokan, *traditional Japanese inns, are usually two- or three-floor wooden buildings with the outward appearance of ordinary houses. They are, in fact, an expensive and exquisite way of experiencing Japanese culture and food.*

JAPANESE INNS

These are inexpensive versions of *ryokan* and they are recommended if you are on a budget and wish to experience traditional Japanese customs and lifestyle. The rooms are *tatami* (straw-matted), divided by paper screens and sparsely but tastefully decorated. Meals are an optional extra.

220

NEW *RYOKAN*

In recent years, some Western hotels have begun to offer a *ryokan* experience for guests staying in *tatami* rooms. There are also a few private *ryokan* set in modern apartment buildings. The ritual and the service are the same as in the traditional *ryokan* and often good value, but the ambience is usually less authentic.

A ryokan interior…

Many *ryokan* are sited in naturally beautiful areas, but even those in cities have traditional inner gardens in which rocks, trees and running water combine to create a feeling of natural scenic beauty. Service is flawless but restrained; as is the expected behaviour of the guests. Room decoration, the timetable of meals, and the general ritual tend to be the same in every inn.

Ryokan are generally costly and some of the more famous establishments in places such as Kyoto and Nara charge more than the best hotels, but they are worth at least one night's stay. The price includes a dinner, *kaiseki ryori* (traditional and classic Japanese cooking), and breakfast in your room, and the services of a personal maid, who serves the 10- or 12-dish meal (of beautifully presented local delicacies). After dinner, the maid converts the living room to a bedroom by pushing back the low, lacquered dining table and putting a futon and cotton-filled quilts on the *tatami* floor.

Furnishings in *ryokan* rooms are simple but elegant. In one corner is an alcove with a flower arrangement and a hanging scroll of a painting or poem. A lacquer dining table is surrounded with cushions and a television set is discreetly available. Most rooms have a veranda overlooking the garden, with chairs outside for periods of quiet contemplation.

Arrival and procedure On arrival, leave your shoes at the entrance; you will be handed a pair of slippers. On reaching your room, leave the slippers at the doorway and enter in your stockinged feet. The maid makes green tea for you and leaves. A perfectly ironed and starched *yukata* (kimono-style dressing gown) is available to wear after you have bathed in your private hot tub. It is perfectly acceptable and expected for you to wear a *yukata* for dinner or if you leave your room to explore your surroundings. In cold weather, a *tanzen* (padded kimono) is provided as well.

The maid arrives later with your dinner arranged on a very large tray of assorted lacquer dishes and pottery bowls. She places the tray just inside the door, bows, picks it up again and carries it to the table, then backs away, bows again and leaves. If you do not want a Japanese breakfast of rice, fish and *miso* soup, the following morning you are able to order coffee, toast and orange juice instead.

Room rates *Ryokan* rooms are designed to accommodate one to four people and charges depend on how many people are staying in the room. Unlike hotels, room rates vary greatly depending on the day and the time of the year. Weekends, public holidays and high season are the most expensive times. In low season, on a mid-week day you can book a *ryokan* for the price of a good hotel. A service charge of 10 to 15 per cent is added to the room rate and tipping is not necessary.

Ryokan are divided into three categories: deluxe, superior and standard. The deluxe establishments do not necessarily accept foreign guests. For further details contact Japan Ryokan Association, 1-8-3 Marunouchi, Chiyoda-ku, Tokyo, tel: 03 231 5310.

...and courtyard

EXILE

For the Japanese, exile was an appalling fate. Their identity was rooted in their place in society, and to be cut adrift from this relationship was akin to death. Depending upon the severity of the crime, banishment could be to a place between 1,100 and 5,000km (700 and 3,000 miles) away. The modern Japanese Penal Code, enacted in 1908, contains no provision for exile.

Taraibune, the washtub boats at Ogi

▶▶ Sado-Shima (Sado Island)   208B2

Exile was once a common Japanese punishment for criminals, politicians, religious leaders, or members of the imperial family who had become unpopular. Many such deposed statesmen, and even emperors, were banished to Sado Island, in the Sea of Japan off the coast of Niigata prefecture, western Honshu. When gold was discovered there during the Edo period, homeless people and prisoners were sent to Sado to work as slaves in the gold mines. Its history has given the island a rather grim image and an air of melancholy; but Sado does have dramatic scenery, well-preserved villages, traditional farming landscapes, lovely beaches and a culture all of its own.

Although relatively small, Sado is Japan's fifth-largest island in size. The population of fewer than 100,000 is increased tenfold by visitors during the summer season. Two mountain chains run east to west along the north and south coasts, divided by an extensive plain where the main towns and farmland areas are found. The old gold and silver mines, major tourist attractions, can be found in the mountains. The storm-battered coastline, with its sheer, plunging cliffs and tiny offshore islands, is also worth exploring.

Three main ferry crossings connect Sado Island with Niigata. Each offers a regular ferry and a hydrofoil. The hydrofoil crossings are approximately twice as expensive, and take half the time. Niigata to Ryotsu (two hours, 20 minutes by ferry) is the most popular and frequent crossing; other alternatives are Niigata to Akadomare (three hours by ferry) or Joetsu (110km/70 miles southwest of Niigata) to Ogi (two hours, 40 minutes by ferry). Ogi is the most attractive port. Ferries do not operate during rough seas. Towns on the island are connected by regular bus services but the main sights are less accessible; the *Sado Teiki Kanko Josha-ken*, a two-day pass, allows

Fishing tackle at Ogi

DRUMS
Taiko are large, barrel-shaped Japanese drums. Village boundaries were determined by the farthest point at which a *taiko* could be heard. In recent times, village drumming rituals have become popular in Japan and many drumming troupes have been established. The most famous is the Kodo (the word means both 'heartbeat' and 'children of the drum') troupe, also known as the 'Ondekoza Demon Drummers'. When not on tour, the drummers live communally on Sado in spartan conditions.

223

unlimited use of all tour buses, the most convenient means of transportation. Comprehensive tours of the island depart from Ogi and Ryotsu (four to eight hours long). Alternatively, cars can be hired at the main ports.

The original hub of the gold mining industry, **Aikawa▶▶**, one hour, 15 minutes by bus from Ryotsu, is one tenth the size that it was during the boom times. Visitors now come here to tour the Sado Kinzan Mine (*Open* 8–5.30) and other related sights. Some of the extensive underground tunnels are open for viewing. Realistic mechanical figures and sound effects are used to re-create the original working conditions of a mine; many men died within a few years of their exile to Sado.

Senkaku Bay▶▶▶, to the north of Aikawa, boasts a stunning coastline with surreal rock formations. Excursion boats operate from Tassha, 15 minutes from Aikawa by bus; a clifftop path also starts from here. The west coast of the island, from Senkaku Bay to Cape Hajiki on the northern tip, is called Soto-Kaifu (Outer Coast); the east coast, south from Cape Hajiki, is known as Uchi-kaifu (Inner Coast). The former has a dramatic, rugged beauty composed of strange rock formations, reefs and cliffs, and is popular with tour buses. The latter is less exciting and quieter.

Ogi▶ is a working port, once best known for its strange, wooden *taraibune* (tub-like boats), used by local women to collect seaweed and shellfish. You can rent one and paddle yourself around on the water. The best reason to visit Ogi is to travel on to **Shukunegi▶▶▶**, 15 minutes to the west by bus. This is a delightful fishing village set in a cove with traditional houses and surrounded by trees and rice paddies.

A seashell mountain on Sado Island

*The Sutra Library
(Kyozo) at Chusonji. The
inner chamber houses a
Monju Bosatsu image,
the Bhodisattva of
wisdom and intellect*

**RIKUCHU-KAIGAN
NATIONAL PARK**
This stretch of rugged,
rocky coastline is
celebrated for its high
cliffs, fantastic rock
formations, small fishing
villages and marine life.
It was, until very recently,
an inaccessible area, but
nowadays, with two private
railways, it is easier to
explore. Buses go from
Morioka to Kuji (about
three hours) and from
here you can take a train
on the Kita Rias line to
Shimano-koshi on the
coast, where buses leave
for the coastal zone of
the park.

Tohoku Central and East

▶▶ Hiraizumi   209D3

Today, Hiraizumi is a small country town, but during
the 11th and 12th centuries the Fujiwara clan paid for the
construction of many temples and palaces with the
proceeds of the gold they mined in the area, and
Hiraizumi competed with Kyoto. Few buildings remain
from this great age, but the Golden Hall (Konjiki-do) of
Chusonji Temple has survived and has recently been fully
restored as one of Tohoku's major cultural attractions.
The farmland areas around Hiraizumi are worth visiting
for their wealth of traditional Japanese houses. Hiraizumi
is 25 minutes from Ichinoseki, which is two hours, 25
minutes by Tohoku Shinkansen from Ueno station,
Tokyo. Alternatively, Hiraizumi is two hours by local
train from Sendai. There is a tourist office on the town's
main street, to the right of the station.

Chusonji Temple▶▶ (*Open* 8–5), a short walk (20
minutes) or bus ride from the station, was founded in 850
and restored in the 12th century. Two halls, Konjiki-do
and Kyozo, remain from this period, whereas the other
buildings in the temple complex date from the later Edo
period. Konjiki-do, a small but impressive structure (now
housed in a fireproof building) has black, lacquered exterior walls and gold-leaf and mother-of-pearl interior
panels. Kyozo, the original temple library, houses a
magnificent Monju Bosatsu image riding a lion.

Once the most important temple complex in Tohoku,
Motsuji Temple▶▶ (*Open* 8–5) is now marked only by the
foundations of the 40 original main temples, but the beautiful Jodo-style paradise gardens (Heian period) have,
remarkably, survived. The Hiraizumi Museum, housing
relics of the Fujiwara clan, is in the garden domain.

▶▶ Morioka   209D4

Morioka is a castle town, founded by the feudal lord
Nambu in the 16th century, and an old-established
provincial university town. It is a charming place with
many temples, an old merchant quarter, a vibrant cultural
life and a successful local craft industry. The Tohoku
Shinkansen to Morioka from Ueno station in Tokyo takes
three hours.

Detail, Chusonji Temple

▶ Sendai
209D3

The largest city in Tohoku was flattened in World War II and has since been rebuilt along the lines of many other modern Japanese cities. It is a good base from which to explore the area of Tohoku, Matsushima (see panel), and the adjoining Yamagata prefecture, a rural district where life follows the traditional Tohoku style. Sendai is two hours by Tohoku Shinkansen (bullet train) from Tokyo's Ueno station.

▶▶ Towada-Hachimantai National Park
209D4

Lying northwest of Morioka, this area is divided into southern and northern sections. Hachimantai, in the south, is a mountainous area of volcanic activity, better known for its *onsen* (hot springs) and thermal resorts than for scenic beauty.

Goshogake Onsen and Toshichi Onsen are both places where people go to soothe away city stress and other ailments. Mixed bathing is the norm. The eastern entrance to the park is via Obuke, 40 minutes on the JR Hanawa line from Morioka (tour buses operate from here).

The Lake Towada area, which lies to the north, is a region of exceptional scenic beauty. The lake itself occupies a giant crater, and the gentle mountain ranges around the lake provide plenty of good hiking and skiing. There are many *onsen* nearby. Sukayu Onsen, to the north, which has a 1,000-person bath, is one of the best known. The pretty Oirase-keiryu (Oirase Valley) district, to the northeast, is also very popular with walkers, particularly in the autumn, when the valley is especially beautiful. There is a frequent bus service from April to October, directly from Morioka to Lake Towada.

MATSUSHIMA BAY
Matsushima Kaigan station is 40 minutes by Senseki line from Sendai. This is the main stop for the famed Matsushima Bay (a very popular Japanese resort destination), which is dotted with small, pine-covered islands, some inhabited and others no more than tiny islets. The bay is regarded as one of Japan's 'Three Famous Views' (the other two are Amano-hashidate, north of Kyoto, and Itsukushima, near Hiroshima), and as such has suffered from commercialism. The islands can be toured by cruiser from Matsushima Kaigan Pier.

225

A bright, airy, covered shopping arcade in modern Sendai

Filled with fresh air and easy to clean, traditional Japanese houses are healthy places, emphasizing simplicity, regularity and refinement. Built of a small number of locally available materials, usually wood, bamboo, paper, woven straw and stone tiles, they sit on stilts above the ground, allowing ventilation and giving protection to the structure from the effects of mildew and damp.

TATAMI ROOMS
Slippers are worn on wooden floors, but the inner *tatami*-matted rooms must be entered in bare or stockinged feet. The street, the *genkan*, the wooden corridors, and the *tatami*-matted rooms represent four levels of decreasing contamination between public and private places. The exclusion of dirt from the *tatami* rooms is important, as the floor is used both as an eating and as a sleeping surface.

A farmhouse lantern

Health and cleanliness The Japanese home contains several standard features for the maintenance of a clean and healthy house. The *genkan* is a paved area at the same level as the garden, with a raised wooden floor, where residents sit to remove their shoes before donning slippers to move into the house. The *engawa*, or veranda, is a well-protected porch that affords shelter from the sun in the summer without blocking low winter rays. The opening onto it allows plenty of air to circulate through the house, even during heavy rain. Like the *genkan*, the veranda has easily maintained floor surfaces, whose proximity to the garden facilitates cleaning. Symbolically, the *engawa* is the link between house and garden. It is associated with meditation in monasteries, where it is the platform from which nature is contemplated.

Tatami (straw mats) line the floors in all major rooms. Futons (Japanese mattresses) are simple, warm, easily cleaned and unobtrusive. Made of canvas and stuffed with cotton batting or other firm material, with no springs inside, futons are easily folded twice and placed in cupboards designed to contain them. Aired frequently in the *engawa*, futons reflect by their number and pattern the age, status and taste of their users.

Seasonal living Rooms are arranged and rearranged according to the way they are used. In the hot and humid summer, all room dividers made of sliding panels can be opened or removed, encouraging the flow of fresh air throughout the house. In winter, the rather loose association of open rooms with large openings to the outdoors can be converted to an arrangement of isolated rooms, which can be closed off from each other and the outside by sliding panels and outside shutters. In cold weather, families gather about the *kotatsu*, a table placed over a *hibachi* (a small brazier), which sits below the floor. This feature is equivalent to the western hearth and is symbolic of the family unit.

To live well in the traditional Japanese house, considerable stress is placed on appropriate dress in summer and winter. The *yukata* is a lightweight, heavily starched, loose cotton garment worn in summer, which allows free circulation of air next to the skin. In winter, it is traditional to wear layers of heavier garments. Their full sleeves allow hand warming and, in a sitting position, the surface area is reduced and the body heat more efficiently retained. Clothing becomes a heavily insulated, personal tent.

Bathrooms In a traditional Japanese house, the lavatory and bath tub are never in the same room. They are regarded as separate and distinct, requiring their own space. The bath is frequently associated with the garden and contains enough room for several people to dress in an atmosphere of natural beauty and social ease. It is designed to give comfort and to allow bathers to be exposed and to relax. The lavatory is sometimes entered only upon leaving the house. It is positioned carefully in order to reduce smells and social embarrassment. The lavatory compartment is always very well ventilated and may contain a flower arrangement.

GENKAN
Many visitors do not pass the *genkan*, thereby reducing the intrusion of dirt into private areas of the house. No animals are allowed past the *genkan*, although they may be allowed to sleep there. These customs ensure that most dirt is left in the *genkan*, where it can readily be removed to the street or garden.

Traditional houses at Ogimachi village

Tohoku West

▶▶ Hirosaki   209C4

Unlike nearby Aomori, this small, compact town escaped wartime bombing. However, it was the postwar planners who destroyed much of the town's architectural heritage. Fortunately, the city does retain some of its old winding alleys and has an appeal enhanced by the friendliness of the townspeople, the thriving local craft traditions, and some well-maintained sites of cultural interest. The tourist office can be found by the station and provides a map of the town and information in English.

Hirosaki is approximately four hours by train from Morioka and 30 minutes by train from Aomori, the busy port town that usurped Hirosaki's position as the cultural and political heart of Tohoku.

Lake Tazawa

▶▶ Kakunodate   209C4

The train journey to Kakunodate from Morioka (55 minutes, JR Tazawa line) passes fine mountain scenery on its way to this small and pretty town, which has one of the best-preserved collections of samurai houses in Japan. Found in the inner town (Uchimachi), the samurai district has about half a dozen original houses and gardens open to the public (9–5), of which Aoyagi, with its turf roof, is especially renowned. Kakunodate's founding lords were originally from Kyoto. They imported with them many weeping cherry trees and the town and its river banks are generously planted, so that, in season, cherry blossoms blow through the streets in clouds. The outer town (Tomachi), once the merchants' quarter, remains the commercial part of town. Kakunodate is well known for items made from cherry bark, a craft that was once the main source of livelihood for poorer samurai.

▶▶ Tazawa-ko (Lake Tazawa)   209C4

This lovely crater lake, the deepest in Japan, has exceptionally clear water. The lake shore is being developed but still maintains a rustic atmosphere. Cruise boats operate from Tazawa-Kohan, where bicycles are also available for rent. In the surrounding countryside there are many isolated inns, with their own open-air hot-spring pools. Nyuto Onsen, connected by bus to Tazawa-ko, is the main resort and has smaller inns scattered around it. To get to Tazawa-ko, take the JR Tazawa line from Kakunodate (16 minutes) or Morioka (40 minutes). The tourist office is to the left of the station. From the station it is a 15-minute bus ride to Tazawa-Kohan on the lake edge.

Tamagawa Onsen►► is an old spa town with a reputation for restorative and curative thermal springs. Many of its individual inns are of wooden construction and conditions are quite basic, but they provide a very interesting experience and a change from Japan's usual over-commercialization of natural resources. Reach the spa by bus from Tazawa-ko (one hour, 30 minutes).

►► Yamagata   209C3

Yamagata city is the capital of Yamagata prefecture, a largely unspoiled region in the heart of Tohoku. The Japanese are promoting the area as one that 'remains largely undiscovered by the international tourist', and there is consequently much information available at the tourist office in Yamagata JR station, one hour, 15 minutes from Sendai by JR express train. Yamagata itself has few attractions and Dewa Sanzan and Mount Zao areas are mainly used by the Japanese as a base for summer hiking and winter skiing. Dewa Sanzan is composed of three peaks (Gassan, Yudono-san and Haguro-san), each one an important sacred site, and the setting for Shinto shrines. Mount Zao is a very popular skiing destination in the winter months. Zao Onsen is the place to find lodging in the region. A cable car operates from there to the mountain summit. Winter snowfall is generally heavy. **Yamadera**►►► is a mountaintop monastery made famous by the *haiku* poet Matsuo Basho. The steep climb to the top is rewarded with wonderful views. The precincts are extensive and worth exploring.

BANDAI-ASAHI NATIONAL PARK
Occupying an area to the west and south of Fukushima and to the west of Yamagata, Bandai-Asahi includes some of the most pretty, interesting, and accessible mountain and lake scenery in Japan. Azuma-san (the Azuma mountains), near Fukushima, has moderate hiking opportunities. Access to Azuma-san is from Jododaira bus station on the Bandai-Asahi Skyline road. Fukushima is one hour, 40 minutes on the Tohoku Shinkansen line from Ueno station in Tokyo. Bandai-Kogen, at the heart of Bandai Plateau, is 40 minutes from Fukushima on the Skyline road or three hours on the scenic Bandai-Asahi Lakeline road.

229

Yamadera, a place of mystery and stillness atop a steep, wooded mountainside

Hokkaido

Sōya-kaikyō

Sōya-misaki

Rebun-tō

Wakkanai

Hamatonbetsu

Rishiri-tō

Esashi

Rishiri-Rebun
Sarobetsu
National Park

K i t a m i - s a n c h i

Teshio

Okoppe

Yagashiri-tō

1032m

Teuri-tō

Nayoro

Haboro

Shibetsu

H O K K A I D

Rumoi

Kamikawa

Asahikawa

Daisetsu-san

1492m

Fukagawa

2290m Sōunkyō
Gorge

Takikawa

Akabira

Asahi-dake

Kamui-misaki

Ishikari-wan

Ashibetsu

**Daisetsuzan
National
Park**

*Shakotan-
hantō*

Otaru

Ishikari

Furano

Shikaribetsu-ko

Iwanai

SAPPORO

Ebetsu

Iwamizawa

Bibai

Shintoku

Yubari

Ishikari-gawa

Sorachi-gawa

Yūbari-sanchi

Hidaka

Obihiro

Motsuta-
misaki

Kutchan

Chitose

Mukawa

Tokachi

Maizuru,
Niigata,
Tsuruga

1898m

Shikotsu-ko

2052m

**Shikotsu-Tōya
National Park**

Hiroshiri-dake

H i d a k a - s a n m y a k u

Tōya-ko

Oshamambe

Abuta

Shiraoi

Tomakomai

Setana

Date

Mukawa

Noboribetsu

Shizunai

Okushiri-tō

Yakumo

Uchira-wan

Muroran

Urakawa

Mori

Samani

O s h i m a - h a n t ō

**Onuma Quasi-
National Park**

Erimo

Esashi

1167m

Nanae

Kamiiso

Esan-misaki

Hakodate

Fukushima

Tsugaru-kaikyō

Ōma-zaki

Matsumae

Ōma

Shiriya-zaki

Seikan Tunnel

*Shimokita-
hantō*

Tappi-zaki

Mutsu

*Tsugaru-
hantō*

HONSHŪ

Mutsu-wan

Goshogawara

Noheji

Ogawara-ko

Hachinohe, Nagoya,
Sendai, Tōkyō

Aomori

A · · B · · C

Mombetsu

Yūbetsu

Saroma-ko

Notoro-ko

Ō

Abashiri

Memambetsu

Abashiri-ko

Rubeshibe

Bihoro

Kitami

Shari

Kawayu

Kussharo-ko

Mashū-ko

Akan-ko

Teshikaga

Naka-
Shibetsu

Akan Kohan

Akan
National Park

Konsen-
daichi

1499m

Nemuro-
wan

Ashoro

Tōren-ko

Nemuro

Kami-
Shihoro

Akan

Kushiro-
Shitsugen
National Park

Kushiro-
heiya

Ikeda

Akkeshi

Shiranuka

Kushiro

Tokachi-gawa

-heiya

Hiro'o

Erimo-misaki

Shiretoko-
misaki

Shiretoko
National Park

1660m

Rausu

Nemuro-kaikyō

RUS

Notsuke-suidō

| 0 | | 50 | | 100 km |
| 0 | 20 | | 40 | 60 miles |

Sendai,
Tokyo

D

E

The unspoiled serenity of Daisetsuzan National Park

SNOW FESTIVALS
Yuki Matsuri (snow festivals) are held throughout the winter in the parts of northern Japan that have heavy snowfalls. The most famous takes place in Sapporo for four days, from the first Wednesday in February. The festival began by chance when, in 1950, some high school students made six ice sculptures in Odori Park. Today, 2 million attend the festival each year. More than 200 elaborate ice carvings are displayed in the park, which is, in fact, a broad avenue, running east to west, bisecting the middle of town.

HOKKAIDO This northernmost and second largest of the four main Japanese islands is the least populous region of Japan. There are few cultural or historical reasons to visit Hokkaido, but if you love the outdoors you will find forests, mountain ranges, lakes, volcanoes, hot springs, open landscapes, and the chance to hike, ski and cycle. Hokkaido also has plenty of rich agricultural, fishing and mineral resources.

Hokkaido is connected to Honshu by the 54km (33-mile) long Seikan Tunnel, the world's longest, which runs under the Tsugaru Straits. The island is bordered by the Pacific Ocean to the south and north, by the Sea of Japan to the west, and by the Sea of Okhotsk to the northeast. Possession of four of the Kuril Islands, in the Sea of Okhotsk, is acrimoniously disputed by Japan and Russia.

JAPANESE COLONISTS Until the beginning of the 20th century, wild and inhospitable Hokkaido was not considered habitable by the Japanese. They visited and settled only the island's coastal regions, to fish and collect seaweed. Some Ainu, one of Japan's original indigenous groups, lived in the interior, but there were no inland Japanese settlements or agriculture. Shortage of space on the other main islands, coupled with the return after 1945 of many Japanese colonists from abroad, led to the first real development of the island, and today more than 5 million people live there.

SAPPORO The large, modern capital city, laid out on a grid system, has many parks, but is not a place to visit for great sights. It does, however, have an active and well-known nightlife, the Susukino district is as lively as anything in Tokyo, and it provides a good base from which to explore the wilderness areas of Hokkaido. The tourist information office is at Sapporo station.

NATIONAL PARKS The national parks of Hokkaido are large, wild and scenic and perhaps the main reason for visiting this remote region of Japan. Three of the major parks are listed here. **Daisetsuzan National Park** is the largest in Japan and one of the most unspoiled. A network of hiking paths gives access to most areas of the park and to many of the mountain peaks, none of which rises much above 2,133m (6,996ft). Most of the lodging available in the park includes access to hot springs. **Akan National Park** is well known for its beauty and wildlife. It is dominated by volcanic peaks, but lakes and vast forests add variety. Akan lies in the east of Hokkaido and can be reached from Kushiro to the south. Kussharo-ko is the largest volcanic lake in Japan, and a focal point of the national park. **Shikotsu-Toya National Park** is in southwest Hokkaido, not far from Sapporo, and is known for its caldera lakes, volcanoes, hot springs and forests. Lakes Toya and Shikotsu (the second deepest in Japan) give the park its name.

GETTING THERE Sapporo is ten and a half hours by train from Tokyo. Chitose, 40km (25 miles) south of Sapporo, is Hokkaido's main airport. The approximate flight time from Tokyo is one hour and 20 minutes, and there are frequent train connections with Sapporo. Japan Air Lines (JAL) flights are scheduled to Chitose from Tokyo, Osaka and Fukuoka. All Nippon Airways (ANA) and JAL also run services from many other Japanese cities.

There are ferry services from Tokyo to Tomakomai or Kushiro, and from many towns on the coast of Tohoku, such as Oma-Hakodate, Aomori-Muroran and Noheji-Hakodate. There is a rail network on Hokkaido and internal flights between major cities.

FOOD
One of the unexpected surprises of visiting Hokkaido is the quality of the regional food. Restaurants tend to be reasonably priced and without pretension. Dishes include shellfish, salmon, herring, squid, sea urchin, potatoes and Chinese noodles (*ramen*). Genghis Khan, a Mongolian-inspired mutton or lamb barbecue cooked by the guest (or a chef) at the table, is another great well-loved dish.

233

Japanese cranes

Abashiri

DUCKWEED
Lake Akan is famous for its rare spherical duck-weed, called *marimo*, which is found in only a few lakes around the world. The green spheres absorb oxygen from the water and then float to the surface, where they exhale and sink. Examples of *marimo* may be seen in shops and information offices and in the *marimo* museum on a small island in the lake. A boat trip on the lake lasts one and a half hours and stops at the museum.

KUSHIRO GREAT MARSH
This is the home of the *tancho* (red-crested crane), brought back from the brink of extinction, and now forming a colony of around 400. They are shy birds who live deep in the marshes in summer. They come out of the deeper reaches in winter, and you can see them at the Red-Crested Crane Natural Park, south of Akan, where some are kept behind high mesh fences. A bus to the Crane Park from Akan Kohan bus terminal takes one hour, 15 minutes (get off at the Tsuru-koen bus stop).

▶▶ **Abashiri**   231D4
Although a small town, this is the main settlement on the Sea of Okhotsk. During the winter, the sea is ice-bound and the floes reach up to the beach. The inhabitants make their living from fishing in the summer months, when the local delicacies of shrimp and 'hairy crab' are taken from the icy seas. Abashiri is the terminus of the JR Sekihoku line; the limited express takes five hours, 40 minutes from Sapporo. There is a tourist information office in the station. Flights from Sapporo's Chitose Airport to Memambetsu (near Abashiri) take 55 minutes by JAS.

The **Municipal Museum**▶▶ (*Open* 8.30–5) houses a collection of genuine Ainu artefacts and preAinu material discovered in the Moyoro Shell Mound, site of an ancient Ainu dwelling place. One part of the Municipal Museum is the Abashiri Prison Museum (Abashiri Kangoku), which records the grim conditions suffered by the convicts who were used to develop the region.

Oroke Kinenkan▶ (*Open* 8.30–5) is a museum dedicated to preserving the heritage of a small tribe of nomadic rein-deer herders who live on Sakhalin island.

About 3km (2 miles) southwest of Abashiri, on route 39, is **Tento-zan**▶▶ hill. From its observation tower, there are views of the Sea of Okhotsk and nearby mountain peaks.

▶▶ **Akan National Park**   231D3
Set in eastern Hokkaido, Akan National Park has three major caldera lakes, volcanic mountains, numerous hot springs and extensive forests of primeval trees. Towns near the park are Bihoro (in the north) and Kushiro (in the south). Buses for the park leave from both towns (neither is of particular interest in its own right). Kushiro has an airport and there are flights there from Tokyo (one hour, 35 minutes) and Sapporo (40 minutes). Bihoro is five hours, 20 minutes from Sapporo by JR Sekihoku line limited express. Kushiro is three hours, 30 minutes on the same line from Bihoro. Within the park, the town of Akan Kohan is the most important resort area. There is a tourist information office near the town's bus terminal.

The easiest way to travel around the park is by sight-seeing buses, although for more freedom you might prefer to rent a car for a few days. The tour buses are noisy and do not stop long at any of the sights; it is worth getting off at one, exploring on foot and then catching another tour bus later (this is allowed if you hold on to your ticket).

Ainu Kotan Village▶, a 10-minute walk west of the bus terminal in Akan Kohan spa town, is a street of souvenir shops and a thatched-roofed building, where displays of Ainu dancing are held six times a day, from May to the end of October.

About 14km (9 miles) from Lake Mashu, **Kawayu Onsen▶▶** is a hot-spring resort near Io-san, an active volcano that vents steam from two ravines. Visitors often buy fresh eggs from the grocery store near the car park and boil them in the small pools of hot water.

Lake Akan▶▶ lies in the western part of the park, surrounded by dense forests and two volcanoes: O-Akandake to the east (dormant) and Me-Akandake to the south (active). Both mountains can be climbed and are popular with hikers.

Lake Kussharo▶▶ is the park's largest lake and it attracts campers and watersports enthusiasts. The lake is at its most attractive in the autumn, when the leaves of the surrounding trees change from green to orange hues.

Lake Mashu▶▶, a 20-minute drive from Teshikaga (one hour, 15 minutes by JR express from Kushiro), is almost 213m (700ft) deep, and surrounded by high rock walls with little or no footholds. The best two viewing spots are on the western side.

Boiling mud at Akan National Park

The still waters of Lake Akan, set beneath two volcanoes and surrounded by forests

235

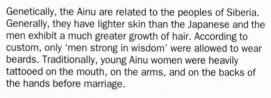

The ancestors of the Ainu were the original inhabitants of Japan. Organized into nomadic tribes who lived by hunting, fishing and gathering, they roamed freely over the central and northern parts of Japan, but as waves of aggressive invaders and settlers moved in from the Asian mainland, they were pushed north. The Ainu were formidable warriors, and constant fighting between them and the Japanese put a great strain on the resources of the emerging Japanese state. However, over the centuries the Ainu were pacified and controlled until, by the 19th century, they were restricted to their present settlements in Hokkaido.

PRAYER STICKS
Kotan-kara-kamui, the Spirit of the World, came from the skies to establish the land of the Ainu. On his return he forgot his chopsticks, and to prevent them rotting he turned them into willow trees. The Ainu still use willow to carve their *inau*, or prayer sticks.

Above: detail of an Ainu totem
Below: Ainu village

Genetically, the Ainu are related to the peoples of Siberia. Generally, they have lighter skin than the Japanese and the men exhibit a much greater growth of hair. According to custom, only 'men strong in wisdom' were allowed to wear beards. Traditionally, young Ainu women were heavily tattooed on the mouth, on the arms, and on the backs of the hands before marriage.

Traditional houses Ainu now live in more modern homes, but traditionally Ainu houses were rectangular wood-framed buildings, with dirt floors covered in reed mats, and thatched walls and roofs. Raised wooden platforms covered in mats or animal (often bear) skins were used for sleeping and an open-fire pit, placed in the middle of the house, was used for cooking, heating and religious purposes. Fire was sacred to the Ainu, and the hearth would often be decorated with *inau*, specially carved wooden prayer sticks, which are still found wherever the Ainu commemorate the spiritual beings they called *kamui* (similar to the Japanese *kami*).

Bear spirits Bears were held in high regard by the Ainu, and an important part of Ainu culture was the festival known as *iomante*, through which they paid their respects to the *kamui* of the bear. In times past, when the bears awoke from their winter hibernation, the men went into the woods and captured a cub, which would be taken to the village and cared for until it was about two years old. The animal was then sacrificed either by strangulation or by being shot with arrows. The head was removed and placed on a pole, and the flesh eaten at a feast that featured dancing by the men and gifts of sake to the bear's head as gratitude for its sacrifice. By sending the spirit of the bear back to its ancestors, the Ainu showed their appreciation for its strength and courage, attributes they hoped would become theirs, as they believed the spirit of the bear would be reborn as an Ainu.

Loss of culture Nowadays, almost all of the 25,000 Ainu living in Hokkaido are descendants of mixed Japanese and Ainu parentage. Sadly, very few either understand the Ainu language or maintain their culture. This loss of identity is partly due to past Japanese government policy that forbids the use of the Ainu language in schools. In the public media, most Ainu customs were banned and in the name of assimilation mixed marriages were actively encouraged. Laws now protect the Ainu, but because of discrimination they remain a poor minority group in Japan. Also, inevitable intermarriage has led them to even greater assimilation into the mainstream of Japanese society. Very recently, there has been some resurgence of interest in Ainu traditions and language among the younger Ainu, plus the Ainu Law of 1997 will hopefully protect what is left of their culture.

The Ainu are often said to be the 'Native Americans' of Japan, and in the same way Ainu culture is now mainly displayed in 'Ainu villages', built specially for the tourist trade. Sadly, most of them are grim, dispirited places. For the tourist, perhaps the best exposition of genuine Ainu traditions is to be found in the Ainu Culture Museum, in Nibutani, near the town of Tomakomai, Hokkaido.

Top: Ainu festival
Above: an Ainu couple

EXORCISM OF EVIL SPIRITS
According to Ainu belief, sickness is caused by evil spirits and healed by driving them away. A crippled man has his legs and arms bound with bulrush stems and cloth and is gently beaten with branches. The bindings are then cut away and thrown into a river, while the Ainu shout at the spirits to flee.

Hakodate by night

▶▶▶ Daisetsuzan National Park   230C3

In the heart of Hokkaido, this is Japan's largest national park and a paradise for hikers. Its scenery is spectacular, with lakes, mountains, deep gorges, waterfalls, forests, hiking trails and the highest mountain in Hokkaido, Mount Asahidake (2,290m/7,511ft). Sounkyo Onsen, at the edge of the spectacular Sounkyo Gorge, is one of the best places to stay (see also Asahidake Onsen, below) while exploring the park, as long as you can ignore the spa hotels, which seem to be designed to brazenly clash with the natural beauty of the surroundings. The only way to travel to Sounkyo Onsen is by bus. If you are journeying from Sapporo, leave the train at Kamikawa (two hours, 30 minutes by JR Sekihoku line) and transfer to the local bus service (35 minutes to Sounkyo Onsen). A tourist information office, called the PC Centre, can be found near the bus station.

Asahidake Onsen▶▶▶ is a quiet, remote village, one hour, 40 minutes by bus from Asahikawa, which is on the JR Sekihoku line from Sapporo. Asahidake Onsen gives access to a two-hour ascent of Mount Asahidake and other mountain trails.

A cable car travels from Sounkyo Onsen to the terminal on **Kurodake Mountain▶▶**. Change here for a chair lift that travels up the mountain to the beginning of the hiking trails. An hour's steady walking will take you to the peak, where you will be rewarded by spectacular views of the surrounding mountains. Be sure to wear sturdy shoes or boots.

Lake Daisetsu▶▶ was created by a rock and earth dam across the Ishikawa (river), which flows through the Sounkyo Gorge. An enjoyable way to visit the lake is to hire a bicycle from Sounkyo's bus terminal and pedal along the path that skirts the edge of the gorge. **Sounkyo Gorge▶▶** itself is 20km (12 miles) long and extends into the park from its northeast entrance. The valley is hemmed in by rocky cliffs almost 190m (625ft) high. There are tremendous views at each turn of the road. Beyond Sounkyo Onsen, the gorge is renowned for its waterfalls; Ryusei-no-taki (Shooting Star) and Ginga-no-taki (Milky Way) are particularly attractive.

▶▶ Hakodate   230B2

On a stumpy peninsula on the southwest coast of Hokkaido, Hakodate has been a fishing port since the 18th century. It was one of the first to be opened to trade with the West by the Treaty of Kanagawa in 1854.

A tourist information office is to the right of JR Hakodate station. The Hokato Kotsu bus company runs a four-hour sightseeing tour of the city, which leaves from the railway station.

A three-minute walk south of the JR station leads to **Asa Ichi▶▶**, a fish and vegetable market open 5am–noon, but at its peak at 8am. More than 400 shops sell a range of food, including *kegani* ('hairy crab'), generally considered to be one of the delicacies of Hokkaido.

Goryokaku▶▶, a Western-style fortress, was built in 1864 in the heart of the city in the shape of a five-pointed star, allowing its defenders to concentrate a murderous crossfire on attackers. Seized by supporters of the Tokugawa family, it fell to troops loyal to Emperor Meiji

DAISETSUZAN HIKING TRAILS
Access to many of Japan's national parks seems to have been considered only in terms of the car driver or tour bus. Daisetsuzan is an exception, providing a network of hiking trails. With adequate maps, equipment and provisions, it is possible to explore this remote and beautiful region on foot. Tenninkyo Onsen, deep in the interior of the park, is a good base, and information is available from the Hokkaido Tourist Association, Keizai Centre Building, Nishi-1-chome, Kita 2, Chuo-ku, Sapporo, tel: 011 231 0941; *Open* 9–5, Sat 9–1; *closed* Sun.

in 1868. All that remain are the outer walls; the grounds have been turned into a park of 4,000 cherry trees. A small museum contains relics of the battle (*Open* 8–8, May–Oct; 9–6, rest of year).

The foreigners' **Motomachi District**▶▶ features several buildings dating from the late 1800s and the early 1900s, and were strongly influenced by Western design, including an Orthodox church founded in 1862. To get there, take a street car from the JR station to Jujigai stop.

Mount Hakodate▶▶ is a small volcanic hill 335m (1,100ft) high, with famous views over the city and a restaurant on the summit. A bus leaves from the JR station for the 20-minute drive to the top.

See also pages 240–241.

IGLOO WEDDINGS
Lake Shikaribetsu is Daisetsuzan park's only natural lake. In the winter the lake freezes over and local people build a village of igloos on the ice, where they hold winter weddings. In March, the igloo village becomes the site of the local Shikaribetsu Kotan Festival.

Hakodate fishing boats

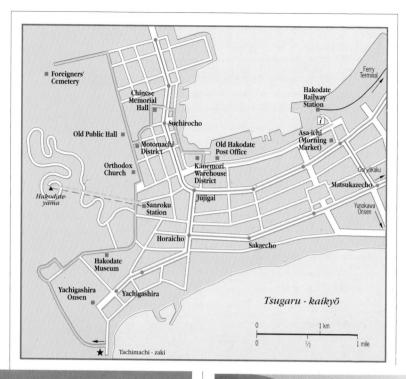

Foreigners' Cemetery

Chinese Memorial Hall

Suehirocho

Old Public Hall

Motomachi District

Orthodox Church

Hakodate-yama

Sanroku Station

Jūjigai

Horaicho

Hakodate Museum

Yachigashira Onsen

Yachigashira

Old Hakodate Post Office

Kanemori Warehouse District

Ferry Terminal

Hakodate Railway Station

Asa-ichi (Morning Market)

Goryōkaku

Matsukazecho

Yunokawa Onsen

Sakaecho

Tsugaru - kaikyō

Tachimachi - zaki

0   1 km
0   ½   1 mile

Walk

Hakodate

Distance: 5km (3 miles); time: around three to four hours.

Hakodate occupies a strategic site on a fine waterfront, backed by Mount Hakodate and overlooking the Tsugaru Straits. This walk starts at Cape Tachimachi on the Pacific Ocean, passes around the base of Mount Hakodate, through the old Western community of Motomachi, and ends at the Foreign Cemetery. There is also a possible detour to the Kanemori Warehouse district with its shops, cafés and restaurants.

Start at Hakodate station (south of the station there is a large **produce market►►**, held Monday to Saturday 5am–noon, which is worth visiting). Take a cab to **Cape Tachimachi►►**, an Ainu word meaning 'a place on the rocks where you wait for fish and catch them with a spear', or take the tram to the **Yachigashira Onsen▶** stop (20 minutes). There is a huge public baths here. Then it is a 15-minute walk south. To the east, in the distance, is Yunokawa Onsen, the oldest hot-spring resort in Hakodate.

Follow the route northwest and then northeast, passing the **Hakodate Museum▶▶**, which houses Ainu relics, before reaching Sanroku station. Here you can take a cable car to the top of **Hakodate Yama (Mount Hakodate)▶▶▶**. The night view from the top is superb, and few Japanese come to Hakodate without visiting the mountain at night to enjoy the spectacular view over the city. There is a café on the summit.

Continuing north, past the green onion domes of the **Orthodox Church▶** on your left, go through the old foreign community area of **Motomachi** (see page 239), a district of Western buildings that developed during Hakodate's period as a treaty port. **The Old Public Hall▶▶**,

completed in 1910, is representative of the architecture of the Meiji period, and has the feel of a British colonial structure.

Continue north along the road to the **Foreigners' Cemetery▶▶**, which is laid out on a hill overlooking the port and is filled with the graves of Russians, Chinese, English, French and Americans. The oldest graves are those of two American sailors who fell ill and died during Admiral Perry's mission in 1854.

Take a cab back to Hakodate station or retrace your steps to the Old Public Hall. From here it is a 15-minute walk to the Suehirocho tram stop, where you can catch a tram. Alternatively, walk to the **Kanamori Warehouse District▶**, a waterfront development of shops and cafés. From here you can walk back along the waterfront to the railway station.

241

Hakodate waterfront, one of the first ports to be opened to foreign trading following the end of Japan's self-imposed period of isolation

Sapporo restaurants

OODLES OF NOODLES
Sapporo is well-known for its *ramen* (noodles), which have Chinese origins. The most popular place to eat them is the Ramen Yokocho, an alleyway of 16 noodle shops one block east of the Susukino subway station.

LISTINGS
The free monthly English language *What's On In Sapporo* gives up-to-date events listings.

SUMMER BEER FESTIVAL
Odori Park in Sapporo is the site of a renowned Summer Beer Festival. Between mid-July and mid-August, numerous Japanese breweries set up shop in the gardens of the park, selling beer from 5pm in the evening. Vendors of noodles and other snack foods are also present, and there is usually a variety of live bands to add to the atmosphere.

The capital of Hokkaido has a population of 1.6 million and is the largest city on the island. More than a century ago it was no more than a collection of Ainu huts, but at the beginning of the Meiji Period the Japanese government decided to colonize the island. Following the advice of American experts, construction of the new city of Sapporo (from the Ainu meaning 'big, dry river') was started in 1871. Streets were laid out in a 100m (328ft) grid system, with wide avenues and parks. There are few interesting buildings, but the grid design is easy to negotiate. The Sapporo transportation information office, in the underground concourse of Odori station, supplies information on the comprehensive and efficient city bus and subway networks (see page 232 for details of how to get to Sapporo and for the snow festival).

Information in English about Sapporo and Hokkaido is available from the Sapporo City Tourism Department, Nishi-2-chome, Kita 2, Chuo-ku, tel: 011 211 2376 (*Open* 9–5, Sat 9–1; *closed* Sun), or from the tourist office in Sapporo station (*closed* on the second and fourth Wed of every month). Sapporo International Communication Plaza, Kita 1, Nishi 3, Chuo-ku (*Open* 9–9), has a reading room with newspapers and books in English.

The **Batchelor Memorial Museum▶▶** (*Open* 9–4, 30 Apr–30 Sep; 9–3, rest of years; *closed* Mon and 4 Nov–29 Apr) is in the grounds of the Botanical Gardens, which grow more than 5,000 plant varieties. It houses the collection of an Englishman, John Batchelor, who was deeply interested in Ainu culture and people.

Sapporo's most famous landmark is its **Clock Tower▶▶**, built in 1878 as part of Sapporo Agricultural College (now Hokkaido University), and now open to the public. Inside is a small museum illustrating the local history.

In 1876, Western influence established the first brewery in Japan; the **Sapporo Beer Garden and Museum▶▶** is built on the site of that original Sapporo Brewery. Free tours of the museum last about an hour, and run daily between 9am and 3.40pm. The Beer Garden is open for the consumption of beer and food from 11.30am to 9pm.

Nakajima Park▶▶ lies about 3km (2 miles) from Sapporo station and has a rose garden, boating lake, Nakajima Sports Centre and two buildings classified as national cultural treasures: the Hasso-an tea house and gardens, and the Hohei-kan, which was originally built as an imperial guesthouse.

▶▶▶ Shikotsu-Toya National Park   *230B3*

See map on page 246.

This 1,000sq-km (386sq-mile) park near Sapporo has lakes, volcanoes and the hot-spring spas of Toyako Onsen and Noboribetsu Onsen. Access is via the JR Sapporo–Hakodate line. For Lake Toya, leave the train at JR Toya station (two hours, ten minutes) and take the bus to Toyako Onsen. For Noboribetsu Onsen, get off at Noboribetsu Station (one and a half hours) and take the bus from there (20 minutes).

Abuta Volcano Science Museum▶▶ (*Open* 9–5), above the Toyako Onsen bus terminal, has photographs and lava displays of the huge eruption of Mount Usu in August 1977, which covered 80 per cent of Hokkaido with volcanic ash. The most interesting feature is the 350-seat 'experience room', duplicating the effects of a volcano.

Jigokudani▶▶ ('Hell Valley'), at the northern edge of Noboribetsu Onsen, is a volcanic crater 450m (1,476ft) in diameter, full of boiling water and mineral formations caused by the volcanic activity. A concrete path (Hell Valley Promenade) follows the left side of the crater, and leads to a lookout point over a large pond of boiling water called Ohyunuma. (*Continued on page 246.*)

INSTANT VOLCANO
Toyako Onsen, on the southwestern shore of Lake Toya, is a much frequented spa town, but it is also the place from which to visit Showa Shinzan, Japan's newest volcano. The volcano first emerged in 1943, appearing in a local farmer's field (much to his surprise). Over the next two years it steadily grew to its present height of 400m (1,312ft). Nearby Showa Shinzan is the volcanic Science Museum (Abuta Kazan Kagakukan), which focuses on the development of this young volcano and other volcanic activity within the Shikotsu-Toya National Park.

243

Shikotsu-Toya National Park

Every large Japanese city has a 'soapland'; an area of bars, massage parlours, nightclubs, restaurants and striptease joints. They used to be called 'Turkoland', but the name was changed after complaints from the Turkish Embassy. The new name derives from the service in Japanese massage parlours of soaping the customer all over while he lies on a rubber mattress.

PACHINKO
Bright, garish, noisy, and smoke-filled, *pachinko* pinball arcades are always found in soapland districts. There are more than 10,000 of these establishments in Japan, and more than half the population admits to playing *pachinko* pinball machines on a regular basis. Players win tokens that they swap for prizes ranging from cigarettes to hi-fi equipment. Apparently *pachinko* was invented by a Korean in Nagoya who, after World War II, wanted to find a use for surplus ball bearings.

244

Outside, massage parlours are generally garishly illuminated with bright neon lighting, and tough-looking individuals stand by the entrances, trying to persuade passers-by to go in.

Inside, soaping is for a basic fee. For an extra payment, the masseuse uses her hands and body to work the soap into a lather. The cost continues to rise depending on the customer's requirements.

A visit to soapland areas, which are quite safe for men and women to walk around, can be instructive about Japanese sensibilities. For example, Japanese men, often company men, usually drunk, socializing after work, are not at all sheepish about their enjoyment of the district, and there is none of the furtiveness found in similar areas elsewhere in the world.

The Yakuza (the Japanese Mafia) are usually involved in the soapland business, and can sometimes be seen cruising through the streets in large Cadillacs that are preferred by top Yakuza men. (Japanese import taxes have raised the prices of these cars, giving them extra status in their owners' eyes.)

The women who work in soapland districts often come from country areas or distant towns. They tend to earn as much money as they can for four or five years and then return home. Family or friends need not know what they have been doing, and there is no loss of face; many of the women go on to set up businesses, or find eligible husbands, and often do well. Japanese newspapers occasionally carry stories revealing that a well-known company boss or politician is married to a 'soapland girl'.

The Japanese government legalizes particular soapland areas as part of a long tradition in Japanese society. In the 17th and 18th centuries, entertainment for townsmen and for visitors alike (and often the main reason for going to town) was the brothel and the playhouse. In large towns and at stage posts along main roads, such as the Tokaido, red-light districts were established and

Amusement arcade

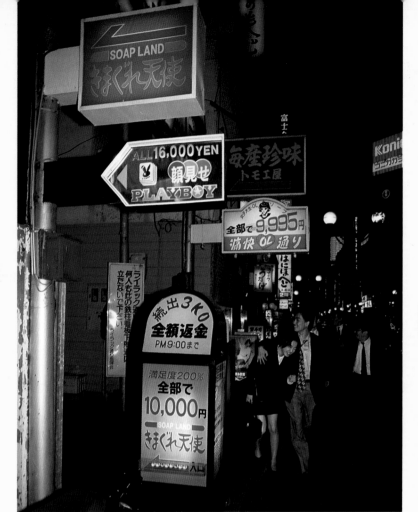

Signs for soapland

legalized by the government. Women in brothels were graded and priced according to their class and background and their skills in such arts as singing, dancing, the tea ceremony, music and dress. Those of the highest rank were entitled to reject a customer they did not like. All, however, were controlled by pimps and were virtual slaves.

Nowadays, visiting a prostitute is not freely condoned in Japanese society, although there is still much less stigma attached than there is in the West. Technically, it is now against the law, but thrives in soapland districts, especially in the so-called Pink Salons, the seedier cabaret clubs where the hostesses are available for extra services, and in the guise of 'health' and 'fashion' massages. Prostitution is often linked to organized crime.

For Japanese women, attitudes are gradually changing. It was recently reported in a respectable Japanese news-paper that some soapland districts now have Adonis bars staffed by handsome waiters and barmen available to their female customers to hire for sex. Apocryphal or not, such a story would certainly have failed to make it into print only a few years ago.

ALCOHOL

For the Japanese, there is no shame in getting drunk; in fact, in some circum-stances, your hosts may expect you to drink too much. Beer and/or sake are the usual accompani-ments to a meal. Guests do not pour their own drinks but allow their companions to do it, and are expected to pour theirs. An empty cup or glass is a signal that a fill-up is required.

Jigokudani (Hell Valley)

SILENT SPRINGS
Most people tend to stop over in Toyako Onsen and other hot-spring resorts in Shikotsu-Toya National Park only one night before moving on to explore another area. If you decide to stay another night or two, you will discover that you have the lodging and the hot baths to yourself daily, between check-out and check-in times.

(*Continued from page 243.*) **Noboribetsu Onsen►►** is a resort famous for its variety of hot-water springs. Eleven different types of mineral-saturated hot water, ranging in temperature from 45°C (113°F) to 91.5°C (197°F), with a total of more than 10,000 tonnes a day, spring from the ground. Though not a sophisticated resort, this is the most popular spa town in Hokkaido, and is always crowded during holiday periods.

Toyako Onsen►►, the main holiday focus for the park, is a typical Japanese resort with many hotels, inns and souvenir shops. Lake Toya is nearby and boat trips across the lake are available. The hot-spring waters are renowned for their curative qualities.

Travel Facts

Kansai International Airport

Arriving

By Air The arrival and departure point for international flights to and from Tokyo is **Narita**, officially called New Tokyo International Airport. The best ways to get to and from the airport, which is 64km (40 miles) from the heart of the city, are by bus or train. The airport's limousine bus information and ticket office is in the arrivals hall, just outside the exit from the customs hall. There are limousine bus services to Tokyo City Air Terminal (TCAT), Tokyo station and major hotels (the bus goes from one hotel to the next in a circular route). Depending on traffic, the journey can take up to two hours. For travel back to the airport, take the bus at least three hours before departure time. If you leave from TCAT, you can check in for your flight and hand in your luggage, which is taken to the airport and put on your flight. (Some airlines do not provide this service.)

Japanese Railways (JR) offers two services from Narita to Tokyo station: the Narita Express (53 minutes) runs at least once every hour from 7.43am to 9.43pm; Airport Narita (one hour, 24 minutes) runs every hour on the hour. Keisei Line Skyliner is a privately operated express train between Narita Airport and Keisei-Ueno station in Tokyo. It runs every 40 minutes between 6am and 8pm, and takes exactly 61 minutes. From Ueno station you can take a taxi or subway (not recommended for your first visit) to your destination. There is a shuttle bus from the arrival hall at the airport to Keisei station, a short distance away. The Keisei information counter and ticket office is near the exit from the customs hall. You will have to pay airport tax on departure from Narita; buy a ticket at TCAT or at a tax counter at the airport (before entering the departure lounge).

The main tourist information office in Narita airport is in Terminal 2. It is open daily 9–8 (tel: 04 7634 6251). Information about all of Japan is available here. There is a smaller office in Terminal 1, open the same hours. If you have a Japan Rail Pass exchange order, it can be ratified for immediate or later use at the JR travel agent in the basement. Ask at the TIC office for directions or look for signs (in English).

Kansai International Airport is another state-of-the-art construction work. In response to ever-growing demands for international and internal flight services, especially in the Kansai area (around Kyoto and Osaka), national government and private investors have spent 1.5 trillion yen building the airport. It is a huge man-made island, lying 5km (3 miles) off the Senshu Coast at the southern end of Osaka Bay, with air connections to 44 countries and 22 areas within Japan. It is joined to the land by a two-tiered access bridge, which carries rail and road services.

The airport is serviced by two rail lines, JR West and Nankai Electric RR. JR's Haruka Express runs directly to Kyoto through Shin-Osaka and Tennoji stations. Nankai runs two limited express trains from Namba. The first operates nonstop between Namba and the airport (29 minutes). The second stops at Sakai (taking 11 minutes) and certain other express points along the way. It is also possible to take nonexpress trains from other points to the airport.

Limousine bus services is available to and from most areas in Kansai.

At present, Kansai Airport has two runways. Plans for the future include the construction of a third runway, which will facilitate takeoffs and landings during difficult wind conditions.

High-speed sea services exploit the airport's waterfront. The Jet Foil service to K-CAT on Port Island (Kobe) runs from 6.30am to 11.15pm daily, taking just 30 minutes. The high-speed catamarans to Awaji and Tokushima take 34 and 90 minutes, respectively.

Customs regulations Clear passport control and collect your luggage before moving on to the 'non-resident' customs counters. Drugs, pornography and firearms are strictly prohibited. Non-residents are allowed to bring in duty free: 400 cigarettes *or* 100 cigars *or* 500g tobacco; 3 bottles (760cc each) alcohol; 50gm/2 fl oz perfume; other goods up to ¥200,000 in value. No allowance is given to people aged 19 or younger.

The import of wildlife souvenirs sourced from rare or endangered species may be either illegal or

Public telephones can be found everywhere in Japan

require a special permit. Before purchase you should check your home country's customs regulations.

Travel insurance Standard travel insurance is advisable, including cover for medical care. Remember to check your policy. Japanese hospitals have high standards but they are expensive, as are dental treatments. English- and, to a lesser extent, German-speaking doctors and dentists are not uncommon.

Visas, health matters Japan has agreements with 52 countries exempting their citizens from the necessity of applying for a visa before entering Japan. Citizens from these countries are allowed to stay in Japan for between three to six months. Check requirements before you leave. Visas are required by anyone who intends to obtain employment, engage in any paid activity, or stay past the specified period. No vaccinations are required for entering Japan.

249

Old and new walk side by side

Climate In general, the climate of Japan resembles the temperate climate of the east coast of the US, although the subtropical, southern island of Kyushu is warmer and the snowy, northern island of Hokkaido is colder. The best times to travel are in spring and autumn. There are four distinct seasons. Spring begins in March (early April in northern Honshu and Hokkaido) and lasts until the beginning of June. April and May are warm and dry, a good time for visiting. From late March to mid-April, the *sakura* (cherry blossoms) ripen northward from Kyushu to Hokkaido. The summer and rainy seasons start in early June; a hot and humid time (except in Hokkaido). From mid-July to early September it remains hot, but not wet. Mountain areas are refreshing at this time of the year. Autumn has clear skies and comfortable temperatures, although late September can be wet. Winter in the north and at high altitudes is cold, snowy and beautiful. In other areas, temperatures rarely drop below freezing.

WEATHER CHARTS

Money matters Credit cards are widely accepted in Japan, but cash is still the preferred way of paying bills in normal transactions, and the Japanese often carry huge wads of money around with them (a reflection of their safe society). Japanese currency is the yen and there are three types of notes and six different coins: 1,000, 5,000, and 10,000 yen notes; and 1, 5, 10, 50, 100, and 500 yen coins. Diners Club, MasterCard, Visa and American Express are the major credit cards. Travellers' cheques in yen or dollars are easily exchanged for cash at the banks, but are not readily accepted at small shops and restaurants.

A network of 21,000 ATMs has been created in Post Offices throughout Japan. Most major credit cards may be used to withdraw cash. Look for Post Offcies with the international ATM service symbol.

Regions of Japan There are eight official regions in Japan, as follows: Hokkaido, Kyushu and Shikoku, and the five regions of Honshu, the largest island: Tohoku, the mountainous rural northeastern region; Kanto, east central Honshu, Japan's most urban region (includes Tokyo); Chubu, the mountainous central region of Honshu, including the Japan Alps; Kinki, lying to the west and including Japan's second-largest industrialized area, based around on the cities of Osaka and Kobe, and the historical capitals of Kyoto and Nara; and finally,

Chugoku on west Honshu, an agricultural and fishing region.

Time differences All of the islands of Japan are in the same time zone. London is nine hours behind (eight hours during British Summer Time), New York and Los Angeles 14 and 17 hours behind, respectively. Australia is one or two hours earlier; New Zealand is three hours earlier; Canada is 12.5 to 18 hours later.

Tipping Tips are neither given nor expected. Large hotels and restaurants may, however, add a 10 to 15 per cent service charge to your bill. A government tax of 3 per cent is added to food bills of ¥7,500 or less and 6 per cent to bills over that sum; to combined food and accommodation bills of ¥15,000 or less, 3 per cent is added; over ¥15,000 6 per cent is added.

When to go The Japanese all tend to take their holidays between similar dates and it is best to avoid these times. The three major holiday periods are: two or three days before and after New Year's Day; the week following Greenery Day (29 April), known as Golden Week; and the week that includes 13–16 August, the Obon Festival, when many Japanese return to their home towns.

The torii *(gate) at Itsukushima Shrine, Hiroshima. Founded in the sixth century, the shrine took its present form during the Heian period (795–1185). Since then it has been rebuilt seven times*

Trains Also see page 92. Trains are the quickest way of exploring Japan. Japan Railways (JR) run 28,000 trains daily, and there are numerous private railway lines. The fare system is complex and needs to be understood to avoid paying the highest prices. There is a basic fare for any train, calculated by the distance of the journey. Added to this fare are various surcharges, mainly dependent on how fast the train is, but also on whether you reserve a seat or not, and on the class of travel.

There are four categories of train; the slower they are, the less you pay. The bullet trains (Shinkansen) are the fastest; limited stop express (Tokkyu or Cho-tokkyu) next to fastest; express (Kyuko) next to slowest; and local trains (Futsu) the slowest.

If you have limited time and no restrictions on your expenses, Shinkansen are the trains to use. On a budget (and in no great hurry), the best trains are a combination of the limited express for long journeys and then the local trains for exploring a particular area.

If you wish to stop at places *en route* to your destination, purchase a ticket for the whole journey; you are allowed to make as many stops as you wish, as long as the date on your ticket remains valid for the whole journey. The period of validity is one day for 100km (60 miles), two days for 200km (125 miles), and then one day for each additional 200km (125 miles). Some restrictions may apply on Shinkansen routes; information on 03 3423 0111. You can get refunds on unused tickets and change routing once without any handling charge.

If you are not sure how much your fare is or where you are going, buy the cheapest ticket and pay any balance due at your destination; most stations have a fare adjustment counter.

Purchase reserved tickets at the 'green windows', called *midori-no-madoguchi* in Japanese.

If you intend to make a reasonable number of train journeys, it is worth buying a national or regional Japan Rail Pass. These are valid for one to three weeks and can save you quite a lot of money. You can purchase them only outside Japan, and they allow you unlimited travel on all JR rail, bus and boat services. Get a voucher from an authorized sales agent (lists available from JNTO) in your own country and exchange it for a rail pass at Tokyo or Osaka stations on your arrival, or better still from the JR counter at Narita Airport (*Open* 7am–11pm every day). Visit www.world.eki-net.com for rail reservations outside Japan.

Do not carry a lot of luggage; busy trains usually have space for only one medium-size suitcase.

Most trains have buffet cars and/or food and drink available from carts that are pushed up and down the aisles. They also sell *eki-ben* (lunchboxes), but those sold at the station are often cheaper and fresher.

All reasonably sized stations and all those on JR lines display station names in *kanji* (Chinese characters) and *Romaji* (Japanese Roman script). The name of the station is in the middle of the nameboard with the preceding and following stations above and beneath it. Keep a careful watch for these nameboards when approaching a station. Sometimes there is only one, and it can flash past before you have seen it.

Try to avoid making a journey during the peak rush hours (7–9am and 5–7pm). All of the major stations are equipped with an information counter where you can get maps, lodging advice, and assistance with your train travel from English-speaking assistants.

The following Japanese phrases may be useful for train travel.

At what time does the train for Tokyo leave? *Tokyo yuki no densha wa nanji ni demasu ka?*
From which platform? *Nanban sen kara demasu ka?*
Where is platform 1? *Ichi ban sen wa doko desu ka?*
Does the train for Osaka leave from here? *Osaka yuki no densha wa koko kara demasu ka?*
I want to get off at Tokyo station. *Tokyo eki de oritai desu.*
Will you tell me when to get off? *Itsu oritara yoi ka oshiete kudasai?*
How many stations (before) I get off? *Koko kara nanbanme no eki de oriruno desu ka?*

Subways Many large Japanese cities have subway systems, most of them providing the quickest and most inexpensive way of moving about town. Subway maps are provided at station information counters or local tourist offices.

Buses Japan has an excellent network of local city and rural buses, and the bus terminals are often adjacent to train stations, so it is easy to make use of both buses and trains. For long journeys, buses are slower and less comfortable than trains but they are somewhat cheaper.

Japanese Railways provides a service of overnight long-distance buses on which the Japan Rail Pass (see pages 254–255) is valid.

Buses come into their own for local journeys. Unfortunately, many do not show their destination in *Romaji*, so it is important to be sure of the number you wish to take, in which direction you want to take it, and where, if at all, you need to change buses. This information can be obtained from tourist offices.

Once you know your bus number and destination, write them on a piece of paper so that people can help you. Knowing how much to pay once you are on board is much easier than catching the right bus.

As you enter the bus (at the back), take a ticket from the dispensing machine inside the door. It has a number on the back. A meter above the driver's head matches the cost of the fares against the numbers on the backs of the tickets. It rotates during the bus journey, increasing the fare against the ticket numbers accordingly.

As you get off, put your fare into the collecting machine by the side of the driver. There is a box attached to the machine that will give change for coins and bills.

Taxis Taxis are quite expensive, but the fare shown on the meter is exactly what you pay. However, tipping is not the custom. It is a good idea to carry the address and telephone number of your destination in *Romaji* and to show the taxi driver, to clarify where you wish to go.

After hailing a cab do not try to open the taxi door. The driver will open the kerbside door by remote control. Similarly, do not try to close the door on leaving.

A red light on the dashboard indicates an available taxi; a green light means it is occupied.

The International Student Identity card, available in many countries from student organizations, entitles the holder to discounts at several art galleries, museums, and so on, plus youth rail passes and reductions on some local transportation.

Car rental Cars can be reserved through Hertz-Japan (tel: 03 3356 8002) and other major companies including Nippon (tel: 03 3485 7196, English-speaking operator available) and Nissan Car Lease (tel: 03 5424 4123, English-speaking operator). An international and national driving licence is required. Traffic drives on the left, the steering wheel is on the right, and speed limits vary, but generally the limit is 80kph (50mph) on highways and 40kph (25mph) in urban areas.

Renting a car locally to explore the immediate area can be a sensible proposition, but for visiting the rest of the country, driving is not the best option. Eki Rent-a-car tickets (*kippu*) offer a combination option of rail ticket and discounted car rental at your destination. Details can be obtained from JR Travel Service offices at major railway stations.

Ferries Frequent ferry services connect the main islands of Japan and local ferries connect all populated small islands to the nearest main ports as well as to other islands in the same group. Tokyo or Osaka to Kyushu, Shikoku, or Hokkaido are popular main routes. Ferries are less expensive than air or rail, although obviously slower. Economy passengers occupy one large *tatami* (straw floor mat) room where they eat, sit and sleep together.

On longer routes, a small Japanese public bath is on the same deck on the ferry. Private cabins also are available. Tickets and information can be obtained from travel agents based in Japan.

Visitors with disabilities In recent years, local authorities have invested a lot of time and money to make public buildings and means of transportation more accessible. Braille is in increasing evidence at ticket booths and alongside place names on public maps, elevators and government building floor plans, etc.

In addition, visitors to Japan will notice that many streets in modern cities now have special markings so that the visually impaired can 'touch-feel' their way as they walk.

254

© Communicarta Ltd, 11/2004

Loudspeakers have also been fitted at road crossing points.

With advance warning, visitors with disabilities can receive assistance at Narita Airport and the limousine bus service is also accessible.

Written enquiries can be sent, well in advance of travel, to: Physically Handicapped Lifestyle Centre, 1-44-2 Umegaoka, Setagaya-ku, Tokyo 154, or visit www.wakaoma.org/aj .

*Line under construction (due to open 2007)

Map user Ref: 9C02117/EXP/NYC/GB

U.D.N.6a

Uniformity is an early lesson for Japanese school children

Language The Japanese spend many years at school learning English but very few are confident of speaking it, though it is probable that their English is better than most visitors' Japanese. The following Japanese phrases are among those that are likely to be most helpful. (In general, 'u' at the end of a word is not pronounced.)

256

Mr or Mrs *san* after the surname (but don't ever append it to your own name)
Yes *hai*
Yes, I agree *hai, so des*
Thank you (*domo*) *arigato*
Yes, please *hai onegaishimasu*
No (rarely used) *iie*
No, I disagree *chigaimasu*
I am sorry *gomen-nasai*
Excuse me (also used to call waiter) *sumimasen...*
Good morning *o-haiyo-gozaimasu*
Good afternoon *konnichi-wa*
Good evening *konban-wa*
Good night *oyasumi nasai*
Goodbye *sayonara*
Excuse me, do you speak English? *sumimasen, Eigo dekimasu-ka?*
Yes, just a little *hai, sukoshi dake*
No, I can't *iie, dame desu*
(On starting a meal) *itadakimasu*
Cheers! *kampai!*
Thank you (for kindness) *domo arigato gozaimash'ta*
Thank you (after a meal) *gochiso-sama desh'ta*
What is your name? *o-namae wa?*
My name is 'Smith' *watashi wa 'Smith' desu*

(I'm) ill (*watashi wa*) *byoki desu*
Help! *tasukete (kudasai)!*
hospital *byoin*
Police *Keisatsu*
How much is it? *ikura desu ka?*
for bed-and-breakfast *choshokutsuki*
for full board *sanshokutsuki*
excluding meals *sudomari desu*
does that include...? *wa tsuite imasu-ka?*
meals *shokuji* or *go-han*
service *saabisu*
Have you anything cheaper? *Nanika motto yasui no wa (arimasen ka?)*
Menu, please *menu o kudasai*
Bill, please *go-kanjo onegaishimasu*
Do you accept credit cards? *credit cardo tsukaemasu ka?*
coffee shop *kissaten*
restaurant *restoran*
beer *biru*
water *mizu*
milk *milku*
coffee *kohee*
Indian tea *kocha*
Japanese or Chinese tea *ocha*
sugar, please *satoh, kudasai*

For details of the Japanese writing system, see pages 20–21.

The following are a few helpful Japanese suffixes and terms:
-dera temple
-dori street or avenue
gai-jin foreigners
-gawa river
-ji temple
-jo castle
-ko lake
-koen park or gardens
-mon gate
onsen hot spring spas
ryokan traditional Japanese inns
sakura cherry blossoms
-san mount
sento public communal bath houses
shoji paper room-dividing screens
tatami closely woven straw floor mats
torii gate

Emergency telephone numbers
Police: 110; Ambulance/Fire: 119. Press the red button on the telephone and dial. No money is required. The operator will answer in Japanese so you will need the assistance of a Japanese speaker. See page 249 for details of English-speaking operators.

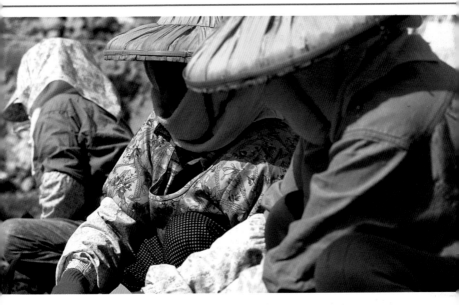

Health The Japanese have the highest life expectancy in the world. Japan is a clean, hygienic country and doctors are highly trained. Health insurance is recommended for visitors. Clinics with English-speaking doctors include: Hibiya Clinic, Hibiya Mitsui Building, 1-1-2 Yurakucho Chiyoda-ku, Tokyo (tel: 03 3502 2681) and Japan Baptist Hospital, 14 Yamanomotocho Kitashirakawa, Kyoto, Sakyo-ku (tel: 075 781 5191). English is spoken at the following hospitals: Ginza area: St. Luke's International Hospital (Sei Roka Byoin), 9-1 Akashi-cho, Chuo-ku (tel: 03 3541 5151); Shinjuku area: International Catholic Hospital (Seibo Byoin), 2-5-1 Naka Ochai, Shinjuku-ku, (tel: 03 3951 1111).

Lost property If you forget something or leave it in a public place there is every chance it will still be there when you return. All public trans-portation systems, including taxi companies, have a lost-and-found service. In Tokyo:
Taxis (tel: 03 3648 0300)
JR (tel: 03 3231 1880)
Subway (tel: 03 3834 5577)
Buses (tel: 03 3815 7229)
The Tokyo Central Lost and Found Police Office is at 1-9-11, Koraku, Bunkyo-ku (tel: 03 3814 4151).

Archaeologists excavating a site on Ishigaki Island

Pharmacies Japanese pharmacies sell the same range of goods as Western shops. Pharmacies are easily found in any town, in Tokyo, there is an English-speaking one at the American Pharmacy, Hibiya Park Building, 1-8-1, Yurakucho, Chiyoda-ku (tel: 03 3271-4034/5), open 9–7 Mon–Sat, 11–7 Sunday and public holidays.

Police Robbery is very rare in Japan and violent crime is even less likely. Japanese policemen and women are helpful and approachable, but very few speak any English. Every Japanese district has its own 'police box' (*koban*), usually near a busy intersection or station. The police on duty will help you find an address if you can show them a map of its location.

Media Japan has four daily English-language newspapers on sale in hotels or at major train stations. There are English editions of the *Asahi*, *Yomiuri* and *Mainichi*, and the fourth is the independent *Japan Times*. The monthly English-language *Tokyo Journal* gives comprehensive reviews and lists of plays, film, art shows and restaurants.

framework of the newspaper's editorial policy.

English-language television and radio are available at most large hotels.

Post offices The Japanese postal service is very efficient in delivering both domestic and foreign mail. Post offices are open Mon–Fri 9–5, with cash deposits or withdrawal until 3pm; Sat 9–12.30 (main offices only); closed on Sunday and national holidays. The Central Post Office next to Tokyo station is open 24 hours a day. Smaller post offices close on the second Saturday of each month. Post boxes are red.

Takyubin (express delivery) service exists for sending heavy or bulky goods between hotels. This takes 24 hours, and those wishing to use the service should check that there will be someone at the other end to receive the goods.

Letters addressed in *Romaji*, sent to Japan or within Japan, should have the address printed in large, bold

Japanese newspapers differ from their Western counterparts in two main areas. A clear-cut stance in articles is avoided, and the publisher, rather than the reporter, assumes responsibility for the content of a story. A journalist is always expected to work closely within the

The distinctive red Japanese post boxes are easy to spot

The urban architecture of Tokyo, ancient and modern

print to make it easier for the Japanese sorter to read. To send a letter or postcard in Japan, take it to the post office and have it weighed. Post office clerks read *Romaji*. Large post offices may be used as *poste restante* addresses.

Telephones Public telephones are found virtually everywhere in Japan. Grey and green telephones accept both 10-yen and 100-yen coins and telephone cards. Red phones accept 10-yen coins only. Direct intercity calls can all be made from these phones but international calls must be made from 'International and Domestic Card/Coin Telephones'

found at international airports and hotels, and in some major office buildings.

To get the international information service dial 0057; for the international operator, dial 0051. Dial direct international calls (using KDDI network) as follows: 001 + the national number of the country being called + area code + local phone number. The national number of Australia is 61; Canada is 1; Ireland is 353; New Zealand is 64; the UK is 44 and the US is 1. If the area code starts with a 0, omit it. To call Japan from Australia dial 0011 81; from Canada 011 81; from the UK, Ireland, and New Zealand 00 81; the US 011 81. Again, omit the area code's initial 0. Fax is widely used in Japan and most offices and hotels have their own fax machines.

Bottles of sake ready to be enjoyed

CONVERSION CHARTS

FROM	TO	MULTIPLY BY
Inches	Centimetres	2.54
Centimetres	Inches	0.3937
Feet	Metres	0.3048
Metres	Feet	3.2810
Yards	Metres	0.9144
Metres	Yards	1.0940
Miles	Kilometres	1.6090
Kilometres	Miles	0.6214
Acres	Hectares	0.4047
Hectares	Acres	2.4710
Gallons	Litres	4.5460
Litres	Gallons	0.2200
Ounces	Grams	28.35
Grams	Ounces	0.0353
Pounds	Grams	453.6
Grams	Pounds	0.0022
Pounds	Kilograms	0.4536
Kilograms	Pounds	2.205
Tons	Tonnes	1.0160
Tonnes	Tons	0.9842

MEN'S SUITS

UK	36	38	40	42	44	46	48
Rest of Europe	46	48	50	52	54	56	58
US	36	38	40	42	44	46	48

DRESS SIZES

UK	8	10	12	14	16	18
France	36	38	40	42	44	46
Italy	38	40	42	44	46	48
Rest of Europe	34	36	38	40	42	44
US	6	8	10	12	14	16

MEN'S SHIRTS

UK	14	14.5	15	15.5	16	16.5	17
Rest of Europe	36	37	38	39/40	41	42	43
US	14	14.5	15	15.5	16	16.5	17

MEN'S SHOES

UK	7	7.5	8.5	9.5	10.5	11
Rest of Europe	41	42	43	44	45	46
US	8	8.5	9.5	10.5	11.5	12

WOMEN'S SHOES

UK	4.5	5	5.5	6	6.5	7
Rest of Europe	38	38	39	39	40	41
US	6	6.5	7	7.5	8	8.5

Camping and self-catering organizations There are some campsites in Japan, but they tend to be difficult to find and primitive. Camping is neither a popular nor common pastime. People on a tight budget who wish to cater for themselves would be better advised to stay in youth hostels. The Japan Youth Hostel Association is at Hoken Kaikan, 1-1 Ichigaya Sadohara-cho, Shinjuku-ku, Tokyo (tel: 03 3269 5831).

Children Young visitors are well provided for in Japan and there are theme parks, aquariums, zoos, video display exhibitions and other child-orientated events readily available throughout the country. There is also a Disneyland on the outskirts of Tokyo. Local tourist information offices have full details of their area's amenities.

Children in Japan are allowed to walk, cycle and travel on public transportation on their own from a very early age, and family homes and schools are still found in the heart of the cities.

Japanese children really enjoy meeting foreign boys and girls and becoming pen pals with them. If you take children to Japan, they will have no difficulty in making friends, despite the language differences.

Electricity From Tokyo east to Hokkaido, the current is 100 volts at 50 cycles. Western Japan operates on 100 volts at 60 cycles. North Americans with electronic equipment that operates at 110/60 will have no problems. Europeans using devices designed to operate at 240/50 cycles will need to adjust them or, if they are not convertible, use a transformer. Some of the major hotels have 240/50 outputs.

Entrance fees Most Japanese museums, galleries, monuments, and nationally known temples and gardens charge entrance fees, which usually fall in the ¥300–¥800 range.

Opening times

Banks open Mon–Fri 9–3, Sat 9–noon; closed Saturday afternoon, Sunday and national holidays.

Museums usually open 9–5, Apr–Oct; 9–4.30, rest of year; closed Monday and 29 Dec–3 Jan. Most museums stop letting people in half an hour before closing time. If a national holiday falls on a museum's weekly closing day, it closes on the following day instead.

Shops open from around 10am. Some close around 6pm; others stay open until much later. Many, but not all, in the central business district are open on Sundays and holidays.

Department stores all open six days a week at 10am. Some stay open to 8pm, although most close at 6 on Saturday and Sunday and holidays. Some are closed on Mondays, and others on Wednesdays and Thursdays.

Photography A huge array of cameras, processing facilities and film of every sort is available in even the smallest Japanese town.

Places of worship The following places of worship in Tokyo hold services in English:
Anglican: St. Alban's, 3-6-25 Shibakoen, Minato-ku (tel: 03 3431 8534).
Baptist: Tokyo Baptist Church, 9-2 Hachiyama-cho, Shibuya-ku (tel: 03 3461 8425).
Catholic: St. Ignatius, 6-5 Kojimachi, Chiyoda-ku (tel: 03 3263 4584).
Jewish: Jewish Community of Japan, 3-8-8 Hiroo, Shibuya-ku (tel: 03 3400 2559).

261

Lavatories Most of the modern facilities in large towns provide Western-style lavatories, but in rural areas Japanese squat-style lavatories are still quite common. There are public lavatories in train stations and public parks (they do not provide paper) but those in department stores and coffee shops are always cleaner.

Information on hand at the Grand Shrines of Ise

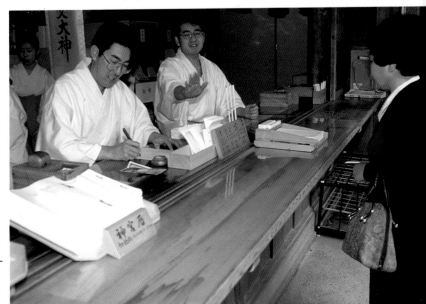

Customs and etiquette However Westernized modern Japan may appear, traditional etiquette continues to be very important. Most Japanese expect that, as a visitor, you will not understand the complexities of their social customs, and that you will behave according to Western rules. However, evidence of a basic understanding of Japanese values and a respect for them will certainly be appreciated, enjoyed and acknowledged by the people you meet.

Status Japanese society is even today hierarchical and spoken Japanese contains a battery of expressions that, used appropriately, set both the relative social positions and the gender of the speaker and the person spoken to. Both parties immediately know where they stand on the ladder of inferiority, equality, or superiority. Visitors, especially on business, are accorded a relatively high status, and may respond to this by being polite and effusive in expressing thanks even for minor kindness. For receivers of hospitality, be it drinks, a meal, or a gift, it is customary to say *Arigato gozaimasu*, a polite 'Thank you', at the time of receiving and at the next meeting. Saying 'Thank you' several times symbolizes a long-term rather than a transitory relationship.

Groups versus individuals The Japanese have a tendency to think in terms of the social group they belong to, rather than as individuals. This leads to an intrinsic recognition of the rights of the group over those of an individual member, and a close observance of family morals and taboos. Social harmony (*wa*) is highly valued in the workplace and at home. In business and politics, consensus opinion is vital before decisions or policies are made public, and an open display of conflict is viewed as deeply embarrassing.

Thinking ahead Forethought is another distinctive feature of Japanese manners. It is always best to do things for others before being asked. For example, a host will try to anticipate what a guest might want or need. Tea or coffee and even a meal may be served without you asking for it. Room dividers (*fusuma* and *shoji*) in a traditional Japanese house do not have locks. If the *fusuma* is closed a person wishing to enter needs to choose correctly between knocking, calling out, or just going away.

Bowing The Japanese bow a lot to each other on meeting or departing. The depth and frequency of the bows depends on the status of the people involved. To be on the safe side, imitate any bows you receive. Hold both arms straight and bow with the

Bid for good luck at Motsuji Temple

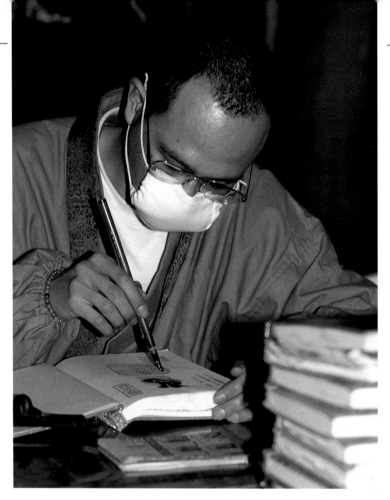

upper body. Shaking hands is an alternative way of introducing yourself and is still a novelty to the Japanese. However, a strong hand-shake is not needed and would not be understood.

Conversation and smiling In conversation, it is common for the listener to nod and utter approving sounds. These do not, however, necessarily mean consent or agreement. In fact, in most cases they signal only that the listener is concentrating on what you are saying. Another possible source of misunderstanding is smiling. For a Japanese smiling may be a way of hiding embarrassment; don't take it to mean assent all the time. Smiling may even disguise inner sadness. Genuine happiness is indicated more accurately by creases in the corners of

A monk signs pilgrims' log books at Koya-san Temple

the eye. According to general Japanese thinking, disclosing such emotions would be to foist off one's problems onto another, to burden the listener and thereby show a lack of consideration.

Nose-blowing It is normal in Japan to clear your throat or sniff if you have a cold or a running nose (and even acceptable to spit discreetly in the street). However, it is considered rude to blow your nose in public. People you see wearing masks over their mouth and nose do so because they have a cold, not because of pollution. It is best to go to some other private place if you need to blow your nose.

Embassies and consulates in Tokyo
The following have embassies and/or consulates based in Tokyo.
Australia: 2-1-14 Mita, Minato-ku
(tel: 03 5232 4111).
Canada: 7-3-38 Akasaka, Minato-ku
(tel: 03 5412 6200).
Ireland: Ireland House, 2-10-7
Kojimachi, Chiyoda-ku
(tel: 03 3263 0695).
New Zealand: 20–40 Kamiyama-cho,
Shibuya-ku
(tel: 03 3467 2271).
UK: 1 Ichiban-cho, Chiyoda-ku
(tel: 03 3265 5511).
US: 1-10-5 Akasaka, Minato-ku
(tel: 03 3224 5000).

Japanese embassies and consulates abroad
Australia: 112 Empire Circuit,
Yarralumla, Canberra, ACT 2600
(tel: 06 273 3244).
Canada: 255 Sussex Drive, Ottawa,
Ontario K1N 9E6
(tel: 613 241-8541).
New Zealand: Level 18, Majestic
Central, 100 Willis Street, Wellington 1
(tel: 04 473 1540).
UK: 101–104 Piccadilly, London
W1J 7JT
(tel: 020 7465 6500).
US: 2520 Massachusetts Avenue
NW, Washington DC 20008
(tel: 202 238-6700).

Tourist offices The Japanese National
Tourist Office (JNTO) operates two
main Tourist Information Centres
(TIC) in Japan. They give advice on
travel arrangements and accommodation and stock lots of useful free
literature. Most towns have their
own tourist offices, normally within
or near the main railway station.
Tokyo office: 10F, Tokyo Kotsu
Kaikon Building, 2-10-1 Yurakucho,
Chiyoda-Ku, Tokyo 100-006 (tel: 03
3201 3331; fax: 03 3201 3347). Open
weekdays 9–5, Sat 9–noon; closed Sun
and national holidays.
Tokyo International Airport office:
Airport No. 2 Terminal Building,
Narita Airport, Chiba Prefecture
(tel: 0476 34 6251). Open 9–8.

JNTO also operates a main office in
Tokyo and others abroad.
Japan (main office): Tokyo Kotsu
Kaikan Building, 2-10-1 Yurakucho,
Chiyoda-ku, Tokyo 100
(tel: 03 3216 2905).
Worldwide JNTO web site address:
www.jnto.go.jp
Australia: Level 18, Australia Square
Tower, 264 George Street, Sydney,
NSW 2000 (tel: 02 9251 3024).
Canada: 165 University Avenue,
Toronto, Ontario M5H 3B8
(tel: 416 366 7140).
UK: Heathcoat House, 20 Savile Row,
London W1S 3PR
(tel: 020 7734 6870).
US: One Rockefeller Plaza, Suite 1250,
New York, NY 10020
(tel: 212 757 5640).

Receiving a helping hand

264

Hotels and Restaurants

HOTELS

There is no shortage of places to stay in Japan. In the cities there is a wide variety of options, while in rural areas there are usually *minshuku* (see pages 80–81), small inns, hotels and sometimes *ryokan* (see pages 220–221).

The Japan Hotel Association has its own website for booking and information at www.j-hotel.or.jp. Welcome Inns, a network of 700 small, reasonably priced hotels and inns, provide information and a booking facility at www.itcj.or.jp. Visit www.eryokan.co.jp for *ryokan* booking and information.

The range of average prices for different categories of accommodation is as follows:

Hotel accommodation:
Expensive (¥¥¥): ¥30,000–45,000
Moderate (¥¥): ¥15,000–29,000
Inexpensive (¥): ¥6,000–14,000

Other accommodation:
Ryokan: ¥20,000–40,000 (includes breakfast and dinner)
Business hotels: ¥8,000–12,000
Minshuku: ¥6,000–8,000
Japanese inns: ¥5,000–7,000
Youth hostels: ¥1,000–3,000

TOKYO

Akasaka Excel Hotel Tokyu (¥/¥¥)
2-14-3 Nagata-cho, Chiyoda-ku
tel: 03 3580 2311; www.tokyuhotel.com
Convenient for the central area, rooms not big but with all facilities, wide variety of restaurants. It's popular, so book well ahead.

Akasaka Prince Hotel (¥¥¥)
1-2 Kioi-cho, Chiyoda-ku tel: 03 3234 1111; www.princehotels.co.jp/english
The service is first-class; the rooms have excellent views and tasteful modern furnishings. The building has quality postwar architecture.

ANA Hotel Tokyo (¥¥¥)
1-12-33 Akasaka, Minato-ku
tel: 03 3505 1111; www.anahotels.com
In the Ark Hills area, between Roppongi and Akasaka, a 37-floor, 903-room block with a sober exterior and vast areas of marble inside. Facilities include a health club and pool, executive floor and several restaurants.

Asakusa View Hotel (¥¥)
3-17-1 Nishi-Asakusa, Taito-ku
tel: 03 3842 2111; www.viewhotels.co.jp
The only hotel with international facilities in this lively entertaining district, but nevertheless manages to retain a very Japanese feel. The facilites include a swimming pool, gymnasium and Japanese garden.

Atamiso (¥¥)
4-14-3 Ginza, Chuo-ku
tel: 03 3541 3621
This small hotel (74 rooms) has a friendly personal service. It is close to central Ginza's nightlife and shopping.

Capitol Tokyu (¥¥¥)
2-10-3 Nagatacho, Chiyoda-ku
tel: 03 3581 4511; www.capitoltokyu.com
In the heart of Tokyo's governmental district, this is a meeting place for the city's power brokers. Quality service, fine cuisine, excellent Japanese garden and pond.

Edmont (¥¥)
3-10-8 Iidabashi, Chiyoda-ku tel: 03 3237 1111
Unexpected back-street location for a very modern hotel with a warm inviting lobby and lounge. The double rooms are a reasonable size.

Elegant Inn Yasuda (¥)
1-56-28 Matsubara, Setagaya-ku
tel: 03 3322 5546
Japanese inn offering Western- and Japanese rooms, air-conditioned. Good value.

Fairmont Hotel (¥/¥¥)
2-1-17 Kudan Minami, Chiyoda-ku
tel: 03 3262 1151
For Tokyo, this is an older style hotel (built in 1952). Small and quietly positioned near the Imperial Palace. Highly recommended during the cherry blossom season in spring.

Ginza Ocean (¥¥)
7-18-15 Ginza, Chuo-ku tel: 03 3545 1221
A cut above the usual business hotel, with friendly staff and a good Japanese restaurant.

Hotel Okura (¥¥¥)
2-10-4 Torano-mon, Minato-ku
tel: 03 3582 0111; www.okura.com
Stately, formal, one of the first of the postwar grand hotels, with 883 spacious rooms, many restaurants, an art gallery, and indoor and outdoor pools. It is quietly sophisticated and popular with diplomats and businessmen.

Hotel Seiyo Ginza (¥¥¥)
1-11-2 Ginza, Chuo-ku tel: 03 3535 1111; www.seiyo-ginza.co.jp
Very expensive, small and luxurious hotel with highly personalized service. Staff-to-guest ratio is three to one. Reservations a must.

Ibis (¥)
7-4-14, Roppong, Minato-ku tel: 03 3403 4411
Straightforward business hotel. Basic, no-frills, but very convenient for Roppongi and its full-on nightlife.

Imperial (¥¥¥)
1-1-1 Uchisaiwaicho, Chiyoda-ku
tel: 03 3504 1111; www.imperialhotel.co.jp
On the edge of Ginza, facing Hibiya Park, this is a city-within-a-city, with 1,059 rooms, more than 20 restaurants, dozens of shops, a health club and pool. Rooms are beautifully appointed, with superb views from the upper stories.

Keihin Hotel (¥¥)
4-10-20 Takanawa, Minato-ku
tel: 03 3449 5711
Slightly out of the way in Shinagawa district, but an excellent value, straightforward, modest hotel. There is usually somebody at the desk who can speak English.

Kikuya Ryokan (¥)
2-18-9 Nishi-Asakusa, Taito-ku
tel: 03 3841 6404
Very small, with eight Japanese-style rooms, some with private bathroom. It is just off Kappabashi-dori.

Kimi Ryokan (¥)
2-36-8 Ikebukuro, Toshima-ku
tel: 03 3971 3766
A friendly little place with Japanese-style rooms, it is popular with Westerners and often full. Seven minutes' walk northwest of Ikebukuro station.

Mitsui Urban (¥)
8-6-15 Ginza, Chuo-ku   tel: 03 3572 4131
Efficient, clean, economy hotel with some character. The facade is painted orange and this together with an accompanying metal-tree sculpture has resulted in the hotel becoming a local landmark and meeting place. Handy for the Shimbashi business and bar district.

Miyako Hotel Tokyo (¥¥¥)
1-1-50 Shirogano-dai, Minato-ku
tel: 03 3447 3111;
www.miyako-hotel-tokyo.co.jp
A quiet comfortable hotel with a delightful Japanese garden. This sister hotel of the more famous Kyoto branch of the same name retains a restrained provincial air that offers a welcome rest from the hustle and bustle of Tokyo life.

New Otani Hotel (¥¥¥)
4-1 Kioi-cho, Chiyoda-ku   tel: 03 3265 1111;
www.newotani.co.jp
Huge hotel complex, largest in Japan, with restaurants and services to match. An attractive feature is its surprisingly large garden.

Palace (¥¥¥)
1-1-1 Maruno-uchi, Chiyoda-ku
tel: 03 3211 5211; www.palacehotel.co.jp
Overlooks the moats of the Imperial Palace. Elegant public areas and 394 beautifully appointed guest rooms. A subway stop from Ginza.

President Hotel (¥¥)
2-2-3 Minami Aoyama, Minato-ku
tel: 03 3497 0111; www.president-hotel.co.jp
The only small, moderately priced hotel, in the expensive Aoyama district. Rooms equipped to high standard and restaurants are recommended.

Roppongi Prince (¥¥¥)
3-2-7 Roppongi, Minato-ku   tel: 03 3587 1111;
www.princehotels.co.jp
Compact 216-room hotel close to Roppongi's entertainments. The courtyard with a café and swimming pool are assets.

Sakura Ryokan (¥)
2-6-2 Iriya, Taito-ku   tel: 03 3876 8118
Close to Ueno and Asakusa, with Western and Japanese rooms.

Shiba Daimon (¥¥)
2-3-6 Shiba-Daimon, Minato-ku
tel: 03 3431 3716;
www.shibadaimonhotel.co.jp
This friendly hotel, which sees few Western guests, is in the Tokyo Tower area. It has a good Chinese restaurant.

Shigetsu Ryokan (¥)
1-31-11 Asakusa, Taito-ku   tel: 03 3843 2345
Friendly, inexpensive Japanese inn, almost on the doorstep of Asakusa Kannon Temple.

Shinagawa Prince Hotel (¥)
4-10-30 Takanawa, Minato-ku
tel: 03 3440 1111; www.princehotels.co.jp
Acceptable budget, reasonably sized rooms. Part of a sports complex; mainly young clients; 24-hour coffee bar.

Shinjuku Prince Hotel (¥¥)
1-30-1, Kabuki-cho, Shinjuku-ku 160
tel: 03 3205 1111; www.princehotels.co.jp
A business hotel on the edge of Kabuki-cho, Shinjuku's red-light district. Reasonably priced restaurants, 24-hour room service, small rooms, but good value for money.

Shinjuku Washington (¥¥)
3-2-9 Nishi-Shinjuku, Shinjuku-ku
tel: 03 3343 3111
A shiny, modern business hotel near the Shinjuku skyscrapers, with 1,310 compact rooms and largely impersonal or automated services. Five minutes' walk from Shinjuku station.

Star (¥¥)
7-10-5 Nishi-Shinjuku, Shinjuku-ku
tel: 03 3361 1111
A small, functional but friendly hotel with 80 rooms, only a couple of minutes' walk from Shinjuku station and the entertainment district.

Tokiwa Hotel (¥¥)
7-27-9 Shinjuku, Shinjuku-ku
tel: 03 3202 4321
A good-value *ryokan*-style hotel with character, and has Western and Japanese rooms. Well placed in the heart of Shinjuku.

Tokyo Hilton International (¥¥¥)
6-6-2 Nishi-Shinjuku, Shinjuku-ku
tel: 03 3344 5111; www.hilton.com
One of the high-rises of Shinjuku, with great views from the upper floors, 807 rooms, 5 restaurants, indoor and outdoor pools, and tennis courts.

Tokyo Kokusai International Youth Hostel (¥)
Central Plaza 18F, 2-1-1 Kagurazaka,
Shinjuku-ku   tel: 03 3235 1107
Simple lodgings in a modern tower block. Reservations in advance are required. Send a letter with a self-addressed postcard for reply.

Tokyo Station Hotel (¥¥)
1-9-1 Maruno-uchi, Chiyoda-ku
tel: 03 3231 2511; www.tshl.co.jp
Built in 1915, this hotel occupies much of the distinctive red-brick section of Tokyo station. Spacious, comfortable rooms with a rather faded elegance, but with slightly eccentric air.

Westin Tokyo (¥¥¥)
Ebisu Garden Place, 1-4-1 Mita, Meguro-ku
tel: 03 5423 7000; www.westin.co.jp
A stylish hotel with richly decorated public areas and 445 guest rooms, part of a new leisure development on the former Sapporo Brewery site.

Yaesu Fujiya (¥¥)
2-9-1 Yaesu, Chuo-ku   tel: 03 3273 2111;
www.yaesufujiya.com
Modern business hotel behind Tokyo Station. The rooms are small but the restaurants are decent.

Yaesu-Ryumeikan (¥¥)
1-3-22 Yaesu, Chuo-ku   tel: 03 3271 0971;
www.ryumeikan.co.jp
Japanese inn offering Western and Japanese rooms with air-conditioning. Good value.

YMCA Asia Youth Centre (¥)
2-5-5 Saragaku-cho, Chiyoda-ku
tel: 03 3233 0611
All welcome. Rooms are basic, but Western and Japanese breakfasts served, indoor pool available. Doors close at midnight; seven to eight minutes' walk from Suidobashi or Jinbo-cho stations.

Hotels and Restaurants

Nikko

You can see Nikko on a day trip from Tokyo. Most of the rooms are in Japanese inns.

Nikko Kanaya Hotel (¥¥)
1300 Kami Hatsuishi-cho, Nikko
tel: 0288 54 0001
Very old, spacious and busy iinn. The staff are very helpful.

Pension Turtle (¥)
2-16 Takumi-cho tel: 0288 53 3168
This inn is well placed, near to the Toshogu shrine. It is recommended for this and its comfortable rooms.

CENTRAL HONSHU

Hakone

Fuji-Hakone Guest House (¥)
912, Sengokuhara, Hakone-machi, Kanagawa 250-06 tel: 0460 4 6577
A simple but clean Japanese inn in quiet surroundings. The owners speak English. Worth a couple of nights' stay (two nights minimum) to explore the region.

Fujiya Hotel (¥/¥¥)
359 Miyanoshita, Hakone-machi, Ashigarashimogun 250-04 tel: 0460 2 2211
Built in 1878—one of the oldest Western-style hotels in Japan. Charming character and traditional Japanese service. Fine gardens.

Naraya Ryokan (¥¥¥)
162 Miyanoshita, Hakone-machi, Ashigarashimogun 250-04
tel: 0460 2 2411
Opposite the Fujiya Hotel. A *ryokan* that has been in the same family for many generations. Elegant, *tatami* rooms with mountain views. First-class Japanese cuisine and hot-spring baths.

Fuji Five Lakes

Hotel Ashiwada (¥¥)
395 Nagahama, Ashiwada-mura, Minami-Isuru-gun, Yamanashi 401-4 tel: 0555 82 2321
On the shore of Lake Kawaguchi, a new, functional Japanese-style hotel; good base for climbing Mount Fuji in season.

Kawaguchiko Youth Hostel (¥)
Eight-minute walk from Kawaguchiko station
tel: 0555 72 1431
Busy during the Fuji climbing season, otherwise you are likely to have the place to yourself. Closed Nov to late Mar.

Ise-shima National Park

Asa (¥¥)
109 Nakano-cho, Ise-shi 516 tel: 0596 22 4101
A family-run wooden-built *ryokan* with 12 rooms in a traditional area. The room price includes two meals, which usually include house specials. The *ryokan* has a good local reputation for its food. The rooms themselves contain delightful antique features and each room is different.

Hoshide Ryokan (¥)
2-15-2 Kawasaki, Iseshi, Mie Prefecture 516
tel: 0596 28 2377
A simple, traditional *ryokan*. The owners serve macrobiotic food for breakfast and dinner. Seven minutes walk to Iseshi station.

Ise City Hotel (¥¥)
1-11-31 Fukiage, Iseshi, Mie Prefecture 516
tel: 0596 28 2111
Close to the Hoshide *ryokan*, this business hotel offers friendly service and quite small but comfortable rooms.

Izu Peninsula

Ginsuiso Hotel (¥¥¥)
2977-1 Nishina, Nishi Izumachi, Kamo-gun, Shizuoka 410-35
tel: 0558 52 2211
Very expensive, classy resort; *ryokan*-style hotel with superb clifftop setting. Book well in advance.

Haji Minshuku (¥)
708 Sotoura-Kaigan, Shimoda City
tel: 0558 22 2597
A friendly *minshuku*, which is helped by the fact the owner speaks English. It is close to the beach and the price includes two meals.

Kaikomaru Minshuku (¥)
Nishi-Kamo-gun, Shizuoka 410-35
tel: 0558 52 1054
At the opposite end of the scale to Ginsuiso, this is a simple, family-run *minshuku*, with its own hot-spring bath. No English spoken.

New Fujiya Hotel (¥¥)
1-16 Ginza-cho, Atami, Shizuoka 413
tel: 0557 81 0111
A straightforward, efficiently-run, resort hotel, with indoor and outdoor hot-spring baths. It is a functional base for exploring Izu Peninsula.

Shimoda Tokyu Hotel (¥/¥¥)
5-12-1 Shimoda, Shimoda, Shizuoka 415
tel: 0558 22 2411; www.shimodatokyu.com
On a hill overlooking Shimoda Bay, with sea and mountain views. Large and impersonal but very practical, with outdoor swimming pool and hot-spring baths.

Kobe

Arcons Hotel (¥¥)
3-7-1 Kitano-cho, Chuo-ku tel: 078 231 1538
Small but well-run hotel on Kitano-cho Hill. Some rooms with sea views. Take a cab if you arrive at the main station.

Hana Hotel (¥¥)
4-2-7 Nunobiki-cho, Chuo-ku
tel: 078 221 1087
A smallish, well-run business hotel with more character than one usually expects from this style of establishment. The rooms are comfortable, if small, and have a good range of facilities. Handy coffee shop serves snacks.

Hotel Okura Kobe (¥¥¥)
2-1 Hatoba-cho, Chuo-ku, Kobe 650
tel: 078 333 0111; www.kobe.hotelokura.co.jp
Set in Merikan Park and close to shopping areas; this 35-floor hotel has elegantly furnished rooms and impeccable service.

Kobe Portopia Hotel (¥¥¥)
6-10-1 Minatojima, Nakamachi, Chuo-ku
tel: 078 302 1111; www.portopia.co.jp
A sleek, modern hotel with elegant rooms with large picture windows that look out over the city or the sea. To arrive in appropriate style, take the Portline monorail from Sannomiya station or a 15-minute taxi ride from Shin-Kobo station.

Kobe Washington Hotel (¥¥)
2-11-5 Shimoyamate-dori, Chuo-ku, Kobe 650
tel: 078 331 6111
An efficiently-run business hotel with an atmosphere more pleasant than is usually found in such establishments. Convenient for a one-night stop.

Ryokan Takayama-so (¥)
400-1, Arima-cho, Kita-ku, Kobe, Hyogo Prefecture 651-14 tel: 078 904 0744
Set in one of the oldest spas in Japan. Manager speaks English. Good food, and a hot-spring spa on the premises.

Nagoya

Hotel Sunroute Nagoya (¥¥)
2-35-24 Meieki, Nakamura-ku, Nagoya 450
tel: 052 571 2221
An unexpectedly bright and cheerful business hotel, very close to Nagoya station. The public areas are quite spacious, but the rooms are small.

International Hotel Nagoya (¥/¥¥)
3-23-3 Nishiki, Naka-ku, Nagoya 460
tel: 052 961 3111
High-quality, long-established popular hotel with a European feel. Western and Japanese restaurants available.

Nagoya Miyako Hotel (¥¥)
4-9-10 Meieki, Nakamura-ku, Nagoya 450
tel: 052 571 3211
A medium-priced hotel offering good service and convenient to the city.

Osaka

Hotel Granvia Osaka (¥¥)
3-1-1 Umeda, Kita-ku, Osaka 530
tel: 066 344 1235
Within the Osaka station complex, the lobby opens onto the station. Busy but very convenient for a one-night stop. Fortunately, the hotel rooms are sound-proofed. Some have fine views over the city.

Hotel New Otani (¥¥¥)
1-4-1 Shiromi, Chuo-ku, Osaka 540
tel: 066 941 1111; www.osaka.newotani.co.jp
One of the best hotels in Osaka, set in a new, futuristic building that towers over Osaka Castle. Services are comprehensive, prices are steep. Excellent fitness club.

Hotel Riva Nankai (¥¥)
2-5-15 Shinsai-bashi-suji, Chuo-ku, Osaka 542
tel: 066 213 8281
Close to Namba station, shopping and nightlife areas. Spacious rooms; children under 12 stay free. Western and Japanese restaurants.

Shin-Osaka Sen-1 City Hotel (¥)
2-2-17 Nishi-Miyahara, Yodogawa-ku, Osaka 532 tel: 066 394 3331
A basic but adequate business hotel if you are on a budget. Some rooms have private baths; otherwise, there are public baths. The hotel lobby is on the sixth floor of the building.

KYOTO

Higashiyama Youth Hostel (¥)
112 Shirakawabashi-goken-cho, Sanjo-dori, Higashiyama-ku tel: 075 761 8135
Convenient to Kyoto station. Guests obliged to take dinner and breakfast. Book ahead in season.

Hiiragiya Ryokan (¥¥¥)
Aneyakoji-agaru, Fuyacho,
tel: 075 221 1136
Expensive; extremely distinguis

Hiraiwa Ryokan (¥)
314, Hayao-cho, Kaminoguchi-a
Ninomiyacho-dori, Shimogyo-ku
tel: 075 351 6748; www.hiiragiya.c
Popular, central Japanese inn. Showers communal bath only.

Hotel Alpha (¥¥)
Kawaramachi, Sanjo-agaru, Nakagyo-ku
tel: 075 241 2000; www.hotwire.co.jp/alpha
Excellent location in central Kyoto. Comfortable, business-style hotel. Deluxe rooms brighter and bigger, worth the extra outlay. Restaurant serves classic Japanese cuisine.

Kyoto Century Hotel (¥¥)
680 Higashishiokoji-cho, Shiokoji-sagaru, Higashinotoin-dori, Shimogyo-ku
tel: 075 351 0111
Near Kyoto station. Good-value Japanese-style rooms available.

Kyoto Holiday Inn (¥¥)
36 Nishihiraki-cho, Tekano, Sakyo-ku
tel: 075 721 3131
Far from city centre, but provides good facilities and the best hotel sports complex in Kyoto. Shuttle bus into town. Rooms for visitors with disabilities.

Kyoto Park Hotel (¥¥)
Sanjusangendo Side, Higashiyama-ku
tel: 075 525 3111; www.kyopark.co.jp
In eastern Kyoto opposite National Museum. Combines Western and Japanese features.

Kyoto Royal Hotel (¥¥)
Sanjo-agaru Kawaramachi, Nakagyo-ku
tel: 075 223 8489; www.kyoto-royal.co.jp
Great position on central Kawamachi-dori. The quality of service is good.

Kyoto Utano Youth Hostel (¥)
29 Nakayama-cho, Uzumasa, Ukyo-ku
tel: 075 462 2288
Near Ryoanji Temple. Simple concrete structure offering basic lodgings. Bicycle rental and laundry facilities available.

Matsuba-ya Ryokan (¥)
Nishiiru Higashinotoin, Kamijuzuya-machi-dori, Shimogyo-ku tel: 075 351 3727
Inexpensive Japanese inn close to Kyoto station and Sanjusangendo Temple. No private facilities.

Miyako Hotel (¥¥¥)
Sanjo-Keage, Higashiyama-ku
tel: 075 771 7111; www.miyakohotel.co.jp
Well-established hotel with first-class reputation. Western- and Japanese-style rooms.

Nashinoki Inn (¥)
Agaru Imadegawa, Nashinoki-dori, Kamigyo-ku
tel: 075 241 1543
North of Imperial Palace; a family-run *ryokan* in a quiet district.

New Miyako Hotel (¥¥)
Hachijo-guchi, Kyoto Station
tel: 075 661 7111; www.newmiyako.co.jp
Sister hotel to the classier and more expensive Miyako Hotel. Across from Kyoto station. Rooms small but many restaurants and bars. Popular with younger Japanese visitors and tour groups.

...nbutsuji Kaikan (¥)
...oincho, Ohara, Sakyo-ku
tel: 075 744 2540
One hour by bus from Kyoto station. Take bus from stop 1 in front of Kyoto Central Post Office to Ohara.

Pension Higashiyama (¥)
Sanjo-sagaru, Shirakawa-suji, Higashiyama-ku
tel: 075 882 1181; www.kid97.co.jp/st-kyoto
In eastern Kyoto, by the Shirakawa canal. Clean, small hotel, constructed in 1985. Western- and Japanese-style rooms available. Doors close at 11.30pm.

Takaragaike Prince Hotel (¥¥¥)
Takaragaike, Sakyo-ku
tel: 075 712 1111; www.princehotels.co.jp
In the north of the city, with large rooms and views of mountains and forests.

Tani House (¥)
8 Daitokuji-cho, Murasakino, Kita-ku
tel: 075 492 5489
Japanese inn run by friendly couple. Popular with visitors on a tight budget. Near Koto-in temple.

Tawaraya Ryokan (¥¥¥)
Fuyacho, Aneyakoji-Kita, Nakagyo-ku
tel: 075 211 5566; www.ryokan.or.jp/kyoto
Very expensive, traditional *ryokan*, generally acknowledged as one of the finest in Japan. Booked months in advance.

Three Sisters Inn Annex (¥¥)
Heian Jingu, Higashi Kita Kado, Sakyo-ku
tel: 075 761 6333
A traditional Kyoto *ryokan*-style inn accustomed to visitors. Quiet and comfortable lodgings.

Temple Accommodation

The following temples accept foreign guests; book in advance by letter. Vegetarian breakfast usually included in the price. Dormitory-style lodging is the norm.

Hiden-in Temple (¥)
35 Sennyuji Sandai-cho, Higashiyama-ku
tel: 075 561 8781
From Kyoto station take bus 208 to Sennyuji-michi stop.

Myokenji Temple (¥)
Teranouchi Horikawa, Kamigyo-ku
tel: 075 414 0808
From Kyoto station take bus 9 to Horikawa Teranouchi stop.

Myorenji Temple (¥)
Teranouchi Omiya higashi, Kamigyo-ku
tel: 075 451 3527
Same as for Myokenji Temple.

WESTERN HONSHU

Hagi

Hokumon Yashiki Ryokan (¥/¥¥)
210 Horiuchi, Hagi-shi, Yamaguchi Prefecture 758 tel: 08382 2 7521; www.hokumon.co.jp
Ryokan inn, with spacious rooms, in old samurai district near castle grounds.

Tomoe Ryokan (¥¥)
608 Hijiwara, Hagi-shi, Koboji Yamaguchi Prefecture 758 tel: 08382 2 0150
An elegant old inn with lovely gardens. The food is excellent. Bath and lavatories shared.

Himeji

Himeji Castle Hotel (¥¥)
210 Hojyo, Himeji 670 tel: 0792 84 3311
Near the station and the castle, this hotel serves Western food and has an outdoor swimming pool.

Hiroshima

ANA Hotel Hiroshima (¥/¥¥)
7-20 Nakamachi, Naka-ku, Hiroshima
tel: 082 241 1111; www.anahotels.com
One of Hiroshima's best hotels, this is five minutes' walk from the Peace Park and the local business district. The rooms themselves are spacious.

City Hotel Hiroshima (¥¥)
1-4 Kyobashi-cho, Minami-ku, Hiroshima
tel: 082 263 5111
Regular business hotel right across from the station. Convenient for a one-night stop.

Ikedaya Minshuku (¥)
6-36 Dobashi, Naka-ku, Hiroshima
tel: 082 231 3329
This is good, standard lodging, set near to the Peace Park. Dinner and breakfast are included in the price.

Mitakiso (¥¥¥)
1-7 Mitaki-cho, Nishi-ku
tel: 082 237 1402
A highly recommended traditional *ryokan*. The better rooms look in onto a delightful Japanese garden. The public baths are an absolute treat and the cuisine, served in your rooms, first class. Room rates include dinner and breakfast. Worth a night's stay if you can afford a room overlooking the garden.

Kurashiki

Ryokan Kurashiki (¥/¥¥)
4-1 Honmachi, Kurashiki 710
tel: 0864 22 0730
Splendid *ryokan* in the heart of old Kurashiki. Constructed from an old merchant's house and connecting rice and sugar warehouses. Excellent restaurant attached that serves classic *Kaiseki* Japanese food.

Matsue

Horaiso Ryokan (¥¥)
Tonomachi, Matsue 690 tel: 0852 21 4337
Pleasing *ryokan* in a secluded setting near the castle.

Matsue Tokyu Inn (¥¥)
590 Asahimachi, Matsue 690
tel: 0852 27 0109
Across the street from Matsue station, this is part of a business hotel chain. The rooms are of reasonabe size and have most of the facilities that you might require.

Miyajima

Jyukeiso Ryokan (¥¥)
Miyajima, Saeki-gun 739-05
tel: 0829 44 0300
A family run *ryokan*, on a small hill east of the pier. English is spoken here and to complement this, a Western breakfast is available on request.

Okayama
Culture Hotel (¥¥)

1-3-2 Gakunan-cho, Okayama City 700
tel: 0862 53 2233
Imaginatively designed hotel with cheerful rooms and a friendly staff. The restaurant serves Western food.

Tsuwano
Meigetsu Ryokan (¥¥)

Tsuwano-cho, Kanoashi-gun 699-56
tel: 08567 2 0685
Excellent traditional *ryokan* in the middle of town.
Wakasagi no Yado Minshuku (¥)

Tsuwano-cho, Kanoashi-gun 699-56,
Shimane-ken tel: 08567 2 1146
Small, family-run *minshuku*. Japanese and Western breakfast. Japanese dinner.

SHIKOKU

Kochi
Hotel Takasago (¥)

2-1 Ekimae-cho, Kochi-shi, Kochi 780
tel: 0888 22 1288
Slightly scruffy *ryokan*, but food is fine and price reasonable.
Washington Hotel Plaza (¥)

1-8-25 Otesuji, Kochi-shi, Kochi 780
tel: 0888 23 6111
Within easy reach of the castle. Fairly large rooms, friendly staff.

Matsuyama
ANA Hotel Matsuyama (¥¥¥)

3-2-1 Ichiban-cho, Matsuyama 790
tel: 0899 335511; www.anahotels.com
Matsuyama's best hotel, in the central area. Near the cable car for Matsuyama Castle and cable-car stop for Dogo Onsen. Variety of bars and restaurants.
Shinsen-en Youth Hostel (¥)

22-3 Dogohimezaka Otsu, Matsuyama 790
tel: 0899 336366
Near Dogo Onsen, busy during the high season. Laundry and bicycle rental facilities are available.
Taikei Business Hotel (¥¥)

3-1-15 Heiwa Dori, Matsuyama 790
tel: 0899 43 3560
Cheerful, pleasant business hotel with more character than most of its kind. Public baths and saunas on the premises.

Shodo island
There are numerous *minshuku* on the island. Book when you arrive in Tonosho, or at the tourist office in Takamatsu before you leave (see pages 182–183).

Takamatsu
Hotel Kawaroku (¥¥)

1-2 Hyakken-machi, Takamatsu 760
tel: 0878 21 5666
A combination of *ryokan* and ordinary hotel, to be found in the heart of the city. Western- and Japanese rooms, with Japanese food served in your room or Western food in the hotel restaurant.

Takamatsu Grand Hotel (¥¥)

1-5-10 Kotobuki-cho, Takamatsu 760
tel: 0878 51 5757
Near the station, shopping arcades, and the pier. Lobby on third floor with views over Tamamo Park.

KYUSHU

Aso National Park
Pension Flower Garden (¥)

3096-4 Takamori, Takamori-machi, Kumamoto-ken tel: 09676 2 3012
Western-style pension in pretty setting. Good food. Cab ride from Takamori station, or call and the hotel will arrange to pick you up.
Yamaguchi Ryokan (¥¥)

Tarutama Onsen, Choyo-son, Kyushu
tel: 09676 7 0006
Mountain *onsen* set in delightful countryside. Cab ride from Aso-Shimoda station.

Beppu
Sakaeya Minshuku (¥)

Ida, Kannawa, Beppu 874 tel: 0977 66 6234
Well-established *minshuku* with its own hot-spring baths. House is old and has character. Food basic but well cooked. Book ahead.
Suginoi Hotel (¥¥¥)

Kankaiji, Beppu 874 tel: 0977 24 1141;
www.suginoi-hotel.com
Beppu's best known, largest and most opulent hotel, more like a mini resort. Gigantic baths. Not the ideal place if you are seeking peace and quiet.
Tamanoyu (¥¥¥)

Yufin-cho, Oita-ken tel: 0977 84 2158;
www.tamanoyu.co.jp
Yufin hot-spring resort is one hour by bus from Beppu and an elegant, fashionable and sophisti-cated alternative to it. The Tamanoyu is expensive but an exceptionally refined and charming trad-itional inn. Despite this, the atmosphere is relaxed, which does make the stay here even more worth the premium.

Fukuoka/Hakata
B&B Guest House Dazaifu (¥)

1-18-1 Sanjo, Dazaifu 818-01
tel: 092 922 8740
Open to visitors with or without a YH card, this is clean, budget lodgings with self-catering facilities. The rooms are *tatami*-floored and sleeping is on futons.
Chisan Hotel Hakata (¥¥)

2-8-11 Hakata-eki-mae, Hakata-ku
tel: 092 411 3211; www.chisan.co.jp/hotel
A friendly, well-run business hotel, five minutes' walk from the Guchi exit of Hakata Station. Higher-priced rooms are larger with sea views. The Japanese and Western breakfast are good value.
Hotel Clio Court Hakata (¥¥)

5-3 Hakataeki-Chuogai, Hakata-ku 812
tel: 092 472 1111
Modern, chic hotel designed by Rei Kurokawa. Rooms are decorated in a variety of styles; you can choose when you book. Western and Japanese restaurants and cheaper food bars. No single rooms.

Hotels and Restaurants

Hotel New Otani (¥¥¥)
1-1-2 Watanabe-dori, Chuo-ku, Fukuoka 810
tel: 092 714 1111; www.newotani.co.jp
First-class hotel with services to match. Rooms large and tastefully decorated.

Mitsui Urban Hotel (¥¥)
2-8-15 Hakata-ekimoe, Hakata-ku
tel: 092 451 5111; www.mitsuikanko.co.jp
A straightforward business hotel. The rooms have good facilities and, despite being small, feel airy because of their relatively large windows. A ten-minute walk from the Guchi exit of Hakata station.

Toyo Hotel (¥¥)
1-9-36 Hakata-eki, Higashi, Hakata-ku 812
tel: 092 474 1121; www.toyohotel-fuk.co.jp
Business hotel convenient to Hakata station. Functional but comfortable enough. Rooms on top floors have more light.

Kagoshima
Kagoshima Hayashida Hotel (¥¥)
12-22 Higashisengoku-cho, Kagoshima 892
tel: 099 224 4111
In the centre of town. Rather eccentric, space-age theme in the decor.

Shigetomiso Ryokan (¥¥¥)
31-7 Shimizu-cho, Kagoshima 890
tel: 099 247 3155
Very expensive *ryokan* that is set in a former villa; once belonging to the Shimizu ruling clan.

272

Kumamoto
Kumamoto Shiritsu Youth Hostel (¥)
5-15-55, Shimazaki-machi, Kumamoto 860
tel: 096 352 2441
Efficiently run youth hostel, open to both men and women. A useful addition is that the proprietor can speak English.

Maruko Hotel (¥¥)
11-10 Kamitori-cho, Kumamoto 860
tel: 096 353 1241
Japanese inn-cum-hotel with mainly *tatami* rooms, which are comfortable and air-conditioned. Western and Japanese meals are available.

New Sky Hotel (¥¥)
2 Higashiamidaji-cho, Kumamoto 860
tel: 096 354 2111; www.anahotels.com
Modern, large, and attractive hotel that offers excellent amenities at a reasonable price. Enjoys a good location near Kumamoto Castle and Suizenji Park.

Miyazaki
Hotel Kensington (¥¥)
3-4-4 Tachibana-dori-higashi, Miyazaki City 880-0805 tel: 0985 20 5500
Simple, inexpensive hotel. Rooms are small; ask for one with a window not facing another building. All rooms have bathroom, TV and phone. Central location.

Nagasaki
Nagasaki Grand Hotel (¥¥¥)
5-3 Manzai-machi, Nagasaki 850
tel: 095 823 1234
Well-established, small and discreet hotel, which has a beer garden. Laid out in a tropical setting and open in spring and summer.

Nagasaki Youth Hostel (¥)
2 Tateyama-cho, Nagasaki 850
tel: 095 823 5032
Near Nagasaki station, it is open to non-members. Accommodation is basic, but laundry facilities are provided for residents.

Nagasaki Washington Hotel (¥¥)
9-1 Shinchi-machi, Nagasaki 850
tel: 095 828 1211
Part of a dependable chain of business hotels. Convenient for sightseeing, it is to be found in the Hamano-machi shopping district and close to Chinatown.

Sakamoto-ya Ryokan (¥¥¥)
2-13 Kanaya-machi, Nagasaki 850
tel: 095 826 8211
An elegant wooden *ryokan* that provides a personalized service to its guests. *Shippoku* (a Nagasaki meal of various dishes) served on request.

Tanpopo Minshuku (¥)
21-7 Hoeicho, Nagasaki 852 tel: 095 861 6230; www3.ocn.ne.jp/~tanpopo7
Basic *tatami* rooms at budget prices. The concrete building is ugly but within walking distance of Peace Park. The nearest station is Urakami; if you call from the station, then the hotel will arrange to pick you up.

OKINAWA

Central Okinawa
Okinawa Hotel (¥/¥¥)
1478 Kishaba, Kitagusuku-son, Nakagami-gun, Okinawa tel: 098 935 4321; www.okinawahotel.co.jp
On a hill in central Okinawa, the hotel has fine views and comprehensive service. The outdoor swimming pool is surrounded by tropical plants.

Naha
Okinawa Harbour View Hotel (¥¥¥)
2-46 Izumizaki, Naha-shi, Okinawa
tel: 098 853 2111; www.anahotels.com
On the island, providing a combination of the best city and resort hotel.

Pacific Hotel Okinawa (¥¥)
3-6-1 Nishi, Naha-shi, Okinawa
tel: 098 868 5162; www.pacifichotel.co.jp
Comfortable and slightly less expensive version of the Harbour View.

NORTHERN HONSHU

Kakunodate
Hyakusuien Minshuku (¥)
31 Shimonaka-machi, Kakunodate, Senboku-gun tel: 0187 55 5715
This central *minshuku* is set in a converted 19th-century warehouse. There is an old-fashioned *irori* hearth and mini-museum included on the premises.

Ishikawa Ryokan (¥/¥¥)
32 Iwase-machi, Kakunodate, Senboku-gun
tel: 0187 54 2030
Modern but quite unpretentious and welcoming Japanese inn, run by friendly family who serve good food.

Kamikochi
Kamikochi Imperial Hotel (¥¥¥)
Kamikochi, Azumi-mura, Nagano-ken
tel: 0263 95 2001; www.imperialhotel.co.jp
Modern, high-class lounge hotel run by the Imperial
Hotel of Tokyo.
Nishi-Itoya Sanso Inn (¥¥)
Kamikochi, Azumi-mura, Nagano-ken
tel: 0263 95 2206
This is a traditional wooden inn, and meals come
with the rooms. It can be found near Kappabashi
bridge.

Kanazawa
Garden Hotel (¥¥)
2-16-16 Honcho, Kanazawa 920
tel: 076 263 3333
A rather welcoming business hotel close
to the station. Rooms are small, but beds are a
comfortable size and windows open. Practical for
a short stay.
Kanazawa Tokyu Hotel (¥/¥¥)
2-1-1 Kohrinbo, Kanazawa 920
tel: 076 231 2411; www.tokyuhotel.com
New hotel in the heart of the city. Public areas spacious. Guest rooms are small but rooms on the
higher floors have good views.
Miyabo Ryokan (¥¥¥)
3 Shimo-Kakinokibatake, Kanazawa 920
tel: 076 231 4228
Traditional and very expensive inn surrounded by
the oldest private garden in the city. The best
rooms open on to the garden.
Murataya Ryokan (¥)
1-5-2 Katamachi, Kanazawa 920
tel: 076 263 0455
Relaxed Japanese inn in the middle of town. No
private baths, but *tatami* rooms comfortable.

Matsumoto
Hotel New Station (¥/¥¥)
1-1-11 Chuo, Matsumoto 390
tel: 0263 35 3850; www.hotel-ns.co.jp
Convenient for the railway station. Friendly
business hotel offering good value. The in-house
food is delicious.
Matsumoto Tokyu Inn (¥¥)
1-3-21 Fukashi, Matsumoto 390
tel: 0263 36 0109
This is a better class of business hotel, close to
train station. The inexpensive rooms are small, the
bigger rooms rather expensive, but a pleasant
place to stay if you are using it as a base for
exploring the area.

Morioka
Hotel Metropolitan Morioka (¥/¥¥)
1-44 Morioka, Ekimae-dori, Morioka, Iwate 020
tel: 0196 25 1211; www.metro-morioka.co.jp
Within the station complex. Rooms are designed
for sleeping rather than lingering, but there is a
good Chinese restaurant on the premises.

Ogimachi
Places to stay in Ogimachi are restricted to
thatched farmhouses, *minshuku* bed, breakfast,
and dinner accommodation. Book at the village
tourist office (tel: 0576 96 1751).

Sado Island
Sado Seaside Hotel (¥)
80 Sumiyoshi, Ryotsu-shi, Sado Island
tel: 0259 27 7211;
www2u.biglobe.ne.jp/~sado
A cheerful, inexpensive hotel, which is a short cab
ride away from the Ryotsu ferry port. Japanese-
style rooms with private bath.
San Kei Kan Minshuku (¥)
Negai 260, Ryotsu-shi, Sado Island
tel: 0259 26 2440
Friendly, family-run *minshuku* by the beach. No
English spoken.

Sendai
Dochuan Youth Hostel (¥)
*31 Kitayashiki, Ohnoda, Taihaku-ku, Sendai,
Miyagi 98* tel: 022 247 0511
Thirty minutes by bus or cab from the station, this
is the best youth hostel in the region. A converted
thatched-roofed farmhouse set on the edge of the
countryside.
Sendai Hotel (¥¥)
1-10-25 Chuo, Sendai, Miyagi 980
tel: 022 225 5171; www.sendai-hotel.com
Modern, but well-established, reputable hotel,
close to the station.

Takayama
Hishuya Ryokan (¥/¥¥)
1-464 Kami Okamotocho, Takayama 506
tel: 0577 33 4001
Good traditional inn near Hida-no-sato village
outside Takayama. There is a quiet and
refined atmosphere.
Kinnikan Ryokan (¥/¥¥)
48 Asahimachi, Takayama 506
tel: 0577 32 3131
First-class traditional Japanese inn in the heart of
old Takayama. Small and popular; best to book
ahead.
Yamakyu Minshuku (¥)
58 Tenshoji, Takayama 506
tel: 0577 32 3756
A cross between a *minshuku* and a *ryokan*. It
has a reputation for good food and a delightful
public bath.

Yamagata
Goto Matabei Ryokan (¥¥)
2-2-30 Hatago-machi, Yamagata 990
tel: 0236 22 0357
Old, fairly comfortable Japanese inn. Plenty of
character and simple but well-prepared food.
Yamagata Nanokamachi Washington Hotel (¥¥)
1-4-31 Nanoka-machi, Yamagata 990
tel: 0236 25 1111
A functional business hotel, forming part of a chain
that generally provides good service.

HOKKAIDO

Abashiri
Sakura-so Minshuku (¥)
27-41 Omagari, Abashiri-shi, Hokkaido
tel: 0152 44 2337
A straightforward place to stay with a pleasant
atmosphere and helpful, friendly owners.

273

Hotels and Restaurants

Akan Kohan
Akan Angel Youth Hostel (¥)
*5-1 Shuri Komanbetsu–Akan-Kohan, Akan 085,
Hokkaido tel: 0154 67 2309*
Well-run youth hostel. Busy in season.
Nibushi no Sato Minshuku (¥)
*Kusshiro-Kohan, Teshikaga-cho, Kawakami-
gun, Hokkaido tel: 0154 83 2294*
A cab ride out of Akan-Kohan village. Has its own
hot-spring baths. No English spoken.
Yamaura Hotel (¥¥)
*Akan-Kohan, Akan 085, Hokkaido
tel: 0154 67 2311*
Small hotel on the lakeside at the southern end
of Akan-Kohan village. Mainly Japanese-style
tatami rooms. Western rooms tend to look away
from the lake.

Hakodate
Hotel Hakodate Royal (¥¥)
*16-9 Omori-cho, Hakodate 040
tel: 0138 26 8181; www.hakodate.or.jp*
Western-style hotel. Efficient, cheerful staff. Cab
ride from the station.
Niceday Inn (¥)
*9–11 Otimachi, Hakodate 040
tel: 0138 22 5919*
The proprietors speak no English but give visitors
a warm welcome. No food, but many restaurants
nearby.

Noboribetsu Onsen
Kiyomizuya Ryokan (¥)
*60 Noboribetsu, Onsen-cho, Noboribetsu 059,
Hokkaido tel: 01438 4 2145*
Japanese inn a short walk from the bus terminal
serving good *tempura*.
Ryokan Hanaya (¥¥)
*Noboribetsu Onsen, Noboribetsu 059,
Hokkaido tel: 01438 4 2521*
This modern, mid-range *ryokan* offers both
Western- and *tatami*-style rooms. The staff is
English speaking.
Suzuki Ryokan (¥¥)
*Karurusu Onsen, Noboribetsu-shi, Hokkaido
tel: 01438 4 2285*
A 30-minute cab ride out of Noboribetsu Onsen in
a quiet mountain setting. Large old inn equipped
with a traditional hot-spring bath.

Sapporo
Fujiya Santus Hotel (¥¥)
*Nishi 7, Kita 3, Chuo-ku, Sapporo 060
tel: 011 271 3344*
Small hotel offering a warm welcome and very
good value for money. Near to JR Sapporo station
and shopping district.
Hotel Alpha Sapporo (¥/¥¥)
*Nishi 5, Minami 1, Chuo-ku, Sapporo 060
tel: 011 221 2333*
Classy city hotel near shopping district and the
Susukino nightlife area. Good service, friendly
staff.
Nakamuraya Ryokan (¥)
*Nishi 7, Kita 3, Chuo-ku, Sapporo 060
tel: 011 241 2111*
Japanese inn with modern facilities and local food.
Near to the station and central area.

Sapporo Washington Hotel II (¥¥)
*Nishi 6, Kita 5, Chuo-ku, Sapporo 060
tel: 011 222 3311*
Better class of business hotel. Part of a reputable
chain of hotels.

Sounkyo Onsen
Daisetsu zan Shirakaba-so Youth Hostel (¥)
*1418 Higashikawa-machi, Kamikawa-gun,
Hokkaido tel: 0166 97 2246*
Accessible by bus from Asahikawa or Sounkyo
Onsen, the hostel has its own hot-spring baths,
good food and pretty scenery.
Kumoi Ryokan (¥¥)
*Sounkyo, Kamikawa-gun, Hokkaido
tel: 01658 5 3553*
New Japanese inn with its own hot-spring bath and
some rooms with private bath. Western breakfast
is provided on request.
Sounkaku Grand Hotel (¥¥)
*Sounkyo, Kamikawa-gun, Hokkaido
tel: 01658 5 3111*
A *ryokan*-style hotel. One of the better and more
reasonably priced of the many resort establish-
ments in the area. Always busy in summer.

Toyako Onsen
Okoiso Minshuku (¥)
*83 Sobetsu-cho, Sobetsu-Onsen, Hokkaido
tel: 01427 5 2522*
In a small *onsen* district 2km (1 mile) west of
Toyaku Onsen. Good, clean establishment serving
fine food.
Showa Shinzan Youth Hostel (¥)
*103 Sobetsu-cho, Sobetsu-Onsen, Hokkaido
tel: 01427 5 2283*
The hostel is slightly shabby but has a good
hot-spring bath.
Toya Park Hotel (¥¥)
Toyako Onsen, Hokkaido tel: 01427 5 2445
Small hotel offering attractive views of the lake.
Excellent service provided. The manager speaks
English.

RESTAURANTS
Almost all large Japanese towns and cities
have an abundance of restaurants to suit every
imaginable taste and budget. At home, space
is usually too limited for socializing, and eating
and drinking out is very much a part of the
Japanese way of life.
Whether you are buying street food or dining in
an expensive restaurant, service and hygiene
standards are first class. With such a large
choice available, the Japanese tend to dine out
in their own districts and to travel only to
establishments with a particular reputation or a
special style of food.
Keep in mind the strategic problem of finding a
restaurant in a strange district. The Japanese
address system is complex and even cab
drivers often have to stop and phone a place
on the way there.
If you see a likely establishment during the
day, ask for a business card as they usually
have a map on the back, which can be shown
to the cab driver.

Cash is preferred to credit cards, especially in smaller establishments.

Restaurants prices:
Lunch
Expensive (¥¥¥): over ¥4,000
Moderate (¥¥): ¥2,000–4,000
Inexpensive (¥): ¥1,000–2,000

Dinner
Expensive (¥¥¥): over ¥8,500
Moderate (¥¥): ¥2,500–8,500
Inexpensive (¥): under ¥2,500

TOKYO

Ajanta (¥)
3-11 Nibancho, Chiyoda-ku
tel: 03 3264 6955 Subway: Kojimachi
This Indian restaurant is much-loved, with the simplest of settings but one of the most comprehensive menus in Tokyo. The vegetarian and non-vegetarian, south and north Indian dishes are particularly good.

Antonio's (¥¥)
Dai 22, Daikyo Building, First Floor, 7-3-6 Minami Aoyama, Minato-ku tel: 03 3797 0388
Subway: Omotesando
This is an excellent Italian restaurant, serving good food at a reasonable price. Service is traditional and the surroundings are classic, for example the tables are covered in starched white tablecloths. It is set alongside a busy expressway, however, once inside the noise and bustle can be forgotten.

Bengawan Solo (¥¥)
7-18-13 Roppongi, Minato-ku
tel: 03 3408 5698 Subway: Roppongi
Indonesian restaurant serving good *rijsttafel* (a variety of dishes served on one tray) at a fairly reasonable price.

Bentenyama Miyako (¥¥)
2-1-16, Asakusa, Taito-ku tel: 03 3844 0034
Subway: Asakusa
Famous sushi and *sashimi* restaurant founded in 1866. The atmospheric interior seems to have been changed little since then. Popular with the sushi cognoscenti. To taste a range of sushi, order the set 12-piece menu.

Bougainvillea (¥¥)
Romanee Building 2F, 2-25-9 Dogenzaka, Shibuya-ku tel: 03 3496 5537
Subway: Shibuya
Vietnamese food may yet challenge Thai for the 'ethnic' crown. This popular place has a wide choice of dishes: noodle soups, crab, spring rolls, sweet-and-sour pork or chicken, meatballs, crisp salads.

Chez Pierre (¥¥¥)
1-23-10 Minami Aoyama, Minato-ku
tel: 03 3475 1400 Subway: Nogizaku
Classic French cooking that has been maintained at a consistently high standard over a period of many years. They have an excellent range of pastries and gateaux, so make sure you leave room for a dessert. There is a comfortable, very French interior, with a bar and stools where you can eat alone and not feel out of place.

Edo-Gin (¥¥)
4-5-1 Tsukiji, Chuo-ku tel: 03 3543 4401
Subway: Tsukiji
Well-established and popular, serving *sashimi* and sushi made from the freshest fish from the nearby market. You can see some swimming in a tank.

Flo (¥¥)
4-3-3 Jingu-mae, Harajuku
tel: 03 5474 0611 Subway: Omotesando
French food served in French bistro surroundings. Good value, especially the all-you-can-eat buffet upstairs.

Fukusushi (¥¥)
5-7-8 Roppongi, Minato-ku tel: 03 3402 4116
Subway: Roppongi
Traditional Japanese sushi served in sleek, fashionable surroundings. English-language menus available. Cocktail bar for pre-dinner drinks.

Futaba (¥)
2-8-11 Ueno, Taito-ku tel: 03 3831 6483
Subway: Ueno
Ueno is well-known for *tonkatsu* (fried pork cutlet), eaten with rice, soup and pickled vegetables; this is one of the oldest restaurants serving the dish.

Goemon (¥¥)
1-1-26 Hon-Komagome, Bunkyo-ku
tel: 03 3811 2015 Subway: Hakusan
An excellent restaurant known for its tofu dishes. Delightful, tiny Japanese garden. Outdoor eating in warm weather.

Gold Leaf (¥¥¥)
Taisei Koki Building B1F, 5-4-12 Hiroo, Shibuya-ku tel: 03 3447 1212
Subway: Hiroo
In Tokyo, Thai food is booming. This is one of the most attractive places in the city to eat it, with a decor of teak wood and black lacquer complementing the vibrant dishes. Bangkok-trained chefs prepare subtly spiced salads, soups and delicious curries. Service is polished and the menu explains it all in English.

Hakkaku (¥)
NS Building, 29th Floor, 2-4-1 Nishi-Shinjuku
tel: 03 3345 1848
A popular place with fine views over Yoyogi Park. There is a varied Japanese menu. Set meals (good value) only at lunchtime

Han (¥¥)
4-3-20 Torano-mon, Minato-ku
tel: 03 3578 8293 Subway: Kamiya-cho
One of a chain, with traditional Japanese cooking. An eager young man kneels to take your order, tapping it into his hand-held terminal. Lots of small dishes give you a chance to try new experiences.

Hard Rock Café (¥¥)
5-4-20 Roppongi, Minato-ku
tel: 03 3408 7018 Subway: Roppongi
Hamburgers, salads, snacks, ice creams and pie, to the sound of loud music. Expect a long wait on weekends.

Hayashi (¥/¥¥)
4th Floor, Sanno Kaikan Building, 2-14-1 Akasaka tel: 03 3582 4078
Serves the dishes of Hida, a mountainous region in central Honshu. Pleasant old farmhouse atmosphere. Known for its food grilled over *hibachi* at your table.

Hotels and Restaurants

Heichinrou (¥¥)
*Shibuya Hillside building, Second Floor, 1-19-3
Jinnan, Shibuya-ku tel: 03 3464 7888
Subway: Shibuya*
The Heichinrou opened its doors many years ago
and has been busy ever since, serving classic
Chinese food of consistently high quality.
Popular with Japanese and Chinese customers
alike. Lunchtime prix fixe and afternoon dim sum
are good value.

Heirokunzushi (¥)
*5-8-5 Jingumae, Shibuya-ku
tel: 03 3498 3968 Subway: Meiji Jingu-mae*
This is an economical way to eat (or try) sushi.
Little dishes, each containing a pair of pieces,
circle past you on a conveyor belt and you pick
the dishes that take your fancy. The chefs work
to replace the sushi while they chat with
customers.

Higono-ya (¥¥)
*AG Building 1F, 3-18-17 Minami-Aoyama,
Minato-ku tel: 03 3423 4462
Subway: Omotesando*
Tasty combinations of fish, shellfish, vegetables
and meats grilled on bamboo skewers. Traditional
decor of black wood and white screens.

Honke Ponta (¥¥)
*3-23-3, Ueno, Taito-ku tel: 03 3831 2351
Subway: Ueno-hirokoji*
Opened before World War II and still run by the
same family, this *tonkatsu* restaurant has a
deserved reputation for serving the best pork in
town. Seafood is also available. Worth a visit just
for the interior decor, which has remained pretty
much unchanged in the last 50 years.

Jinya (¥¥)
*My City Building 7F, Shinjuku Station, 3-38-1
Shinjuku-ku tel: 03 3352 0018
Subway: Shinjuku*
Family-style Japanese cooking, all beautifully
presented. There is a choice of *tatami* (mat) or
conventional table and chairs.

Johnny Rockets (¥)
*Coco Roppongi Building 2F, 3-11-10 Roppongi,
Minato-ku tel: 03 3423 1955
Subway: Roppongi*
This restaurant serves good, freshly made
hamburgers, french fries and salads, along with
other fast food staples.

Kisoji (¥)
*Ginza Jujiya Building 5F, 3-5-4 Ginza, Chuo-ku
tel: 03 3567 0406
Subway: Ginza*
A convenient Ginza spot for inexpensive prix fixe
lunches of soup and rice with fish or chicken.

Kitchen Five (¥¥)
*4-2-15 Nishi Azabu, Roppongi tel: 03 3409
8835*
Small, very popular restaurant serving freshly
made Mediterranean/North African-style dishes.
The delightful proprietor is a food enthusiast.

Komagata Dojo (¥¥)
*1-7-12 Komagata, Taito-ku tel: 03 3842 4001
Subway: Asakusa*
Dojo are small river fish, and this establishment
has been serving them in a variety of dishes
for nearly 200 years. There is *tatami* (mat)
seating.

Konomi (¥¥¥)
*1-7-2 Nishi-Asakusa, Taito-ku
tel: 03 3843 7773 Subway: Tawaramachi*
A small restaurant in the Kappabashi district,
serving Kyoto cuisine. *Kyobento*, a double-decker
lacquered lunchbox of two dozen little seasonal
dishes, is an aesthetic treat.

Kyubei (¥¥¥)
*8-7-6 Ginza, Chuo-ku tel: 03 3571 6523
Subway: Higashi-Ginza*
Founded many years ago, and still going strong,
this restaurant has some of the most expertly
made sushi to be found anywhere in Japan.

La Tour d'Argent (¥¥¥)
*New Otani Hotel, 4-1 Kioi-cho, Chiyoda-ku
tel: 03 3239 3111
Subway: Akasakamitsuke*
The first branch outside Paris of the celebrated
La Tour d'Argent. Absolutely the finest French and
Japanese-inspired dishes in opulent surroundings.
Do expect a very expensive evening out.

Lintaro (¥¥)
*BIF Seigetsudo Building, 5-9-15 Ginza, Chuo-ku
tel: 03 3571 2037 Subway: Ginza*
Lintaro Mizuhama is the friendly owner of the
restaurant that bears his name, and he is often
found chatting to the diners or directing the
service. He's a Ginza native and expert as his
family has been here for centuries. The deep
basement room is a surprise, with its high ceiling
and Italian Renaissance pictures. The food is
Italian but with Japanese flair. Superbly fresh
salads and vegetables come from the
restaurant's gardens.

Little Okinawa (¥¥)
*8-7-10 Ginza, Chuo-ku tel: 033572 2930
Subway: Ginza or Shinbushi*
Busy, happy place serving food from Japan's
southern-most main island, with a Chinese
influence.

Mai-Thai (¥¥)
*1-18-16 Ebisu, Shibuya-ku
tel: 03 3280 1155 JR: Ebisu*
This small, cheerful and popular spot on a side
street, serves a typical Thai menu at reasonable
prices. One of a growing choice of eating places in
the fast-developing Ebisu area.

Mominoki House (¥)
*2-18-5 Jingu-mae, Harajuku
tel: 03 3405 9144 Subway: Harajuku.*
Excellent natural foods restaurant serving
idiosyncratic menu inspired by macrobiotic/
French/Japanese foods and cooking styles.
Good value lunches.

Nakase (¥¥¥)
*1-39-13 Asakusa, Taito-ku
tel: 03 3841 4015 Subway: Asakusa*
A famous and long-established *tempura* restaurant
near Nakamise-dori. Follow your nose to the delicious smells, but be prepared to wait. Often diners
are waiting outside the door well before opening
time. Lunch is the best for economy, and because
the area shuts early.

Nanbantei (¥¥)
*4-5-6 Roppongi, Minato-ku
tel: 03 3402 0606 Subway: Roppongi*
A popular *yakitori* (grilled food) restaurant with
very friendly atmosphere.

Rice Terrace (¥¥)
2-7-9 Nishi-Azabu, Minato-ku
tel: 03 3498 6271 Subway: Nogizaka
A relaxed setting for some of the best Thai food in
Tokyo. The service is friendly but polished. Try to
get a table downstairs; the upper level is cramped.

Robata (¥/¥¥)
1-3-8 Yuraku-cho, Chiyoda-ku
tel: 03 3591 1905 Subway: Yuraku-cho
Set in a replica of an old Japanese farmhouse with
a rustic interior. Good regional cuisine.

Rock 'n' Roll Diner (¥)
Big Ben Building B1F, 2-5-2 Kitazawa,
Setagaya-ku tel: 03 3411 6565
Subway: Yoyogi-uehara
American salads, hamburgers and sand-
wiches in a big, busy 1960s environment.

Roppongi Sumida (¥¥¥)
Aoba Roppongi Building B1F, 3-16-33
Roppongi, Minato-ku tel: 03 5570 5777
Subway: Roppongi
Teppanyaki grilled delicacies expertly prepared
from fresh crab, abalone, prawns, seafoods
and steak.

Ryu Sushi (¥)
5-2-1 Tsukiji, Chuo-ku tel: 03 3541 9517
Subway: Tsukiji
It is hard to get any nearer to the source of supply
than this little sushi bar next to the market halls.
Unusual for the Tsukiji location, the owner is not the
senior chef but another sort of artist, the painter
Ryutaro Shiina. He is normally in attendance from
an early hour, greeting the customers who mostly
work in the market. It's a great place to satisfy
your hunger, after a predawn visit there.

Sakafuji (¥)
1-6-1 Asakusa, Taito-ku tel: 03 3843 1122
Subway: Asakusa
A bright and friendly modern restaurant on three
floors, next to Hotel TOP.

Samovar (¥¥)
2-22-5 Dogenzaka, Shibuya-ku
tel: 03 3462 0648 Subway: Shibuya
Well-prepared Russian stews and soups, kebabs,
rye bread, beers and vodkas.

Samrat (¥)
Shojikiya Building 2F, 4-10-10 Roppongi,
Minato-ku tel: 03 3478 5877
Subway: Roppongi
One of the first of the Indian wave and still popu-
lar, serving tandoori dishes and curries on the
milder side. The all-day buffet is a bargain.
Branches include: Koyas One Building 6F, 13-7
Udagawa-cho, Shibuya-ku.

Sanjugo Danya (¥)
B1F, Shibuya City Hotel, 1-1 Maruyama-cho,
Shibuya-ku tel: 03 3770 9835
Subway: Shibuya
The '35 Steps' is a Japanese bistro with East-West
country cooking to suit most tastes. Take your
shoes off and choose a seat at the counter or one
of the low tables. The staff don't speak much
English, but a few words go a long way.

Sasanoyuki Restaurant (¥¥)
2-15-10, Negishi, Taito-ku tel: 03 3873 1145
Near JR station Uguisudani
Known for its tofu dishes. A good selection of
vegetarian fare available.

Shabu Zen (¥¥)
5-17-16 Roppongi, Minato-ku
tel: 03 3585 5600 Subway: Roppongi
A big restaurant, and good at *shabu-shabu*,
including 'all-you-can-eat' deals. The American
beef is less costly than the local.

Shigeyoshi (¥¥¥)
Olympia Co-op Olympia B1F, 6-35-3 Jingu-mae,
Shibuya-ku tel: 03 3400 4044
Subway: Meiji Jingu-mae
A small counter and a few tables, with the chefs in
full view. The cooking is utterly traditional, from the
Nagoya area. Lunch prices are reasonable.

The Siam (¥)
World Town Building 8F, 5-8-17 Ginza, Chuo-ku
tel: 03 3572 4101 Subway: Higashi-Ginza
This one has been around for years, and it is still
serving tasty Thai standards at prices that are
economical for Ginza, especially at lunchtime.

Takeno (¥¥¥)
6-21-2 Tsukiji, Chuo-ku tel: 03 3541 8698
Subway: Tsukiji
Fine *sashimi* and sushi; fish fresh from the
market. Most of the lunch customers are market
professionals, the evening crowd comes from far
and wide, drawn by the Takeno's reputation. At the
sushi counter, the chefs keep their jewel-like
creations coming until you reluctantly call a halt.

Tamazushi (¥)
B2F Ginza Core Building, 5-8-20 Ginza, Chuo-ku
tel: 03 3573 0057 Subway: Higashi-Ginza
Quick service of good sushi, with economical prix
fixe menus and à la carte, depending on what is in
season. At lunchtime, you may have to wait for the
business crowd to clear.

Ten-Ichi (¥)
6-6-5 Ginza, Chuo-ku tel: 03 3571 1949
Subway: Ginza
Well-known *tempura* establishment founded in
1930 by Isao Yabuki, who raised the standard of
tempura-making to an art.

Tokai-en (¥)
1-6-3 Kabukicho, Shinjuku-ku
tel: 03 3200 2934 Subway: Shinjuku
An enormous Korean operation, with all-you-can-
eat bargain lunches. Spicy seafood, stews and
bulgogi barbecues are particularly good.
Boisterous in late evening.

Tokyo Kaisen Ichiba (¥¥)
36-1 Kabukicho, 2-chome, Shinjuku-ku
tel: 03 5273 8301
Above a 24-hour fish market. Choose from a huge
variety of fish downstairs, take it upstairs, and the
staff will prepare it for you.

Torigin (¥)
4-12-6 Roppongi, Roppongi tel: 03 3403 5829
Subway: Roppongi
A simple *yakitori* also serving rice casseroles in
their own pots. Popular with local office workers,
but there is an English menu. Good for a quick,
tasty meal and drink.

Tsukiji (¥¥)
Miyuki Building B1F, 5-6-12 Ginza, Chuo-ku
tel: 03 3571 0071
Subway: Higashi-Ginza
A bright and busy all-day restaurant in the heart of
Ginza. The menus at lunchtime are attractive and
reasonably priced.

Hotels and Restaurants

Tsunahachi (¥)
3-31-8 Shinjuku tel: 3352 1012
Subway: Shinjuku (east exit)
This is the largest of a chain of inexpensive *tempura* restaurants. Popular with young people. Prix fixe represents the best value.

Yabu Soba (¥)
2-10 Awajicho, Kanda tel: 3251 0287
Subway: Awajicho
Established in 1880, this is one of the most famous *soba* noodle shops in Tokyo. There is an English menu available.

Zakuro (¥¥)
Basement TSB Kaikan Building, 5-3-3 Akasaka tel: 3582 6841 Subway: Akasaka
Popular *shabu-shabu* restaurant, which also serves inexpensive *sukiyaki* and *obento* (lunchboxes). Alternatively, there is an English menu.

CENTRAL HONSHU

Hakone
Fujiya Hotel Dining Room (¥¥)
Fujiya Hotel, 359 Miyanoshita, Hakone machi tel: 0460 2 2211
In the graceful old dining room of a classic period hotel in Miyanoshita on the Hakone Tozen railway. Expect good service.

Kobe
Gaylord (¥¥)
Basement, Meiji Seimei Building,
8-3-7 Isogami-dori, Kobe tel: 078 251 4359
Good Indian food, especially tandoori dishes, in smart Indian restaurant surroundings. Lunchtime specials are excellent value. This resturant is well-liked by foreign residents.

Marrakech (¥¥)
Maison de Yamate basement, 1-20-15 Nakayamata-dori tel: 078 241 3440
North African food prepared by the friendly (English-speaking) Moroccan owner and chef. The interior is particularly well-designed. This establishment get very busy, so book in advance to be sure of a table.

Masaya Honten (¥)
1-8-21 Nakayamate-dori, Kobe
tel: 078 331 2890
A very popular restaurant that serves good noodles and is fast and inexpensive.

Misono (¥¥¥)
1-7-6 Kitanagasa-dori, Kobe tel: 078 331 2890
One of Kobe's oldest steakhouses. The beef comes from local cattle reared in a traditional manner and is cooked at your table.

Nagoya
Kishimen-tei (¥)
3-20-4 Nishiki, Naka-ku, Nagoya
tel: 052 951 3481
This tiny place has a large reputation for serving the best *kishimen* noodles (a Nagoya classic) in town.

Yaegaki Tempura Restaurant (¥¥)
4-2-10 Nishiki, Naka-ku, Nagoya
tel: 052 263 1818
Long-established restaurant serving fresh fish and vegetable *tempura*. English menu available.

Osaka
Capricciosa (¥)
2-8-110, 105 Nambanaka tel: 066 631 5155
A relaxed Italian establishment, serving large portions of pizza and pasta at low prices.

Fuguhisa (¥¥)
3-14-24 Higashi-ohashi, Higashinari-ku, Osaka tel: 066 972 5029
Known for its *fugu ryori* (blowfish cuisine). Good, unpretentious cooking at a price difficult to beat.

Hankyu Grand Building Restaurants (¥/¥¥)
32 Bangai, Osaka.
The top four floors of this building near Osaka station have a wide range of eating establishments serving Japanese and Western food.

Kuidaore (¥¥)
1-8-25 Dotonbori, Osaka tel: 066 211 5300
A popular restaurant serving a variety of Japanese food. With four floors, prices rise as you go. Watch out for the mechanical clown outside the entrance.

Le Rendevous (¥¥¥)
The Plaza, 2-2-49 Oyodo-Minami
tel: 066 453 1111
Seasonally based French cooking of the highest standard at Osaka's most famous restaurant. Small intimate establishment; service formal and discreet. Men are asked to wear jackets and ties.

Mimiu (¥¥)
6-18 Hiranomachi 4 chome, Chuo-ku, Osaka
tel: 066 231 5770
Old tea house establishment, the home of *udon-suki*, noodles simmered at your table in a pot.

The Seasons (¥¥¥)
Hilton International, Osaka, 8-8 Umeda 1-chome, Kita-ku tel: 066 347 7111
Elegant European food in plush, but friendly surroundings. Very close to Osaka station.

KYOTO

Agatha (¥¥)
2nd floor, Yurika Building, Kiyamachi-dori, Sanjo-aguru, Nakagyo-ku tel: 075 223 2379
Robatayaki (charcoal grill) restaurant. Creative cooking, fun atmosphere and popular.

Ajiro (¥¥)
Myoshinji Minami-mon-mae, Hanazono, Sakyo-ku tel: 075 463 0221
Shojin ryori temple cooking in a restaurant setting. Meals served in private rooms. Near south gate of Myoshinji temple. Open to 6pm only.

Ashiya Steak House (¥/¥¥)
172–13 Kiyomizu 4-chome, Higashiyama-ku tel: 075 541 7961
Friendly establishment in a charming traditional house, serving excellent Kobe beef.

Gontara (¥)
Fuyacho Dori, Shijo-aguru
tel: 075 221 5810
This is an 80-year old noodle shop selling handmade *Udon* and *soba* noodles. It's good food and good value.

Hirano-ya (¥¥)
Maruyama Koen, Chion-in, Minami-mon-mae, Higashiyama-ku tel: 075 525 0026
Attractive tea house serving traditional 300-year-old Kyoto dish, made from simmered yams or potatoes and dried cod.

Hyotei (¥¥¥)
Kusakawa-cho 35, Nanzenji tel: 075 771 4116
One of the best *kaiseki* restaurants in Kyoto.
Beautifully presented meals served in a small but
handsome house opening onto a lovely garden.
Tatami mat seating in private rooms.

Izusen (¥)
*Daijiin-nai, Daitokuji-cho, Murasakino, Kita-ku
tel: 075 491 6665*
Fast service, inexpensive temple food in a sub-
temple of Daitokuji. Open to 5pm only.

Kaihoji (¥¥)
*Masamune 20, Momoyama-cho, Fushimi-ku
tel: 075 611 1672*
Unusual Chinese-style *shojin ryori* food from Zen
temple of the Obaku sect. There are shared
dishes to be had. Open to 5pm only.

Mankamero (¥¥¥)
*Inokuma-dori, Demizu-agaru, Kamigyo-ku
tel: 075 441 5020*
Very expensive, traditional, old establishment
(1716) serving food of the *Yusoku-ryori* style, once
the cuisine of the imperial court. If you can afford
it, it is a very special night out. To try the food at a
more reasonable price, eat here for lunch and
order the prix fixe *take-kago-bento.*

Minokichi (¥/¥¥)
*Sanjo-agaru, Dobutsuen-mae dori, Sakyo-ku
tel: 075 771 4185*
Established in 1735, this is one of Kyoto's best-
known restaurants. A variety of menus is served in
a complex of buildings, which also has a delightful
garden. The highlight is the *Kyo-kaiseki*, a meal of
eight dishes.

Misoka-ankawamichiya (¥)
*Fuyacho-dori, Sanjo-agaru
tel: 075 221 2525*
Perhaps the most famous *soba* noodle shop in
Kyoto. Small, with tiny rooms, opens out onto a
courtyard. Based here, in old Kyoto, for the past
300 years.

Nishiki (¥¥)
*Nakano-shima, Koen-uchi, Arashiyama, Ukyo-ku
tel: 075 871 8888*
Set on an island right in the middle of the Oi River.
The tea house serves excellent *Kyo-ryori.*

Oiwa (¥)
*Nijo-sagaru, Kiyamachi-dori, Nakagyo-ku
tel: 075 231 7667*
A variety of deep-fried kebabs served in a
renovated treasure house.

Okutan (¥¥)
*86-30 Fukuchi-cho, Nanzenji
tel: 075 771 8709*
Founded more than 300 years ago as a vegetarian
restaurant, this is one of the oldest and best tofu
places in Kyoto. There is also a beautiful garden
to admire.

Rokusei (¥¥)
*71 Nishitenno-cho, Okazaki, Sakyo-ku
tel: 075 751 6171*
Good Kyoto cuisine in a tasteful modern restaurant
overlooking tree-lined canal.

Takasebune (¥)
*Nishikana, Chiyamachisagaru,
Shijo-nishi, Shimogyo-ku tel: 075 351 4032*
Excellent *tempura* and *sashimi* dishes served at
very reasonable prices.

WESTERN HONSHU AND SHIKOKU

Hagi
Fujita Soba-ten (¥)
*59 Kumagai-cho, Hagi
tel: 08382 2 1086*
Friendly, handmade *soba* restaurant, which
also sells *tempura*. However, it does close at
7pm and second and fourth Wednesday of each
month.

Hiroshima
Okononi Mura (¥)
5-21 Shin-tenchi, Hiroshima tel: 082 241 8758
Two floors of outlets each selling their own versions of *okonomi-yaki*, a Japanese pancake with a
variety of fillings.

Suishin (¥¥)
*6-7 Tatemachi, Naka-ku, Hiroshima
tel: 082 247 4411*
Serving *kamameshi*, a rice casserole cooked
with fresh fish and other ingredients, this is a
very busy restaurant in the middle of town. This
might have something to do with five floors of
dining rooms.

Kurashiki
Kamoi-zushi (¥)
1-3-17 Chuo, Kurashiki tel: 0864 22 0606
Very reasonably priced sushi in a grand old rice
granary. *Nuku-sushi*, a steamed rice and fish dish,
is the house special.

Matsue
Minami-kan (¥/¥¥)
*14 Suetsugu Honmachi Matsue
tel: 0852 21 5131*
Excellent *kaiseki* cuisine and local seasonal
dishes in modern surroundings.

Matsuyama
Shin-Hamasaku (¥¥)
*Sanban-cho-4-chome, Matsuyama
tel: 0899 33 3030*
Spacious restaurant in the middle of town. Serves
fresh inland sea fish dishes, local dishes, and a
variety of other Japanese fare.

Unkai (¥/¥¥)
*6th floor, ANA Hotel, 3-2-1 Ichiban-cho,
Matsuyama tel: 0899 33 5511*
Eat here and indulge in the excellent service and
sophisticated surroundings. It is convenient to the
middle of the city and close to the castle.

Takamatsu
Maimai-tei (¥¥)
*18-5 Higashita-machi Takamatsu
tel: 0878 33 3360*
Serving extremely good *sanuki-udon* (thick,
white, wheat-flour noodle) dishes, this is a small,
unpretentious place to eat. The owner/chef even
makes some of his own cooking utensils.

Takamatsu Grand Hotel (¥¥)
*1-5-10 Kotobuki-cho, Takamatsu
tel: 0878 51 5757*
There is a choice of two good Japanese restaurants on the hotel's second floor. It can be found
near the station and port.

279

Hotels and Restaurants

Tenkatsu (¥¥)
Hyogomachi, Takamatsu tel: 0878 21 5380
Popular *tempura* and sushi restaurant in the Hyogomachi shopping mall near the station. The *sashimi* is prepared from fish that swim around, oblivious, in a tank in the restaurant. Seating is on *tatami* (mats), or on stools at the counter.

KYUSHU AND OKINAWA

Beppu
Amamijaya (¥)
1-4 Jissoji, Beppu tel: 0977 67 6024
Known for its handmade flat noodle dishes. There is also a wall display of local crafts.
Fugumatsu (¥¥)
3-6-14 Kitahama, Beppu tel: 0977 21 1717
Simple, straightforward blowfish (*fugu*) restaurant. *Fugu* and other fresh fish dishes are of good quality.

Fukuoka
Gourmet City (¥)
Basement, Hotel Centraza, 4-23 Hakataeki-Chuogai, Fukuoka tel: 092 461 0111
Collection of about ten restaurants offering variety, economy and convenience (near bullet-train exit of Hakata station).
Hakuryu (¥)
A food stall with seats in front of the Mitsubishi Bank in Tenjin. Serving inexpensive noodles and dumplings. No telephone; evening only.
Ichiki (¥)
1-2-10 Maizara, Chuo-ku tel: 092 751 5591
A friendly, relaxed bar/restaurant. Try the skewered fish or meat dishes.
Tsukushino (¥¥¥)
15th Floor, ANA Hotel, 3-3-3 Hakata-Eki-mae, Fukuoka tel: 092 471 7111
The best classic Japanese food. Impressive views over the city. English menu available.

Kagoshima
Ajimori (¥¥)
13-21 Sennichicho tel: 0992 24 7634
Shabu-shabu establishment serving *satsuma kuroshabu*, a Kagoshima dish made from the meat of a small black pig reared locally. The flesh, lighter and more tender than regular pork, is cooked by you at your table by dipping into a boiling broth. Delicious, generous portions and good value.
Noboraya (¥)
2-15 Horie-cho tel: 0992 26 6697
Popular *ramen* restaurant in the middle of town. Large portions at low prices. Watch the kitchen staff at work while you eat. Good place to relax and enjoy the local atmosphere.
Yudofu Gonbe-e (¥)
8-12 Higashi Sengoku-machi tel: 099 222 3867
Small, friendly establishment selling good quality tofu dishes. Try the tofu with lemon dipping sauce.

Kumamoto
Mutsugoro (¥¥)
Basement, Kumamoto Green Hotel, 12-11 Hanabata-cho, Kumamoto tel: 096 325 2222
Small restaurant serving local dishes (mainly horse meat) and various seafood.

Senri (¥¥)
Suizenji Koen Park, Kumamoto tel: 096 384 1824
Within Suizenji Park itself, this restaurant serves dishes made of local delicacies, including horse meat, eel and river fish. The option of Western or *tatami* seating is available.

Miyazaki
Kuretake (¥)
Basement, Nikko Building, 3-2-10 Nishi, Tachibana-Dori, Miyazaki tel: 0985 24 2818
There are a number of local dishes on offer. In particular, try *hiyajiru*, a cold fish soup served over hot rice.

Nagasaki
Fukiro (¥¥¥)
146 Kami Nishiyama-machi, Nagasaki tel: 095 822 0253
Old wooden building with *shoji* screens and *tatami* mats, set on a clifftop stone staircase near Suwa Shrine. The house special is *shippoku*, a Nagasaki meal in which a variety of small dishes are served all together. Four or more diners are usually required for a *shippoku* feast.
Hamakatsu (¥¥)
1-14 Kajiya-machi, Nagasaki tel: 095 823 2316
Modern restaurant serving reasonably priced *shippoku* (minimum two people) and a variety of prix fixe with local dishes. This is a good place to try the local cuisine.
Shikai-ro (¥)
4-5 Matsugae-machi, Nagasaki tel: 095 8822 1296
Five floors seating more than 1,500 people. Popular restaurant that was responsible for inventing *champon*, a Chinese-inspired, thick noodle dish, two centuries ago. English menu available.

Naha
Heiwa Dori Shopping Arcade (¥)
Heiwa Dori, Naha, Okinawa.
Food outlets in the arcade sell a very wide variety of Japanese dishes. You can eat your meal there without ceremony or take it away.
Ryotei Naha (¥/¥¥)
2-2-11 Tsuji, Naha, Okinawa tel: 098 868 2548
Good local cuisine combined with a floor show of Okinawa folk dance.
Sam's by the Sea (¥¥)
3-25-5 Gushi, Naha City tel: 098 857 0339
The Sam's chain is run by an American ex-military family, and their restaurants combine Western and Japanese cooking. The portions are large and the service is good; the lighting may be a little dim for some tastes.

NORTHERN HONSHU

Kanazawa
Kaga Tobi (¥)
Kohrinbo 109, 2-1 Kohrinbo, Kanazawa tel: 076 262 0535
Set on a back street just behind the Kohrinbo 109 department store, the Kaga Tobi serves a wide variety of good Japanese dishes.

Kanko Bussankan (¥)
2-20 Kenrokumachi, Kanazawa
tel: 076 222 7788
In the Ishikawa Prefectural Products Centre, near
the Kenrokuen Garden main entrance. Open during
the daytime only (10–6), serving *sashimi*, noodles
and the local cuisine, *kaga-ryori*, which uses
mountain vegetables, shellfish (particularly tiny
sweet shrimp) and river fish.
Miyoshian (¥¥)
1-11 Kenrokumachi, Kanazawa
tel: 076 221 0127
In the Kenrokuen garden; established for over a
century. *Tatami* mats and views over the pond.
Kaga-ryori considered to be the best in Japan.

Matsumoto
Kura (¥¥)
2-2-15 Chuo, Matsumoto tel: 0263 33 6444
Sushi and *tempura* restaurant in a mud-walled,
moated old house in the heart of town.
Naja (¥)
4-3-20 Ote, Matsumoto tel: 0263 36 9096
Vegetarian establishment with English menu
available. The food is well-prepared.
Taiman (¥/¥¥)
4-2-4 Ote, Matsumoto tel: 0263 32 0882
Deservedly well-known French restaurant serving
excellent food in rustic Japanese setting.
Furnished with Matsumoto *mingei* furniture.

Sendai
Aji Tasuke (¥)
4-4-13 Ichiban-cho, Sendai tel: 022 225 7672
Small, popular place serving simple, but delicious
fare at inexpensive prices. Known for its grilled
beef tongue, which is served at lunch and dinner
with oxtail soup and rice mixed with barley. Perfect
for a cold northern Honshu day. Closed Tuesdays.
Gintanabe Bekkan (¥¥)
2-9-34 Kokubun-cho, Sendai
tel: 022 227 3478
A busy fish restaurant serving everything from
sashimi to a whole baked fish. Informal light meals
served at the counter, more complete meals
served in rooms at the back.
Iwashiya (¥/¥¥)
4-5-42 Ichiban-cho, Sendai tel: 022 222 6645
Probably the best seafood restaurant in town, with
tatami seating.
Kakitoku (¥¥)
4-9-1 Ichiban-cho, Sendai tel: 022 222 0785
A very long-established, locally famous oyster bar.
Not to be missed if you enjoy eating oysters.
Steak and nonshellfish dishes are also available.
Santarom (¥¥¥)
1-20 Tachi-machi, Sendai tel: 022 224 1671
An elegant restaurant serving traditional dishes
such as *tempura*, *shabu-shabu*, *fugu* and *suriyaki*.
Service and food are excellent. Weekday set
lunches offer the best value.

Takayama
Kakusho (¥/¥¥)
2-98 Baba-cho, Takayama tel: 0577 32 0174
In an old mansion house in the eastern part of
town near Shorenji temple, this nationally known
restaurant serves top-class *shojin-ryori*.

Kofune (¥)
Hanasato-cho 6-6, Takayama
tel: 0577 32 2106
A noodle shop conveniently close to the station,
selling inexpensive fare. An English-language menu
is available, which is quite unusual in such an
establishment.
Suzuya (¥¥)
24 Hanakawa-cho, Takayama
tel: 0577 32 2484
Small restaurant, decorated in a rustic Takayama
style, serving local dishes. Try the *sansai-ryori*,
mountain vegetables and *ayu*, a river fish grilled
with soy sauce or salt.

HOKKAIDO

Hakodate
Bay Restaurant (¥¥)
11-5 Toyokawa-cho, Hakodate
tel: 0138 22 1300
Housed in a waterfront warehouse, its seafood
dishes come in unusual combinations, such as
tuna fish in coconut milk.
Matsumae (¥¥)
Hakodate Kokusai Hotel, 8th Floor, 5–10
Otemachi, Hakodate 040
tel: 0138 23 5151
A seafood restaurant that has good views
of the waterfront and serving well-prepared
Hokkaido dishes.

281

Sapporo
Hyosetsu-no-Mon (¥¥)
S5W2 tel: 011 521 3046
Popular restaurant in the Susukino district. If
you like crab, this is the place to visit because
the menu is entirely composed of king crab
dishes. It is a noisy, lively place. They have a
menu written in English with accompanying
photos of the dishes.
Ramen Yokocho (¥)
A small alley in Susukino (one block south and
running vertical to Susukino Avenue) packed with
shops selling Sapporo *ramen* (Chinese-style
noodles). Waits can be long.
Round Midnight (¥¥)
Hotel Arthur, S1OW6, Sapporo
tel: 011 561 1000
This refined but relaxed well-run establishment
offers good value set lunches and dinners, which
include a bargain all-you-can-eat option. Mixed
Japanese, Chinese and Western food. Very highly
recommended.
Sapporo Biru-en (¥¥)
N6, E9 Sapporo tel: 011 742 1531
Sapporo's original brewery, now a German-style
beer garden. The house special is a cook-it-your-
self lamb and vegetable barbecue called Genghis
Khan, washed down with lots of beer.
21 Club (¥¥¥)
Hotel Arthur, S1OW6, Sapporo
tel: 011 561 1000
An elegant restaurant with an art deco theme. It
is the highest dining room in the city and the
views are breathtaking. As you would expect, it
serves good quality Western and Japanese food
and has excellent service.

Index

282

Index

283

Index

Index

285

Index

Index

Picture credits

The Automobile Association would like to thank the following photographers, libraries, and associations for their assistance in the preparation of this book.

ALAMY 58t (Jon Bower), 59 (Jim Zuckerman), 180b (Iain Masterton); **BRIDGEMAN UK LTD** 60r Victoria & Albert Museum, London, UK; **BRUCE COLEMAN COLLECTION** 233 Japanese cranes; **CORBIS UK** 58b (Michael S. Yamashita), 112 (Jon Hicks); **MARY EVANS PICTURE LIBRARY** 33t Courtesan, 34t Jingu, 34b Amaterasu (sun goddess), 36b Amitabha buddha, 37t Fujiwara era, 39 Samurai warrior, 41t Jesuits in trade, 41b Japanese ladies, 42c Commodore Perry, 42c Perry's expedition, 43 New Japanese constitution, 45t Emperor Meiji, 45b Peach tree blossom, 104/5t Daimo & Suite, 110t Yokohama earthquake 1923, 110c Earthquake cartoon; **M. GOSTELOW** 51t Tokyo Asakusa, 61 Sengakuji, 64b Market Tsukiji, 65 Marking tuna (Tsukiji), 66 Yasakuni Shrine war memorial museum, 248b Tokyo Ikebukuro; **ROBERT HARDING PICTURE LIBRARY** 24b Preparing for sumo wrestling, 237t Ainu 'Marimo' festival Hokkaido; **MICHAEL HOLFORD** 38b Akita armor, 77 sword play; **GETTY IMAGES (HULTON)** 46b US Marines, Okinawa, 47 Pearl Harbor; **JAPAN NATIONAL TOURIST ORGANISATION** 16 & 17t Kansai International Airport, 32b Okutsu Onsen, 80b Minshuku, 99 L. Yamanaka, 220t Ryokan; **PICTURES COLOUR LIBRARY LTD** 4t 10b Mount Fuji, 27 Shinjuku, Tokyo, 265t Tokyo snack stall; **POPPERFOTO** 111t & 111b Kobe earthquake; **REX FEATURES LTD** 44b Emperor Hirohito; **D. SCOTT** 104 Kanbara stage sixteen of the Tokaido, 104/5 Shono stage forty-six of the Tokaido, 105 Fukuroi stage twenty-eight of the Tokaido; **SPECTRUM COLOUR LIBRARY** 5br Cherry blossom (Ueno Park), 9t Sanja festival, 12t Robots, 13b Assembly line, 16b Bullet train, 18t Yushima shrine, 24t Sumo wrestlers, 25 Sumo wrestling, 31 Karatsu festival, 36t Kasuga shrine Nara, 93 Shinkansen bullet train, 94/5 Mt. Fuji, 98 Mt. Fuji & Kawaguchi Lake, 101b Mt. Fuji & Hakone Komagatake ropeway, 103 Hakone Mt. Fuji & L. Ashi, 124 Zen Garden Daitokuji Temple, 135t Daisen-in-Zen Garden, 162 Himeji Castle, 175t Wakayama Mt. Koya Ryn Onsen, 207t Naginata Martial Art, 220b Tsumago interior of Waki Hojin, 225 Miyagi Sendai shopping center, 247t Tokyo Shibuya; **VICTORIA & ALBERT MUSEUM** 76t & 76–77 Swords.

All remaining pictures are held in the Association's own library (AA PHOTO LIBRARY) and were taken by JIM HOLMES with the exception of pages 2, 11, 26t, 18b, 19t, 20b, 28t, 29b, 30b, 50, 51b, 52t, 53t, 55, 56, 63, 64t, 68/9, 73t, 78/9, 84b, 88t, 91t, 92t, 117, 131t, 137, 142t, 143, 158, 159t, 159b, 167b, 201, 219, 249, 251, 264 which were taken by D. Corrence and page 62t which was taken by R.T. Alford.

The Automobile Association would also like to thank Nicolas Soames of Naxos Audiobooks and the Japan National Tourist Organisation (JNTO) in London for their help during the preparation of this book.

Acknowledgments

The author would particularly like to thank Harry Cook and Simon Halewood for their assistance with the research for some sections of this book, Helen Morgan for her expert typing of the manuscript. The author would also like to thank Terry Randsley, Philip Quirk, Glen Walford and David Hodgson.

Contributors

Original copy editor: Nia Williams
Revision verifier: David Scott
Revision copy editor: www.lodestonepublishing.com